C. S. Lewis

a reference guide

1972–1988

A
Reference
Guide
to
Literature

Ronald Gottesman
Editor

C. S. Lewis

a reference guide
1972–1988

SUSAN LOWENBERG

G.K. Hall & Co.
An Imprint of Macmillan Publishing Company
New York

Maxwell Macmillan Canada
Toronto

Maxwell Macmillan International
New York   Oxford   Singapore   Sydney

G.K. Hall & Co.
An Imprint of Macmillan Publishing Company
866 Third Avenue
New York, NY 10022

Maxwell Macmillan Canada, Inc.
1200 Eglinton Avenue East Suite 200
Don Mills, Ontario M3C 3N1

Macmillan Publishing Company is part of the Maxwell Communication Group of Companies.

Library of Congress Catalog Card Number: 92-42316

Printed in the United States of America

Printing number
1 2 3 4 5 6 7 8 9 10

Library of Congress Cataloging-in-Publication Data

Lowenberg, Susan

    C.S. Lewis : a reference guide, 1972-1988 / Susan Lowenberg.
      p. cm. — (A Reference Guide to Literature)
    Includes bibliographical references and index.
    ISBN 0-8161-1846-9 (alk. paper) : $55.00
    1. Lewis, C.S. (Clive Staples), 1898-1963—Bibliography.
I. Title. II. Series.
Z8504.37.L68 1993
[PR6023.E926]
016.823'912—dc20 92-42316

                                                    CIP

Contents

The Author

Susan Lowenberg received a bachelor of arts degree in English and French from California State University, Dominguez Hills, in 1979, a master's degree in library science from the University of California, Los Angeles, in 1981, and a master's degree in business administration from Bradley University in 1986. She was the business librarian at Bradley University Library from 1981 to 1986, chair of the circulation department at California State University, Northridge Libraries, 1986–89, head of the access services department, 1989–90, and science librarian and curator of the map library, 1991–92, at the University of Colorado at Boulder Libraries. She is currently Information Resources/Theatre-Dance Librarian at the California Institute of the Arts. She has published several articles on library related subjects in professional journals.

Preface

In the 1970s, Joe R. Christopher and Joan K. Ostling compiled *C. S. Lewis: An Annotated Checklist of Writings about Him and His Works* (Kent, Ohio: Kent University Press, 1974), which identifies material about Lewis published from 1919, when he began his writing career, to the cutoff date of June 1972. Christopher also began compiling an "Inklings Bibliography" on C. S. Lewis, J. R. R. Tolkien, and Charles Williams in each quarterly issue of *Mythlore* beginning in June 1976.

Since July 1972, however, material about C. S. Lewis has been scattered throughout many books and articles, and listed in many national and commercial bibliographies as well as periodical indexes and abstracts. An update of Christopher and Ostling's checklist was needed to bring together in one list, and to provide bibliographic control over, all the books, essays, or chapters in books, periodical articles, and doctoral dissertations about Lewis and his work. That compiling is accomplished in this bibliography.

Bibliographic sources used to identify material on Lewis are the following:

Abstracts of English Studies

American Book Publishing Record

Arts and Humanities Citation Index

Bibliographic Index

Biography Index

British Humanities Index

British National Bibliography

Catholic Periodical and Literature Index

Cumulative Book Index

Dissertation Abstracts International

Essay and General Literature Index

Humanities Index

Library of Congress Catalog. Books: Subjects

Modern Humanities Research Association. *Annual Bibliography*

Modern Language Association. *MLA International Bibliography*

Philosopher's Index

Reader's Guide to Periodical Literature

Religion Index One: Periodicals

Religion Index Two: Multi-Author Works

Religious and Theological Abstracts

The Year's Work in English Studies

Materials included in this bibliography are English language items published between July 1972 and December 1988, containing biographical, bibliographical, or critical information about C. S. Lewis and his works. Following the very helpful precedent set by Christopher and Ostling's checklist, this work also includes book reviews of works by Lewis published for the first time or published in a new collection.

Materials excluded from the bibliography are reprints, excerpts or adaptations of Lewis's works, and reprints of any item listed in Christopher and Ostling's checklist unless it has been substantially altered, enlarged, revised, or published in a new form. Book reviews of books about Lewis, master's theses, audio and visual materials, games and software by or about Lewis or that are adaptations of any of his works, reviews or articles about such audio or visual materials, reports of meetings of C. S. Lewis Societies, and letters to the editor that are not specifically about an article previously published in that periodical are also excluded.

Annotations for each entry cited are descriptive, detailing the major concern, topic, argument, or thesis as it is presented in the entry. The entries are arranged chronologically by the date of publication. Each entry is listed only once and is uniquely numbered by its order in the bibliography. Items not actually examined have an asterisk before the entry number. A combined author and subject index is included. The subject index identifies the major topics discussed in the cited entry and the works by Lewis referenced to in the entry.

This bibliography is very similar to the one compiled by Christopher and Ostling with the following exceptions. Christopher and Ostling's checklist is arranged in broad subject categories: general, biography, fiction and poetry, religion and ethics, literary criticism, and selected book reviews. This one is arranged in chronological order by date of publication. Christopher and Ostling included master's theses: this bibliography excludes them because of their marginal value and general inaccessibility.

Acknowledgments

I thank the University of Colorado at Boulder University Libraries for providing financial support for this project. I am also grateful for funding from the Council on Research and Creative Work at the University of Colorado at Boulder as well as additional funding from California State University, Northridge Libraries in the form of a Meritorious Performance and Professional Promise Award.

I thank the Marion E. Wade Center at Wheaton College for supplying me with hard-to-get Lewis material. The Interlibrary Loan Departments at the University of Colorado at Boulder, California State University, Northridge, and the University of California, Los Angeles, provided invaluable assistance in locating materials.

Mary Pecchio helped prepare this manuscript for publication and gave much helpful advice on word-processing techniques.

I thank Leah Morrison for her help in obtaining Lewis material.

I especially thank Anton D. Lowenberg, who initially encouraged me to undertake this project, for invaluable help in editing and obtaining library materials.

C. S. Lewis

a reference guide

1972–1988

Introduction

C. S. Lewis—His Life and Work

Clive Staples Lewis, known as "Jack," was born on November 29, 1898, in Belfast, Northern Ireland. His father, Albert, was a solicitor and his mother, Flora (née Florence Hamilton), was a clergyman's daughter who had been a promising mathematician, receiving a B.A. degree from Queen's College. Lewis had an older brother, Warren Hamilton, who was born on June 16, 1895.

Lewis began to write when he was six years old. He later explained he had been driven to writing in an attempt to overcome his extreme manual clumsiness, caused by having only one joint in his thumb; this was a physical defect inherited from his father. In later life, Lewis characterized his childhood writings about Animal-Land as prosaic, lacking poetry or romance. However, he believed that in undertaking this work as a child, he was in effect training himself as a novelist.

Several times during his childhood Lewis experienced a feeling or sensation that was to have a profound influence on his life. These experiences of intense desire, which he called "Joy," had no uniform cause, but the common quality of being "an unsatisfied desire which is itself more desirable than any other satisfaction." [1]

When Lewis was nine years old, his mother died of cancer and all his previous happiness and security vanished. Flora's death drove the two brothers away from their father but closer to each other. Passages in *Surprised by Joy* imply "that in the weeks leading up to Flora's death, the survivors all hurt one another in an irremediable way." [2] In his grief over losing his wife, father, and brother within a short time, Albert was emotionally unable to care for his sons.

Two weeks after his mother's death, Lewis was sent away to Wynyard, a boarding school in England. He was subjected to incompetent and brutalizing teaching before the school collapsed in 1910 and its headmaster declared insane. After a brief stay in a school close to his home, Lewis was sent in January 1911 to Cherbourg School in Malvern, England. He appears to have been reasonably happy there, and, in fact, his brilliant mind suddenly began to blossom under the influence of excellent teaching.[3] However, while at Cherbourg, Lewis, through various influences, came to reject the Christian faith of his boyhood.

During this time Lewis underwent an imaginative "renaissance," a return of Joy, which had vanished from his life after his mother's death. The experience was reawakened on his discovering several reproductions of Arthur Rackham's illustrations to *Siegfried and the Twilight of the Gods.* This episode sparked in Lewis a desire for "Northernness," which he described as "a vision of huge, clear spaces hanging above the Atlantic in the endless twilight of Northern summer, remoteness, severity," [4] which he discovered in Wagner, Norse mythology, and nature. During the next several years he lived almost two separate lives, an inner one concerned with Joy and an outer one filled with day-to-day realities.

In 1913 Lewis won a scholarship to Malvern College and entered the school that September. He was desperately unhappy there. Under the fagging system, in effect at most English public schools, a clique of senior boys more or less ran the school and freely bullied unpopular or resentful boys, one of whom Lewis appears to have been. School life was totally dominated by a struggle for social position that even manifested itself in pederasty—younger, effeminate looking boys, "Tarts," offering their favors to the senior boys, "Bloods," in return for influence and privilege. Also contributing to Lewis's unhappiness at Malvern was his dislike of the athletic games that students were forced to play, and his loss of privacy, resulting in fatigue of both mind and body.

During holidays in April 1914, Lewis made friends with Arthur Greeves, who shared his love of "Northernness." He described Greeves as his "First Friend," an alter ego, the "man who first reveals to you that you are not alone in the world by turning out (beyond hope) to share all your most secret delights." [5]

Albert Lewis, realizing that public school did not suit his son, sent him to William T. Kirkpatrick, his former headmaster. "Kirk," who had retired, was taking in private pupils, and from 1914 to 1917 Lewis lived with him and his wife in Surrey. Lewis wrote that "if ever a man came to being a purely logical entity, that man was Kirk." [6] He was ruthlessly rational and felt language was solely for the purpose of communicating or discovering truth. Lewis had always felt two impulses, the imaginative and the rational; Kirk satisfied the latter. To a large extent Lewis's own acutely logical mind was formed and sharpened by Kirk. [7]

In December 1916 Lewis won a scholarship to University College, Oxford, and had started to study there when he was called into the army in June 1917. While quartered with other cadets at Oxford, Lewis shared a room with E. F. C. ("Paddy") Moore. Although he did not particularly like Paddy, he became acquainted with his mother, Mrs. Janie Moore, and was soon spending weekends in the company of Mrs. Moore, her son, and daughter, Maureen. Mrs. Moore was forty-five and had been separated from her husband for many years. Lewis appears to have become infatuated with her.

Lewis was sent to France in November 1917 and was wounded on April 15, 1918, during the Battle of Arras. When he was sent to a London hospital, Mrs. Moore moved there to be near him. She wrote to Albert Lewis that his son had promised Paddy to look after her if something should happen to Paddy.[8] Paddy was killed in combat, and when Lewis returned to Oxford in 1918, he set up housekeeping with Mrs. Moore and her daughter.

This arrangement and the relationship between Lewis and Mrs. Moore always remained a mystery to both family and friends, probably as a result of Lewis's total reticence on the subject. In his autobiography Lewis omits all mention of Mrs.

Moore, merely alluding to a "huge and complex episode" in which his "earlier hostility to the emotions was very fully and variously avenged." [9] He tried to keep his living arrangement secret from his father, with whom he had become increasingly estranged. His brother, Warren, to whom he was probably closer than anyone, wrote that this was "'perhaps the only subject which Jack never mentioned, for on the only occasion when I hinted at my curiosity he silenced me with an abruptness which was sufficient warning never to re-open the topic.'" [10]

While some Lewis scholars [11] have speculated that there was a sexual relationship between Mrs. Moore and Lewis, publicly the relationship was that of son and adopted mother. Mrs. Moore would constantly interrupt Lewis's writing or studying to have him help her with housework or to run erands. Mrs. Moore's "main virtue was kindness, especially to those in any sort of need. Her main fault, that of being too autocratic and controlling, was the almost inevitable result of having to take charge, at an early age, of a large house and family." [12] Lewis accepted her demands with unvarying good humor and without complaint. He wrote Warren of "'the perpetual interruptions of family life—the partial loss of liberty'" yet added that "'I have definitely chosen and don't regret the choice. Whether I was right or wrong, wise or foolish, to have done so originally, is now only an historical question: once having created expectations, one naturally fulfills them.'" [13]

At Oxford, Lewis took a First Class in classical moderations in 1920 and another First in *Literae Humaniores* (commonly called "Greats"), ancient history, and philosophy, in 1922. Since there were no positions open in philosophy at Oxford, Lewis decided to read English language and literature. He completed the three-year course in one and took First Class Honors in June 1923. He applied for several positions without success, held a temporary post in philosophy for a while, and then, in May 1925, was elected Fellow and Tutor in English language and literature at Magdalen College, Oxford, a position he held until 1954.

While an undergraduate, Lewis became friends with Owen Barfield, whom he described as his "Second Friend," "The man who disagrees with you about everything. He is . . . the antiself. Of course he shares your interests . . . but he has approached them all at a different angle." [14] Barfield greatly influenced and modified Lewis's thought. Through his "Great War" with Barfield, he "ceased to separate his emotional experiences from his intellectual process, and came to regard 'Joy' and poetic vision, in their way, as truthful as rational argument and objective fact." [15] Barfield also turned Lewis against "chronological snobbery," the assumption that whatever has gone out of date is on that account discredited, and showed him "that Myth has a central place in the whole of language and literature." [16]

Lewis's conversion to Christianity was a gradual and complex process that occurred between 1923 and 1931 and that he fully described in *Surprised by Joy*. Lewis was helped along by the writers he most admired, George MacDonald, G. K. Chesterton, Johnson, Spenser, Milton, and Dante, who all had the common link of Christianity. In addition, his closest friends, Greeves, Barfield, and J. R. R. Tolkien, a professor of Anglo-Saxon at Oxford whom Lewis met in 1926, were all Christians. Lewis progressed from realism to philosophical idealism to pantheism to theism and finally to Christianity when on September 28, 1931, while on the way to the zoo with his brother, he came to a belief in Jesus Christ as the Son of God.

Once Lewis became a Chritian, he lost interest in Joy as an experience. He wrote in *Surprised by Joy* that "the old stab, the old bittersweet, has come to me as often and as sharply since my conversion as at any time in my life whatever" but concludes that "it was valuable only as a pointer to something other and outer," namely God.[17] Lewis wrote his fiction, especially *Perelandra* and the Chronicles of Narnia, to elicit this experience of Joy in his readers and to show them the way to God.

Lewis had become reconciled to his father and nursed him during the weeks before Albert's death in September 1929. With the proceeds from the sale of the family home in Ireland, he and Warren purchased a house in Headington Quarry, outside Oxford, which was known as the Kilns. The Lewis brothers, with Mrs. Moore and her daughter, moved into the Kilns in October 1930. Lewis spent most nights at his rooms in Magdalen College during the school term and most of his weekends and vacations at the Kilns. Mrs. Moore lived at the Kilns until the summer of 1948 when she became ill and retired permanently to a nursing home. Lewis visited her there every day until her death on January 12, 1951, at the age of seventy-nine.

Warren was an officer in the Royal Army Service Corps (R.A.S.C.), had served in France during World War I, in England and the Far East, and retired in 1932 with the rank of captain. He lived at the Kilns arranging and editing the Lewis family papers. In 1939 Warren returned to the R.A.S.C., served in France, and obtained the rank of major; he became ill and left the army permanently in 1940. Warren lived at the Kilns, spending most of his time during the day at his brother's rooms at Magdalen. He wrote and published a number of books on seventeenth-century French history and biography. During the late 1940s Warren began to have a serious problem with alcoholism, which greatly concerned Lewis and restricted his activities.

Sometime during the 1930s, Lewis began to meet informally with a small group of friends, usually on Thursday evenings in his rooms at Magdalen and on Tuesday mornings at their favorite pub, "The Eagle and Child," which they nicknamed "The Bird and Baby." More or less regular members included Lewis, Warren, Tolkien, Barfield, Christopher Tolkien, Hugo Dyson, Nevil Coghill, Adam Fox, Dr. R. E. Havard, Lord David Cecil, Gervase Mathew, Colin Hardie, and John Wain.[18] They called themselves "Inklings," which Tolkien said "'was a pleasantly ingenious pun in its way, suggesting people with vague or half-formed intimations and ideas plus those who dabble in ink.'"[19] The Thursday evening meetings would usually consist of someone reading aloud his work in progress, followed by discussion, commentary, and criticism. Charles Williams, whom Lewis met in 1936 after writing to him in praise of one of his works, became a regular member of the Inklings when the Oxford University Press, where he was an editor, moved to Oxford in 1939 because of the war.

During the 1940s and 1950s Lewis continued to lecture and instruct pupils in English literature at Oxford and then at Cambridge when he was elected professor of medieval and Renaissance English there in 1954. Lewis's lectures, filled with amusing analogies and packed with information, were generally popular with students. He "was a conscientious tutor who tried to keep the balance right between amiability or conviviality (not always possible between incompatible types) and his duty to the pupils to give them sufficient preparation for their examinations."[20] His students responded to Lewis largely in accordance with their own temperaments. Some found Lewis to be a bully; they considered him combative and felt that he used them as targets to sharpen his power of argument. Other students found Lewis to be exhilarating, invigorating, and inspiring in challenging them to think for themselves.

In 1952 another woman entered Lewis's life. Helen Joy Davidman was an American with a Jewish background; for a time she was a member of the Communist party and married a fellow communist, William Lindsay Gresham, in 1942. They had two sons, David and Douglas, born in 1944 and 1945, respectively. Both Greshams abandoned communism and converted to Christianity in 1948, partly through the influence of C. S. Lewis's religious books. "Partly because of her lifelong ambition to be a writer, and because of her deep appreciation for the great help Lewis' books had given both her and her husband," [21] Joy began a correspondence with Lewis. When Joy went to England in 1952 in the hope that some months of separation would help her troubled marriage, Lewis "invited her to Oxford and gave a lunch party in her honour at Magdalen." [22] Lewis's friends found her "foul-mouthed, bad-tempered and self-assertive" while Lewis was charmed by hers.[23] One biographer states that "the vivacity and depth of her mind, the quick and logical response to argument, and the considerable breadth of literary knowledge embracing many fields in which he was deeply interested" made it inevitable that Lewis would find Joy a splendid companion.[24] Another biographer maintains that Joy was well read but not an intellectual and argues that her personal qualities that Lewis's friends "found repugnant were precisely the ones which he found alluring." [25]

When Joy returned to the United States in January 1953, she discovered that her husband was in love with another woman. She allowed him to divorce her for desertion and returned to England with her two sons. She sent the boys to preparatory school in Surrey and lived for a time in London before moving to Oxford in 1955 to be near Lewis. When the Home Office refused to renew her permit to remain in Great Britain, Lewis secretly married Joy in a civil ceremony on April 23, 1956, giving her and her children British nationality. The marriage was a matter of friendship and expediency; Joy remained living in her own house as Mrs. Gresham.

In 1956, Joy became ill with cancer and was admitted to the hospital in October of that year; it was feared she was dying. In order to make public his relationship to Joy, Lewis announced in *The Times,* on December 24, 1956, simply that a marriage had taken place between himself and Joy. Then on March 21, 1957, a religious marriage ceremony was performed at Joy's hospital bedside "because Joy did not want to die in hospital and Lewis could not bring her to the Kilns unless he was married to her in the sight of God as well as in the sight of man. " [26] Joy miraculously recovered for a time and the period between 1957 and 1960, when Joy and he were able to lead a more or less normal married life, "saw Lewis at his happiest and most relaxed." [27] Lewis "felt that he had achieved full maturity and manhood only through marriage. . . . In living with Joy, he was being himself." [28] Joy died on July 13, 1960. Douglas Gresham, Joy's son, wrote that, although Lewis tried to conceal his grief from his friends, "Jack was never again the man he had been before Mother's death." [29]

Lewis's work *A Grief Observed*, "in its shooting stabs of pain, its yelps of despair, its tears, its emotional zigzagging," bears testimony to the shattering effect of Joy's death on Lewis. [30] In this work he wrestled with unbelief, describing God as a "Cosmic Sadist"; he found he still believed in God but could not find any evidence of His goodness. Eventually, he felt that the whole process of his wife's death and his own grief had smashed his earlier illusions about God and made his faith stronger.

Lewis continued to lecture at Cambridge and to write, but his health slowly deteriorated until his death on November 22, 1963.

Biographers of Lewis, as well as his own autobiographical works, reveal him as a complex individual. He apparently relished drinking beer and smoking heavily. He loved arguing and debating to such an extent some thought him a bully. He was a patient teacher and a loyal friend. He befriended strangers who wrote to him for advice and wrote thousands of letters to them filled with loving spiritual counsel. He was reticent about his personal life and his religious beliefs, even with his closest friends. He viewed introspection as a form of egoism and avoided it, yet several of his works are autobiographical. He projected a strong persona in each of his works, so that the reader is made to feel that he or she knows Lewis. In his literary criticism, the persona was that of "a fluent, highly intelligent man talking about books in a manner which is always engaging." [31] In the Chronicles of Narnia, he is the kindly uncle. In his apologetics, he is the skeptical seeker after truth. But the "real" Lewis probably was known only to a few close family members and friends.

C. S. Lewis's major works can be divided into three categories—fiction, apologetics, and literary criticism. His fiction includes the three novels that make up the Ransom or Space Trilogy: *Out of the Silent Planet* (1939), *Perelandra* (1943), and *That Hideous Strength* (1945). Although Lewis did not plan the trilogy in advance, these novels are linked together by the character of Ransom, who journeys to Mars in the first novel, travels to Venus in the second, and leads a small group on Earth in a fight against evil in the third.

The Chronicles of Narnia are probably Lewis's best-known and best-loved works of fiction. The seven novels that make up this series for children are *The Lion, the Witch and the Wardrobe* (1950), *Prince Caspian* (1951), *The Voyage of the "Dawn Treader"* (1952), *The Silver Chair* (1953), *The Horse and His Boy* (1954), *The Magician's Nephew* (1955), and *The Last Battle* (1956).

Lewis's last novel was considered by him, and probably by most critics, to be his best. *Till We Have Faces* (1956) is unlike anything else Lewis wrote, which may be why it is not as popular as the rest of his fiction. The novel is a retelling of the Cupid and Psyche myth in the form of a complaint against the gods told in a first person narrative by the female protagonist, Orual.

The Screwtape Letters (1942) is Lewis's best-known apologetic work, and, next to the Chronicles of Narnia, his most popular work. These epistles consist of advice from an experienced devil, Screwtape, to his nephew, Wormwood, engaged on his first assignment on earth—the temptation of a young Christian. This work became a best-seller and almost overnight made Lewis internationally famous. Other apologetic works include *The Problem of Pain* (1940), *Mere Christianity* (1952), which grew out of a series of radio broadcasts Lewis gave between 1941 and 1944, *The Great Divorce* (1945), *Miracles* (1947), *Reflections on the Psalms* (1958), *The Four Loves* (1960), and *Letters to Malcolm: Chiefly on Prayer* (1964). Lewis also wrote two accounts of his conversion—the first as an allegory, *The Pilgrim's Regress* (1933), and the second as an autobiography, *Surprised by Joy* (1955). *A Grief Observed* (1961) was written in response to his wife, Joy's, death.

Lewis's scholarly works of literary criticism include *The Allegory of Love* (1936), which traces the idea of courtly love, *A Preface to "Paradise Lost"* (1942), *English Literature in the Sixteenth Century Excluding Drama*, the third volume of the *Oxford History of English Literature* (1944), *Studies in Words* (1960), *An Experiment in Criticism* (1961), and *The Discarded Image* (1964) as well as many additional individual essays.

The critical response to Lewis's works has concentrated on his fiction, especially the Ransom Trilogy and the Chronicles of Narnia, and his apologetic works. His literary criticism, although extremely influential when first published since it opened up completely new areas of research, has not excited as much current interest. Two good surveys of his entire works are Joe R. Christopher's *C. S. Lewis* (1987) and Chad Walsh's *The Literary Legacy of C.S. Lewis* (1979).

For the most part the critical response to Lewis has been overwhelmingly positive. Critics praise his clarity, his intelligence, his erudition, his rational defense of traditional Christianity, his unique combination of reason and imagination, the mythopoetic art in his fiction, his portrayal of the numinous, his imaginative power, his diversity and complexity, and his depiction of the dialectic of desire. Some negative aspects of his works that are cited are his dogmatic attitude, his use of straw-man and either/or arguments, and the didactisicm in his fiction. Most critics agree that Lewis's lasting reputation will be based on his fiction—the Ransom Trilogy, the Chronicles of Narnia, *Till We Have Faces*, and *The Screwtape Letters*.

Some recent critics [32] find that Lewis's apologetics fail to prove logical arguments for the existence of God. Most concede that while his arguments are still valid and helpful, they are not as successful as his imaginative works. Recent critics of Lewis's fiction find that his earlier works are dogmatic, more concerned with Christian beliefs than in telling a story or realizing a fictional world. [33] Lewis's later works are considered to be mythopoeic, successfully combining Christianity, myth, and romanticism.

A few critics of late have attacked Lewis's portrayal of female characters as subordinate to men and see his works as reflecting the author's prejudice against women. [34] Others disagree, [35] however, viewing Lewis's depiction of women characters as supporting their right to develop their own talents.

In the 1980s, a debate developed over *A Grief Observed*. John Beversluis sees it as a repudiation of Lewis's earlier apologetics. Others [36] maintain it is an affirmation of his Christian faith. George Musacchio [37] considers it fiction rather than Lewis's outpouring of grief after his wife's death.

Another debate in the 1980s centered on the authorship of some works published as Lewis's. Kathryn Lindskoog [38] has charged that Walter Hooper, one of the trustees of Lewis's estate and the editor of Lewis's posthumous works, has passed off inferior works, namely *The Dark Tower* (1977), as Lewis's when they were in fact written by Hooper's friend Anthony Marchington.

The response to Lewis, unlike the response to most scholarly authors or novelists, has developed something of a cult following. Among his devotees, as A. N. Wilson states, a great schism has occurred in the sense that "two totally different Lewises are being revered by the faithful, and it is this which makes the disputes so painfully acrimonious." [39] On one side is the High Church group led by Hooper, who believe in "the Perpetual Virginity of C. S. Lewis" and have made him into some sort of Catholic saint. [40] On the other side are Lewis's Protestant devotees in the United States, who deny his fondness for alcohol and tobacco. Wilson states that "Lewis idolatry, like Christianity itself, has resorted to some ugly tactics as it breaks itself into factions." [41]

Given C. S. Lewis's popularity, it is not surprising that there are a number of periodicals devoted solely or in part to him and his works. Individual articles from these are included in the bibliography when they meet the selection criteria. The periodicals are:

CSL: The Bulletin of the New York C.S. Lewis Society 1 (November 1969–). The New York C. S. Lewis Society. Monthly. Editor: Jerry L. Daniel. 84-23 77th Avenue, Glendale, NY 11385. $10 per year.

The Canadian C. S. Lewis Journal, no. 1 (1979–). Quarterly. Editor: Stephen Schofield. Dunsfold, Godalming, Surrey GU8 4PF, England. $10 per year.

Chronicle of the Portland C. S. Lewis Society, 1–13 (1972–84). The Portland C. S. Lewis Society. Quarterly. No address; ceased publication in 1984.

Inklings: Jahrbuch für Literatur und Ästhetik 1 (1983–). Inklings-Gesellschaft. Annual. Articles published in German with English abstract or in English with German abstract. Editor: Gisbert Kranz. Erster Rote-Haag-Weg 31, 5100 Aachen, Germany. 50 DM per year.

Lamp-Post of the Southern California C. S. Lewis Society 1 (1977–). The Southern California C. S. Lewis Society. Quarterly. Editor: Terry Mathis. P. O. Box 533, Pasadena, CA 91102. $8.00 per year.

Lewis Legacy, no. 1 (1989–). C. S. Lewis Foundation for Truth in Publishing. Quarterly. Editor: Kathryn Lindskoog. 1344 East Mayfair Avenue, Orange, CA 92667. $10 per year.

Mythlore: A Journal of J. R. R. Tolkien, C. S. Lewis, Charles Williams, General Fantasy and Mythic Studies 1 (January 1969–). The Mythopoeic Society. Quarterly. Editor: Glen H. Goodknight. P.O. Box 6707, Altadena, CA 91003. $20 per year.

Seven: An Anglo-American Literary Review 1 (1980–). Wheaton College. Annual. Editors: Barbara Reynolds, Beatrice Batson, Lyle Dorsett, Brian Horne, and Normandi Ellis. Bookmakers Guild, Inc., 9655 W. Colfax Avenue, Lakewood, CO 80215.

CSL, the *Chronicle*, and the *Lamp-Post* are all published by regional Lewis societies and contain articles by society members and reports of society meetings; the quality of the articles ranges from scholarly to pedestrian. *The Canadian C. S. Lewis Journal* is eccentric in character, containing nonscholarly articles, and covers controversies in Lewis studies. The *Lewis Legacy* is concerned solely with the controversy over the Lewis oeuvre. *Inklings*, *Mythlore*, and *Seven* publish articles on the other "Oxford Christians" such as Tolkien and Williams, as well as articles on Lewis. *Inklings* and *Mythlore* both have short academic articles while *Seven* publishes long articles of scholarly interest.

There are two major collections of Lewisiana. The Marion E. Wade Center, located at Wheaton College, Wheaton, Illinois 60187, with Marjorie Lamp Mead as acting curator, was begun in 1965 as a collection only of C. S. Lewis. Since then it has expanded to include works by and about Owen Barfield, G. K. Chesterton, George MacDonald, Dorothy L. Sayers, J. R. R. Tolkien, and Charles Williams. Lewis holdings include first editions of most of his works, some manuscripts, original letters, the Lewis papers edited by W. H. Lewis, and family photographs. There are also biographical, bibliographical, and critical studies on Lewis as well as the periodicals devoted to Lewis studies.

The Department of Western Manuscripts, Bodleian Library, Oxford OX1 3BG, England, contains an extensive collection of Lewis's books—every edition published in Britain as well as a large number of foreign editions. Holdings include most of the books written about Lewis and copies of almost all articles published by Lewis in British periodicals with the exception of some very obscure local journals. Manuscript holdings include several hundred letters written by Lewis to various individuals. A few books and article manuscripts are also on deposit. Both the Bodleian and the Wade Center have photocopies of each other's unique letters and manuscripts by Lewis.

NOTES

1. C. S. Lewis, *Surprised by Joy* (New York: Harcourt Brace Jovanovich, 1955), pp. 17–18.
2. A. N. Wilson, *C. S. Lewis: A Biography* (New York: Norton, 1990), p. 21.
3. Roger Lancelyn Green and Walter Hooper, *C. S. Lewis: A Biography* (London: Collins, 1974), p. 30.
4. Lewis, p. 73.
5. Ibid., p. 199.
6. Ibid., p. 135.
7. Green and Hooper, p. 41.
8. Wilson, p. 59.
9. Lewis, p. 198.
10. Walter Hooper, "Introduction," *They Stand Together: The Letters of C. S. Lewis to Arthur Greeves (1914–1963)*, ed. Walter Hooper (London: Collins, 1979), p. 21.
11. See Wilson, and Kathryn A. Lindskoog, *The C. S. Lewis Hoax* (Portland, Ore.: Multnomah, 1988).
12. George Sayer, *Jack: C. S. Lewis and His Times* (San Francisco: Harper & Row, 1988), p. 76.

13. Humphrey Carpenter, *The Inklings: C. S. Lewis, J. R. R. Tolkien, Charles Williams, and Their Friends* (Boston: Houghton Mifflin, 1979), p. 14.
14. Lewis, p. 199.
15. Carpenter, p. 37.
16. Ibid., p. 41.
17. Lewis, p. 238.
18. Hooper, p. 27.
19. Carpenter, p. 67.
20. Wilson, p. 97.
21. Hooper, "Note," *They Stand Together*, p. 535.
22. Carpenter, p. 236.
23. Wilson, p. 240.
24. Green and Hooper, p. 259.
25. Wilson, p. 272.
26. Green and Hooper, p. 268.
27. Ibid., p. 295.
28. Sayer, p. 232.
29. Douglas H. Gresham, *Lenten Lands: My Childhood with Joy Davidman and C. S. Lewis* (New York: Macmillan, 1988), pp. 130–133.
30. Wilson, p. 282.
31. Wilson, p. xvii.
32. For example, see John Beversluis, *C. S. Lewis and the Search for Rational Religion* (Grand Rapids, Mich.: Eerdmans, 1985) and Richard Harris, *C. S. Lewis: The Man and His God* (Wilton, Conn.: Morehouse-Barlow, 1987).
33. For example, see Randel Helms, "All Tales Need Not Come True" (*Studies in the Literary Imagination*, no. 2 (1981):31–45) and Lee D. Rossi, *The Politics of Fantasy: C. S. Lewis and J. R. R. Tolkien* (Ann Arbor, Mich.: UMI Research Press, 1984).
34. For example, see James D. Merritt, "'She Pluk'd, She Eat'" in *Future Females: A Critical Anthology*, ed. Marleen S Barr (Bowling Green, Ohio: Bowling Green State University Popular Press, 1981, pp. 37–41) and Susan Cassandra Henthorne, "The Image of Woman in the Fiction of C. S. Lewis" (Ph.D. dissertation, State University of New York at Buffalo, 1985).
35. For example, see Nancy-Lou Patterson, "*Guardaci Ben*: The Visionary Woman in C. S. Lewis' Chronicles of Narnia and *That Hideous Strength*," *Mythlore* 6 (Summer 1979):6–10 and 6 (Fall 1979):20–24 and Karla Faust Jones, "Girls in Narnia: Hindered or Human?" *Mythlore* 13 (Spring 1987):15–19.
36. For example, see Robert Walter Wall, "The Problem of Observed Pain: A Study of C. S. Lewis on Suffering," *Journal of the Evangelical Theological Society* 26, no. 4 (1983):443–451 and Marilyn Chandler Teichert, "A Healing Art: Autobiography and the Peotics of Crisis" (Ph.D. dissertation, Princeton University, 1984).
37. George Musacchio, "C. S. Lewis' *A Grief Obsreved* as Fiction," *Mythlore* 12 (Spring 1986):24–27.
38. Lindskoog, pp. 27–44.
39. Wilson, p. xv.
40. Ibid, p. xvi.
41. Ibid.

Writings by C. S. Lewis

Spirits in Bondage: A Cycle of Lyrics. London: William Heinemann, 1919. Under the pseudonym of Clive Hamilton.

Dymer. London: J. M. Dent, 1926. Under the pseudonym of Clive Hamilton.

The Pilgrim's Regress: An Allegorical Apology for Christianity, Reason and Romanticism. London: J. M. Dent, 1933.

The Allegory of Love: A Study in Medieval Tradition. Oxford: Clarendon Press, 1936.

Out of the Silent Planet. London: Bodley Head, 1938. New York: Macmillan, 1943.

Rehabilitations and Other Essays. London: Oxford University Press, 1939.

The Personal Heresy: A Controversy. London: Oxford University Press, 1939. With E. M. W. Tillyard.

The Problem of Pain. London: Centenary Press, 1940. New York: Macmillan, 1943.

The Screwtape Letters. London: Geoffrey Bles, 1942. New York: Macmillan, 1943.

A Preface to "Paradise Lost": Being the Ballard Matthews Lectures Delivered at University College, North Wales, 1941. Revised and enlarged. London: Oxford University Press, 1942.

Broadcast Talks: Reprinted with Some Alterations from Two Series of Broadcast Talks ("Right and Wrong: A Clue to the Meaning of the Universe" and "What Christians Believe") Given in 1941 and 1942. London: Geoffrey Bles, 1942. Published as *The Case for Christianity*. New York: Macmillan, 1943.

Christian Behaviour: A Further Series of Broadcast Talks. London: Geoffrey Bles, 1943. New York: Macmillan, 1943.

Perelandra. London: Bodley Head, 1943. New York: Macmillan, 1944.

The Abolition of Man: Or Reflections on Education with Special Reference to the Teaching of English in the Upper Forms of Schools. Riddell Memorial

Lectures, Fifteenth Series. London: Oxford University Press, 1943. New York: Macmillan, 1947.

Beyond Personality: The Christian Idea of God. London: Geoffrey Bles, 1944. New York: Macmillan, 1945.

That Hideous Strength: A Modern Fairy-tale for Grown-ups. London: Bodley Head, 1945. New York: Macmillan, 1946.

The Great Divorce: A Dream. London: Geoffrey Bles, 1945. New York: Macmillan, 1946.

George MacDonald: An Anthology. London: Geoffrey Bles, 1946. New York: Macmillan, 1947.

Miracles: A Preliminary Study. London: Geoffrey Bles, 1947. New York: Macmillan 1947. With revised Chapter III. London: Collins-Fontana Books, 1960.

The Arthurian Torso: Containing the Posthumous Fragment of "The Figure of Arthur" by Charles Williams and "A Commentary on the Arthurian Poems of Charles Williams" by C. S. Lewis. London: Oxford University Press, 1948.

Transposition and Other Addresses. London: Geoffrey Bles, 1949. Published as *The Weight of Glory and Other Addresses.* New York: Macmillan, 1949.

The Lion, the Witch and the Wardrobe: A Story for Children. Illustrated by Pauline Baynes. London: Geoffrey Bles, 1950. New York: Macmillan, 1950.

Prince Caspian: The Return to Narnia. Illustrated by Pauline Baynes. London: Geoffrey Bles, 1951. New York: Macmillan, 1951.

Mere Christianity: A Revised and Amplified Edition, with a New Introduction, of the Three Books "Broadcast Talks," "Christian Behaviour," and "Beyond Personality." London: Geoffrey Bles, 1952. Published as *Mere Christianity: A Revised and Enlarged Edition, with a New Introduction, of the Three Books "The Case For Christianity," "Christian Behaviour," and "Beyond Personality."* New York: Macmillan, 1952.

The Voyage of the "Dawn Treader." Illustrated by Pauline Baynes. London: Geoffrey Bles, 1952. New York: Macmillan, 1952.

The Silver Chair. Illustrated by Pauline Baynes. London: Geoffrey Bles, 1953. New York: Macmillan, 1953.

The Horse and His Boy. Illustrated by Pauline Baynes. London: Geoffrey Bles, 1954. New York: Macmillan, 1954.

English Literature in the Sixteenth Century Excluding Drama. The Completion of "The Clark Lectures," Trinity College, Cambridge, 1944. The *Oxford History of English Literature*, vol. 3. Oxford: Clarendon Press, 1954.

The Magician's Nephew. Illustrated by Pauline Baynes. London: Bodley Head, 1955. New York: Macmillan, 1955.

Surprised by Joy: The Shape of My Early Life. London: Geoffrey Bles, 1955. New York: Harcourt, Brace & World, 1956.

The Last Battle: A Story for Children. Illustrated by Pauline Baynes. London: Bodley Head, 1956. Published as *The Last Battle*. New York: Macmillan, 1956.

Till We Have Faces: A Myth Retold. London: Geoffrey Bles, 1956. New York: Harcourt, Brace & World, 1957.

Reflections on the Psalms. London: Geoffrey Bles, 1958. New York: Harcourt, Brace & World, 1958.

The Four Loves. London: Geoffrey Bles, 1960. New York: Harcourt, Brace & World, 1960.

Studies in Words. Cambridge: Cambridge University Press, 1960.

The World's Last Night: And Other Essays. New York: Harcourt, Brace & Co., 1960.

A Grief Observed. London: Faber and Faber, 1961. Greenwich, Conn.: Seabury Press, 1963. Under the pseudonym of N. W. Clerk.

An Experiment in Criticism. Cambridge: Cambridge University Press, 1961.

They Asked for a Paper: Papers and Addresses. London: Geoffrey Bles, 1962.

Beyond the Bright Blur. New York: Harcourt, Brace & World, 1963.

Letters to Malcolm: Chiefly on Prayer. London: Geoffrey Bles, 1964. New York: Harcourt, Brace & World, 1964.

The Discarded Image: An Introduction to Medieval and Renaissance Literature. Cambridge: Cambridge University Press, 1964.

Poems. Edited by Walter Hooper. London: Geoffrey Bles, 1964. New York: Harcourt, Brace & World, 1965.

Screwtape Proposes a Toast and Other Pieces. London: Collins—Fontana Books, 1965.

Letters. Edited, with a memoir, by W. H. Lewis. London: Geoffrey Bles, 1966. New York: Harcourt, Brace & World, 1966.

Studies in Medieval and Renaissance Literature. Collected by Walter Hooper. Cambridge: Cambridge University Press, 1966.

Of Other Worlds: Essays and Stories. Edited by Walter Hooper. London: Geoffrey Bles, 1966. New York: Harcourt, Brace & World, 1967.

Christian Reflections. Edited by Walter Hooper. London: Geoffrey Bles, 1967. Grand Rapids, Mich.: Eerdmans, 1967.

Letters to an American Lady. Edited by Clyde S. Kilby. Grand Rapids, Mich.: Eerdmans, 1967. London: Hodder and Stoughton, 1969.

Spenser's Images of Life. Edited by Alastair Fowler. Cambridge: Cambridge University Press, 1967.

A Mind Awake: An Anthology of C. S. Lewis. Edited by Clyde S. Kilby. London: Geoffrey Bles, 1968. New York: Harcourt, Brace & World, 1969.

Narrative Poems. Edited by Walter Hooper. London: Geoffrey Bles, 1969. New York: Harcourt Brace Jovanovich, 1972.

Selected Literary Essays. Edited by Walter Hooper. London: Cambridge University Press, 1969.

God in the Dock: Essays on Theology and Ethics. Edited by Walter Hooper. Grand Rapids, Mich.: Eerdmans, 1970.

Undeceptions: Essays on Theology and Ethics. Edited by Walter Hooper. London: Geoffrey Bles, 1971.

Fern-seeds and Elephants, and Other Essays on Christianity. Edited by Walter Hooper. London: Fontana, 1975.

The Dark Tower, and Other Stories. Edited by Walter Hooper. London: Collins, 1977. New York: Harcourt Brace Jovanovich, 1977.

The Joyful Christian: 127 Readings from C. S. Lewis. New York: Macmillan, 1977.

They Stand Together: The Letters of C. S. Lewis to Arthur Greeves (1914–1963). Edited by Walter Hooper. London: Collins, 1979. New York: Macmillan, 1979.

The Visionary Christian: 131 Readings from C. S. Lewis. Selected and edited by Chad Walsh. New York: Macmillan, 1981.

Of This and Other Worlds. Edited by Walter Hooper. London: Collins, 1982. Published as *On Stories, and Other Essays on Literature*. New York: Harcourt Brace Jovanovich, 1982.

The Business of Heaven: Daily Readings from C. S. Lewis. Edited by Walter Hooper. London: Fount, 1984. San Diego: Harcourt Brace Jovanovich, 1984.

Boxen: The Imaginary World of the Young C. S. Lewis. Edited by Walter Hooper. London: Collins, 1985. San Diego: Harcourt Brace Jovanovich, 1985.

C. S. Lewis Letters to Children. Edited by Lyle W. Dorsett and Marjorie Lamp Mead. London: Collins, 1985. New York: Macmillan, 1985.

First and Second Things: Essays on Theology and Ethics. Edited by Walter Hooper. London: Collins, 1985.

Present Concerns. Edited by Walter Hooper. London: Fount, 1986. San Diego: Harcourt Brace Jovanovich, 1986.

Timeless at Heart: Essays on Theology. Edited by Walter Hooper. London: Fount, 1987.

The Essential C. S. Lewis. Edited and with an introduction by Lyle W. Dorsett. New York: Macmillan, 1988.

Letters: C. S. Lewis [and] Don Giovanni Calabria: A Study in Friendship. Translated and edited by Martin Moynihan. London: Collins, 1988. Ann Arbor, Mich.: Servant Publications, 1988.

The Quotable Lewis. Edited by Wayne Martindale and Jerry Root. Wheaton, Ill.: Tyndale House, 1989.

Christian Reunion and Other Essays. Edited by Walter Hooper. London: Collins, 1990.

All My Road before Me: The Diary of C. S. Lewis, 1922–1927. Edited by Walter Hooper. London: Harper Collins, 1991. San Diego: Harcourt Brace Jovanovich, 1991.

Writings about C. S. Lewis

1972

1 BABBAGE, STUART B. "C. S. Lewis and the Humanitarian Theory of Punishment." *Christian Scholar's Review* 2:224–235.

Lewis felt the humanitarian theory of punishment, which treats crime pathologically and the criminal with psychiatry, reduces the criminal to the level of nonrational being and deprives him of his humanity. "'Mercy, detached from Justice, grows unmerciful.'" He wished society to be protected but put the rights of the individual ahead of those of society. He wanted punishment and loss of liberty to be on retributive grounds and felt the survival of our humanity was at stake.

2 "C. S. Lewis's Dedicatees." *CSL: The Bulletin of the New York C. S. Lewis Society* 3 (August):4–5.

This article lists twenty-five books Lewis dedicated to individuals or groups. It provides brief identification of dedicatees not well known.

3 CARLETON, JIM. "Wondelone." *Parma Eldalamberon: The Book of Eleven Tongues* 1, no. 2:4.

Several words in Old Solar are very close to human language even though Ransom states that no human languages descended from Old Solar. The *hnau* use Old Solar for communication between the species but each uses a separate language for communication within species, reflecting the needs of their specialized fields. Lewis has the modifier follow the word modified.

4 CHRISTOPHER, JOE R. "C. S. Lewis vs. Restoration Comedy." *CSL: The Bulletin of the New York C. S. Lewis Society* 4 (November):4–5.

Lewis's romanticism and desire for magnitude could not be satisfied in Restoration comedy, which depicted a "world of elegant cuckoldry and cynic wit." He objected to the agnostic humanism in the "world devoid of ultimate meaning" of Restoration comedy. Lewis believed in and defended traditional morality and "stock responses."

1972

5. ———. "A Serious Limerick." *The Chronicle of the Portland C. S. Lewis Society* 1, no. 8 (8 September):4–5.

    Lewis's "Epitaph" published in *Time and Tide* June 6, 1942, on page 460 and reprinted in Poems as number 11 of Epigrams and Epitaphs has a limerick's rhyme scheme (AABA) and metrical stresses (3.3.2.2.3.). The irony in using the same description for the girl and the bomb is accomplished by breaking the usual limerick rhythm. Lewis's "shifts in rhythm turn the poem into a statement rather than a jingle."

6   COMO, JAMES T. "C. S. Lewis in Milton Criticism." *CSL: The Bulletin of the New York C. S. Lewis Society* 3 (October):5–6.

    Lewis's *A Preface to "Paradise Lost"* "tells us much about the art of poetry and about poetry in the West," as well as about Milton's poem. His explanation of Milton's treatment of Satan is an important contribution to Milton criticism. But "perhaps Lewis's greatest accomplishment . . . was to define the genre of *Paradise Lost* as that of Secondary Epic, wherein the theme is great, unchanging, and remote, and the manner is ceremonial."

7   ———. "Myth and Belief in *Perelandra*." *CSL: The Bulletin of the New York C. S. Lewis Society* 4 (December):2–7.

    The novel's structure is narrative framework: Eden, temptation, descent and ascent; the form is epical. It is about the Christian myth and is intended, in part, to teach; the power of myth accounts for its success. Symbols employed are psychoracial archetypes that create a strong and affirmative response. Mythic elements are a story that has extraliterary value, provides numinous experience, "conveys a meaning embodied in itself," "deals with impossibles and preternaturals," and exposes a reality, a truth, that we have always wanted.

8   DAY, JACK E. "Notes on *The Great Divorce*." *Chronicle of the Portland C. S. Lewis Society* 1, no. 6 (7 July):4–6.

    The Great Divorce retells the *Refrigium*, the respite given to souls of the damned. Lewis wrote it to show that only through the surrender of self-will can one come into God's presence. The characters are bundles of common sins. We learn about the personality types the narrator finds offensive and about his less attractive traits.

9   GARNER, ROSS. "In Praise of Fairy Tales." *Chronicle of the Portland C. S. Lewis Society* 1, no. 10 (3 November):3–4.

    Fairy tales "introduce us *into* reality." The Land of Faerie is a different dimension, with arbitrary rules that cut through to essentials. Lewis's Space Trilogy is a fairy tale because it has the distinguishing marks of wonder, difference of place, arbitrariness of rules, and decisions made without regard to their practical effects.

10 GREEN, CAROLE. "Lewis in *The Lion, the Witch and the Wardrobe*." *Chronicle of the Portland C. S. Lewis Society* 1, no. 11 (1 December):4–7.

There are problems of inner consistency in the novel such as the Narnians speaking English and celebrating Christmas. The novel shows Lewis's philosophy on English grammar schools, sex roles, the Lilith myth, the moral law, chronological snobbery, and miracles. Narnia is Lewis's myth at its best. "The themes of deep magic, ancient truth, and prophecy run through the book." The character of Edmund shows the process of giving in to evil and of redemption. The novel also reveals Joy in the characters' experiences and arouses it in the reader.

11 HILDERBRAND, GERALD. "C. S. Lewis' *Miracles*, a Brief Look." *Chronicle of the Portland C. S. Lewis Society* 1, no. 9 (6 October):5–6.

The purpose of *Miracles* is to consider "the philosophical question as to whether miracles can happen or not [which] determines the answer to the historical question."

12 HODGENS, RICHARD [M.]. "J. B. S. Haldane, Jailor." *CSL: The Bulletin of the New York C. S. Lewis Society* 3 (July):6–7.

"Haldane certainly served as an irritant for Lewis." The Jailor in *The Pilgrim's Regress* parrots Haldane's *Daedalus or Science and the Future* (New York: Dutton, 1924) and Weston in *Out of the Silent Planet* parrots his *Last Judgment: A Scientist's Vision of the Future of Man* (New York: Harper & Brothers, 1927). Haldane's attack on the Ransom Trilogy in "Auld Hornie, F. R. S." is "a pathetic tissue of misunderstandings and non-sequiturs, and not often very funny."

13 ———. "The Planetology of C. S. Lewis: A Summary." *CSL: The Bulletin of the New York C. S. Lewis Society* 3 (July):2–5.

The features of Mars, Venus, and the Moon as Lewis describes them are "traditional"; in peopling these planets he "followed a long optimistic tradition begun in ancient times, revived in the Renaissance and followed by a majority of astronomers to his own time." At the time he wrote, his astronomy was modern and tenable. He does make mistakes in his descriptions but only in details that would escape the "common reader"; these errors do not indicate a contempt for science. Lewis disapproved of actual space travel: he was afraid that "if Malacandra and Perelandra existed, we would ruin them."

14 HUTTON, MURIEL. ". . . And I quote." *CSL: The Bulletin of the New York C. S. Lewis Society* 3 (September):5–16.

Hutton cites instances where Lewis quoted MacDonald "admiringly, suggesting that his 'master' has made the point better than he can." In compiling *George MacDonald: An Anthology* Lewis selected, emphasized, and repeated those opinions of MacDonald he most strongly held himself. Lewis

1972

may have been "compiling a sort of anthology à clef, offering all the main clues to students of his work and its debt to MacDonald."

15   KIMBALL, WILLIAM CLAYTON. "The Christian Commitment: C. S. Lewis and the Defense of Doctrine." *Brigham Young University Studies* 12 (Winter):185–208.

This overview of Lewis's life and work shows that he "understood the problems and frustrations that accompany the Christian quest." His insights into human weakness, his sheer common sense, his emphasis on the practical, and his style made him effective in presenting his religious message. His imaginative works are infused with an "atmosphere of desperate courage, of wild romance, of great deeds done in the face of hopeless odds." Latter-day Saints can turn to Lewis, not to learn what to believe, because there are doctrinal differences between Lewis and the Mormon Church, but in order to learn how to become better Christians.

16   KIRKPATRICK, HOPE. "Some Preliminary Thoughts on Lewis and Freud." *CSL: The Bulletin of the New York C. S. Lewis Society* 3 (September):2–4.

The dangers Lewis saw in Freud's work were his attack on religion and "immortal longings," his distortion of perspective, and his belief that sexual satisfaction was man's highest pleasure. Lewis felt psychoanalysis was consistent with Christianity as long as the science or method remained separated from the philosophy, the analyst's interpretation. However, he felt there was something morbid and egotistical in such curiosity about oneself.

17   LANDER, JOYCE. "On *Preface to 'Paradise Lost.'*" *Chronicle of the Portland C. S. Lewis Society* 1, no. 8 (8 September):6–7.

Lewis was more than qualified to judge Milton because he was a medieval scholar and a Christian. His criticism is constructive. "In order to understand what Milton was actually saying, Lewis saw the importance of understanding the epic form, the style, and the content of *Paradise Lost.*"

18   "Major Warren H. Lewis." *CSL: The Bulletin of the New York C. S. Lewis Society* 3 (August):1–4.

Warren's scholarly career centered on seventeenth-century France. He has clarity of style and nicety of expression, he creates the historical sense and feeling of the period, he treats his characters with sympathy and respect, and his history has "an anecdotal style, centered on individuals, their actions and influences." A bibliography of his works is included.

19   NOEL, HENRY. "My Kind of Lewis." *Chronicle of the Portland C. S. Lewis Society* 1, no. 7 (4 August):3–7.

Approximately 85 percent of those who admire Lewis are people who enjoy one or more kinds of Lewis's writing. About 14 percent also admire him as a person. A very large number of his admirers are not Christians. Most know and like only parts of his writings or certain aspects of his personality. The real Lewis is full of surprises in the things in which he believed. In his poetry, "his skill in metric patterns is masterly, his rhymes are never forced, his vocabulary is immense and versatile, his images are often memorable, his insights are subtle and profound." One can affirm that Lewis's poetry is "good" only by affirming that modern poetry is not "good."

20 PURCELL, JAMES MARK. *"Narrative Poems." CSL: The Bulletin of the New York C. S. Lewis Society* 4 (November):2–3.
    Lewis's greatest desire was to be a poet; "his novels and other books are often only prose redactions of earlier poems." He attempted to revive the tradition of long verse narrative. He "distrusted the style of contemporary verse" and his poetry is in conscious revolt against the poets whose "stories come closer to the realistic novel than to pure romance." "Queen of Drum" is in iambic pentameter rhymed couplets and shows the influence of Morris and Browning. "Lancelot" is meant to be read as "Elizabethan iambic pentameters, with two extra unstressed syllables and . . . a double pause in each line."

21 ROBERTS, DONALD A. *"A Preface to 'Paradise Lost.'" CSL: The Bulletin of the New York C. S. Lewis Society* 3 (October 1972):2–5.
    Lewis "bravely and defiantly reaffirmed Milton's primacy among the masters of heroic poetry, and . . . reasserted the profoundly Christian character of his writing." He had lapses in taste and judgment in complaining of the anthropomorphism of God, the treatment of the war in heaven and various aspects of heavenly living, and in concluding that it was not a religious poem. He deserves ultimate praise for demolishing the "absurd notion that Satan is the 'Hero' of *Paradise Lost.*"

22 ROGERS, DEBORAH CHAMPION WEBSTER. "The Fictitious Characters of C. S. Lewis and J. R. R. Tolkien in Relation to Their Medieval Sources." Ph.D. dissertation, University of Wisconsin, 220 pp.
    Medieval literature influenced Lewis and Tolkien but they diverged from it. Their heroes start small and grow into a balanced superiority. They are concerned with the theme of couples rather than the medieval love triangle. They have "a vivid consciousness of companionship and friendship." Their villains have the greatest qualities but have perverted them; Lewis's villains are "the bad rulers, ability to govern perverted to lust for domination; and the bad intellectual, brain-power perverted to self-serving and prying." He stressed the danger of magic to humans; most of his magicians are bad. "With his abundance of realistic detail, Lewis's characterization seems more in the prevailing twentieth-century mode," but his view of man and of "how much man needs allegiance to a higher Being before he can do anything" is in harmony with the Middle Ages.

21

1973

*23 ROSSI, LEE DONALD. "The Politics of Fantasy: C. S. Lewis and J. R .R. Tolkien." *DAI* 33 (1973):5195A. Cornell University, 264 pp.

Lewis's best works attempt to create alternative worlds where one can escape the evils of the modern world. "His heroes are confronted by the impoverishment of social and political life," and metaphors of flight and escape are central to his works. Lewis's fantasies are a response to the threatening realities of his family, his schools, and Europe during World War I; his attention turned inward away from the public world to imaginary worlds and questions of personal salvation. He concentrated on a search for alternative realities and values.

24 VAN WAASDIJK, E. J. "Letter from Holland." *CSL: The Bulletin of the New York C. S. Lewis Society* 4 (November):5–6.

The Screwtape Letters is Lewis's best-known work in the Netherlands. In theological circles in Amsterdam he is virtually unknown, but he is familiar to those who study English literature. Lewis's "first concern was to 'undeafen' the ears of his readers to the voice of Our Lord," and so he did not concern himself with what each denomination believed.

25 WILLIAMS, TERRI. "Lewis's Hell—A Bugbear?" *Chronicle of the Portland C. S. Lewis Society* 1, no. 6 (7 July): 7–8.

Lewis's hell in *The Great Divorce* is frightening because the danger is not apparent or predictable at first. The unexpected, the unpredictable, causes real fear.

*26 WONG, FRAN. "Between the Paws of the True Aslan." Crux 10, no. 1:10–15.

Source of citation: *Religious and Theological Abstracts*, vol. 17, 1974.

1973

1 BABBAGE, STUART B. "C. S. Lewis and the Humanist Dilemma." *The Reformed Theological Review* 32 (September–December):73–81.

Lewis wrote *The Pilgrim's Regress* to indicate a middle path between the philosophies of the North, rigidly skeptical or dogmatic, and those of the South, open to every sort of intoxication. He said we live in a post–Christian age; the humanists are wrong, the Great Divide did not occur between the Middle Ages and the Renaissance but between Jane Austen's age and our own. Humanism is negated by the "congenital weakness of human nature." Awareness of failure leads the Christian to repentance, the humanist to self-contempt. Humanists "can tell us what we ought to do but they cannot tell us how."

2 CHRISTOPHER, JOE R. "An Introduction to Narnia Part IV: The Literary Classification of The Chronicles." *Mythlore*, no. 9:12–15, 27.

Following Graham Hough's classification, certain elements in the chronicles are "'Humor' Literature and Romance of Types," mainly the non-human characters, and "Freestyle Allegory," where allegorical significance comes and goes at will. They have many similarities with Spenser's allegory *The Faerie Queen*—both deal with holiness, temperance, friendship, and justice. In Northrop Frye's classification scheme they are "Myth" in the parts dealing with Aslan, "Romance" because of the talking animals and witches, and "High Minesis" as the hero is superior to other men but not the environment.

3 ———. "Joseph Wood Krutch and C. S. Lewis: A Comparison and a Letter." *CSL: The Bulletin of the New York C. S. Lewis Society* 4 (October):3–4.

Krutch in "Life, Liberty and the Pursuit of Welfare" (Saturday Evening Post 234 [15 July 1961]:18–19, 56–58) states that the source of absolute standards is "'something permanent in human nature itself.'" Lewis in the first chapter of *Mere Christianity* goes from Krutch's beginning, that everyone has a sense of justice, the moral law, and states that this implies the existence of a Law-Giver, "a moral God who has built morality into the conscious aspects of this universe."

4 DAY, MARGIE. *"The Problem of Pain."* *Chronicle of the Portland C. S. Lewis Society* 2, no. 7 (3 August):2–3.

The Problem of Pain is an intellectual study. Lewis argues that nature cannot be used to prove the existence of God because He is outside nature. All religions involve three elements: experience of the numinous, morality, and the Numinous Power as guardian of morality. Christianity adds the element of a historical man who claims to be the Giver of the moral law. Lewis proves that God uses pain to shatter our illusions that all is well and to prompt us to surrender our self-will.

5 DYE, CLARENCE FRANCIS. "The Evolving Eschaton in C. S. Lewis." Ph.D. dissertation, Fordham University, 288 pp.

Lewis's central theological theme is eschatology as a dynamic process that starts at birth. His basic premise is man's immortality and the vehicle for the process is man's free choice. Though man and God were separated in the Fall through man's free choice, God has not abandoned man. He has given him *Sehnsucht*, "a memory of what was and a hope for what might be," and Tao, the moral pattern in nature. Each person must choose God or himself; hell "will be an eternal process of turning in on oneself" while heaven "will be the ultimate experiencing of God." The danger Lewis saw in science and technology is their view that man is an end in himself. Lewis's weakness is his "lack of regard for modern biblical criticism" that "denies the action of the Holy Spirit in our present day and age." His greatest contribution is "his insistence on the free will of man."

6   FITZPATRICK, JOHN. "Myth in the Apologetic Works." *CSL: The Bulletin of the New York C. S. Lewis Society* 4 (September):4–7.

Lewis insisted "that the myths in Scripture are important *in themselves* as well as for the meanings they convey." He does not insist they be accepted literally but does not rule out the possibility that they may be literally true. Lewis said Christianity lacks the grandeur and richness of other mythologies but represents " 'the humiliation of myth into fact.' " As a literary critic, Lewis insisted that the "gospels are either truth, or lies, or a very early example of psychological realism." He felt that the story of Christ demands from us a religious, historical, and imaginative response.

7   FRANCESCHELLI, AMOS. "Anthroposophy—The Teachings of Rudolf Steiner with Special Reference to C. S. Lewis." *CSL: The Bulletin of the New York C. S. Lewis Society* 4 (May):2–6.

The author quotes passages in Lewis's works that refer directly to anthroposophy. Common elements in Lewis and Steiner are the role of thought as an activity "through which we strive toward Truth," the denial of chronological snobbery, and the affirmation of the operative presence of Christ.

8   "Further Up and Further In." *Christianity Today* 18 (9 November):38–39.

Christianity is the solid base of all Lewis's writings. He deals "specifically with man's longing for God, the sin-created gulf separating God and man, and the problem of evil, which often causes man to reject the idea of God's existence." His imagination, through the "use of rhythm, geographic detail, vowel music and onomatopoeia," infuses *Till We Have Faces* and the Chronicles of Narnia with *Sehnsucht*, the longing for God and heaven which is part of every person.

9   GILBERT, DOUGLAS, and KILBY, CLYDE S. *C. S. Lewis: Images of His World*. Grand Rapids, Mich.: Eerdmans. 192 pp. Reprint. London: Hodder and Stoughton, 1973.

Photographs of people and places important to Lewis are accompanied by brief text, often in Lewis's own words, detailing their relationship to him, his feelings or thoughts about them, or the individual's reaction to Lewis. The source of each quotation is provided. The collection also contains reproductions of Lewis's earliest manuscripts, stories of Animal-Land, with his illustrations. It provides a brief chronology of Lewis's life and a separate account of his conversion to Christianity.

10 GOODKNIGHT, GLEN [H.], and BRENION, FREDERICK. "Walter Hooper: A Thank You." *Mythlore*, no. 9:28.

This article lists the works by Lewis collected or edited by Hooper as well as the articles he wrote on Lewis.

11 HANNAY, MARGARET P[ATTERSON]. "C. S. Lewis and Homosexuality." *CSL: The Bulletin of the New York C. S. Lewis Society* 5 (November):2–5.

Lewis found homosexuality "opaque to the imagination." He viewed it as a sin and an affliction but felt that "sins of the spirit are always worse than sins of the body." He was angered by those who try to read homosexuality into male friendships. Lewis treated pederasty in classical Greek authors as he did the faults of other great writers: he abstracted the philosophy from its context. Since he was not a classicist, this inability to understand erotic attraction between males is not a serious handicap to his literary scholarship.

12 HARMS, PAUL W. F. "C. S. Lewis as Translator." Ph.D. dissertation, Northwestern University, 306 pp.

Lewis's intention in his apologetics was to translate "classical Christianity, stated in learned English, into the language of the English vernacular." His style consists of close attention to his audience, a discriminating choice of language, irony, wit, humor, illustration, metaphor, free use of reason and imagination, and an air of the spoken word. *Mere Christianity*, *Miracles*, *Letters to Malcolm*, and *The Great Divorce* are each studied in depth. Lewis's contribution to rhetoric was "the capacity for 'rendering imaginable what before was only intelligible.'"

13 HENDRICKSON, DAVID. "An Appreciation of G. K. Chesterton Inspired by C. S. Lewis." *Chronicle of the Portland C. S. Lewis Society* 1, no. 12 (5 January):3–10.

Both Chesterton and Lewis longed for truth and pursued it intellectually and emotionally. Chesterton "made such an immediate conquest of Lewis because they met in Fairyland, a place where pessimism, atheism and hatred of sentiment are revealed as the unreal things they are." Lewis found in Chesterton honesty, humor, and goodness. In Chesterton he "discovered that the pagan sentiments weren't so much in need of changing as of expansion and completion."

14 HOLBROOK, DAVID. "The Problem of C. S. Lewis." *Children's Literature in Education*, no. 10 (March):3–25.

The Narnian Chronicles have their origins in Lewis's psychic hunger for the mother who died when he was an infant. In the "other world" of Narnia, that of the unconscious, of death, the mother encountered has not been humanized by child and is the all-bad, all-hate, "castrating mother," the White Witch. We are dealing with deep primitive symbolism and "because so many bodily

1973

feelings are involved the imagery is very sexual." Evil is represented by the non-human and thus justifies immediate hostility; in Narnia the primary ethical requirement is to be ready to fight. The children never make choices, they never escape magical control and determinism. The hate, fear, and sadism in the Chronicles is not relieved by humanizing benignity. See response 1977.25 and reply 1978.17.

15   JANSSEN, GUTHRIE E. "*The Abolition of Man*: A Review." *Chronicle of the Portland C. S. Lewis Society* 2, no. 4 (4 May):2–6.
      Lewis criticizes scientism, environmentalism, and pragmatism. He is concerned with issues of epistemology and cognition. Lewis argues that there are constants, the Tao, which God has ordained. Current philosophical orientations—the doctrine of progress, that everything is relative, that the only constant is change, and that truth can be affirmed only from experience—will be the destruction of the society that accepts them.

16   KILBY, CLYDE S. Interview. *Chronicle of the Portland C. S. Lewis Society* 2, no. 3 (20 April):1–6.
      There is something supernatural about Lewis's books; in his works coincidence is the act of the sovereign God. His genius was to be off-hand when witnessing to people. He was antagonistic to modernism in religion and firmly on the side of orthodoxy. Lewis "*assumed* the Holy Spirit." He has written more powerfully on joy than anyone since St. John on Patmos. He believed in purgatory for saved people and felt that everyone in heaven would learn to worship God in his or her unique way.

17   ———. "The Lewis Collection at Wheaton College." *CSL: The Bulletin of the New York C. S. Lewis Society* 5 (November):6.
      This article details the Lewis holdings as of September 1973.

18   KIRKPATRICK, HOPE. "Lewis *contra* Freud." *CSL: The Bulletin of the New York C. S. Lewis Society* 4 (February):2–6.
      Lewis disagreed with Freud's idea that art is produced from daydreams and wish fulfillment. He said art evokes "immortal longings" and is the product of disinterested imagination. He disagreed that religion and literature show an unconscious interest in sex. He also disapproved of analyzing the artist rather than the work of art.

19   ———. "A Reply to Dr. Plank." *CSL: The Bulletin of the New York C. S. Lewis Society* 4 (April):8–9.
      Lewis had no quarrel with the technique of psychoanalysis but feared that an analyst, using his own values, would try to help a patient view himself and the world more realistically by curing him of Christianity. See 1973.33.

20 KRANZ, GILBERT. "Dante in the Works of C. S. Lewis." Translated by Hope Kirkpatrick. *CSL: The Bulletin of the New York C. S. Lewis Society* 4 (August):1–8.

Lewis felt Dante was the most sublime Christian poet and that *The Divine Comedy* was the greatest achievement of medieval art and thought. Lewis and Dante had in common "a strong Christian faith, an outspoken ethical conviction, sensitivity to language and knowledge of the ancient and medieval poets and philosophers"; they differed in temperament and character. Dante made a large impact on Lewis's imagination; Lewis used many quotes from Dante, his verses as chapter headings, and "Dantesque expressions to illustrate philosophical or religious insights or to characterize some situations in his own life." *The Pilgrim's Regress*, *The Great Divorce*, and the Ransom Trilogy show Dante's influence most strongly.

21 "Lewis, The Christian Rhetorician." *CSL: The Bulletin of the New York C. S. Lewis Society* 4 (September):1–4.

Lewis as a rhetorician adapted himself to the post–Christian world, using an intellectual militancy in defense of Christianity against the enemy, Satan. He chose a non-expert audience and deliberately presented himself as relatively ignorant, with humility, and as a real convert from atheism. Much of his appeal comes from his reliance on reason; he did not use many emotional appeals but instead appealed to the imagination. His organization is almost faultless. His style accounts for much of his success; its qualities are simplicity, popular tone, personal intimacy, variety of sentence structure, and clarity.

22 "Lewis's Revision of *Miracles*, Chapter 3." *CSL: The Bulletin of the New York C. S. Lewis Society* 4 (July 1973):4–6.

Lewis objected to the naturalist's view of thought as a product of nonrational causes because it means surrendering a belief in the validity of reason. G. E. M. Anscombe argued that thought, like other human behavior, can be observed and the causes of a particular thought can be discovered; nothing will have been determined about the validity of the thought itself since this was not examined. Lewis conceded several points to Anscombe but maintained confidence that "valid reasoning" can lead us to the truth. His solution is to say that one thought can "stand in a Cause–Effect relationship to another thought by *being seen to be* a ground for it." This "act of inference" is a unique mode of causation which can only be accounted for as being derived from divine reason.

23 LINDSKOOG, KATHRYN ANN. *C. S. Lewis: Mere Christian.* Glendale, Calif.: Regal Books, 242 pp.

Lindskoog summarizes Lewis's views on the key topics of God, nature, man, death, heaven, hell, miracles, prayer, pain, love, ethics, and truth. The book includes a short biography, lists key places in Lewis's life, provides a list of special resources, and includes a chronological list of Lewis's books. See 1981.37 for revised and expanded edition.

24   LINTON, CALVIN D. "C. S. Lewis Ten Years Later." *Christianity Today* 18 (9 November):4–7.

One of Lewis's major contributions as a literary historian was to show that the shift from "a God-centered universe of order, hierarchy, purpose and 'dance and harmony' to a man-centered (that is self-centered) cosmology of the psyche" occurred with the Romantic movement, not in the Renaissance. He increased our understanding of the nature of the romantic hero as rebel. His contributions to philosophy include demonstrating that Christianity "need fear no intellectual assault" and pointing out the futilities of science and the deficiencies of materialism, naturalism, and romantic sentimentalism as ways to know ourselves and the world. His novels dislocate us from reality and convince us of another existence. His personality shines through his works; technical aspects of his style are precision, felicity of phrase, intricate but clear syntax, and rhythmic grace. "One century cannot hope to see again such an assemblage of gifts." Reprinted: 1976.28.

25   LLOYD, JOAN. "Transcendent Sexuality as C. S. Lewis Saw It." *Christianity Today* 18 (9 November):7–10.

Lewis viewed sexuality or gender as a metaphysical reality defined by God that transcends biological reality. Masculine is grounded in the demand for obedience, feminine in obedience; thus God is ultimately masculine and His creation feminine. *Perelandra, That Hideous Strength*, and the Chronicles of Narnia demonstrate some aspects of masculine and feminine. Humans display characteristics of both genders; marriage is "the mystical image of the union between God and man," a union of the personalities of both husband and wife into a new one.

26   LOBDELL, JARED C. "The True Narnia." *Triumph* 8 (January):37–38.

The Chronicles attempt to "clothe the bones of Christianity in new flesh." Lewis is most himself when he is most literary, as he is here, using the inventions of others, if not his own.

27   McGOVERN, EUGENE. "Obstinacy in Belief at the Socratic Club." *CSL: The Bulletin of the New York C. S. Lewis Society* 4 (January):2–5.

Lewis felt that "questions worth discussing have objective answers which are accessible to reason"; the Socratic Club was a means to discover some answers about the Christian religion. A Christian believes and no evidence can convince him otherwise. In his essay "On Obstinacy in Belief," Lewis showed this attitude is "a *logical* requirement of the *meaning* of the statement 'I am a Christian.'" Christianity involves a relationship with a Person and is well worth the risk of being wrong.

28 MOBLEY, JONNIE PATRICIA. "Toward Logres: The Operation of Efficacious Grace in Novels on C. S. Lewis, Charles Williams, Muriel Spark, and Gabriel Fielding." Ph.D. dissertation, University of Southern California, 155 pp.

Logres, a dream that haunts people in every age, is a mythical city founded on unselfish love, a kingdom of complete humanity with the beauty and splendor of order. Efficacious grace, the "divine impulse moving a person to perform acts above his natural powers," is the force that creates Logres. Lewis in *That Hideous Strength* shows how this grace affects Jane and Mark Studdock and leads them toward Logres.

29 MORRIS, CLIFFORD. "A Non-Academic Portrait of C. S. Lewis (1898-1963)." *Chronicle of the Portland C.S. Lewis Society* 2, no. 10 (2 November):5–12.

Morris was Lewis's driver during his last years. He remembers Lewis as a dear and lovable man, a true friend and splendid companion, a Christian warrior of the highest order. He "was a man to whom one would go in any sort of trouble and be sure that one would receive *all that could possibly be given* of Christian love, understanding, and helpfulness." Reprinted: 1979.76

30 NOEL, HENRY. "Lewis vs. Bultmann in L'Aigle." *CSL: The Bulletin of the New York C. S. Lewis Society* 4 (April):9–10.

The claim that the Gospel account of Christ's birth is not historical reality but merely symbolic and poetic is straight out of Rudolf Bultmann's *Die Geschichte der Synoptischen Tradition* (Göttingen: Vandenhoeck and Ruprecht, 1921). Lewis wrote in "Modern Theology and Biblical Criticism" that he has been reading poems, legends, and romances all his life, that he knows what these are like, and that the Gospel is neither legend nor romance.

31 ———. "Was C. S. Lewis a Calvinist?" *Chronicle of the Portland C. S. Lewis Society* 2, no. 8 (7 September):2–4.

In *The Problem of Pain* and in *Letters to Malcolm* Lewis "made it abundantly clear that he did not subscribe to the basic tenets of Calvinism," which is the idea of that some people are predestined by God to go to hell.

32 O'HARE, COLMAN. "Charles Williams, C. S. Lewis and J. R. R. Tolkien: Three Approaches to Religion in Modern Fiction." Ph.D. dissertation, University of Toronto, 413 pp.

Lewis, Williams, and Tolkien differed in what they saw as the dangers to Christianity, the solutions they proposed to these dangers, and the form in which they presented their concerns. Lewis used the technique of *reductio ad absurdum*, Chesterton's method, in *The Screwtape Letters* and the Ransom Trilogy to attack the historical point of view and scientism. He used material from the art and life of Williams in *That Hideous Strength* thus weakening the artistic credibility of the trilogy as a whole.

1973

33 PLANK, ROBERT. "Can Lewis and Freud Be Reconciled?" *CSL: The Bulletin of the New York C. S. Lewis Society* 4 (March):5–7.

This is a reply to Kirkpatrick's article "Lewis *contra* Freud" [see 1973.18]. Freud thought human behavior was determined by the conflict between the drive to love and life and the drive to destruction and death. He recognized literature that transcended self-centered daydreams. He said symbols of sex are found in religion and literature, not that they are only a substitute. A psychoanalyst would never attempt to convert his patient away from Christianity. For Kirkpatrick's response, see 1973.19.

34 PURCELL, JAMES MARK. "Lewis vs. Empson: Was Eden Plato's or OGPU's?" *CSL: The Bulletin of the New York C. S. Lewis Society* 4 (April):6–8.

Lewis in *Preface to "Paradise Lost"* and William Empson in *Milton's God* (London: Chatto & Windus, 1961) are both concerned with Milton's "theme of the revolt against Omnipotence." Both describe the working order of the "traditional European Christian monarchist state as it functioned *c* 1300—the French Revolution." However, Lewis saw rebellion as treason against God and the Christian–Platonic order. Empson saw rebellion as morally heroic, that the system created its rebels because it demoralized its creatures. Their debate is "over the social structure of the traditional European Christian state."

35 RICE, ROBERT C. "*Sehnsucht* and Joy." *CSL: The Bulletin of the New York C. S. Lewis Society* 4 (June):2–4.

Lewis is the only writer to deal successfully with *Sehnsucht*; he does so masterfully, decorously, and with true *pietas*. Lewis came to realize that Joy was not attached to anything or was not in the thing that evoked it; he realized that Joy was a reminder but did not understand, until he converted to Christianity, that what Joy pointed to was the "true End or Object of our deepest desiring," God.

36 ROBERTS, DONALD A. "C. S. Lewis and the Worship of the Church." *CSL: The Bulletin of the New York C. S. Lewis Society* 4 (April):5-6.

Lewis discusses the confused state of the church today, its divisions in body and spirit; he deals firmly but discreetly with the coercive and immature alterations in the liturgy, in the mode of worship, and in traditional doctrine.

37 ROUTLEY, Erik. "The Prophet Lewis." *CSL: The Bulletin of the New York C. S. Lewis Society* 4 (January):5–7.

At Oxford, 1939–1945, Routley heard Lewis's sermons "Learning in Wartime" and "The Weight of Glory." He "had a superbly unaffected delivery . . . used words as precision tools, the effortless rhythm of the sentences, the scholarship made friendly, the sternness made beautiful." His great secret was that he hated casual contacts; human contact had to be serious, concentrated, and attentive, regardless of its length, or it was best avoided. Reprinted: 1979.89, 90; 1983.64.

38   SMITH, CHARLES. "*Out of the Silent Planet.*" *Chronicle of the Portland C. S. Lewis Society* 2, no. 1 (2 February):3–5.
      Lewis's science fiction has the marvelous in the grain of each work. The Trilogy's framework is the biblical myth of creation and redemption, its value system is the Tao, its morality is a "blend of rigorous duty, scrupulous justice, and blinding magnanimity."

39   SOTH, CONNIE. "Reflections on *The Horse and His Boy.*" *Chronicle of the Portland C. S. Lewis Society* 2, no. 11 (7 December):4–6.
      In the novel Lewis slyly pokes fun at human pretensions. The Chronicles offer a welcome escape from the frenetic world and, because of Lewis's refreshing worldview, they provide a renewed sense of God's goodness and humor.

40   STEVENSON, KAY. "On 'Religious Controversy and Translation': An Introduction to *English Literature in the 16th Century.*" *CSL: The Bulletin of the New York C. S. Lewis Society* 4 (March):1–5.
      This chapter shows Lewis at his worst and his best. He uses labels, such as "Drab" and "Papist," which are not meant to be dyslogistic but have that connotation. Lewis's likes and dislikes are evident throughout. He is incapable of entering sympathetically into the Renaissance. He makes the writers into living personalities, "his style is a source of delight," and he brings a "sense of freshness, of alertness and responsiveness to the reading" of these works.

41   SWEENEY, JAMES. "C. S. Lewis: Speaker." *Chronicle of the Portland C. S. Lewis Society* 2, no. 2 (2 March):2–9.
      Lewis is "the living example of what real inter-personal communication is supposed to be and do." He cultivated communicative techniques in speech, was aware of the effects of speech communication, possessed a communicative attitude that caused him to desire interaction with people, relished provocative communication, and possessed the capability to make his listener or reader an active partner. Lewis also had an esteem and appreciation for language, was able to identify with the audience to which he wanted to communicate, had a disciplined mind, made ideas sparkle, was brilliant at metaphor and analogy, possessed a faculty of vividness, and achieved perfection in the marriage of the written and spoken word.

1973

42 *"That Hideous Strength." CSL: The Bulletin of the New York C. S. Lewis Society* 4 (March):1–5.

    Ransom is not the hero as he was of the first two novels; the focus is on the Studdocks and their marriage. The influence of Williams is evident in the Arthurian material; Tolkien and Chesterton also influenced the novel. The novel uses an omniscient narrator, unlike the first two, perhaps because of the complications of the plot, the "violent kineticism of the evil that Lewis wished to depict," or because of the various strands interwoven, in which case the narrative mode might be considered "polyphonic." Lewis attacks "behaviourism, bureaucracy, technology, modern education, newspapers, misguided feminism, 'the Inner Ring,' 'Men Without Chests,'" and the degradation of language.

43 WENNBERG, ROBERT. "Legal Punishment and Its Justification." *Christian Scholar's Review* 3:99–112.

    Lewis is correct in his arguments "that considerations of deterrence and treatment are not by themselves adequate to the task of justifying a morally acceptable system of punishment." However, the retributive theory as Lewis espoused it does not provide against inhumane treatment of the guilty and it is too restrictive in ruling out the victimization of the innocent because it excludes all offenses of strict liability. Each of these mono-value approaches "—deterrent, therapeutic, or retributive—fails to reckon with other values that ought to be taken into account." See Richards's response, 1985.67.

44 WHITE, WILLIAM LUTHER, and PETERSON, JAN. "Some Books by C. S. Lewis in Foreign Translations." *CSL: The Bulletin of the New York C. S. Lewis Society* 5 (November):5.

    The article offers a selected list of thirteen translations of Lewis's works in various languages.

45 WRONG, CHARLES. "Meeting with C. S. Lewis in Broad St., Oxford, this Afternoon (August 8, 1959)." *CSL: The Bulletin of the New York C. S. Lewis Society* 4 (February):6–8.

    Wrong was Lewis's student in the 1930s for a short time and met him occasionally after that relationship ended. Lewis's writing, because of his massive erudition and concern for exactly the right words, was a little heavy, never pompous, but "almost oppressively dignified and formal." His conversation was "friendly, brilliant and fascinating—entirely suited to the company in which he found himself." On this occasion they discussed *Till We Have Faces, English Literature in the Sixteenth Century Excluding Drama*, homosexuality, his books in general, his brother, his wife and her illness, Pascal, Oliver Cromwell, suicide, Tolkien, Malvern (Lewis's public school), the problems of authorship, and the Chronicles of Narnia. Reprinted: 1979.119.

46 ZIEGLER, MERVIN LEE. "Imagination as a Factor in the Works of C. S. Lewis." Ph.D. dissertation, University of Florida, 158 pp.

In *The Pilgrim's Regress*, the Ransom Trilogy, the Chronicles of Narnia, and *Till We Have Faces*, Lewis uses imaginative discourse as a rhetoric mode. Imagination has both an objective dimension, which constitutes its metaphorical component, and a subjective dimension, which constitutes its *Sehnsucht* or emotional component. Lewis uses fantasy, symbolism, and allegory to encourage a metaphorical response to the message; he creates a message that will be received as myth to encourage the highest emotional response. Lewis's apologetics are both meaningful, which stems from the metaphorical component, and memorable as a result of his emphasizing beauty, goodness, and estrangement, an element of *Sehnsucht*.

1974

1 ADEY, LIONEL. "The Light of Holiness: Some Comments on Morris by C. S. Lewis." *Journal of the William Morris Society* 3 (Spring):10–22.

Most of Lewis's critical comments on William Morris appear in his letters to Arthur Greeves; he did not account for his love of Morris, whom he had read since adolescence, "until the psychological, religious and domestic settling down of 1929–31." Underlying his appreciation of Morris is "a need for actuality, a sense of loss, a thirst experienced since childhood for a joy fleetingly glimpsed, and an almost life-long immersion in Norse, Celtic and classical myths" as well as a "desire to look back from the sordid present to ages of chivalry, heroism, magic and the supernatural." Lewis and Morris have much in common in background and psychologically; they most differed in political and social philosophies—Morris was a Marxist while Lewis was too ardently individualistic and private to join any social cause or movement.

2 ARNOTT, ANNE. *The Secret Country of C. S. Lewis*. London: Hodder and Stoughton, 127 pp. Reprint 1976. Reprint. Grand Rapids, Mich.: Eerdmans, 1975. Reprint. Basingstoke: Lakeland, 1983.

Arnott has written a biography for young adults that traces how Lewis "became a man with a mind like a sword that cut through all lies and sham and showed up the blinding beauty of true goodness." The book focuses mainly on his childhood, his spiritual journey that culminated in Christianity, and how and why he came to write the Chronicles of Narnia.

3 BRUCE, LENORA. "Thoughts on Two Lewis Essays." *Chronicle of the Portland C. S. Lewis Society* 3, no. 1 (1 February):3–7.

In "Religion: Reality or Substitute?" Lewis discusses how we know which experiences are real and which are substitutes. He rejects immediate feeling as irrational fluctuations that affect all beliefs, not just religious ones.

33

1974

In "Christianity and Literature" he wrote that the modern approach to literature, which values creativeness, spontaneity, and freedom, was directly in contrast to the teachings of the New Testament, which emphasizes imitation and
hierarchical order. The Christian's writing should be the "reflection of eternal
Beauty and Wisdom."

4   CARNELL, CORBIN SCOTT. *Bright Shadow of Reality: C. S. Lewis and the
     Feeling Intellect.* Grand Rapids, Mich.: Eerdmans, 180 pp. Reprint. 1979.
         "*Sehnsucht* is a prevalent theme in literature" but has not been recog-
     nized as such because it has been subsumed in Romanticism. Lewis's search
     for it is chronicled in *Surprised by Joy* and *The Pilgrim's Regress*. Through
     the influence of Williams, Barfield, and MacDonald, Lewis came to under-
     stand the importance and function of the imagination. For him meaning comes
     through both reason and imagination. The search for *Sehnsucht* commonly
     appears in literature as a quest; this motif is evident in *The Pilgrim's Regress*
     and the Ransom Trilogy. Dominant images of *Sehnsucht* in Lewis's work are
     distant hills, exotic gardens, islands, and a special kind of music. Lewis uses
     either allegory or mythopoeic art to convey *Sehnsucht*. His best works are
     those in which he uses myth; *Till We Have Faces* is his most complex and
     beautiful myth. Lewis sees *Sehnsucht* as in, but not totally identifiable with,
     sex, art, the golden past, and paganism. He identifies it as the desire for God,
     and says that such a desire supports the idea of His existence. Lewis's concept
     of *Sehnsucht* is his "most significant contribution to Christian apologetics and
     an important clue for understanding literary history."

5   ———. "The Inklings and the 20th Century: Did They Back Away?" *CSL:
     The Bulletin of the New York C. S. Lewis Society* 5 (October):4–5.
         The Inklings' "works reflect a suspicion of the 20th Century" but "in
     several areas they actually anticipated interests and concerns" that came into
     focus twenty or thirty years later. Ecology: Lewis's works reflect the idea
     that man must respect and use wisely the natural world created by God.
     Sense of community: Lewis's ethics are based on the idea that "men are
     members one of another, that without human community no good thing can
     survive." The role of women: Lewis felt that "equality cannot become the
     highest good without losses." Dangers of relativism: the warning is evident
     in *The Abolition of Man*. Fantasy: the Inklings "affirmed wonder, awe and
     beauty"; they saw that the common reader had a hunger for a "rich imagina-
     tive literature."

6   CHRISTOPHER, JOE R. "An Analysis of 'The Apologist's Evening
     Prayer.'" *CSL: The Bulletin of the New York C. S. Lewis Society* 5
     (October):2–4.
         The poem is in the tradition of John Donne, with his tone, if not his
     actual wording. Elements of Donne's style used by Lewis are use of thy and

thou, parallelism of *From all* in the first and second stanza, and the balanced antithetical phrasing. The theme is based on Lewis's life and concerns the dangers of religious pride.

7 ⸻. "'From the Master's Lips': W. B. Yeats as C. S. Lewis Saw Him." *CSL: The Bulletin of the New York C. S. Lewis Society* 6 (November):14–19.

Lewis read Yeats and visited him twice. He was overawed by Yeats's personality, half fascinated and half repelled by his doctrines of magic and the occult, "'finally the more repelled because of the fascination.'" Lewis wrote that he had a "'ravenous, quasi-prurient desire for the Occult,'" of which he was afraid. He satirized Yeats in *Dymer*, using him for the character of the Wizard. As a literary historian Lewis recognized Yeats's genius but personally preferred William Morris.

8 CHRISTOPHER, JOE R., and OSTLING, JOAN K. "C. S. Lewis: A Biographical Supplement." *CSL: The Bulletin of the New York C. S. Lewis Society* 5 (June):4–6.

This article provides a partial list of items omitted from Christopher and Ostling's annotated checklist. These biographical essays, personality sketches, and new items include entries in standard reference works, letters of reactions to Lewis and his work, announcements tracing his career, and obituaries.

9 ⸻. *C. S. Lewis: An Annotated Checklist of Writings About Him and His Works*. Kent, Ohio: Kent State University Press, 389 pp.

This checklist is the most complete list of material published on Lewis between c. 1919 and June 1972. Subject arrangement includes divisions for general items, biographical material, fiction and poetry, religion and ethics, literary criticism, selected book reviews of Lewis's works. Indexes to master's theses, doctoral dissertations, authors, and works by Lewis mentioned in the annotations are also included.

10 CLARK, ZOIE. "Comments of Three Lewis Addresses." *Chronicle of the Portland C. S. Lewis Society* 3, no. 4 (3 May):3–5.

Three essays in *God in the Dock* show Lewis's adroitness in communicating Christianity to different audiences. "Notes on the Way" (1941) addresses unbelievers and shows them the unreasonableness of their ordinary reasonings. "Answers to Questions on Christianity" (1944) addresses industrial workers with honesty and truth. "Christian Apologetics" (1945) addresses clergy and youth leaders and shows them how to defend and communicate Christianity.

11 DAY, JACK [E.]. "An Examination of *English Literature in the Sixteenth Century (Excluding Drama).*" *Chronicle of the Portland C. S. Lewis Society* 3, no. 6 (July-September):8–14.

The sixteenth century's literary achievement is considered by many as unequaled. The century was also a remarkable period in history that Lewis divided into three styles: Late Medieval, Drab Age, and Golden Age. Examples of the Late Medieval are John Fisher, More and Tyndale, Hugh Latimer, and John Knox. The poetry of the Drab Age was meant as lyrics for songs and so is plain, and sometimes flat and dull. Lewis obviously revels in the writings of the Golden Age. He wrote that the main impression of the sixteenth century "'must be one of narrow escapes and unexpected recoveries.'"

12   FORD, PETER. "C. S. Lewis and Heaven." *Chronicle of the Portland C. S. Lewis Society* 3, no. 2 (15 February):4.
      Walter Hooper's conjecture that the immortality of all men is the central premise of Lewis's writings is correct. The sermon "The Weight of Glory" shows Lewis's desire for heaven and belief in immortality in its fullest form.

13   ———. "The Influence of G. K. Chesterton on C. S. Lewis." *Chronicle of the Portland C. S. Lewis Society* 3, no. 7 (October–December):11–13.
      Lewis wrote that Chesterton's *The Everlasting Man* (London: Hodder & Stoughton, 1925) allowed him to make sense of the Christian outline of history for the first time. By 1932 he had read most of Chesterton's theological works and decided to write about his own spiritual voyage in *The Pilgrim's Regress*. Lewis carried on the tradition of "the English School of Christian Apology, of which Chesterton was one of this century's greatest lights."

14   FULLER, EDMUND. "After the Moon Landings: A Further Report on the Christian Spaceman C. S. Lewis." In *Myth, Allegory and Gospel: An Interpretation of J. R. R. Tolkien, C. S. Lewis, G. K. Chesterton, Charles Williams.* Edited by John Warwick Montgomery. Minneapolis, Minn.: Bethany Fellowship, pp. 79–96.
      The recent advances in space exploration do not destroy the effect of Lewis's Trilogy; they are "symbolic stories and technical developments do not invalidate them." Norman Mailer and Wernher Von Braun have also discussed God's connection with space exploration.

15   GREEN, ROGER LANCELYN, and HOOPER, WALTER. *C. S. Lewis: A Biography.* London: Collins, 320 pp. Reprint. New York: Harcourt Brace Jovanovich, 1974.
      Green, "an English scholar who has written fantasy and children's books," was chosen by Lewis to be his biographer. Hooper, "a theologian who has read English," was Lewis's secretary during his last months and is one of the executors of his literary estate. Their work is a sympathetic, almost reverent memoir of Lewis, which recounts his life, family and friendships, the books and ideas that molded him, his conversion to Christianity, his scholarly career, his everyday life, and how he came to write what he did.

16 GRUENLER, ROYCE GORDON. "C. S. Lewis and Imaginative Theology: In Memoriam." *Ohio Journal of Religious Studies* 2 (November):99–104.

In "Transposition," Lewis argues that our emotional life is richer and higher than that of our sensations. "The transposition of the richer spiritual and emotional realm into the poorer realm of sensations and syllables takes place when elements in the poorer system carry more than one meaning"; this relationship is not symbolic but sacramental—the emotional transforms and transubstantiates the sensation. Lewis constantly addresses the question "how do we know?" His principal contribution to theology and biblical interpretation is his appreciation of the realm of the spiritual, which he felt should be allowed to function along with the realms of sensation and reason and properly to inform them.

17 HARWOOD, A. C. "C. S. Lewis and Anthroposophy." *CSL: The Bulletin of the New York C. S. Lewis Society* 5 (February):1–4.

Lewis had three objections to anthroposophy: "one he withdrew, one he modified, but the third remained an insuperable obstacle." The one he withdrew was whether "it is possible for man here and now, in the phenomenal world, to have commerce with the world beyond." He modified his objection to the idea that, although it recognized the Trinity, anthroposophy gave a higher place to the Son than the Father. The tenet that Lewis could not accept was "the idea that man is on the way to becoming a tenth hierarchy—a unique hierarchy of freedom and love." This was the "great divide" between Lewis and anthroposophy; he said, "I was not born to be free—I was born to adore and obey." Reprinted: 1979.43.

18 HAYNES, JACK. "Eros in *That Hideous Strength*." *CSL: The Bulletin of the New York C. S. Lewis Society* 5 (April):2–4.

The novel "has buried within a veritable marriage manual." Jane is afraid of being invaded and entangled; she has a deep resentment against love and therefore against Mark. Her reeducation begins when she joins Ransom's group and he tells her that she failed in love because she has never attempted obedience; her problem is one of pride. When she realizes that God understands with full seriousness her fear of "'being treated as a thing, an object of barter and desire and possession,'" she surrenders and the change comes over her.

19 HILDERBRAND, GARY. "*Miracles*." *Chronicle of the Portland C. S. Lewis Society* 3, no. 6 (July-September):5–7.

Most arguments against miracles are the result of an anti-supernatural bias. Lewis argues that there are two alternatives, naturalism and supernaturalism, and shows that naturalism cannot account for reason, free will, or moral judgment. Therefore something outside of nature must exist, something that is the source of reason and morality. Lewis shows that miracles are a genuine possibility and that there is a probable basis for each claim to miracle.

1974

20 HIPOLITO, JANE. "Flatland and Beyond: Characterization in Science Fiction." In *Science Fiction: The Academic Awakening*, a CEA Chap Book, Supplement to *The CEA Critic* 37 (November). Edited by Willis E. McNelly. Shreveport, La.: College English Association, pp. 18–21.

Science fiction has traditionally been viewed as a genre of ideas rather than people, and as a result, is often written as a kind of allegory with flat characters designed as symbolic abstractions. Lewis's Ransom Trilogy is the preeminent example. He saw the trend toward fragmentation and specialization as the most alarming weakness in Western civilization and created in the trilogy symbolic characters representing the synthesis of "truths" ignored by specialists.

21 HOOPER, WALTER. "Narnia: The Author, the Critics, and the Tale." In *Children's Literature*. Vol. 3. Edited by Francelia Butler and Bennett A. Brackman. Philadelphia: Temple University Press, pp. 12–22.

Criticism of the tales usually cites their violence as does Holbrook [see 1973.14]. Lewis felt that battles and villains killed at the end of a book did not represent any kind or degree of fear beyond that which an ordinary child wants and needs to feel. These stories are not allegories in the sense Lewis used the term; the moral themes were not in Lewis's mind at the beginning but grew out of the telling and are part of the narrative. *The Last Battle* is the best, "the crowning achievement of the whole Narnia creation." Reprinted: 1977.30.

22 ———. "Warren Hamilton Lewis: An Appreciation." *CSL: The Bulletin of the New York C. S. Lewis Society* 5 (April):5–8.

Warren was a modest and shy man; he was a homebody and liked the out-of-doors. He "had the unmistakable stamp of the professional soldier." He ended living very much to himself, partly due to the loss of his brother and his fears of bankruptcy, drummed into his and his brother's heads by their father, but "his last years were, in the main, happy ones."

23 HUME, KATHRYN. "C. S. Lewis' Trilogy: A Cosmic Romance." *Modern Fiction Studies* 20 (Winter):505–517.

The structure of the typical romance begins with the hero at peace, secure, and relatively passive. He then hears the "call to adventure," which he must obey; for the ego, this is a call to disentangle itself from the unconscious. The hero enters the "special world of the adventure" where the struggle takes place; for the ego, this is the land of the unconscious where entry and exit must be accomplished by a symbolic death and rebirth. The hero wins his battle, departs from the special world, and returns to his proper place; the hero has become a master of both the everyday world and the special realm of his experience. *Out of The Silent Planet* is a conventional romance and follows this pattern. *Perelandra* is not a conventional romance, as Ransom's "situation and experience remain analogous to those of romance but on a higher spiritu-al plane." *That Hideous Strength* also follows the pattern of a conventional romance with Mark and Jane Studdock as joint heroes. The Trilogy itself can be viewed as one whole cosmic romance.

24 KAWANO, ROLAND M. "Reason and Imagination: The Shape of C. S. Lewis." Ph.D. dissertation, University of Utah, 234 pp.
    Lewis found the modern world uncongenial to his spirit and adopted the freedom of the medieval world view. He recognized that a gap existed between an idea and its image and attempted to bridge this gap by immersion in the image, which allows a full exploration of the idea. He saw literature and mythology in the light of sanity and mental health. *Till We Have Faces* can be seen as an instance of the "good dreams" of pagan mythology. Dance was the focal image in Lewis's work and symbolized the highest realities. He was interested in story and mythopoeia rather than character; he emphasized the "succession and pattern of events that tried to catch a state, a taste, a color, or something inexpressible." Lewis's narrative poet-ry exemplifies this doctrine of story and mythopoeia while his lyric poems are "idea poems which corro-brate themes and concepts he treated elsewhere."

25 KILBY, CLYDE S., and EVANS, LINDA J. "C. S. Lewis and Music." *Christian Scholars Review* 4:1–15.
    Music for Lewis was "a glory, a joy, and a fundamental *motif* throughout his works." He uses images of song, play, and dance to represent the highest things. His overwhelming ambition for many years was to write poetry, the most musical of all literature. In his literary criticism, he "makes constant allu-sions to composers and musical works, showing evidence of the manner in which music and literature accentuate each other in his thinking." He disliked modern hymns—the music was that of popular songs, the lyrics mostly bad, sentimental, and lugubrious; he felt their emotional effect was distracting to worship and often mistaken for religious emotions.

26 KIRKPATRICK, HOPE. "'The Humanitarian Theory of Punishment.'" *CSL: The Bulletin of the New York C. S. Lewis Society* 5 (December):1–6.
    Lewis felt that humanitarian theory, because it treats crime as an illness and attempts to analyze and cure the criminal, removes from punishment any connection with justice. He felt there were great opportunities for tyrannical abuses in such a system, that "interference with a man's psyche unless he asks for it is inexcusable."

27 KIRKPATRICK, MARY. "An Introduction to the Curdie Books by George MacDonald, Including Parallels Between Them and the Narnian Chronicles." *CSL: The Bulletin of the New York C. S. Lewis Society* 5 (March):1–6.
    Both authors deal with the idea that something can be visible to one per-

son and not to another, depending on that person's degree of faith in the thing to be seen. Both are concerned with "the idea that all men are in the process of growing, either for the better or the worse." They both use the image of the door as the connection between different worlds and the idea that what one sees once entering through the door is different from what one saw looking from the other side.

28 ———. "Lewis and MacDonald." *CSL: The Bulletin of the New York C. S. Lewis Society* 5 (May):2–4.

Lewis said MacDonald wrote fantasy that hovers between the mythopoeic and the allegorical better than any one else. Both authors deal with the theme of "Inexorable Love." *The Great Divorce* shows MacDonald's influence in its theme that one must give up a thing in order really to have it. MacDonald also appears as Lewis's guide and what the character says is a "condensation of those teachings of MacDonald which made the greatest impression on Lewis."

29 LAMBERT, BYRON C. "The Story of Two Lives: Or, New Joys and Surprises in Rereading *Surprised by Joy.*" *CSL: The Bulletin of the New York C. S. Lewis Society* 6 (November):7–10.

Surprised by Joy is the story of the integration of Lewis's two lives: the inner, imaginative, mythical life and the factual, intellectual, outer one. Lewis's debate with Barfield opened his outer intellectual life to theism; his reading of MacDonald's *Phantastes*, described with lavish care, passionately, brilliantly, and with an artistic devotion unsurpassed in the book, baptized his imagination. A minor theme also present is "the *achievement of objectivity*, the liberation of Lewis from his subjectivity and self-concern." Also evident are Lewis's humor, vivid figures of speech, wisdom, and the homeliness and incongruity of the places of his most momentous decisions. Lewis renders God's persistent wooing of the human heart to Himself with "astonishing accuracy, boldness and subtlety"; it is one of the triumphs of literature.

30 LIEB, LAURIE. "Body and Mind in *That Hideous Strength.*" *CSL: The Bulletin of the New York C. S. Lewis Society* 5 (September):10–12.

The novel is built around a series of opposites, one of which is the polarity between mind and body. Belbury favors mind over body as symbolized by the worship of the bodiless head. St. Anne's represents the body, often taking the form of sexuality; the focus is constantly on Jane's body, marriage, and barrenness. In Jane and Mark, the body often operates independently and superiorly to the mind or rational intellectual processes.

31 LINDEN, WILLIAM. "Tormance and C. S. Lewis." *CSL: The Bulletin of the New York C. S. Lewis Society* 5 (May):4–5.

Lewis stated that he owed a considerable debt to David Lindsay's *A Voyage to Arcturus* (London: Methuen, 1920), which gave him the idea that the appeal of "scientifiction" could be combined with the appeal of the "supernatural." He said that "Lindsay was the first writer to find out what outer space is good for." Lewis was also influenced by Lindsay's central idea that we are only exiles here in this world.

32 McGOVERN, EUGENE. "Some Notes on Chesterton." *CSL: The Bulletin of the New York C. S. Lewis Society* 5 (May):6–8.

Chesterton and Lewis both shared a distaste for "mean-mindedness, brittle skepticism, the urge to debunk." Both used images of battle and war to depict the Christian's relationship with the world. Lewis's work shows some indications of "distributivism," the economic philosophy Chesterton was very interested in. Chesterton is not read very much today, but he was "one of the deepest thinkers who ever existed."

33 McKENZIE, PATRICIA ALICE. "*The Last Battle*: Violence and Theology in the Novels of C. S. Lewis." Ph.D. dissertation, University of Florida, 200 pp.

The struggle between good and evil is a central theme in the Narnian Chronicles, the Ransom Trilogy, *Till We Have Faces*, and "After Ten Years." Violence is often used to resolve this struggle and "functions both as an identifying characteristic of evil and as an instrument for the chastisement of evil." Lewis uses violence as a proof of valor, a means to teach the recalcitrant; as political therapy, "a means of liberation for characters who are caught in a situation that threatens to be paralyzing"; and as a warning, a means to preserve society from attackers and a means of redemption. Chronologically, the novels progress from the preoccupation with actual combat to an internalizing of conflict. Links between violence and Christian theology appear in sacrifices and subterranean struggles followed by an ascent to higher life and eschatological visions.

34 MEMORY, J. D. "C. S. Lewis and the Mind-Body Identity Thesis." *CSL: The Bulletin of the New York C. S. Lewis Society* 5 (August):7–8.

The idea that thought can be reduced to biochemistry and physics, a strict form of materialism, was refuted by Lewis in his chapter on naturalism in *Miracles*. He maintained Samuel Alexander's distinction between contemplating an external object and enjoying the experience, the strict separation between object and subject.

35 MERCHANT, ROBERT. "*Reflections on the Psalms*." *CSL: The Bulletin of the New York C. S. Lewis Society* 5 (January):1–5.

The Psalms are "[a] compendium, a distillation . . . not only of the Jewish religion but also of the Christian faith." Characteristics Lewis noted were their antiquity and parallelism in thought and meter, and that most are of the literary

1974

type *individual lament*. Lewis stated that Scripture is "an untidy and leaky vehicle"; it is not "an unrefracted light giving us ultimate truth in systematic form." He warned against two extremes—"that of thinking that things in their natural state must either be rejected *in toto* or else swallowed whole."

36   MONTGOMERY, JOHN WARWICK. "Introduction: The Apologists of Eucatastrophe." In *Myth, Allegory and Gospel: An Interpretation of J. R. R. Tolkien, C. S. Lewis, G. K. Chesterton, Charles Williams*. Edited by John Warwick Montgomery. Minneapolis: Bethany Fellowship, pp. 11–31.

These four authors display a combination of ingenuousness and genius, and seem "almost to make a fetish out of unoriginality" because they write about Christianity. The "literary apologetic for the Gospel—the Great Eucatastrophe" unites these writers. Lewis presents allegorical myths as an apologetic for the comprehensiveness of Christian truth.

*37   NEULEIB, JANICE WITHERSPOON. "The Concept of Evil in the Fiction of C. S. Lewis." *DAI* 35 (1975):4539A. University of Illinois at Urbana-Champaign, 196 pp.

Lewis's theory is that evil is the choice of a wrong good, "especially the choice of a selfish good over a divinely orientated one." In *The Screwtape Letters*, *The Great Divorce*, the Ransom Trilogy, the Chronicles of Narnia, and *Till We Have Faces*, Lewis's evil characters are "selfish, unpleasant people who are working untiringly for whatever personal whim motivates their lives" and all have that "particular quality of schoolboy nastiness that is Lewis's trademark." In *Till We Have Faces*, as the result of his growth and development as both man and artist, Lewis was "able to create a character who demonstrated all the narrowness of evil but who also experienced the expanding effects of self-awareness and salvation."

38   NOEL, HENRY. "Some Little-Known Books in Lewis's Background." *CSL: The Bulletin of the New York C. S. Lewis Society* 5 (July):2–8.

Books were Lewis's lifeblood; "he was forever tossing off the name of authors and titles." This is a list of books "of [which] Lewis has at least on one occasion written appreciatively." Included are references in Lewis's work where the item is mentioned and comments on the work that "suggest similarities with Lewis's own life or thought or . . . show why Lewis admired that writer."

39   NOLAN, CHARLES J., Jr. "The Child Motif in *That Hideous Strength*." *CSL: The Bulletin of the New York C. S. Lewis Society* 5 (August):5–7.

Lewis uses the Christian doctrine that one must become like a little child, be spiritually reborn, in order to obtain salvation as a thematic device in the novel. "The emotional openness of the child equips the person to be spiritually receptive of God's grace because it involves humanity and willingness to obey." Both Jane and Mark Studdock need to undergo this regression to childhood in order to be spiritually reborn.

40   PIPPERT, WESLEY G. "A Home for C. S. Lewis." *Christianity Today* 18 (24 May):49–50.
      The Bodleian Library and Wheaton College are the "leading centers for serious Lewis study." Clyde S. Kilby started Wheaton's Lewis collection, and Marion E. Wade, founder and chairman of Service Master, a Chicago firm, contributed $200,000 to it. Kilby hoped to build a replica of Lewis's house by 1980 to house the collection.

41   PURTILL, RICHARD [L.]. *Lord of the Elves and Eldils: Fantasy and Philosophy in C. S. Lewis and J. R. R. Tolkien.* Grand Rapids, Mich.: Zondervan, 211 pp.
      Fantasy provides escape, recovery, and consolation. Applying Lewis's theory that the value of a book can be determined by the kind of reading it admits, Lewis and Tolkien's fantasies are valuable literature. Key themes in Lewis and Tolkien are: the world is a place of wonder, the modern world seems ugly and miserable, the Christian story provides a happy ending, and in the conflict between good and evil each person chooses his own side. In the secondary worlds they create, language is very important; Lewis identifies language with rationality and sees it as a tool to express ideas and images. Contrary to what Lois and Stephen Rose wrote in *The Shattered Ring* (Richmond, Va.: John Knox, 1970) Lewis's characters are active and believable; in his works evil results from choosing self over God, and God is the only source of goodness. Lewis's fantasies are not formal arguments for God but reveal an imagination that naturally thinks in Christian terms and gives these terms new imaginative concern for other races and cultures, and for ecology.

42   RIGBY, LUKE. "Recollections of C. S. Lewis." *CSL: The Bulletin of the New York C. S. Lewis Society* 5 (January):6–7.
      Lewis was Rigby's tutor for a year at Oxford in 1944. Lewis was "the true master, the true teacher. He shared his appreciation and enthusiasm and thereby instilled confidence and demanded effort." "The kindness, sensitivity, the zest for life, the fun, the deep sense of humor, the seriousness, the depths, the unexpectedness: they combined to make a man who was exhilarating to be with." Reprinted: 1979.85.

43   SHEILS, MERVILL. "Chuck Colson's Leveler." *Newsweek* 84 (9 September):72–73.
      Colson was drawn to Christianity through Lewis's works. His appeal to believers and skeptics is due to "the amiable wit of his writings," his formidable logic, and "his own reluctant religiosity." The popularity of his works

"does seem to bespeak a fascination with the metaphysical questions that pervade them."

44   SPEROU, CAROLE. *"Prince Caspian." Chronicle of the Portland C. S. Lewis Society* 3, no. 7 (October–December):8–11.
   "Prince Caspian is the story of setting Narnia to rights after invasion and conquest had turned it away from its original beauty." Through its varied creatures, the story shows Lewis's mastery at communicating sights and feelings as well as his realism and humor. In the story there is a respect for roles but roles may be discounted with a demand from the higher Authority. Parts of the narrative echo Charles Williams's idea of how people turn into the kinds of beings they have spent their lives becoming. Lewis shows how Christians can believe many things unbelievers do not, how Christians must allow their concept of God to grow, and how Christians become like Christ through their contact with God.

45   STAHL, JOHN T. "Austin Farrer on C. S. Lewis as 'The Christian Apologist.'" *Christian Scholar's Review* 4:231–37.
   Farrer, in his essay "The Christian Apologist" (in *Light on C. S. Lewis*, pp. 23–43. Edited by Jocelyn Gibb. New York: Harcourt, Brace and World, 1965), objects to Lewis's rationalistic-idealistic philosophy as outmoded. Although some of Lewis's works have a rationalistic orientation, especially his *reductio ad absurdum* argument against naturalism and his moral argument for God's existence, not all scholars reject the *reductio* type of argument as invalid, and the moral one may serve a psychological function. Farrer objects to certain arguments in *The Problem of Pain*; however, "Lewis did not believe that his explication was an irrefutable chain of deduction, nor the result of such." His purpose was to use "the vast repertoire of literary genre and imagery at his command" to explain clearly the biblical perspective on life.

46   TENNYSON, G. B. "The Ancients versus the Moderns: Thoughts on *The Abolition of Man*." *The Occasional Review*, no. 1:63–80.
   The Ancients believe things are getting worse, that the world is decaying; the Moderns believe things are getting better, that modern knowledge is superior to earlier knowledge and renders it obsolete. The controversy is not primarily about science but rather what human life is about; whether to seek truth among words or among things. Lewis says that Moderns do not accept the Tao, and thus exhibit an irreverence toward life, reality, and practical reason. "Man makes himself, the modern temper says, and he can thus unmake himself or anything else at will." Lewis points out that "this attitude may come so to dominate our lives by its misuse of technology that we no longer have a basis for judging whether anything at all is good or bad." Reprinted: 1978.44.

47 WESTERLUND, LOIS. "Excerpts from *The Great Divorce*: Life after Death in Metaphor." *CSL: The Bulletin of the New York C. S. Lewis Society* 5 (June):2–4.

In *The Great Divorce* hell is the isolation of an individual's own mind. Lewis used images of shadow and light. "The human shapes are metaphors expressing the dehumanizing effect of choosing illusions instead of truth." The Solid People symbolize "the true humanity man is intended for and which he may realize by coming to the light of truth."

48 WILLIAMS, JAN. "Digory's Conflict." *The Lamp-Post of the Southern California C. S. Lewis Society* 2 (October):1–2.

Digory's conflict in *The Magician's Nephew* is between honoring his mother and following Aslan. His concern for his dying mother influences all his adventures in Narnia and tempts him to disobey Aslan. His faith in Aslan's goodness is shaky and this adds to and continues the conflict. In the end Digory goes from obeying Aslan's rules, taught to him by his parents, to obeying Aslan in person and maintaining allegiance to Him.

49 WILLIAMS, TERRI. "Lewis on Punishment." *Chronicle of the Portland C. S. Lewis Society* 2, no. 12 (4 January):3–6.

In "The Humanitarian Theory of Punishment" Lewis urges a return to the retributive theory of punishment for the sake of the criminal. The humanitarian theory of punishment abolishes justice and treats the criminal's actions as involuntary, which dehumanizes the criminal. In "Delinquents in the Snow" Lewis argues that treating crime as a harmless prank does an injustice to society. If society does not live up to its obligation to punish criminals the victimized individuals may take matters into their own hands.

50 ———. "'On Stories' and 'On Fairy Stories.'" *Chronicle of the Portland C. S. Lewis Society* 3, no. 6 (July–September):2–3.

The core concept of Lewis's and Tolkien's essays is that stories give us a glimpse of reality beyond what is directly experienced. Tolkien lists recovery, escape, and consolation as gifts of the fairy tale for readers. "Story allows us to look at invisible things. Fairy story allows us to understand their meaning."

1975

1 ADEY, LIONEL. "The Barfield–Lewis 'Great War.'" *CSL: The Bulletin of the New York C. S. Lewis Society* 6 (August):10–14.

The "Great War" between Barfield and Lewis concerned two issues. Barfield maintained that imagination conveys truth while Lewis felt it merely shows "what difference a given statement might make if true, without establishing its truth or falsehood, which depend on rational judgment." The other issue was the nature of metaphor. Barfield thought metaphor was a relationship perceived by a flash of intuition while Lewis said metaphor was a concrete mental picture. This academic tournament shaped and sharpened the combatants' wits and developed the central issues both expounded in their subsequent works. See also 1978.1.

2 AQUINO, JOHN. "Shaw and C.S. Lewis's 'Space Trilogy.'" *Shaw Review* 18 (January):28–30.

Lewis's Trilogy is an open and exact refutation of George Bernard Shaw's philosophy of the Life Force and Creative Evolution as depicted in his *Back to Methuselah* (London: Constable, 1921). Weston is a caricature of Shaw—speaks like him, and shares his philosophy and egotism. Lewis attacks Shaw's philosophy on the basis of its vagueness and randomness. Shaw and Lewis both "combine fantasy and science to develop religious beliefs" and are celebrators of life—but "Shaw's Life Force organizes and perfects; Lewis's Life is something one should experience and cherish."

3 ARLTON, BEVERLY. "Belief: A Functional View." *CSL: The Bulletin of the New York C. S. Lewis Society* 6 (October):1–5.

Lewis defined belief as assenting to a proposition felt to be so overwhelmingly probable that, although logically it cannot be proved to the exclusion of dispute, psychologically there is no room for doubt. He also felt that the object of one's faith had to be valid in order for there to be any virtue in the faith. Lewis distinguished between faith on a "propositional level," a belief in doctrine, and faith based on the "logic of personal relations"—a Christian has a relationship with a Person, and has faith because He is Who He is.

4 BARFIELD, OWEN. "C. S. Lewis and Historicism." *CSL: The Bulletin of the New York C. S. Lewis Society* 6 (August):3–9.
Reprint of 1975.5.

5 ———. "C. S. Lewis and Historicism." In *Man's "Natural Powers": Essays for and about C. S. Lewis*. Edited by Raymond P. Tripp, Jr. Church Stretton, England: The Society for New Language Study, pp. 1–8.

Lewis "emphatically denied any recognizable, certainly any *significant* evolution or development of consciousness in the course of human history." A self-consistent system of Lewis's epistemology can be derived from his published works: the two sources of knowledge are divine revelation and scientific method. Our present worldview seems to be based on the scientific method but is a myth, one that could destroy civilization unless it can be complemented with knowledge derived from divine revelation. Our knowledge of the past is limited to "documentary and archaeological records plus what has been divinely revealed." Reprinted: 1975.4.

6   CHRISTOPHER, JOE R. "The Labors of Psyche: A Sorting of Events." *CSL: The Bulletin of the New York C. S. Lewis Society* 7 (November):7–10.

The sequence of events in Psyche's labors in the original story by Apuleius is compared with the four visions in Lewis's *Till We Have Faces*. The first version is the retelling by a priest where the events agree with Apuleius's version; the second identifies Orual with Psyche; the third story is told in pictures as Orual and Fox follow Psyche's progress. The second and third versions merge when the vision and the labors come together. The last version is contained in a note following the text in the American edition.

7   COBB, LAWRENCE [W.]. "The Beginning of the Real Story: Images of Heaven in C. S. Lewis and Dante." *CSL: The Bulletin of the New York C. S. Lewis Society* 7 (December):1–5.

The Great Divorce and *The Divine Comedy* both depict relationships with other human beings in heaven, human bodies rather than disembodied spirits, although Dante's are less substantial than Lewis's. Lewis depicts nature as heaven's setting while Dante sets his heaven in the universe apart from nature. Each soul in Lewis's hell must face a humiliating confrontation similar to Dante's with Beatrice; both authors depict a broken and contrite heart as a sacrifice acceptable to God. Lewis did not just borrow from Dante but transmuted certain elements into something new and different.

8   COLBERT, JAMES G., Jr. "The Common Ground of Lewis and Barfield." *CSL: The Bulletin of the New York C. S. Lewis Society* 6 (August):15–18.

Both Lewis and Barfield viewed the present as just another historic period and did not patronize the ideas of the past. Both objected to Freud's teachings as well as to the theory of evolution. Both used the existence of intelligence in the universe to prove God's existence. Barfield attempted to judge the epistemological truth or falsehood of philosophical principles. Lewis treated philosophical principles either implicitly or incidentally; he makes us imagine and feel what he said we cannot know.

9   COLISH, MARIA L. "Medieval Allegory: A Historigraphical Consideration." *Clio* 4 (June):347.

Lewis, in his influential book *The Allegory of Love*, made the distinction between allegory and symbol. "'The allegorist leaves the given . . . to talk of that which is confessedly less real, which is a fiction. The symbolist leaves the given to find that which is more real.'" Lewis felt that the medieval poets must be read allegorically because that is the way they wrote.

10 COLMAN, E. A. M. "Hamlet: The Poem or the Play?" *Sydney Studies in English* 1:3–12.

Colman examines Lewis's British Academy Shakespeare Lecture, given in 1942, "Hamlet: The Prince or the Poem?" in which Lewis argued that critics should concentrate on the whole dramatic poem rather than just on the character of the prince. He argues that the poetry of the play should be constantly related to its stage action.

11 COMO, JAMES T. "*Till We Have Faces*: A Preface to Comprehension." *CSL: The Bulletin of the New York C. S. Lewis Society* 7 (November):1–3.

Thematically the novel "is Lewis from beginning to end." In it, he is concerned with the truthfulness of myth, the barrenness of reason without imagination and faith, sacramentalism and semantics, the dialect of desire, grace, membership, and the law of inattention. In form the work is the opposite of his usual technique of mythologizing—here he de-mythologizes. The structure is the asking in Part I and answering in Part II; this arch is supported by another inner layer consisting of the maturity of Orual. Other elements are those of time and the overlapping, intertwining of description, and careful control of emphasis, which manipulates the emotions.

12 DINNAGE, ROSEMARY. "Allegories of Childhood." *TLS: Times Literary Supplement*, 4 April, p. 363.

The enormous extent of Lewis's reading and scholarship is a handicap to him in writing the Chronicles of Narnia. It gets in the way of his originality and overloads the books with influences and echoes and also appears in the unnatural way his children sometimes speak. "And yet the books are at least two parts original inspiration to one of pastiche." The greatest impact of the tales comes through their sequences of visual images, in which, "at his best, Lewis draws as much on dream as on literature." The major concerns of the stories are the struggle between good and evil, and the validity and limits of the imagination.

13 DOCKERY, CARL DEE. "The Myth of the Shadow in the Fantasies of Williams, Lewis, and Tolkien." Ph.D. dissertation, Auburn University, 180 pp.

The "imaging of darkness," the myth of the shadow, unites the fantasies of these three authors, not their Christianity. "The shadow myth . . . is generally characterized by: (a) the threat, or action initiated by the forces of darkness; (b) the encounter, or the forces of light responding to and defeating darkness; and (c) transformative renewal of the forces of light." The shadow in the Ransom Trilogy is scientism. The perspective of all three writers "is that of the preservation or renewal of life and order against threatening forces of destruction, chaos and death."

14 DONEY, RICHARD, and LAMBERT, BYRON C. "Paul Elmer More and C. S. Lewis." *CSL: The Bulletin of the New York C. S. Lewis Society* 6 (January):5–8.

More was impressed by *The Pilgrim's Regress*, saying it has "'a style that will make you chuckle with joy'"; he quotes it in *On Being Human* (Princeton: Princeton University Press, 1936) wherein he attacks French symbolist poets for their "lust of irresponsibility," which he says Lewis renders as the flight from God. Lewis wrote a letter to More, now lost, pointing out the weaknesses in his rejecting the absolute in *The Sceptical Approach to Religion* (Princeton: Princeton University Press, 1934); More's reply is reprinted herein.

15   FICHTE, JOERG O. "The Reception of C. S. Lewis' Scholarly Works in Germany." In *Man's "Natural Powers": Essays for and about C. S. Lewis.* Edited by Raymond P. Tripp, Jr. Church Stretton, England: The Society for New Language Study, pp. 17–20.

Lewis's scholarly works have not been translated into German but have evoked a fairly large response from German literary critics. Lewis is praised for his erudition, "refreshing style, unencumbered by the academic predilection for pedantry and turgidity, for his originality, and for his indifference to time-honored critical dogmas and literary evaluations." Krog seriously questions Lewis's definitions of allegory and symbolism in *The Allegory of Love*; Lewis's discussion of the mode and function of allegory is unnecessarily restrictive. *English Literature in the Sixteenth Century Excluding Drama* was considered the most original of the three volumes of the *Oxford History of English Literature*, which had appeared by 1956. *Studies in Words* is praised for Lewis's awareness of verbal nuances and treated with uneasiness due to his "idiosyncratic rendering of certain phrases." *An Experiment in Criticism, The Discarded Image*, and *Studies in Medieval and Renaissance Literature* were also praised by their reviewers.

16   FROST, NAOMI. "Life after Death: Visions of Lewis and Williams." *CSL: The Bulletin of the New York C. S. Lewis Society* 6 (April):2–6.

In Lewis's and Williams's fantasies, death is the irreversible metamorphosis of the body or the soul. The distinction between life before and after death is blurred for both the saved and the damned: "The process of new life or second death progresses with every choice made during mortality." Both depict choices made after death as extensions of mortal decisions. The law required that the will of the damned be permitted; fulfillment of the law requires heaven to triumph over hell, in that evil is allowed to have its way only among those who choose it and does not affect the good.

17   GRAHAM, W. FRED. "Fantasy in a World of Monochrome: Where C. S. Lewis Continues to Help." *Christianity Century* 92 (26 November): 1080–1082.

Lewis's frankly apologetic works are inadequate in convincing people of God's existence because of "the inevitable narrowing and flattening effect,

1975

the prosaic quality that results when anyone must treat great and often para-doxical themes in brief compass." Because what is unimaginable is unthinkable, it is unprovable; argument, then, is not the place to start. Stories that startle the imagination and whet the appetite for mystery, which Lewis's fantasies do, are far more effective in evoking the existence of God. Reprinted: 1977.26.

18 GREEN, ROGER LANCELYN. "C. S. Lewis and Andrew Lang." *Notes and Queries* 22 (May):208–209.

The source of the couplet that appears on the title page of Lewis's *Spirits in Bondage: A Cycle of Lyrics* is Lang's *History of English Literature from "Beowulf" to Swinburne* (New York: Longmans, Green, 1912, p. 579). Lewis misquoted from memory. Lang in turn misquoted Baudelaire from memory. The original is from the poem "The Moon's Minion":

> The lover thou shalt never meet,
> The land where thou shalt never be:

and appeared in the periodical *London*, March 2, 1878, and in *Ballades in Blue China*, vol. 22 (1880), p. 64–65.

19 GRIFFIN, BRIAN. "The Two Jacks: J. B. Priestly and C. S. Lewis." *Library Review* 25 (Spring/Summer):215–17.

Both Priestly and Lewis lost their mothers when young and as boys "tended to be dreamy, and played against a background of distant, magical hills." Both were manually clumsy and so were drawn to writing as therapy; both were influenced by MacDonald's *Phantastes*. Both were essentially bourgeois and had a profound sense of real democracy, although they were apolitical. Both had the "'image': pipe-smoking, middle-aged, altogether very English." Both wrote a surprisingly wide range of works that are entertaining and have an immense popular appeal. Both stood for being merely human, merely Christian, a "blend of simplicity-plus-integrity-plus-sheer humanity."

20 GRUBER, LOREN C. "Old English Maxims and Narnian Gnoms." In *Man's "Natural Powers": Essays for and about C. S. Lewis*. Edited by Raymond P. Tripp, Jr. Church Stretton, England: The Society for New Language Study, pp. 59–63.

Lewis uses maxims to "instruct others in the specific qualities of reality, human and divine." The similarities between Old English maxims and those in Narnia are the use of "religious poetry and secular heroic formulas," descriptions of the natural world that are factual, and the use of concrete images. Both sorts of maxims "lead those individuals who will attend to their symbolic content on a quest which concludes in higher levels of wisdom."

21 HALL, THOMAS G. "Narnia: The Gospel According to C. S. Lewis." *Cresset* 38 (June):29–33.

The archetypal quest for self, a spiritual journey, is "the central organizing principle in Lewis's narrative art and the metaphorical agency of his witness to Christ in fantasy." An unfit, weak hero encounters evil, becomes conscious of his limitations and his possibilities, wins the battle, is purged and baptized in the imagination, and thus achieves a Christ-like ideal selfhood. Other recurring motifs are (1) illusion-reality, (2) destruction of nature and animal life, (3) discipleship. "The realism of Narnia is the consequence of its believable inner life and its coherence as a tale about a preferred order of things in a wished-for universe of poetic justice."

22 HARWOOD, A. C. "A Toast to the Memory of C. S. Lewis Proposed at Magdalen College, July 4th 1975." *CSL: The Bulletin of the New York C. S. Lewis Society* 6 (September):1–3.

Harwood had an abiding friendship with Lewis that "defied all differences of opinion, outlook and interests." Lewis lived in the present moment; he was interested in people, not institutions, and had enormous sympathy for the "little man"; "he opened windows for many people into realms hitherto unknown to them." Reprinted: 1976.17; 1979.44.

23 JEANES, GEOFF. "'Other World' in Fiction: Reflections on a Body of Literature." *CSL: The Bulletin of the New York C. S. Lewis Society* 6 (June):1–4.

Fantasy exhibits its deepest possibilities "in the blending of physically other-world locales with spiritual or numinous unearthliness." Otherness is not merely physical strangeness or spatial distance; it is another dimension. It is "putting something new into the world; seeing old things from a new angle . . . drawing attention to mundane glories taken for granted: that's what this sub-creative milieu is about." Lewis's descriptions produce "unearthly visions of psychedelic strangeness yet vivid conviction." By depicting "otherness," fantasy authors make us realize what we are truly like, "that something different is pictured shows us how we differ from it."

24 JOHNSON, WILLIAM C., Jr. "Lewis, Barfield and Imagination." In *Man's "Natural Powers": Essays for and about C. S. Lewis*. Edited by Raymond P. Tripp, Jr. Church Stretton, England: The Society for New Language Study, pp. 35–42.

Lewis and Barfield both recognized the problem of scientism, "the domination of the rational principle in mental life." In the Ransom Trilogy "Lewis attempts to place and answer the modern, epistemological dilemma: he juxtaposes imaginative cognition with the fallacy of perception without imagination taking his reader on a journey of discovery and challenging him to suspend and eventually transform his empiricism and isolation."

1975

25 KEEFE, CAROLYN. "Mystic Experience in *Till We Have Faces.*" *CSL: The Bulletin of the New York C. S. Lewis Society* 7 (November):4–7.

Psyche and Orual attain self-knowledge "through directly apprehending divine majesty, authority and compelling sweetness." William James, in *The Varieties of Religious Experience* (New York: Random House, 1929), describes four elements in a mystic experience: (1) ineffability, the inability to express or communicate the experience; (2) "noetic quality," the overwhelming conviction of revelation—the experience generates its own proof; (3) transiency—the elevated state of emotion caused by the experience cannot be maintained for long; (4) passivity, being "grasped and held by a superior power." Psyche's experience fits into each of these categories. Orual's can slip into three but she has less verbal inadequacy in writing about her mystic experience. She is "an inveterate narrator; almost nothing stopped the flow."

26 KIRKPATRICK, HOPE. "Hierarchy in C. S. Lewis." *CSL: The Bulletin of the New York C. S. Lewis Society* 6 (February):1–6.

Lewis's hierarchical system is evident in his works: a vertical hierarchy includes God, man, and beast, and a horizontal hierarchy exists between unequals on earth. Lewis believed in the inequality of humans; he felt social and political equality was necessary because we are fallen, but felt it is rigid and flat. He believed hierarchy between people was a dance "with changing responsibilities as situations change," a principle of order "essentially flexible and alive."

27 LADBOROUGH, RICHARD W. "C. S. Lewis in Cambridge: Some Personal Impressions." *CSL: The Bulletin of the New York C. S. Lewis Society* 6 (July):7–10.

Lewis's aggressiveness was an attempt to cover his fundamental shyness. He was a man's man. His memory was prodigious and he seemed to have read everything; he was interested in ideas and things. Because of his modesty and reticence, he rarely discussed his own work and few undergraduates got to know him. He was not interested in the affairs of the university. He had little interest in organized religion or in ritual. "He seemed . . . to lead a curiously detached life, even when undergoing mental or physical agony." Reprinted: 1979.60.

28 LEITENBERG, BARBARA. "The New Utopias." Ph.D. dissertation, Indiana University, 226 pp.

Compares and contrasts the new utopias depicted by Ayn Rand, Lewis, B. F. Skinner, and Aldous Huxley. They all "emphasize the creation of a utopian man rather than just a utopian environment." Lewis concentrates more on criticizing traditional utopias than clearly describing his own. He finds that the modern scientific attitude that denies absolute values and the dignity of man is the greatest threat to Christianity. Only in surrendering self to God can man achieve freedom and happiness. The Ransom Trilogy "dramatizes a modern cosmic battle between the universal forces of Good and the forces of Evil, or Tao *vs.* science."

29 LINDSKOOG, KATHRYN [ANN]. "Getting It Together: Lewis and the Two Hemispheres of Knowing." *Journal of Psychology and Theology* 3 (Fall):290–293.

In Lewis's poem "Reason," the virgin goddess Athene stands for reason and the mother goddess Demeter personifies imagination. Images he uses for reason in the poem and in other works are light, purity, and clarity; images for imagination are warmth, darkness, and fertility. Scientists have discovered that reason is a function of the left hemisphere of the brain and imagination a function of the right. Lewis "wishes that his two modes of knowing, reason and imagination, would together teach him truth . . . since neither mental function is complete without the other." Reprinted: 1979.68.

30 LOGANBILL, DEAN. "Myth, Reality, and *Till We Have Faces*." In *Man's "Natural Powers": Essays for and About C. S. Lewis*. Edited by Raymond P. Tripp, Jr. Church Stretton, England: The Society for New Language Study, pp. 55–58.

As a myth, the novel must be experienced as a concrete reality, must be received before the reader can abstract truth from the full reality. Lewis attempted to reconstruct the primitive mythopoeic consciousness; he has broken the confinement of the historical moment. The reader therefore must "adopt his own consciousness in order to receive whatever *reality*" the work expresses.

31 MANLOVE, C. N. "C. S. Lewis (1989–1963) and *Perelandra*." In *Modern Fantasy: Five Studies* Cambridge: Cambridge University Press, pp. 99–151.

Lewis "avoids his own time and place" in his fiction because he disliked the modern world. He had the urge to transcend the limits of his own environment and had a "simple curiosity about things which appear beyond knowledge." He tried to recreate *Sehnsucht* in his fantasy. Lewis attempted to portray innocence in *Perelandra* by reconciling or fusing opposites such as youth and maturity, abundance and restraint, delight and order. In depicting the Lady's innocence, Lewis made her insusceptible to temptation; her motive for disobeying would have been love. Ransom's physical defeat of the Un-man is justified only if mind and body are one so that mental weapons and physical ones are the same. Lewis's philosophical idealism, his belief that mind is higher than body, makes his attempt to represent them as an organic unity unconvincing. See response 1979.47.

1975

32   MERCHANT, ROBERT. "An Evening with Walter Hooper: Report of the 69th Meeting, July 11, 1975." *CSL: The Bulletin of the New York C. S. Lewis Society* 6 (July):1–7.

In a question and answer format, Hooper discusses Lewis's attitudes toward science fiction, "mere Christianity," the Anglican Church, mass, mystical experiences, music, and women.

33   ———. "What Christians Believe." *CSL: The Bulletin of the New York C. S. Lewis Society* 6 (September):3–6.

Like most Christians, Lewis modified and reshaped his inherited convictions to arrive at his Christian beliefs. The three possible sources of Christian doctrine are Scripture, tradition, and reason; each of these is found wanting by itself. Jesus was a fundamentalist (he cited Scripture as authority), a traditionalist, and a rationalist (he urged his followers to use their intellectual faculties). In Lewis's description of what Christians believe there are several strands of Scripture, tradition, and reason.

34   MYERS, W. A. "C. S. Lewis's Argument for Natural Law Ethics." In *Man's "Natural Powers": Essays for and about C. S. Lewis*. Edited by Raymond P. Tripp, Jr. Church Stretton, England: The Society for New Language Study, pp. 43–46.

Lewis in *The Abolition of Man* claims that "the principles of natural law must be taken as self-evidently obligatory," that values cannot be grounded in anything other than natural law, and that real values cannot be justified. He fails to address two problems, however: we have no guideline for recognizing real objective values in natural law, and values may be particular to a culture.

35   NEULEIB, JANICE WITHERSPOON. "The Empty Face of Evil." *Christianity Today* 19 (28 March):14–16.

Till We Have Faces, through Orual and the development of her self-understanding, focuses on the definition and habitation of evil. Essentially, evil is the wrong kind of love; it "is the face of blank, malicious selfishness," and "the desire to have, to own, to devour others rather than to let them be and grow in their own ways and times."

36   ———. "Technology and Theocracy: The Cosmic Voyages and Wells and Lewis." *Extrapolation* 16 (May):130–136.

Out of the Silent Planet and H. G. Wells's *The First Men in the Moon* (London: G. Newnes, 1901), both cosmic voyages (a minor genre of fantasy), are parallel in style and technique: they use similar means of travel developed by scientists who first will not and then cannot reveal their secret, they describe similar emotional effects produced by space travel, and they depict characters of "scientist-turned-space traveler accompanied by a money-hungry sidekick." The differences in these novels are thematic: Wells "wished to satirize and thus, perhaps, reform human nature by showing another race that had, by chance . . . developed without human foibles"; Lewis created a metaphor for Christianity without using the usual Christian symbols and showed creatures morally and spiritually superior because they have not been separated from God.

37   "Reactions to *A Grief Observed.*" *Chronicle of the Portland C. S. Lewis Society* 4, no. 1 (January–February):6–8.

       The Problem of Pain and *A Grief Observed* show the difference "between comprehending truth and the struggle of living through the reality of that truth." In *A Grief Observed* emotion at first partially overwhelms reason and faith. Lewis analyzes his feelings instead of mistaking them for truth. After the anguish and anger are cleared away, reason becomes clearer and faith stronger.

38   SOTH, CONNIE. "The Space Theology of C. S. Lewis: An Introduction." *Chronicle of the Portland C. S. Lewis Society* 4, no. 2 (March–June):13–20.

       In the essay "Religion and Rocketry," Lewis questions whether humankind should attempt to explore other planets and suggests that the vast distances of space may be God's method of quarantine. In *Out of the Silent Planet* he strikingly develops this theme. He also points out in the essay that missionaries might not be able to recognize an unfallen race if it exists on other planets. He feels that a discovery of rational beings on other planets would not invalidate Christianity.

39   SPEROU, CAROLE. "*Voyage of the 'Dawn Treader.*' " *Chronicle of the Portland C. S. Lewis Society* 4, no. 4 (October–December):6–9.

       Lewis's sense of humor and his common-sense asides in the story are delightful. Personal aspects he put into the story are the old-fashioned character of Reepicheep, Lucy's fear of insects, and her experience of Joy. Eustace's conversion, brought about by his realizing the emptiness of his goals, his acknowledging that he needs other people, and his encounter with the numinous in Aslan, is the major theme of the story. The narrative also deals with God's relationship with man and man's response to God.

40   SPEROU, MIKE. "Prayer." *Chronicle of the Portland C. S. Lewis Society* 4, no. 4 (October–December):3.

       In his essay "Work and Prayer," Lewis says that God allows us to cause events by action as well as prayer, but while action is limited only by natural boundaries, God puts stipulations on prayer because of its unlimited power and potential danger. In "Petitionary Prayer: A Problem without an Answer" Lewis's problem is with God saying "He will grant us 'whatever' we ask and at the same time reserving a discretionary power to refuse." Our assumed definition of faith leads to this contradictory implication.

1975

41 STARR, ROB. "*Till We Have Faces*." *Chronicle of the Portland C. S. Lewis Society* 4, no. 1 (January–February):2–5.

Throughout the novel there are two threads: "Orual's outward righteousness and passion for truth and her subtle inward sins." The novel is an excellent example of one of Lewis's favorite techniques, that of representing the opponent's argument in a convincing manner.

42 TALBOTT, BROWNIE. "CSL on Humility." *Chronicle of the Portland C. S. Lewis Society* 4, no. 2 (March–June):2–9.

Lewis finds the essence of Christian morality in humility. He says humility is an attitude toward God, recognizing and revering His nature, which leads to our accepting our prideful, flawed nature. He finds "self-renunciation not a diminishing of one's individuality but a fulfillment of it."

43 TAMAIZUMI, YASUO. "The Conditions of Happiness in Our Age—A Japanese Impression of C. S. Lewis." In *Man's "Natural Powers": Essays for and about C. S. Lewis*. Edited by Raymond P. Tripp, Jr. Church Stretton, England: The Society for New Language Study, pp. 47–54.

Japan is basically a non-Christian society and Lewis is an alien figure there. Lewis's critical stance is more emotional than rational; the stronger his feeling, the more rational he becomes. Lewis uses reason "(1) as a means by which to distinguish his likes and dislikes, (2) as a weapon with which to attack his dislikes, and (3) as a shield of defense with which to rationalize and justify his likes." Lewis both attracts and repulses. His "self-definition as the spokesman of the Old Western Culture gives him a certain toughness and simplicity that make him grand, magnificent, sublime, and pure, and at the same time, strict, parochial, uncompromising."

44 TIMMERMAN, JOHN H. "C. S. Lewis: Reciprocity and Human Freedom." *Cresset* 39 (December):6–10.

"Modern man has imprisoned himself in a self-imposed isolation." Lewis's response to this is evident in the Doctrine of Reciprocity: "the harder one reaches out for God, the more this searching is reciprocated by God." In his view one may either make oneself supreme or subject oneself totally to God. Such a subjection to God "snaps the bars on the human spirit" and results in spiritual freedom. This belief is most explicitly expressed in *The Great Divorce*, with examples in *Out of the Silent Planet* and *Perelandra*.

45 TRIPP, RAYMOND P., Jr. "Chiliastic Agnosticism and the Style of C. S. Lewis." In *Man's "Natural Powers": Essays for and about C. S. Lewis*. Edited by Raymond P. Tripp, Jr. Church Stretton, England: The Society for New Language Study, pp. 27–33.

Since Christianity is an attitude or condition rather than a worked-out metaphysics, Lewis, insofar as Christianity determines his writing, is an inconsistent thinker. "He must rely upon the strength of his personal convictions and is thus precluded from arguing. . . . he is limited to rhetorical assertion and illustration." Lewis attacks attitudes and disciplines outside Christianity on the basis that men cannot arrive at the truth by the natural power. He rejects all forms of knowledge except Christianity, in spite of the fact that Christianity does not provide knowledge. Lewis's "style is marked by a negative and categorical postponement of knowledge."

46   ———, ed. *Man's "Natural Powers": Essays for and About C. S. Lewis.* Church Stretton, England: The Society for New Language Study, 63 pp.
       Lewis "represents the central, Christian epistemology of the West: an instinctive empiricism which requires all greater than material knowledge to be held 'on faith.'" These essays engage Lewis on the issue of man's "natural powers," how much a man can or cannot know. These essays are listed individually in this bibliography.

47   UNRUE, JOHN C. "Beastliness in Narnia: Medieval Echoes." In *Man's "Natural Powers": Essays for and about C. S. Lewis.* Edited by Raymond P. Tripp, Jr. Church Stretton, England: The Society for New Language Study, pp. 9–16.
       The motif of bad beasts or beastliness represents the decadence or lost state to which creatures descend when they lose sight of God and His purpose. It was a concept common in medieval literature and is evident throughout the Chronicles of Narnia. Edmund in *The Lion, the Witch and the Wardrobe* and Uncle Andrew in *The Magician's Nephew* are prime examples of beastliness.

48   VIDAL, JAIME. "The Ubiquitous Center in Bonaventure and Lewis, with Application to the Great Dance on Perelandra." *CSL: The Bulletin of the New York C. S. Lewis Society* 6 (March):1–4.
       St. Bonaventure expressed the "logic of Coincidence of Opposites, a logic especially applicable to God, who is . . . the Coincidence of Opposites." Christ, in "his central position within the inner life of the Trinity," is the center of everything. Bonaventure's ideas explain the ending of *Perelandra*, the longest and most detailed mystic passage in Lewis's work.

49   WATT, DONALD. "The View from Malacandra." *CSL: The Bulletin of the New York C. S. Lewis Society* 6 (June):5–7.
       Out of the Silent Planet owes a debt to Wells's *The First Men in the Moon* (London: G. Newnes, 1901). There are many similarities between the two novels; however, Lewis surpasses Wells in creating a narrative method that gives the reader a "credible first-hand impression of a non-human Gestalt." He renders a vivid and comprehensive view of the Malacandrian hierarchy as well as a critical perspective on human beings from the Malacandrian point of view.

1975

50 WILLIAMS, TERRI. "Odyssey of a Traitor." *Chronicle of the Portland C. S. Lewis Society* 4, no. 3 (July–September):8–12.

Edmund in *The Lion, the Witch and the Wardrobe* is a sensualist and does not think of the results of his actions. "Pain and discomfort finally lead him to see (and follow) truth." While Edmund's choices are motivated by self-ishness, Nikabrik in *Prince Caspian* becomes a traitor through pride and mis-guided loyalty to the Dwarves. Both Edmund and Nikabrik, through the preparation of their choices, betray their friends.

51 WIRT, SHERWOOD. Interview. *Chronicle of the Portland C. S. Lewis Society* 17 March:1–9.

Wirt interviewed Lewis in May 1963 for *Decision* magazine and felt out of his depth because Lewis was a first-class intellectual and theologian. Lewis's view of Scripture is not the same as that of Billy Graham—verbal inspiration. Lewis felt that God brought people to Him by means they espe-cially disliked. Lewis used a light approach because he felt it would have the greatest appeal to readers. He had a sincere respect for the church and the clergy. He smoked incessantly during the interview, and Wirt feels Lewis was trying to kill himself, that he had no more zest for living after his wife's death. Lewis felt that it would be terrible to bring sin to other planets. He always had a spiritual message in his books. Lewis "was spiritually a semite just like we are." Wirt believed that Lewis had more influence on this century than any other Christian.

52 WOLFE, GARY K. "Symbolic Fantasy." *Genre* 8 (September):195–209.

Wolfe develops the characteristics of symbolic fantasy through the work of MacDonald, Lindsay, and Lewis's Ransom Trilogy. The form is prose fiction interspersed with lyrics, ballads, and highly descriptive pas-sages. The intent is to transcend "the limitations of human existence to attain new perspectives and insights." The protagonist starts with a projected image and is then stripped of all but the characteristics essential to the created myth or story. He is usually naive and laboring under a vice or illusion, which his development, an educational process, strips away. Action takes place in another world, a spiritual landscape in which any element may carry a moral meaning and which has a different time scheme. There is usually a tutelary figure, a guide native to this world; the antagonist is usually an invader from our own world. The structure is highly episodic, the style highly descriptive. Symbolic fantasy usually results when the dominant cultural attitude is too narrow and does not allow for the expression of man's psychological or spir-itual makeup.

53 WRONG, CHARLES. "Christianity and Progress." *CSL: The Bulletin of the New York C. S. Lewis Society* 6 (August):19–24.

Lewis said the belief in progress, that we stand at the highest point humanity has so far reached and that mankind will continue to advance, is based on the fallacious idea of evolution. He had reason to think that the world was moving from bad to worse and sometimes he seemed to embrace this belief. For the most part, however, he regarded "history as a record of interrupted but discernable progress." He valued consistency but did not invariably achieve it; he "saw different patterns at different times." Lewis also did not hesitate to cast moral judgments on past events or on those responsible for them.

54 ZOGBY, EDWARD [G.]. "C. S. Lewis: Christopoesis and the Recovery of the Panegyric Imagination." Ph.D. dissertation, Syracuse University, 528 pp.

Lewis's thought forms a triadic pattern. Through the dialect of desire he discovered in his life the pattern of delight, pain, and fruit; he explored this pattern in literature and found that it was "coincidental with the universal pattern of new creation found in *Evangelium*." Lewis's literature is Christopoesis; he so "moves the imagination of the reader or the exercitant as to awaken a desire for God." He uses the key metaphor of the downward ascent of God to activate the panegyric imagination, the "action of the central man recovering that inner unity which has only been intimated by the longing for Joy, *Sehnsucht*."

55 ZUCK, JOHN E. "Religion and Fantasy." *Religious Education* 70 (November–December):586–604.

The works of Lewis, Tolkien, and Williams illustrate how religion and fantasy can be successfully combined and how appropriate this is for our present cultural situation. The important relationship between religion and fantasy is developed through two themes: "fantasy can enlarge our sense of what is actual, possible, and valuable" and fantasy can "revivify our capacity to experience the sacredness that is in and with our world." These authors write mythopoesis, " 'stories about the gods,' about the fundamental powers and realities of the universe and the primordial events which have made the world what it is."

1976

1 BARFIELD, OWEN. "Some Reflections on *The Great Divorce*." *Mythlore* 4 (September):7–8.

There were two Lewises: an atomic Lewis whose thinking was "ruthlessly cause-and-effect" and uncompromisingly logical, and a mythopoetic Lewis who had "a firm intuition in the Substantial reality." They came as close as they ever did to remarriage in *The Great Divorce*. Lewis's outstandingly

1976

original touch in this work is his use of "not only material shapes but *materiality itself* to symbolize immateriality." He uses twentieth-century man's principle of reality to point to a greater reality.

2 BASSETT, WILLIAM CLYDE. "The Formulation of a Basis for Counseling from a Christian Theory of Personality as Represented by C. S. Lewis and Watchman Nee." Ph.D. dissertation, University of Arkansas, 221 pp.

Both Lewis and Nee believed that man comprises spirit, soul, and body, each of which has a specific function and is supposed to operate in harmony with God's design. They advocated a Christian view of man that can provide all the answers to his problems; a Christian theory of personality can explain man's uniqueness and give significance to life.

3 BROWN, CAROL ANN. "The Land Where the Shadows Fall: The Idea of Heaven in C. S. Lewis." *CSL: The Bulletin of the New York C. S. Lewis Society* 7 (October):1–2.

"Faced with a generation conditioned to despise happiness, and in the pursuit of pleasure, and repelled by the traditional symbols of Heaven, Lewis had to forge his own symbolism and imagery using them not as illusion but as illustration." He drew from the medieval model of the universe and from the twists and surprises of science fiction. "From the shadows and hints on Earth, and the experience of Joy, he awakened a hunger for the reality of Heaven."

4 ———. "The Three Roads: A Comment on 'The Queen of Drum.' " *CSL: The Bulletin of the New York C. S. Lewis Society* 7 (April):14.

The road to hell taken by the King and the road to heaven taken by the Archbishop are known to us by experience. The road to Elfland, that "half-light between Heaven and Hell," taken by the Queen, "thirsty with desire for the deeper realities beyond the senses," represents a present danger in our lives.

5 CHAPMAN, ED[GAR L.]. "Toward a Sacramental Ecology: Technology, Nature and Transcendence in C. S. Lewis's Ransom Trilogy." *Mythlore* 3 (June):10–17.

Lewis establishes a link "between egotism or moral failure and ecological disaster." He warns against technology with its sterile rationalism, self-righteousness, and greed, forces that have dominated Western civilization. He saw that "we conquer nature through our technology and exploit it only to have a damaged nature threaten to destroy us." Some modern thinkers have recently arrived at the same conclusion. Nature has a sacramental meaning for Lewis: it is "an image of and a window to the numinous world."

6 CHENNELL, VIRGINIA VERNON. *"Till We Have Faces." English Journal* 65 (January):67–68.

Chennell reveals how she uses Lewis's novel to teach mythology to senior high school students. Through the novel, they can "relate the plots and themes of ancient myths to their own lives" and discover "the relevance of mythology today."

7   CHRISTOPHER, JOE R. "An Inklings Bibliography." *Mythlore* 3 (June):30–38.

Beginning with the June 1976 issue of *Mythlore*, Christopher's bibliography is contained in each issue of the periodical. The annotated checklist covers both primary and secondary works on the Inklings, principally J. R. R. Tolkien, C. S. Lewis, and Charles Williams. Materials included are books, essays, periodical articles, and some book reviews. In addition to items primarily about these authors, brief references to the writers in other works are cited. Later issues of the *Mythlore* bibliography, which continues through 1988, are not listed separately.

8   ———. "Transformed Nature: 'Where Is It Now, the Glory and the Dream?'" *CSL: The Bulletin of the New York C. S. Lewis Society* 7 (September):1–7.

"Nature writing" and a joy or vision found in and through nature is evident in the poetry of Wordsworth and Kathleen Raine as well as in Lewis's prose. These visions are in some sense mystical and occurred in childhood but became lost to Wordsworth and Raine; they can no longer see the glory in nature but can remember that they saw it. This vision was not lost to Lewis; the First Image, the true image, when lost to intuition must be recovered through the Second Image and the intellect; "the Final Image will be the First Image, but known differently." Lewis postulated a "risen, resurrected eternal nature upon the New Earth which followed the Day of Judgment."

9   CLARK, ZOIE. "Notes on 'The Seeing Eye.'" *Chronicle of the Portland C. S. Lewis Society* 5, no. 2 (April–June):2.

The Christian doctrine of prevenient grace means that God must first seek man before man can seek Him. In his essay "The Seeing Eye," Lewis details how to avoid God. He makes four points: "1) man needs a peculiar apparatus for finding God, 2) God is not a fixed object or a diffused essence, 3) there are many convenient ways to avoid God, and 4) essentially God is the hunter."

10   COMO, JAMES T. "An Introduction to *The Allegory of Love*: Report of the 75th Meeting, January 9, 1976." *CSL: The Bulletin of the New York C. S. Lewis Society* 7 (January):1–3.

The Allegory of Love traces "the evolution from late antiquity through the Middle Ages . . . [of] that literary genre which claimed romantic love as its subject and allegory as its form." Courtly love's elements are an adulterous liaison between lovers, requited love results in the spiritual ennobling of the

1976

lover, high courtesy marks the lovers' demeanor, and the relationship has the status of a religion.

11 FORBES, CHERYL. "Narnia: Fantasy, But . . ." *Christianity Today* 20 (23 April):6–10.
    Lewis wrote the Chronicles of Narnia for the childlike. He did not write them with a didactic purpose in mind but they do contain a potency of Christianity. He "offers children . . . a vivid story filled with familiar details and extraordinary events. He also presents to them logic, differing concepts of time, loyalty, how to tell whether someone is telling the truth or lying, common sense, love, sacrifice, evil and goodness, war and violence, death, and the importance of the imagination. Children learn what pride is, how difficult obedience can be, and how temptation works. In short, Lewis introduces them to reality, both physical and spiritual."

12 GREENFIELD, ROBERT. "C. S. Lewis and Oxford." *Chronicle of the Portland C. S. Lewis Society* 5, no. 1 (January–March):4–9.
    Greenfield heard Joy Davidman lecture on Hassidic Judaism and felt she was thoroughly delightful and effervescent. Lewis spoke after the lecture, bantering with Joy; he was incredibly witty and brilliant. Greenfield believes that Lewis suffered from intellectual snobbery at Oxford. Lewis lived there, surrounded by cruel academic intrigues, a witness to Christ in a quiet way through his books and lectures.

13 HALL, SUSAN. "Screwtape, Satan, and Sophistication." *CSL: The Bulletin of the New York C. S. Lewis Society* 7 (March):1–4.
    The popularity of *The Screwtape Letters* "is due in part to the fact that Lewis takes fuzzy, capricious, amorphous Evil and gives it structure." He sees evil as a parasite: "it can only feed on what has been created by God." Lewis instructs by showing good, which cannot be attributed to our own efforts, till the unbeliever must confront the notion of an operative God.

*14 HANNAY, MARGARET P[ATTERSON]. "Rehabilitations: C. S. Lewis' Contribution to the Understanding of Spenser and Milton." *DAI* 37 (1977):1564A. State University of New York at Albany, 400 pp.
    "In *The Allegory of Love* Lewis set up the Art/Nature distinction between the Bower of Bliss and the Garden of Adonis," which provoked reevaluation of Spenser's philosophic and moral purpose in *The Faerie Queene*. His thoughts on allegory, symbol, and myth generated a controversy that redefined the genre of allegory. In *Preface to "Paradise Lost"* Lewis cleared away misconceptions about Milton's poem. The areas he clarified are the architectonic quality of the verse, Milton's theory of creation, his Christology, and the romantic identification of Satan as hero. *Perelandra* is Lewis's most surprising contribution and is a door into the world of *Paradise Lost*.

15 ———. "*Surprised by Joy*: C. S. Lewis' Changing Attitudes toward Women." *Mythlore* 4 (September):15–20.

"When Joy Davidman became first [Lewis's] friend and then his wife, she radically altered his presentation of women in his fiction, his use of masculine as a term of praise and perhaps more significantly, his pronouncements on marriage." *Perelandra* and *That Hideous Strength* reflect on male superiority, at least in a hierarchical sense. In *Till We Have Faces*, dedicated to Joy, "Lewis has become capable of entering into a woman's mind"; Orual is significant in her relation to God, not to men. Lewis finally saw that women are fully human. In *The Four Loves* he also demonstrated his new understanding of the relationship between men and women; he learned that a wife can be a friend as well as a lover. See reply 1977.39.

16 HARRIS, MASON. "Science Fiction as the Dream and Nightmare of Progress: Part 3, C. S. Lewis: Cosmic Politics and the Fall of Woman." *West Coast Review* 10, no. 4:3–10.

Lewis's fantasy is enjoyable but his antimodern, nonparadoxical Christianity is unpalatable; his views of women, sex, and marriage offend readers of every persuasion. In *Out of the Silent Planet* Lewis satirizes Wellsian utopia and attacks racism. Ransom's mission in *Perelandra* and *That Hideous Strength* is to preserve the innocence of the young women. There are elements of Oedipal fantasy in these two novels: the Green Lady is the virgin mother, Ransom is the good father, and the Un-man and directors of NICE are bad fathers. Lewis only offers submission to a good authority rather than a bad authority as an answer, but the authoritarianism of the good characters, especially Ransom, is apparent. Lewis's celebration of innocence is both his strength and weakness: "the attempt to preserve childhood innocence at any cost must be paid for by a self-defeating return to authority."

17 HARWOOD, A. C. "A Toast to the Memory of C. S. Lewis Proposed at Magdalen College." *Mythlore* 3 (June):3–5.
      Reprint of 1975.22. Reprinted: 1979.44.

18 HENDRICKSON, DAVID. "*The Discarded Image*." *Chronicle of the Portland C. S. Lewis Society* 5, no. 1 (January–March):11–16.
      Lewis's delight in the medieval spirit led him to describe that world in *The Discarded Image*. He describes medieval people as bookish and organizers, characteristics that led them to construct "'a harmonious mental Model of the Universe,'" which appealed to the imagination and the emotions. Lewis identifies ideas behind the model: the body is irrelevant, heaven is for statesmen, "perfect things precede imperfect things," man's place in the universe is low. He ignores the differences in customs of earlier periods, disregards geography and physical perspectives, and does not distinguish between fiction and history.

1976

19 HODGENS, RICHARD [M]. "Notes on *Narrative Poems.*" *CSL: The Bulletin of the New York C. S. Lewis Society* 7 (April):1–14.

For Lewis the story came first and should be told clearly. For him "obscurity was a very serious fault," but it is the cause of *Dymer's* failure. The weird story of the poem came first and was an obsession of Lewis's. "The Queen of Drum," considered Lewis's best poem, deals with three different realms: the real world, the Christian supernatural world of heaven and hell, and dreamland and fairyland. Lewis uses mixed meter to depict the disintegration between the characters and their world.

20 HOLMER, PAUL L. *C. S. Lewis: The Shape of His Faith and Thought.* New York: Harper & Row, 116 pp. Reprint. London: Sheldon, 1977.

Lewis felt that literature "is not a disguised theory, nor an implied didacticism. Instead, it communicates in such a way that, when successful, it creates new capabilities and capacities in the human personality." He distinguished between *connaître*, which is knowledge by "becoming another self, sharing the feeling, pathos and hope, and *savoire*, which is knowledge in the 'about' mood, theories and views, laws and hypotheses." Lewis felt that the areas covered by literature, philosophy, theology, and psychology (i.e., the nature of reality, the nature of man, and the nature of beauty and goodness) were not knowable through theories or general laws. He believed that the world around us was an objective moral order and that the individual must find the means within his own personality to become its qualified reader. Lewis's apologetic works cause "us to create for ourselves all kinds of these aptitudes and propensies we simply did not have before" in order to achieve a moral consciousness.

21 HOOPER, WALTER. "Reminiscences." *Mythlore* 3 (June):5–9.

Hooper remembers Lewis's conversation as formidable and rich, a "combination of wit, charm and humour"; he "chose to talk about things which give pleasure." He adapted his manner to fit whomever he was with, and he was interested in other people's comfort. He gave two-thirds of his income to charity and could not bring himself to buy anything he thought he could live without.

22 KAWANO, ROLAND M. "C. S. Lewis and the Great Dance." *Christianity and Literature* 26 (Fall):20–38.

Dance is "used by the mystic to translate into human terms his heavenly vision." Lewis uses images of play and dance to express "the highest things" in his apologetics, criticism, and fiction. Play and dance contain some of the most important elements of Joy, which is the "serious business of heaven." The central element in Lewis's images of play and dance is the reconciliation of order and freedom. *The Silver Chair* and *Perelandra* contain the most extensive images of dance in Lewis's fiction.

*23 KEMBALL-COOK, JESSICA. Title unknown, subject: sex discrimination in Tolkien and Lewis. *Mallorn.*
Source of citation: *Year's Work in English Studies*, 1976, p. 354.

24 KILBY, CLYDE [S.]. "Some Insight on Emeth." *Chronicle of the Portland C. S. Lewis Society* 5, no. 4 (October–December):11.
"Lewis often taught that any step honestly taken in what one judges to be the right direction will result in light for another step of the same kind."

25 KIRKPATRICK, HOPE. "An Approach to *The Personal Heresy.*" *CSL: The Bulletin of the New York C. S. Lewis Society* 7 (June):1–8.
Lewis attacked the position that "poetry is an expression of the poet's personality." He states that the personality expressed is not necessarily that of the poet. The personaltiy in a work of literature appears in the grip of strong emotion from which the poet has already escaped in order to see it objectively. He says that we approach the poet by sharing his consciousness, not by studying it. E. M. W. Tillyard, however, sees a fundamental paradox in that an artist is "most himself when he is least himself," when he abandons himself and surrenders to his art; it is then the audience sees his unmistakable personality.

26 KIRKPATRICK, JOHN. "The Great Dance in *Perelandra.*" *CSL: The Bulletin of the New York C. S. Lewis Society* 7 (February):1–6.
This may be the supreme fulfillment of Lewis's poetic aspirations, not in verse but an exalted poetic prose or free verse. The aim is "to picture an antiphonal ceremony, enacted in a state of trance, lasting a whole year." Themes in the stanzas are eternity, change, order, immanence, differences, circles, ancient worlds, incarnation, redemption, other worlds, dust, individuals, courtesy, love, bounty, plans and patterns, and cosmic space.

27 LINDSKOOG, KATHRYN [ANN]. "C. S. Lewis: Reactions from Women." *Mythlore* 3 (June):18–20.
Lewis was not a misogynist in his personal life. His mother was probably the most important woman in his life; her death ended his happy childhood. He became temporarily infatuated with Mrs. Moore when he was nineteen and she forty-six, the same age his mother was when she died. Lewis enjoyed the happiest time of his life during his marriage to Joy Davidman. Lindskoog and several other women who were briefly acquainted with Lewis have nothing but praise for him and his kind acceptance of them. Reprinted: 1983.41, 42.

28 LINTON, CALVIN D. "C. S. Lewis Ten Years Later." *CSL: The Bulletin of the New York C. S. Lewis Society* 7 (July):104.
Reprint of 1973.24.

1976

29   McGOVERN, EUGENE. "On the Objectivity of Moral Values." *CSL: The Bulletin of the New York C. S. Lewis Society* 7 (September):8–12.

The concept that moral values are objective and express truths about realities outside ourselves is part of the foundation of Lewis's work. In "The Poison of Subjectivism" he advances two propositions: the human mind is incapable of inventing a new value, and "every attempt to do so consists in arbitrarily selecting some one maxim of traditional morality, isolating it from the rest and erecting it into an *urium necessarium*." Those, like Lewis, who force us to recognize the unbridgeable chasm between right and wrong deserve our greatest thanks.

30   MEILAENDER, GILBERT. "The Social and Ethical Thought of C. S. Lewis." Ph.D. dissertation, Princeton University, 273 pp.

Lewis's central premise is that "all human beings are made for life in community with God (and thereby with one another)." The Christian undergoes a process of sanctification and is properly to delight in things without seeking security in them, both to enjoy and to renunciate. Love is essential to true community—it "overcomes the problems of selfishness and self-centeredness." Lewis saw hell as a "retreat into the self, a denial of community." He viewed community as a hierarchy that allows for diversity in individual personalities. Other elements include Tao and the idea that pain is a reminder to the Christian that the sinful self must be killed, the belief that the natural loves need to be transformed. Revised for publication: 1978.26.

31   MERCHANT, ROBERT. "An Approach to *Miracles*." *CSL: The Bulletin of the New York C. S. Lewis Society* 8 (November):1–5.

A naturalist believes nothing exists but nature; a supernaturalist believes that something exists above and beyond nature. Reason is independent of nature but comes into nature from without, from supernature. Moral judgments are valid only if they are offshoots of absolute reason or wisdom. The incarnation is the pivotal miracle; "it elucidates, clarifies, pulls together all the other Christian Miracles and indeed the whole of life." There are two types of miracles: those of old creation "reproduce operations we have already seen"; those of new creation "reproduce operations yet to come." The premier example is the Resurrection.

32   MEYER, ERIC C. "C. S. Lewis' Problem with Petitionary Prayer." *CSL: The Bulletin of the New York C. S. Lewis Society* 7 (February):8–12.

Lewis believed that Jesus taught two opposing patterns of petitionary prayer that cannot be reconciled. Pattern A: to condition all prayers on God's will; Pattern B: that we shall receive precisely what we ask for if we pray with undoubting faith. Lewis, however, misunderstood key passages (Matthew 21:21–22 and Mark 11:22–24). Jesus's words "you shall receive whatever you ask for" are the hyperbole rather than the image He used, as Lewis suggests.

Lewis also misunderstood the unhesitating belief as applying to the specific thing asked for rather than general faith in God. Thus, Pattern B can and does fit into Pattern A. Reprinted: 1977.40.

33 MORGAN, GERALD. "The Self-Revealing Tendencies of Chaucer's Pardoner." *Modern Language Review* 71, no. 2 (April):241–255.
    Lewis's psychological interpretation of *The Romance of the Rose* in *The Allegory of Love* is incorrect. He "is mistaken in the fundamental distinction that he draws between secular and creative allegory on the one hand and religious and exegetical allegory on the other." The psychological approach must be abandoned for a moral one and so Lewis's central strategy is undermined. An objective interpretation of *The Pardoner's Tale* shows it as the Pardoner's attempt to exploit the pilgrims for his own gain.

34 MORRISON, JOHN. "Obedience and Surrender in Narnia." *CSL: The Bulletin of the New York C. S. Lewis Society* 7 (October):2–4.
    The theological definitions of surrender and obedience are "to yield possession of" and "to give power over to another." Examples are Eustace's conversion in *The Voyage of the "Dawn Treader"* and Lucy's decision in *Prince Caspian* to follow Aslan. Lewis makes it clear that true conversion is a free choice and means commitment to Aslan (Christ).

35 MURPHY, BRIAN. "Enchanted Rationalism: The Legacy of C. S. Lewis." *Christianity and Literature* 25 (Winter):13–29.
    Lewis's themes and concerns are contrary to our contemporary cultural assumptions. His technique of "rational opposition," intellectual battle with his peers, allowed him to discover what he believed and gave him an opportunity to defend his beliefs. The validity of reason is one of Lewis's major themes and is part of all his works. His juxtaposition of the fantastic with the prosaic or homely makes his fiction enchanted. Lewis is "a shining example of what the intellectual life can be—everything from fun to profound. . . . Lewis combines the fun and the profound in an altogether inimitable way."

36 PATTERSON, NANCY-LOU. "Narnia and the North: The Symbolism of Northernness in the Fantasies of C. S. Lewis." *Mythlore* 4 (December):9–16.
    Northernness is a basic element in the symbolic structure of the Narnia Chronicles, especially *The Horse and His Boy*. Northernness evokes feelings of exultation and ecstasies of desolation; for Lewis it was the way to God. In world culture, north is the primary direction, represents light, corresponds to Yang, and is located at the top of the head. South is dark, corresponds to Yin, and is the lower region of the body "where the passions and heats of the flesh are located." "The backbone is the column of the universe" that connects them. The union of north and south occur in *The Horse and His Boy*, with the marriage of dark-skinned southern Arvis and light-skinned northern Shasta.

1976

37 SAMMONS, MARTHA C. "The God Within: Reason and Its Riddle in C. S. Lewis' *Till We Have Faces.*" *Christian Scholar's Review* 6:127–139.

The conflict between faith and reason is the basis of the structure and purpose of *Till We Have Faces*. The novel depicts three different worldviews: sacrificial primitive religion and superstition, Greek rationalism, and faith in an unseen god. Orual and her rationalist viewpoint are the center of the story; the central image is the veil, which is both intellectual and spiritual, separating Orual from both knowledge of herself and knowledge of the god. "Lewis' use of a first person narrative technique, the 'complaint' format, and an undefined setting allows the reader to fully experience Orual's view of things," and thus to create the story himself. Lewis evokes numinous responses through the techniques of transforming characters and meanings, and transposition, "the restatement of ideas in new terms."

38 ———. "Lewis's View of Science." *CSL: The Bulletin of the New York C. S. Lewis Society* 7 (August):1–6.

Lewis stated that the Fall caused a separation between subject and object; science sees only fact or object without meaning or subject. He does not attack science but "scientism"—the popular belief that "science puts us in touch with reality while other types of thought" do not. Lewis distinguished between reality perceived and reality experienced but finds both vital. He saw that the ideal way to unite reason and imagination, the two modes of experience, is through metaphor, which puts things into their context and restores relationships among them. Myth, for Lewis, is the most perfect form of metaphor.

39 SHENKER, ISRAEL. "Faithful Gather to Recall a Dinosaur: C. S. Lewis (1898–1963)." *New York Times* 10 December, p. B1.

The New York C. S. Lewis Society held a conference on Lewis, who wrote "witty, lucid books in defence of Christian orthodoxy, delighting in rigors of reason, not empty piety, with no water in the wine but lots of heady bubbles." Reprinted: 1979.106.

40 SPEROU, CAROLE. "*The Silver Chair.*" *Chronicle of the Portland C. S. Lewis Society* 5, no. 4 (October–December):8–10.

The Silver Chair is different from the other Narnia Chronicles with its long, moving passages, its emphasis on plot, and Lewis's use of suspense and surprise. He also uses realistic touches and humor in the story. He does an interesting job of creating beings and keeping them true to their characteristics. Lewis's theology is revealed through Aslan: he is not tame, he calls Jill to him, he has definite expectations of the children, he wants Jill to use her discipline and intellect to carry out her task, and he expects the children to follow him even through difficult circumstances.

41   STAHL, JOHN T. "The Nature and Function of Myth in the Christian Thought
      of C. S. Lewis." *CSL: The Bulletin of the New York C. S. Lewis Society* 7
      (January):3–8.
            Lewis viewed myth as a literary genre and defined its six characteris-
      tics. His most superb myth is *Till We Have Faces*, whose central theme is
      that "what we are is what we become by what we do day in and day out." In
      an allegory characters are personified abstractions; the function of allegory
      is to reveal what cannot be said well in literal speech. *The Pilgrim's Regress*
      is an allegory of a spiritual journey. "Myth and its fulfillment or embodi-
      ment in history" are mixed in Christianity. A Christian must grasp the
      mythical significance of the Bible, accept it as historical fact, and commit
      himself to the person revealed in the myth as God Himself. Reprinted in
      part: 1978.42.

42   TETREAULT, JAMES. "C. S. Lewis and T. S. Eliot." *CSL: The Bulletin of the
      New York C. S. Lewis Society* 8 (December):1–5.
            Lewis was unwaveringly hostile toward Eliot's poetry and criticism for
      over thirty years. Eliot was the representative of the Modernist movement,
      which Lewis found "antithetical in mood and form to all he loved and respect-
      ed." Toward the end of his life, Lewis came to "recognize the sincerity of
      Eliot's faith and to realize that literary and temperamental differences were
      minor compared with this solid ground."

43   WOOD, DOREEN ANDERSON. "The Pattern in the Myth: Archetypal
      Elements in C. S. Lewis's *Till We Have Faces.*" Ph.D. dissertation, University
      of Tulsa, 163 pp.
            Lewis wrote first in allegory and then, as his skill developed, he turned
      toward the archetypal and mythic in his stories. This progress is evident from
      The Pilgrim's Regress to *Till We Have Faces*, the apex of his art. He presents
      several mythic truths through archetypes in *Till We Have Faces*: "God
      demands worship and obedience; a man must know himself; true vision is see-
      ing things as they are, not as they appear; love and sacrifice may take many
      forms; a man may bear the burdens of another."

44   ZARETZKE, KENNETH. "Ethics, Environment, and Society: On Being
      Uncompromising, Ornery, Militant, Rigorous, Imperious, and Invincibly Self-
      Righteous or A Critique of Everything." In *Soli Deo Gloria: Essays in
      Reformed Theology, Festschrift for John H. Gersther*. Edited by R. C. Sproul.
      Phillipsburg, N. J.: Presbyterian and Reformed, pp. 164–193.
            Lewis is mentioned several times in passing. Zaretzke says he admires
      Lewis unabashedly and that intellectuals such as Alan Watts sneer at Lewis
      because he is a threat to their way of life.

1977

1 ADEY, LIONEL. "C. S. Lewis: The Man and What He Stood For." *CSL: The Bulletin of the New York C. S. Lewis Society* 8 (March):1–7.
     Lewis knew a great deal of suffering, grief, and frustration—his mother's death from cancer, a strained relationship with his father, life with the "domineering, crotchety, and totally unbelieving" Mrs. Moore, severe criticism at Oxford for writing popular apologetics, denial of full professorship, and the death of his wife. He tried to undeceive the world of the illusions of chronological snobbery, naturalism and materialism, and reductionist psychology. Lewis was "too humble to realize how exceptional he was"; he had a clear mind, a feeling heart, immense learning, genuine wisdom, and compassion. As a Christian, he was a democrat, "unwilling to allow any fallen creature unlimited power over his fellows." Reprinted: 1979.1.

2 ———. "C. S. Lewis's Annotations to His Shakespeare Volumes." *CSL: The Bulletin of the New York C. S. Lewis Society* 8 (May):1–8.
     Lewis's annotations are glosses, paraphrases of difficult passages, etymological or semantic comments, textual variants, quotations from Shakespeare's sources, comments on *Arden Edition* notes, notes on puns, and comments on other interpretations. He approaches Shakespeare as a working scholar, treating the plays as a classical text. His "most stimulating notes are those on *Hamlet, Othello*, and *The Tempest*."

3 ASHER, RICHARD E. Review of *The Joyful Christian: 127 Readings from C. S. Lewis. Library Journal* 102 (15 December):2505.
     "Fifteen of Lewis' religious works have been extracted on the topic of 'What a Christian can joyfully believe.' Selections range from 'Affection' to 'Where and When to Pray' and extend from six lines ('Scruples') to seven pages ('Incarnation')." Asher captures Lewis at his most humorous and most serious. This collection "will serve as source material for the student and meditative reading for the layman"—a joy to read.

4 BARNES, JULIAN. "Bread." *New Statesman* 93 (25 February):257.
     This review of *The Dark Tower and Other Stories* finds them "donnish and cerebral, with a charmless undertone of misogyny." The prose is lifeless, puritanically down-to-earth, and without much style.

5 BORKLUND, ELMER. "Lewis, C(live) S(taples)." In *Contemporary Literary Critics*. New York: St. Martin's, pp. 344–354.
     Lewis believed that criticism should allow the reader to enter into the author's intentions. Ethically, proper reading allows the reader "to exercise that power of sympathetic understanding which transcends self-interest." When reading properly we do not access the author's consciousness but what

the author saw and felt. Therefore good criticism encourages good reading of worthy literature. "All of Lewis' criticism is designed to enable the reader to 'enter more fully into the author's intentions.'" The article also gives brief biographical information, provides a bibliography of Lewis's criticism, verse, and novels, and presents a short bibliography of secondary works. Reprinted: 1982.2.

6   BRADY, CHARLES A. "Some Notes on C. S. Lewis's *The Dark Tower and Other Stories.*" *CSL: The Bulletin of the New York C. S. Lewis Society* 8 (September):1–10.

Lewis did not finish "The Dark Tower," perhaps because he thought it too derivative—the device of the chronoscope from MacDonald, the White Riders, and the Dark Tower itself too close to Tolkien. The side of the theme that deals with hell may have frightened him "with an immediacy still too naked for his mythopoeic art"; he was not yet ready or equipped to deal with it. The themes evident in the fragment are those that surfaced "so harmoniously in *That Hideous Strength.*"

7   BRESLIN, JOHN B. "Surprised by Lewis, the Law and Long Loyalties." *America* 137 (31 December):486–87.

The Joyful Christian: 127 Readings from C. S. Lewis, provides an illuminating introduction to the breadth and depth of Lewis's religious reflections. Lewis's "genius lay in pouring the rich wine of Christian orthodoxy into crystal goblets of his own devising whose translucence made the old vintage sparkle afresh."

8   BRIDGES, LINDA. "A Consideration of *An Experiment in Criticism.*" *CSL: The Bulletin of the New York C. S. Lewis Society* 8 (January):1–6.

Lewis's innovation is to judge a book by the way it is read. A literary reader receives the author's work; an unliterary reader's own preconceptions are so firmly in the front of his mind nothing new can penetrate. Lewis takes for granted that the literary reader visualizes the images read. Bridges disagrees: some otherwise literary readers do not/cannot visualize as they read; this may account for the unpopularity of poetry. Lewis distinguishes between Poiema, something made, the artifact, and the Logos, the meaning; we can praise or condemn a work for how it is crafted or for its content, but we must not confuse the two.

9   BROWN, CAROL ANN. "Once upon a Narnia." *CSL: The Bulletin of the New York C. S. Lewis Society* 8 (June):1–4.

"Fairy tales are the key to the wisdom of the submerged, both pagan and Christian"; they concern people faced with powers and destinies they cannot control but which they have to confront, usually with the help of a member of some feared or mistrusted group of a different nature or species. This theme of

1977

the hero in danger runs throughout the Chronicles; the hero has to struggle and suffer before there can be a happy ending. The physical description of Narnia has the "tang of our world when it is enchanted."

10 BROWN, JUDITH. "The Pilgrimage from Deep Space." *Mythlore* 4 (March):13–15.
    Out of the Silent Planet deals with the spiritual pilgrimage of Ransom; his entry into Malacandra is described in terms of natural childbirth, the planet becomes his nursery, and he undergoes a ritual initiation into manhood. *Perelandra* has two levels as "an account of the temptation and evil, and an account of man's struggle with the two." Ransom's physical defeat of the Unman is not a cop-out on Lewis's part. The Lady has withstood and rejected temptation, and fulfilled her responsibilities. Perelandra also represents the inner world of man where maturity involves not just the "excellence of knowledge, nor the possibility of knowledge, nor the possibility of a paradisal adjustment of life, but with a grubby hand-to-hand combat of the redeemed nature beating down the unredeemed." In *That Hideous Strength*, as in *The Pilgrim's Regress*, one character moves toward salvation, and once having accepted the Way, he kills a dragon and obtains the missing ingredient of his own character.

11 BURGESS, ANTHONY. "Joy to the World." *New York Times Book Review*, 25 December, pp. 1, 18.
    Review of *The Joyful Christian: 127 Readings from C. S. Lewis*. Lewis "is the ideal persuader for the half-convinced, for the good man who would like to be a Christian but finds his intellect getting in the way." But what would the response of a Jew or a Muslim be to his cool, precise, yet unpedantic arguments?

12 "C. S. Lewis Goes Marching On." *Time* 110 (5 December):92.
    Lewis, the "Pascal of the Space Age, is the only author in English whose Christian writings combine intellectual stature with best-seller success." His works have brought "innumerable souls into the precincts of belief," including Sheldon and Jean Vanauken and Charles Colson. Part of his appeal may be that he started out as an atheist and that, as Walter Hooper claims, he expresses " 'a coherent, universal faith, something permanent in a world of seeming chaos.' " Reprinted: 1979.16.

13 CARNELL, CORBIN SCOTT. "The Meaning of Masculine and Feminine in the Work of C. S. Lewis." *Modern British Literature* 2 (Fall):153–159.
    Lewis saw each individual as being masculine and feminine in gender though male or female in sex. This basic polarity "makes for wholeness, a yin–yang movement deeper than sexual differences, an interdependence which reflects the triune God." He would probably have seen the women's

movement as a reaction against political and economic repression and still have wanted the man to have a ceremonial headship in the home. Lewis's idea that "we are both masculine and feminine, that the roles are always changing, that relatedness is more like a dance than a rule" provides ways for understanding our identities and how they relate to the women's movement.

14 CHAPLIN, DORA. "Some Reflections on *Letters to an American Lady*." *CSL: The Bulletin of the New York C. S. Lewis Society* 8 (May):9–13.

Lewis did not like writing letters but believed "taking time out to advise or encourage another Christian was both a humbling of one's talents before the Lord and also as much the work of the Holy Spirit as producing a book." In these letters, he emphasized the necessity of living in the present, said that forgiving and being forgiven are the same and that one has to just keep on trying, and stressed prayer ("intercessory prayer was interwoven with his whole life"). The letters reveal Lewis's faith as a living thing penetrating every aspect of his life.

15 CHAPMAN, ED[GAR L.]. "Images of the Numinous in T. H. White and C. S. Lewis." *Mythlore* 4 (June):3–10.

"The degree to which a fantasy writer creates (or recreates) a myth to which we experience an intensely numinous response is a measure of his status as a fantasy or mythopoeic writer." Numinous describes the religious experience of confronting the sacred, the holy, or the Being who inspires these feelings. While White does not give much of a numinous dimension to the Arthurian legends, Lewis's mastery in the presentation of numinous myth is evident. Lewis progressed from *Dymer*, where he did not grasp the meaning of the numinous, and *The Pilgrim's Regress*, where he is not too effective in treating his religious beliefs in a numinous way, to the Ransom Trilogy and the Narnia Chronicles, where numinous mythic images play a greater part, to *Till We Have Faces*, where the numinous world is considered the only source of explanation for our "common sense" world.

16 CHRISTOPHER, JOE R. "Archetypal Patterns in *Till We Have Faces*." In *Longing for a Form: Essays on the Fiction of C. S. Lewis*. Edited by Peter J. Schakel. Kent, Ohio: Kent State University Press, pp. 193–212.

Christopher examines Lewis's use of archetypes, which are "universal human patterns," or parallels that "tend to be from literature, biblical or other." In his novel *Till We Have Faces* Lewis uses these archetypes: Psyche as hero, resembling, at times, Christ; the union of the church with God in the marriage of Psyche to the god of the mountain; paradise lost when Psyche disobeys the command of her husband; Orual's queenship and her veil becoming a mask, a second personality she hides behind; *Sehnsucht*, a romantic archetype; Orual's psychological reversal, a well-known pattern if not archetypal; Orual's realization of her true motives; the bearing of a burden for another, which both

1977

Psyche and Orual do, a Christ archetype; "Dantean imagery which reinforces the Christian meaning of Orual's final vision."

17 CLASPER, PAUL. "C. S. Lewis and the Chinese." *CSL: The Bulletin of the New York C. S. Lewis Society* 18 (October):1–2.
  The Chinese appreciate Lewis's logical writing, his use of illustrations, and his discussion of the Tao. They respect his rational romanticism, his appreciation for the mythic and the poetic, his belief that the great myths of humanity are "God-given 'good dreams' sent to prepare and point to the Myth-Fact of Jesus Christ." The Chinese respond to Lewis because he writes from the fully evangelical center of Christianity. Reprinted: 1978.8.

18 COBB, LAWRENCE [W.]. "Masculine and Feminine: The Shape of the Universe." *CSL: The Bulletin of the New York C. S. Lewis Society* 8 (February):1–6.
  Lewis believed there is a fundamental polarity of masculine and feminine gender that divides the universe. God is the ultimate masculine, and the Church, both as a corporate body and as individuals, is the feminine counterpart. Woman is better prepared to surrender to God since she has temporarily surrendered to man in the ceremonial context of marriage. "For a man the reversal of roles may be bitter."

19 COX, JOHN D. "Epistemological Release in *The Silver Chair*." In *The Longing for a Form: Essays on the Fiction of C. S. Lewis*. Edited by Peter J. Schakel. Kent, Ohio: Kent State University Press, pp. 159–168.
  In *The Silver Chair*, "the most important images complement a structural pattern and self-reflective critical commentary that consistently deals with the problem of knowledge." The source or analogue for the image of Prince Rilian is Hamlet, whose world is also "one where doubt and uncertainty prevail"; the image of Queen of the Underworld comes from MacDonald's Lilith and Spenser's monster Error; the central image, the silver chair, also comes from Spenser's *Faerie Queene*. "Five distinct worlds are encountered in the course of the narrative." England and the Underland are worlds of diminished reality, or reductive knowledge; Aslan's Land, Narnia, and Bism are places of freedom and delight.

20 CUNNINGHAM, LAWRENCE S. "C. S. Lewis: *The Screwtape Letters*." *Christian Century* 94 (2 March):190–191.
  Lewis's prose is straightforward and unadorned but there is a less agreeable stylistic element evident in *The Screwtape Letters*: "a certain flippant dismissal of modern challenges to religious belief as simply lapses of good taste and reasonableness." Nevertheless there is much gold in this work: Lewis invites us to see the goodness and mystery in the ordinary and the mundane; he "wants each person to experience Christianity as true and as real as one's own life."

21 CURTIS, ANTHONY. "Remembering Tolkien and Lewis." *British Book News* (June):429–430.

Curtis was a pupil of both Tolkien and Lewis during World War II. "At the end of an hour with Lewis I always felt a complete ignoramus; no doubt an accurate impression but also a rather painful one." He remembers Lewis's skill in argumentation, "beamingly alert manner," and astonishing memory.

22 FOWLER, ALASTAIR. "The Aliens of Othertime." *TLS: Times Literary Supplement*, 1 July, p. 795.

In this review of *The Dark Tower and Other Stories*, Fowler notes that "The Dark Tower" has the same compulsive readability as the Ransom Trilogy. In "After Ten Years" Lewis treats the old story actively and distinctively; nothing is as we expect. The collection is valuable for those interested in the development of Lewis's rational imagination.

23 FROST, NAOMI. "Excerpts from Lewis on Husbands and Wives." *CSL: The Bulletin of the New York C. S. Lewis Society* 8 (July):7–8.

Lewis's views on Christian marriage are too neat—the wishful thinking of a bachelor. Woman's role of submission has been imposed by both State and Church; man's obligation to be "Christ-like" in his relationship to his wife remains unenforceable and impossible.

24 FUTCH, KEN. "C. S. Lewis on the Art of Writing: A Preliminary Study." *The Lamp-Post of the Southern California C. S. Lewis Society* 1, no. 2 (April):1–3; no. 3 (July):3–6.

Lewis said the purpose of writing is communication; an author asks us not to look *at* him but to look *with* him at something else. The author as Author writes because he has material looking for a form—the *Poiema*, something made, pleases. The author as Man wants his work to contribute to the world—the *Logos*, something said, instructs. Lewis offers advice on how to write: substance—write about what interests you; as a Christian your beliefs should be latent in the work; use "the intellectual attack first . . . to undermine [the] reader's intellectual prejudice and then the emotional appeal." Structure—strive for "a unity of diversity, a variety . . . of material fused together into a grand design." Style—use as a means; its only two tests are sound and significance.

25 GOUGH, JOHN. "C. S. Lewis and the Problem of David Holbrook." *Children's Literature in Education*, no. 25 (Summer):51–62.

Holbrook's article [see 1973.14] is bad scholarship and "so internally contradictory as to verge now and then on incoherence." Lewis's mother died when he was nine, not an infant, and his response to her death was conscious and constructive, a reaction that "demolishes the foundation of Holbrook's psychoanalytic criticism." The White Witch is a religious symbol of evil, not

1977

a sexual symbol. The characters continually exercise their free will; they are tested, given choices, and as a consequence grow morally. There are a variety of intelligent creatures, human and non-human, all capable of either good or evil on the basis of their free choice. Holbrook greatly overestimates the extent of the militarism in Narnia. See Holbrook's reply 1978.17.

26   GRAHAM, W. FRED. "Fantasy in a World of Monochrome: Where C. S. Lewis Continues to Help." *CSL: The Bulletin of the New York C. S. Lewis Society* 8 (February):6–8.
        Reprint of 1975.17.

27   GRIFFIN, WILLIAM. "Christian Writers? Take C. S. Lewis." *National Catholic Reporter* 13 (23 September):7+.
        "If sales are signs, then C. S. Lewis is one of the most popular Christian novelists being published in the United States today." What draws people to his works is the golden thread of Christian orthodoxy that runs through them all. According to Hooper, Lewis practiced and lived the sort of Christianity he wrote about.

28   HANNAY, MARGARET P[ATTERSON]. "A Preface to *Perelandra*." In *The Longing for a Form: Essays on the Fiction of C. S. Lewis*. Edited by Peter J. Schakel. Kent, Ohio: Kent University Press, pp. 73–90.
        Lewis altered in his Edenic myth those elements of Milton's *Paradise Lost* he objected to: "the magnificent Satan, the anthropomorphic deity, the undignified corporeality of the angels, the mistaken attempt to describe prelapsarian sexuality." Lewis's Satan is utterly contemptible; he leaves God " 'sufficiently awful, mysterious, and vague' "; the angels are perceived as light; and the King and Queen are separated throughout most of the novel, thus avoiding the problem of sexuality. These differences are of "artistic presentation, not theology." Lewis emulates Milton in presenting the magnificence of the King and Queen, in making the King superior, in giving him special revelation, and in making the problem of the Fall that of free will. "The major departures from *Paradise Lost* come toward the end of *Perelandra*": The Queen is saved by outside intervention, the King refuses to put his wife before obedience to God, the pair prove their worth by obedience, and they are invested with the rulership of their planet.

29   HOGAN, PATRICK G., Jr. "C. S. Lewis, Science Fiction, and Myth." *Helios* 5 (Spring):61.
        "A new and searching exposition is now needed of C. S. Lewis as mythmaker." To accomplish this reexamination it will be necessary to define myth appropriately so it will illuminate Lewis's myth-making processes and, once this concept is established, to identify the myths he planted in his works.

30 HOOPER, WALTER. "Narnia: The Author, the Critics, and the Tale." In *The Longing for a Form: Essays on the Fiction of C. S. Lewis*. Edited by Peter J. Schakel. Kent, Ohio: Kent State University Press, pp. 105–118.
    Reprint of 1974.21.

31 ———. "Reflections of an Editor." *CSL: The Bulletin of the New York C. S. Lewis Society* 8 (August):1–6.
    Hooper became an editor because he came into possession of Lewis's manuscripts and because he felt no one else was sufficiently interested to do the job. He tries to steer a balanced course between the two schools of editing—that of printing exactly what the author wrote and that of printing what the author intended. He wants more than anything for Lewis to be read. He feels that he (Hooper) has no talent for interpretation but rather a gift for "picking up information from unlikely sources and putting it in a prominent place where it can be seen by all."

32 HOWARD, ANDREWS. "*Till We Have Faces* and Its Mythological and Literary Precursors." *Mythlore* 4 (March):30–32.
    Orual's jealousy is similar to that of the two sisters in the original story by Apuleius, but hers is more sophisticated; besides being envious of what Psyche has, she desires to possess her. As in the original, Lewis emphasizes the characters' maturation: Psyche's journey of the soul is the task-filled mythic one while Orual's is one of suffering. The essence of the novel is love transformed.

33 HUTTAR, CHARLES A. "C. S. Lewis's Narnia and the 'Grand Design.'" In *The Longing for a Form: Essays on the Fiction of C. S. Lewis*. Edited by Peter J. Schakel. Kent, Ohio: Kent State University Press, pp. 119–135.
    The Chronicles fall into the genre of "scripture," which comprises varied material loosely united, is a blend of myth and realism, and has the structure of the "grand design"—Creation, Fall, Redemption, and Eschatology. Lewis's creation departs from Genesis: a world already exists and all Aslan actually creates in Narnia are the various forms of life. There is no equivalent of the Fall: humans introduce evil into Narnia in the very moment of creation. The full pattern of Christian redemption is not repeated in Narnia but the principle of voluntary self-sacrifice is evident. Lewis's eschatology in *The Last Battle* has the "Antichrist, Armageddon, final judgement, destruction of the world, the end of time and the new paradisal creation."

34 JOHNSTON, ROBERT K. "Image and Content: The Tension in C. S. Lewis' Chronicles of Narnia." *Journal of the Evangelical Theological Society* 20 (September):253–264.
    Lewis's intent in the Chronicles of Narnia was to create myth, "to ensnare a more ultimate reality in the net of fantastic images transformed into

story by the connective fabric of plot." He felt modern man's myths were false and inadequate, incapable of performing the true mythic task; he strongly believed in the role myth could play in helping man to understand reality. Lewis was also constrained to add a rational side to his storytelling; the logos or content is distinctly Christian. He wanted modern bifurcated man to experience myth as a unified imaginal-rational creature. Lewis failed at this impossible task: his content is unacceptable to much of the audience he wanted to reach. In the Chronicles "the birth of the numinous is aborted by too strenuous a rational exercise, too early in the myth-making process."

35   KAWANO, ROLAND M. "C. S. Lewis and the Formation of *Mere Christianity.*" *CSL: The Bulletin of the New York C. S. Lewis Society* 8 (July):1–7.
    Lewis attempted to delineate a central Christianity that would uncover the historic community of Christian belief. He was influenced by Richard Hooker's defense of the law of human nature and of natural law as well as his principle of the visible Church as "everyone who professed one faith, one Lord, one Baptism." Richard Baxter first used the phrase "mere Christianity" and emphasized the unifying principle—"to 'have unity in things necessary, and liberty in things unnecessary, and charity in all.'" MacDonald influenced Lewis by opening his imagination and allowing "him to consider questions formerly inconceivable, and to see realities therefore hidden."

36   KILBY, CLYDE S. "*Till We Have Faces*": An Interpretation." In *The Longing for a Form: Essays on the Fiction of C. S. Lewis.* Edited by Peter J. Schakel. Kent, Ohio: Kent State University Press, pp. 171–181.
    About true and false love, the story also sets forth "Lewis' belief that even pagan blood is thicker than rationalistic water." Witnesses from the gods to Orual are Psyche, Fox, rain, and the palace, each of which call her to them. Two extreme responses to God are suggested by the characters of Psyche, who seeks God, and Orual, who tries to hide from God. Orual's great defeat was selfishness masquerading as love. Both sisters "pay the price of failure to recognize the divine calling, Psyche for disobeying her husband [love] and Orual for her spiritual blindness" in rejecting love.

37   LeGUIN, URSULA K. Review of *The Dark Tower and Other Stories.* New Republic 176 (16 April):29–30.
    None of the stories is Lewis at his best. Much hatred and self-righteousness are displayed in this work. These stories have a dominant tone of cruelty and are marked by spitefulness toward women.

38   LEYLAND, MARGARET M. "Lewis and the School-girls." *The Lamp-Post of the Southern California C. S. Lewis Society* 1, no. 3 (July):1–2.

Leyland was one of three girls evacuated to the Kilns during World War II. She recounts Mrs. Moore's devotion to Lewis and overprotectiveness toward him, treating him at times like a small boy. Mrs. Moore was very Victorian in outlook and dress. Lewis seemed unconcerned with the war; instead his mind was filled with space and the heavens (he was a keen astronomer), literature, and his church. "He was a kind, sympathetic and very human man, never talking down to us school girls."

39 McGOVERN, EUGENE. "A Reply to Margaret Hannay." Mythlore 4 (March):27–28.
    McGovern claims that Hannay [see 1976.15] exaggerates Joy Davidman's effect on Lewis's thought. She relies too heavily on the term "chauvinism." She makes two serious charges too casually: that the attitude toward women in the church is a "superstitious taboo" and that there is "implicit racism" in the Chronicles of Narnia. Nothing is too small for her to pick over in the presentation of women in *That Hideous Strength*.

40 MEYER, ERIC C. "Petitionary Prayer: C. S. Lewis' Problem." *Spiritual Life* 23 (Spring):19–25.
    Reprint of 1976.32.

41 MILLER, DAN. Review of *The Dark Tower and Other Stories. Booklist* 73 (1 June):1485.
    "The Dark Tower" and "The Man Born Blind," "though lacking the strength of Lewis' other science fiction . . . are rich in mood and characterization and will be eagerly sought by the enormous number of his fans."

42 MILLER, IGNATIUS. "C. S. Lewis—Man for All Readers." *Catholic Library World* 49 (October):118–121.
    In Lewis "is God's plenty: prayer and brilliant polemic, marshwiggles and eldils, philosophy and Christian dogma and Milton criticism—all of a high order and all of a piece." He has a vast array of works, from philosophical/religious writings to autobiography; except for scientific and technological categories, his books fall into every section of the Dewey Decimal Classification System.

43 MORRIS, FRANCIS J. "Metaphor and Myth: Shaping Forces in C. S. Lewis' Critical Assessment of Renaissance Literature." Ph.D. dissertation, University of Pennsylvania, 263 pp.
    Lewis's concept of the function of language and the cognitive value of metaphor is substantially that expressed by Barfield in *Poetic Diction*. Both believe there is a "psycho-physical parallelism in nature that metaphorical images were rooted in and could exploit in order to achieve human knowl-

edge and its communication, especially in literary art." Lewis's understanding of the role of myth is a result of his own life. Myth transcends rational thought, communicating epistemologically in a nonconceptual way; myth partially solves the problem of "tasting" reality or "knowing" it as exclusive alternatives. The value and power Lewis accorded to "metaphor and myth as vehicles of the 'realizing imagination'" give coherence, shape, and continuity to his literary criticism. They also influence and control his choice of authors, of the Middle Ages and the Renaissance, and his judgments about them.

44 MUSACCHIO, GEORGE. "The Three Temptations of Perelandra's Queen." *The Lamp-Post of the Southern California C. S. Lewis Society* 1, no. 4 (October):3–5.
    The central conflict in *Perelandra* is the demonic temptation of the Green Lady. Her perfection is not static but capable of growth or deterioration. The first temptation centers on knowledge, that greater knowledge will make her more lovable. The second is an appeal to independence, "to make one's reason the measure of righteousness." The third centers on price, that self-sacrifice because of love will make her a tragic martyr. All these temptations are an appeal to the self—"when self-awareness is born . . . so is the possibility of choosing self instead of God."

*45 NAKAO, SETSUKO. "A Reading of *Till We Have Faces*." *Sophia English Studies* 2:53–67.
    Source of citation: *MLA Bibliography* 1977.

46 NEULEIB, JANICE WITHERSPOON. "The Creative Act: Lewis on God and Art." In *The Longing for a Form: Essays on the Fiction of C. S. Lewis*. Edited by Peter J. Schakel. Kent, Ohio: Kent State University Press, pp. 40–47.
    Lewis saw God as "the great artist forming the universe in a gigantic eternal pattern" and because of this interpretation he "was able to deal consistently and effectively with the question of free will and predestination." Lewis deals with "the troublesome problems of God's will versus Man's will and free will versus predestination" in the Ransom Trilogy, the Chronicles of Narnia, and *Till We Have Faces*. He treats these not as philosophical questions, but as artistic building blocks that strengthen the creations and make them more subtle and impressive in their structures.

47 NOLAN, CHARLES J., Jr. "The Rhetorical End: 'Venus at St. Anne's.'" *CSL: The Bulletin of the New York C. S. Lewis Society* 9 (November):8–9.
    The final chapter of *That Hideous Strength* knits together the themes and motifs Lewis has used throughout: growth of Mark, fertility motif, destruction of evil, Logres and Britain, love, humility, and obedience.

48 O'REILLY, JAMES D. "A Sentence—Outline of *Mere Christianity.*" *The Lamp-Post of the Southern California C. S. Lewis Society* 1, no. 1 (January): 2–3; no. 2 (April):4–7.

A paraphrase of *Mere Christianity.*

49 OURY, SCOTT. "'The Thing Itself': C. S. Lewis and the Value of Something Other." In *The Longing for a Form: Essays on the Fiction of C. S. Lewis.* Edited by Peter J. Schakel. Kent, Ohio: Kent State University Press, pp. 1–19.

The key to understanding Lewis is his attention to "the value of something other than himself, to 'the thing itself.'" This emphasis on otherness or objectivity appears throughout Lewis's theological, apologetical, and critical works; his method is to describe and define rather than evaluate. He felt myth could somehow convey the object, reality, in its ultimate sense. In the Ransom Trilogy, Lewis's concern for the object is evident in his close attention to setting, each person's uniqueness, and the shape of these individuals' lives. However, he also teaches and instructs, calling attention away from the thing itself, thereby reducing the mythopoeic and imaginative value of the trilogy.

50 PURTILL, RICHARD [L.]. "*That Hideous Strength*: A Double Story." In *The Longing for a Form: Essays on the Fiction of C. S. Lewis.* Edited by Peter J. Schakel. Kent, Ohio: Kent State University Press, pp. 91–102.

In *That Hideous Strength* "the dialectic of the theme is echoed by the dialectic of the tale" depicted through "an intricate and detailed opposition of scenes and characters." The central opposition is between St. Anne's, founded on the love of God and fellow man, and Belbury, founded on love of self. The conflict is a struggle for souls, namely those of Jane, whose problem is a lack of commitment to anything, and of Mark, whose problem is a commitment to the wrong thing. Levels in the story include the adventure of romance, "what happens when two people in a relationship begin to go different ways," and "the adventure of any soul and the different ways in which it may choose good or evil."

51 Review of *The Dark Tower and Other Stories. Kirkus Review* 45 (15 February):181.

One has mixed feelings about editor Walter Hooper's attempt to salvage the uncollected and unfinished pieces of fiction. The reviewer finds it a pleasure to hear Lewis's voice again but not always to hear what he is saying. "The patronizing and avuncular pigeon-holer of other people's departures from the path of true belief" is evident in two of the stories and intermittently visible throughout the rest.

-52 Review of *The Dark Tower and Other Stories. New York Times Book Review,* 15 May, p. 18.

With this volume, carefully edited and annotated, all Lewis's fiction is available for his fans.

1977

53 Review of *The Dark Tower and Other Stories. Publisher's Weekly* 211 (7 March):97.

    The pieces "are not major efforts, but literate and lively, and worth reading as a reminder of one of the best writers to try his hand" at science fiction.

54 Review of *The Joyful Christian: 127 Readings from C. S. Lewis. Publisher's Weekly* 212 (24 October):68.

    "A treasury of delights," this collection focuses on the "penetrating simplicity and ecumenical charity" with which Lewis charmed a generation.

55 RYAN, RICHARD W. Review of *The Dark Tower and Other Stories. Library Journal* 102 (15 April):948.

    This volume completes the publication of Lewis's fiction. "The Dark Tower" and "A Man Born Blind" are published for the first time; the other three short stories and the novel fragment were published in *Of Other Worlds: Essays and Stories.*

56 SAMMONS, MARTHA C. "'The Man Born Blind': Light in C. S. Lewis." *CSL: The Bulletin of the New York C. S. Lewis Society* 9 (December):1–7.

    In this short story, as well as his novels, Lewis associates God and Heaven with the biblical metaphor of light. "God is Reality, the Concrete Light itself, the source of all," but in our world of appearance and perception we often mistake the effects of light for light itself. There are two worlds—the spiritual and the physical; and two kinds of seeing—looking objectively, scientifically, and analytically at experiences and looking along experiences to "see their true subjective value and significance as well as the source to which they point." See 1983.21 for response.

57 SCHAKEL, PETER J., ed. *Longing for a Form: Essays on the Fiction of C. S. Lewis.* Kent, Ohio: Kent State University Press, 234 pp. Reprint. Grand Rapids, Mich.: Eerdmans, 1979.

    The essays examine the form or literary type of Lewis's fiction; the focus is "on the kinds of novels these are, and on their shapes, their patterns, their total effects." Schakel believes "too great an emphasis on Lewis's ideas, unbalanced by attention to what the works really are and how they really work upon the reader, can lead to sheer 'use' of them, usually to reinforce a pre-existing world or life view." The essays are listed individually.

58 SPEROU, CAROLE. "A Look at *The Last Battle*." *Chronicle of the Portland C. S. Lewis Society* 6, no. 4 (October–December):3–6.

    The Last Battle divides into three sections: the first section presents many themes and suggests deep meaning, the middle section is devoted to adventure, and the final section has many references to the end of the world and the afterlife. Puzzle and Shift are the kinds of creatures foretold in the Bible about the endtimes on earth. "Evil destroys nature, increases technology, and sets up more restraints and controls on individuals." Themes in the novel relating to Christian theology are that the mind must guide the feelings, that all gods and all religions are not the same, and that we underestimate "the prisons we create for ourselves." Lewis vividly describes the end of the world and heaven.

59 STARR, ROB. "Notes on 'The Inner Ring.'" *Chronicle of the Portland C. S. Lewis Society* 6, no. 2 (April–June):14–17.
    Lewis describes inner rings as being caste systems where the unfavored are made aware of their inferiority; the systems are volatile and permeate all areas of society. He felt that the desire to be in "an inner ring is a driving force behind much of human action." He gives two reason for the undesirability of inner rings: they are a common cause for turning young people into criminals and they can only lead to frustration. His main point is the comparison of inner rings with wholesome groups; comparisons are central to his writings. The common appeal today is to do something because "everyone does it," to be like "us," attitudes that are reasonably descriptive of an inner ring.

60 STEWART, IAN. "Recent Fiction." *Illustrated London News* 265 (April):59.
    Review of *The Dark Tower and Other Stories*. In "The Dark Tower," the best of the stories, a character is propelled into the world of Othertime and makes "some unnerving discoveries about the nature of time." "We can only regret that so inventive a storyteller did not complete his tale."

61 TIMMERMAN, JOHN H. "The Epistemology of C. S. Lewis: Reason and Belief in *Till We Have Faces*." *Religion in Life* 46 (Winter):497–508.
    This novel is "at once Lewis' most difficult, and yet his best, work." Two themes are evident: the development of the soul and the place of reason and belief in Christian epistemology. "Imagination reaches beyond the grasp of reason to seize the meaning of 'what it is,' or fact. . . . Belief consists of assent to the meaning disclosed through imagination."

62 ———. "Logres and Britain: The Dialectic of C. S. Lewis's *That Hideous Strength*." *CSL: The Bulletin of the New York C. S. Lewis Society* 9 (November):1–8.
    The novel's uniqueness is its use of Arthurian legends. Logres represents the perfect order, "a body politic of human law in complete harmony with God's spiritual law" (St. Anne's); Britain represents the threat of the beast, man's fallen nature, man's will (N.I.C.E. or Belbury). The struggle between

1977

the two reveals their contrasting and conflicting beliefs about nature, man, God, and society. Ransom is the focal point, "the Space-Traveler who is a bridge with the higher powers; the Fisher-King who is spiritual leader and who receives the bruise of the Evil One; the Pendragon who is the political ruler, the King invested with temporal powers by God."

63 TIXIER, ELIANE. "Imagination Baptized, Or, 'Holiness' in the Chronicles of Narnia." In *The Longing for a Form: Essays on the Fiction of C. S. Lewis.* Edited by Peter J. Schakel. Kent, Ohio: Kent State University Press, pp. 136–158.

The Chronicles, through a mode of expression called holiness, appeal to the imagination, "rejuvenate our understanding of religion . . . bring us nearer to the mystery of God, and to a spiritual world we might otherwise have been tempted to reject as outdated and uninteresting." The hints of holiness in the tales are found in the call of longing, in the call to vigilance, and in images of joy, happiness, beauty, and glory. Holiness points to the "land of happiness, the land of Aslan, the land of God," heaven, and to God Himself.

64 TOTTON, NICK. "In Retrospect." *Spectator* 238 (5 March):24.

In this review of *The Dark Tower and Other Stories*, Totton claims that none of the material "begins to approach the standard of C. S. Lewis's previously published fiction. These are scrapings from the very bottom of the barrel."

65 VAN DER WEELE, STEVE J. "From Mt. Olympus to Glome: C. S. Lewis's Dislocation of Apuleius's 'Cupid and Psyche' in *Till We Have Faces*." In *The Longing for a Form: Essays on the Fiction of C. S. Lewis.* Edited by Peter J. Schakel. Kent, Ohio: Kent State University Press, pp. 182–192.

Lewis used Apuleius as a source or influence, not as a model. The patterns of alteration he employed are (1) "the historical reconstruction of life in the city-state of Glome"; (2) telling the story from Orual's point of view; (3) "the episode of Orual's glimpse of the castle and her subsequent enlightenment"; and (4) "the exhibition of the anatomy of love," love in "both its proper forms and the ethical ambiguities which jeopardize its proper expression."

66 VANAUKEN, SHELDON. *A Severe Mercy: C. S. Lewis and a Pagan Love Invaded by Christ, Told by One of the Lovers.* London: Hodder and Stoughton, 238 pp. Reprint. 1979. Reprint. San Francisco: Harper & Row, 1977, 1980, 1987. Reprint. New York: Bantam Books, 1979. Reprint. New York: Phoenix Press, 1987.

A deeply intimate account of Vanauken's marriage and Christianity. The Vanaukens became converts through Lewis's books and letters, and eventually they became friends with him. The "severe mercy" is the death of Vanauken's wife, Davy, an event that ultimately strengthened Vanauken's faith beacuse it allowed him to see, with Lewis's help, his jealousy of God, whom Davy had put first.

67   WALSH, CHAD. "The Reeducation of the Fearful Pilgrim." In *The Longing for a Form: Essays on the Fiction of C. S. Lewis*. Edited by Peter J. Schakel. Kent, Ohio: Kent State University Press, pp. 64–72.

   Lewis was faithful to the traditions of science fiction in the Ransom Trilogy. The overall plot is "the struggle between divine and demonic powers," but *Out of the Silent Planet* has the subplot of "the gradual reeducation of Ransom, as he is taught by his adventures and his contacts with various" creatures to conquer his fears and to trust in God. The symbols of birth and rebirth figure prominently. Each of the subsequent novels continues Ransom's reeducation.

68   WARD, SAMUEL KEITH. "C. S. Lewis and the Nature-Grace Aesthetic." Ph.D. dissertation, University of Pittsburgh, 269 pp.

   Lewis was preoccupied with the need for philosophical unity; the problems he struggled with—the dualism between reason and imagination, fact and value, object and subject—are those of Western culture. His method of resolution is "the Principle of the Triad" in which two incompatible realities are joined together by another reality that acts as a bridge between them. In his anthropology and epistemology, natural intuition and reason are synthesized through imaginative inspiration. Lewis believes the cosmos consists of nature and supernature (grace); he attempts to reconcile them through the process of "Transposition." His aesthetics reconciles the dualities of Logos (meaning) and Poiema (form) through the Joy of myth.

69   WARREN, EUGENE. "The Angel of the Law in *The Great Divorce*." *CSL: The Bulletin of the New York C. S. Lewis Society* 8 (June):4–5.

   In *The Great Divorce* Lewis paraphrased Psalm 91 as a paean to Sara Smith and paraphrased Psalm 110 as the hymn the earth sings after the young man's lust-lizard is killed. This signifies that Man is nature's Messiah; "in man's redemption, all natures that were his enemies, because he used them wrongly, now become his friends and servants, as he is made willing and able to use them rightly." The law, described in Psalm 19 and considered by Lewis to be "luminous, severe, disinfectant, exultant," appears as the angel who kills the lizard. Lewis demonstrated that only by submitting to the law can we be reborn and our natures, and nature herself, be redeemed in and with us.

70   WESTERLUND, LOIS. "It All Depends on the Point of View: C. S. Lewis's *Out of the Silent Planet*." *CSL: The Bulletin of the New York C. S. Lewis Society* 8 (October):2–5.

   Lewis "takes us out of the silent planet into the communication of the heavens" because Malacandra is still an unfallen world and its inhabitants

1978

have retained the clearsightedness of Eden. Ransom's perspective becomes that of the Malacandrians when he sees the totality of human experience through their eyes.

71   WILLIAMS, TERRI. "A Look at 'De Descriptione Temporum.'" *Chronicle of the Portland C. S. Lewis Society* 6, no. 3 (July–September):2–6.
      Lewis believed the great division in history occurred between the age of Jane Austen and Walter Scott and the present because of the change in the political order, the change in the arts, religious change, and the change brought on by machines. He felt the change made by machines was "the greatest change in the history of Western man." Lewis's thesis raises the questions of whether there needs to be "a re-evaluation of the impact of machines on our culture" and whether "there [is] not a more significant change which goes along with the religious change Lewis mentions," that of the rejection of absolute values.

72   ZOGBY, EDWARD G. "Triadic Patterns in Lewis's Life and Thought." In *The Longing for a Form: Essays on the Fiction of C. S. Lewis*. Edited by Peter J. Schakel. Kent, Ohio: Kent State University Press, pp. 20–39.
      "Through the dialectic of desire Lewis discovered a naturally polar relation between reason (mind) and imagination (spiritual sensation), the tensions of the coinciding opposites producing the third thing. The triadic pattern in Lewis's life and autobiographies is *delight: pain: fruit*; in his social criticism—*tradition (Tao): anti-tradition* (being outside of the Tao): *the Tao realized* in the individual person; in his theology—*begetting (Zoe): making (bios): participation* in the life of the Trinity; in his fiction—*masculine: feminine: union* (marriage); in his literary theory—*Logos: Poiema: Evangelium* in the imagination of the reader." Zogby examines these triadic patterns in the Ransom Trilogy, *Till We Have Faces*, and *Surprised by Joy*.

1978

1   ADEY, LIONEL. *C. S. Lewis's "Great War" with Owen Barfield*. English Literary Studies, no. 14. British Columbia: University of Victoria, 136 pp.
      The "Great War" consists of Barfield's *Poetic Diction*, an incomplete pile of letters, and unpublished essays written between 1928 and 1932; it focused on Lewis's attempt to dissuade Barfield from Rudolf Steiner's theory of anthroposophy. Lewis's objections were based on his "disbelief in truth supposedly apprehended by the imagination, together with an extravert distrust" of self-contemplation. The central issue concerns "whether subject and object were ever one or always distinct." Lewis had a psychological need to believe that "nature existed outside his own mind"; he adopted Samuel Alexander's distinction between an individual's contemplating external objects and enjoying his own feelings and sensations. Barfield strongly influenced

Lewis, delivering him from "chronological snobbery." Most important, "through arguing with Barfield, Lewis came to regard imagination as the human spirit's supreme power," thus enabling him to accept the supernatural, and ultimately Christianity, making the rest of his work possible. Barfield "lacked Lewis's expertise in formal logic, his breadth of reading, above all his wit and liveliness in expression." However he, not Lewis, "questions common assumptions about human nature and experience"; his "thought is both more original and more profound" than Lewis's.

2   BAILEY, MARK. "The Honour and Glory of a Mouse: Reepicheep of Narnia." *Mythlore* 5 (Autumn):35–36.

Reepicheep is symbolic of much of the character of Narnia, especially its pride and glory. His pride, however, is actually a proper sense of dignity and worth. He never crosses the line between dignity and arrogance, is firm in his beliefs, remains uncompromising in his standards, and has the virtues of kindness and charity.

3   BLATTNER, PAUL [F., Jr.]. *"Reflections on the Psalms." Chronicle of the Portland C. S. Lewis Society* 7, no. 3 (July–September):11.

Modern Christians feel a dualism between the externals of worship and the worship itself that was not felt by the psalmist. The psalmist revels in the law as is evident by his desire to study and understand it; because it is true and because God has commanded the law, it is good and beautiful.

4   CARPENTER, HUMPHREY. *The Inklings: C. S. Lewis, J. R. R. Tolkien, Charles Williams and Their Friends*. Boston: Allen and Unwin, 287 pp. Reprint. 1981. Reprint. New York: Ballantine, 1978, 1981. Reprint. Boston: Houghton Mifflin, 1979.

A discriminating collective biography mainly concerned with Lewis, Carpenter's work reconstructs an imaginary Thursday evening meeting of the Inklings. Lewis, Tolkien, and Williams were all Christians but did not share common beliefs or attitudes toward Christianity or a common academic view-point. They all wrote stories in which myth played an important part but each used myth in a different way. Tolkien's and Williams's works owe almost nothing to the other Inklings except simple encouragement; Lewis "had not written many of his books before the Inklings began to meet, and there are elements in his later works which can be easily identified as bearing the mark of Tolkien or Williams." He alone was influenced by the others. Lewis gathered around himself men who shared his tastes and interests; the Inklings owe their existence to friendship and Lewis himself.

5   CARTER, MARGARET L. "A Note on Moral Concepts in Lewis' Fiction." *Mythlore* 5 (May):35.

Some critics feel that Lewis's portrayal of good and evil, especially in

1978

The Screwtape Letters and *Perelandra*, is petty. However, his preference for "small targets" was a conscious philosophic choice evident in all his works. Lewis "asserts the central importance of the ordinary human being"; he believes that a "sin's effect on the individual sinner is more important than its spectacular visibility," and that "the most commonplace action of the most obscure person may be of eternal importance."

6 CHARD, JEAN MARIE. "Some Elements of Myth and Mysticism in C. S. Lewis' Novel *Till We Have Faces*." *Mythlore* 5 (Autumn):15–18.
   Lewis drew from Apuleius, the Babylonian love goddess Ishtar, the mystical tradition of Sufism, and the "esoteric traditions underlying alchemy and the tarot." The three aspects of personality—physical, rational, and spiritual—are represented in the three sisters, other characters, and aspects of the god. Names are used as symbols; other symbols are the well and the mirror. Themes include the doctrine of substitution (bearing another's burden), death and rebirth, and fertility versus sterility.

7 CHRISTOPHER, JOE R. "Touring 'The Dark Tower.'" *CSL: The Bulletin of the New York C.S. Lewis Society* 9 (April):9–13.
   "The Dark Tower" resembles Wells's *The Time Machine* (London: W. Heinemann, 1895); both begin with a group of men talking, have unusual machines, depict alien cultures, and have a character visit the alien culture. J. W. Dunne's *An Experiment with Time* (New York: Macmillan, 1927) is referred to in the text and may have stimulated Lewis's imagination with the idea of parallel time tracks. The coming together of parallel time tracks may have come from Murry Leinster's "Sidewise in Time" published in *Astounding Stories*, June 1934. The whole concept of the Stinging-man, while original, may have its source in David Lindsay's *A Voyage to Arcturus* (London: Methuen, 1920). The "dark tower" is an allusion to Browning's "Childe Roland to the Dark Tower Came."

8 CLASPER, PAUL. "C. S. Lewis and the Chinese." *Christianity Today* 22 (15 May):12.
   Reprint of 1977.17.

9 COLAN, DERMOT. "C. S. Lewis and Saint John of the Cross." *Contemplative Review* 11 (Spring):17–21.
   The end of *The Voyage of the "Dawn Treader"* is similar yet different from the notions and images used by Saint John of the Cross. Lewis depicts a journey on the sea toward the end of the world, uses nature images to indicate the bliss of newfound joy, and uses the symbol of childlikeness. Saint John of the Cross depicts the journey of the soul and God moving in the soul; he uses nature to symbolize the rest, refreshment, and recreation that comes with con-

templating God; and uses the symbol of the Bride and Bridegroom to indicate the relationship between humanity and God.

10   COMMIRE, ANNE. "Lewis C(live) S(taples) 1989–1963 (N. W. Clerk, Clive Hamilton)." In *Something about the Author*. Vol. 13. Detroit: Gale Research, pp. 129–146.

Commire has compiled biographical information for young adults, listing personal facts, career information, awards and honors, and writings. Through an extensive use of Lewis's *Surprised by Joy* and his letters, she recounts his life, thought, and creative impulses. She supplies quotes from the Chronicles of Narnia along with some of Pauline Baynes's illustrations as well as a bibliography of secondary works.

11   EVERIST, BURTON. "In the Dentist's Chair or Further Up and Further In?" *CSL: The Bulletin of the New York C. S. Lewis Society* 9 (June):1–5.

Lewis believed in purgatory as a purging or cleansing of the soul in order to be able to come into God's presence. He also believed in prayers for the dead and in the Resurrection but was reticent about the state of the dead until the Resurrection. Lewis did not want to "'arouse factual curiosity about the details of the afterworld.'"

12   FRANCESCHELLI, AMOS. "Words, and the Word." *CSL: The Bulletin of the New York C. S. Lewis Society* 9 (February):1–8.

Lewis's *Studies in Words* examines specific words to bring out "the shifting focus and accumulation of the meanings of a word as it requires new emphasis and new values." He demonstrates that corresponding words in different languages undergo parallel changes in meaning. He states seven principles affecting a word: ramification, the insulating power of the context, the "dangerous sense" or dominant meaning of the word, the word's meaning and the speaker's meaning, tactical definitions, methodological idiom, and moralization of status words.

13   FUTCH, KEN. "Lewis as Ramsden." *The Lamp-Post of the South California C. S. Lewis Society* 2, no. 2 (April): 1–2.

The character Ramsden in Barfield's *This Ever Diverse Pair* (published under the pseudonym G. A. L. Burgeon. London: Gollancz, 1950) is Lewis incognito: Ramsden and Burgeon, the solicitor protagonist, are "intellectual companions sharing 'intellectual intercourse.'" Ramsden is a successful man of letters who writes compulsively, does not want to understand business, and gives away the money earned from royalties.

14   GRIFFIN, EMILIE. "Some Reflections on *The Four Loves*." *CSL: The Bulletin of the New York C. S. Lewis Society* 9 (March):1–6.

Lewis's *The Four Loves* is a delightful antidote to the modern, narrow

1978

definition of all love as sexually based. He identifies the four loves as affection (storge), the love between parents and children and of humans for animals; eros, erotic love, only one of its elements being sexual; friendship (philia), based on common insights or shared experiences; and charity (agape), love for the least lovable or the unlovable. Lewis differentiated between Need-Love and Gift-Love: "Aspects of each may be involved ineach of the Four Loves, except in God's love for his creatures, which is pure Gift-Love."

15 HODGENS, RICHARD [M.]. "Notes on Lewis's 'The Dark Tower.'" *CSL: The Bulletin of the New York C. S. Lewis Society* 9 (April):1–8.
     Lewis wrote "The Dark Tower" without planning it and the plot became impossible. It lacks credibility in the initial discussion of time travel, in the existence of Othertime, in the transfer of a character's mind into the mind of his double in Othertime and the explanation for his being able to cross the language barrier, and in accounting for the Stinging-man. "The Dark Tower" is well written but ill conceived; it "is not a fragment but a tissue of fragments that could not be reconciled."

16 HOFFECKER, W. ANDREW, and TIMMERMAN, JOHN H. "'Watchman in the City': C. S. Lewis's View of Male and Female." *Cresset* 41 (February):16–21.
     Lewis argues against "Priestesses in the Church" on the basis that a woman representing God would change the very nature of Christianity; he felt the masculine imagery of Christianity was inspired and essential. Lewis's view of the genders masculine and feminine as fundamental polarities that divide all created things is evident in *Perelandra*; *That Hideous Strength* demonstrates that one finds "sexual identity only by complete obedience to Christ." However, nowhere does Lewis discuss "rationally" rather than imaginatively what it means to be male or female.

17 HOLBROOK, DAVID. "Letter to the Editors" *Children's Literature in Education* no. 28 (Spring):50–51.
     Reponds to Gough's article [1977.25]. The message of the Narnia books is not Christian at all "but a very idiosyncratic philosophy of life based on hate."

18 HOWARD, THOMAS. "The 'Moral Mythology' of C. S. Lewis." *Modern Age* 22 (Fall):384–392.
     "Lewis struggled to find a way of speaking to an epoch with which he shared virtually no suppositions at all." In his mythic tales, the Ransom Trilogy and the Chronicles of Narnia, he created secondary worlds in order to familiarize people with certain ideas entailed in the Christian vision, ideas that

are alien and incomprehensible to modern man. These worlds have a "moral order—fixed, serene, absolute and blissful." Within this hierarchical order, in obedience and through discipline, freedom and selfhood are found. Ordinariness and stock responses are central to Lewis's vision. "The way of health, in the moral mythology of C. S. Lewis, lies along the well-trodden path, and not in newly blazed trails," which are unstructured, fragmented, and random.

19 KILBY, CLYDE S. "The Heart of Lewis." *Modern Age* 22 (Summer): 323–325.

In his review of *The Joyful Christian: 127 Readings from C. S. Lewis*, Kilby says the collection "might be regarded as an extension of the Apostles' Creed." Lewis acquired the ultimate writing style, which "obliterates itself and focuses the attention on the meaning."

20 ———. *Images of Salvation in the Fiction of C. S. Lewis*. Wheaton, Ill: Harold Shaw, 140 pp.

Kilby summarizes the Ransom Trilogy, the Chronicles of Narnia, *The Screwtape Letters*, *The Great Divorce*, *The Pilgrim's Regress*, and *Till We Have Faces* and draws parallels between them and Christian beliefs.

21 KIRKPATRICK, HOPE. "The Final Essay in *The Personal Heresy*." *CSL: The Bulletin of the New York C. S. Lewis Society* 9 (May):1–8.

Lewis defined poetry as imaginative literature that conveys the reality of experiences by using the extralogical elements of language-rhythm, vowel-music, onomatopoeia, and associations. The poet goes beyond his own personality and limitations "to find that arrangement of public experiences, embodied in words, which will admit him (and incidentally us) to a new mode of consciousness." He was a "poet who knew what goes into the making of a poem and could recognize skill and craftsmanship," while Tillyard was a critic and reader who reacted to poetry chiefly emotionally.

22 "Lewis on Words." *Chronicle of the Portland C. S. Lewis Society* 7, no. 4 (October–September):7–12.

In *Studies in Words*, Lewis gives a practical guide for word use and shows his utter love for words. He believes the study of language is also the study of human intelligence and the nature of God. He warns against committing verbicide by inflating meaning. His general theme is that new word meanings derive from old meanings. He distinguishes between the word's meaning and the user's meaning. He identifies the limitation of language as being uni-linear, not being able to convey a sudden, complex event. He treats emotional language, distinguishing between "words that *express* emotion from words that *arouse* emotion." He felt the proper use of language is critical in communicating Christian truth.

1978

23   LINDSKOOG, KATHRYN [ANN]. "Some Problems in C. S. Lewis Scholarship." *Christianity and Literature* 27 (Summer):43–61.
     Lindskoog raises questions about Walter Hooper's exact relationship with Lewis, his role as Lewis's secretary, executor of Lewis's literary estate, editor and compiler of Lewis's published and unpublished material, and co-author of Lewis's biography. See 1979.5 for reply and 1979.67 for response to this article.

24   McGOVERN, EUGENE. "Lewis's 'Social Morality.'" *CSL: The Bulletin of the New York C. S. Lewis Society* 9 (July):1–7.
     Lewis ignored most social issues; instead he concentrated on "matters that each of us can do something about, actions upon which the fates of our souls depend." For him, social morality is concerned with "'fair play and harmony between individuals.'" He did not believe Christianity required a particular organization of society since both a religious and secular state would face the same problems. He felt the state should have enough power to perform its necessary tasks but should not assume the tasks better handled by other institutions. Lewis's severity in judging materialism and greed resulted in the serious fault of hasty and impatient writing.

25   MARTIN, JOHN. "Chesterton and Lewis: The Necessary Angels." *CSL: The Bulletin of the New York C. S. Lewis Society* 9 (January):1–12.
     Lewis and Chesterton had an angelic gift, "a talent for making others see the earth again—for making them see it more deeply or more truly than before or from some startling new angle of vision." They shared in the angelic tradition of announcing the Savior and casting out the Prince of this world.

26   MEILAENDER, GILBERT. *The Taste for the Other: The Social and Ethical Thought of C. S. Lewis*. Grand Rapids, Mich.: Eerdmans, 245 pp.
     Revision of 1976.30.

27   MERCHANT, ROBERT. "Lewis, the Apologist." *CSL: The Bulletin of the New York C. S. Lewis Society* 10 (December):1–7.
     Lewis said the universe is in the throes of a civil war and the earth is occupied by the rebels. Apologetics has the character of a military operation; Lewis called it the defense of the Christian faith. He defined that faith as an "unchanging, historically revealed and historically defined set of beliefs." He made Christianity understandable and attractive to ordinary people. Lewis the apologist personified tenacity, pluck, bravery, and courage.

28   MILLER, IGNATIUS. "Lewis and Charlotte Yonge." *CSL: The Bulletin of the New York C. S. Lewis Society* 9 (January):13–14.
     Yonge was a best-selling Victorian novelist who, dealing with big social questions, was concerned with the responsibilities of those living on

inherited wealth toward those whose sweat and toil had made the wealth possible. Lewis refers to Yonge in his autobiography, had a number of her novels, and names a character in *Prince Caspian* after Yonge's ancestor Sir Cloudesley Shovel.

29 MONICK, STANLEY. "C. S. Lewis: An Approach to Christian Myth." *Lantern (Pretoria)* 27 (April):62–69.

    For Lewis, myth yields an inner reality, a poetic truth. In the Ransom Trilogy he deals with the myth contained in Genesis: temptation, the Fall, and the loss of paradise. Three facets to his approach are his implicit acceptance of the fallen state of man that results in his isolation from the pattern of the universe, his rejection of scientific humanism, and his use of science fiction to create a new mythology to illuminate traditional Christian myth. Lewis's appeal continues because of the renaissance of myth in literature, and disenchantment with scientific theories of human behavior and with scientific humanism.

30 MUSACCHIO, GEORGE. "War Poet." *The Lamp-Post of the Southern California C. S. Lewis Society* 2, no. 4 (October):7.

    Although not a volume of war poetry as it was advertised when published, *Spirits of Bondage* does contain two poems, "Death in Battle" and "French Nocturne," in which Lewis captures something of the Great War experience.

*31 NAKAO, SETSUKO. "Salvation in the Ransom Trilogy." *Bulletin of Seisen College* 26:1–14.

    Source of citation: *MLA Bibliography* 1979.

32 NELSON, MARIE. "Non-Human Speech in the Fantasy of C. S. Lewis, J. R. R. Tolkien and Richard Adams." *Mythlore* 5 (May):37–39.

    Language in the Chronicles of Narnia does not distinguish non-human from human but rather "seems to distinguish non-virtuous from virtuous creatures." All three authors have themes of survival and life triumphant and succeed in making their characters believable by skillfully endowing them with language.

33 NEULEIB, JANICE [WITHERSPOON]. "Of Other Worlds: Worldly Wisdom as It Grows in Science Fiction." *Extrapolation* 19, no. 2 (May): 108–11.

    Neuleib restates Lewis's five categories of science fiction as found in his essay "On Science Fiction" in *Of Other Worlds* and examines how the characteristics of science fiction fit the definition of mythology. Through the creative experience of science fiction, readers and writers gain knowledge about themselves.

1978

34 OLSEN, DOROTHY ANNE. "First and Second Things: The Theoretical
    Criticism of C. S. Lewis." Ph.D. dissertation, Bowling Green State University,
    107 pp.
        Lewis's principle of First and Second Things—that out of its proper
    place a thing loses its natural good—is evident in his literary criticism. A poet
    must transcend himself and focus the reader's attention on the poem and not
    the poet. The poem should not be overvalued; its worth is in the self-transcen-
    dence it allows. Through literature the audience can transcend its own particu-
    larity and experience the perceptions of other people and other times. This
    aesthetic experience is the unattainable goal of art.

35 PYLES, FRANKLIN ARTHUR. "The Influence of the British Neo-Hegelians
    on the Christian Apology of C. S. Lewis." Ph.D. dissertation, Northwestern
    University, 183 pp.
        F. H. Bradley and Bernard Bosanquet provide the starting point for
    Lewis's philosophical thought. His perspective was basically idealist but he
    did not hesitate to modify his idealism "in order to guarantee knowledge of
    the real world." He was also influenced by Samuel Alexander's dichotomy
    between "the act of knowing and the object of knowing." Lewis's "philosoph-
    ical concerns for the knowledge of reality, the particularity of God and the
    worth of the individual dominated his apologetic writings and shaped them in
    a consistent pattern." The pattern centers around the incarnation, in which all
    dichotomies are overcome.

36 RAMSHAW, WALTER. "C. S. Lewis on Death and Resurrection." *CSL: The
    Bulletin of the New York C. S. Lewis Society* 9 (September):1–7.
        Lewis believed that physical death is the direct result of sin and is a
    Christian's release from sin and suffering; he also believed that personality
    persists after death. He overemphasized the consequences of our own action,
    "with God's role being reduced almost to that of a target which we either
    approach or avoid." Lewis viewed resurrected life for the Christian as being
    with Christ, being like Him, being fed or entertained, and as having some kind
    of official position in the universe.

37 Review of *The Joyful Christian: 127 Readings from C. S. Lewis. Booklist* 74
    (1 March):1066.
        This collection presents "an effective summary of Lewis's easily
    digestible content and exceptionally readable prose."

38 Review of *The Joyful Christian: 127 Readings from C. S. Lewis. Christian
    Century* 95 (18 January):60.
        Lewis "is enjoying renewed vogue." As a publisher, William Griffin
    "cannot miss; as readers, we cannot."

39   RICARDS, PHILIP. "Lewis and Mythology." *The Lamp-Post of the Southern California C. S. Lewis Society* 2, no. 2 (April):3–8.

Myth offers ways of ordering existence and shows the essential structure of reality. It informs man about himself and invokes personal involvement rather than contemplation or conceptual analysis. Myth expresses a saving power in human life; it portrays and conveys a power to transform man's life. Myths provide exemplary patterns for human action. "Myths are enacted in ritual." They are extended symbols standing for a state of feeling or a state of mind. They originate as creations of a consciousness immersed in the world, one that has not distinguished between subject and object.

40   SARDELLO, ROBERT J. "An Empirical-Phenomenological Study of Fantasy, with a Note on J. R. R. Tolkien and C. S. Lewis." *Psychocultural Review* 2 (Summer):215.

Lewis identified fantasy as delusion, as a means of escape, and as "normal castle-building." The latter, when it is disinterested, approaches the mythical.

41   SPEROU, CAROLE. " 'The Dark Tower.' " *Chronicle of the Portland C. S. Lewis Society* 7, no. 4 (October–December):2–5.

In mood and theme "The Dark Tower" is related to *That Hideous Strength*. Lewis's mastery of description is evident in the fragment, especially in gradually building intense dramatic interest. The characters of MacPhee, Camilla, and Michael Scudamour are fairly well developed. Two primary themes are the nature of time (although this may be about other worlds instead), and the evilness of stinging and the Stinging-man.

42   STAHL, JOHN T. "The Nature and Function of Myth in the Christian Thought of C. S. Lewis." *Christian Scholars Review* 7:330–336.

Reprinted from 1976.41.

43   STEWARD, JEFFERSON ALLEN. "Man's Ransom, God's Purchase: Character-Making in C. S. Lewis' Planetary Romances." Ph.D. dissertation, Syracuse University, 331 pp.

There is a dynamic structure in the spectrum of literary, cultural, and religious experience called the open canon that enables us to examine the relationship between Lewis and the reader. This process is reached through character-making. Lewis saw character as the natural organ of sensibility. "Character-making transmits the character of the maker." Ransom's symbolic "unassignedness" is the focal point/characteristic of the Trilogy. Lewis used the Trilogy as a means of psychological exorcism, "transmuting his own character in terms of Christian religio-cultural identity as soul-story."

1978

44 TENNYSON, G. B. "The Ancients Versus the Moderns: Thoughts on The Abolition of Man." *CSL: The Bulletin of the New York C. S. Lewis Society* 9 (August):1–11.
    Reprint of 1974.46.

45 WAGGONER, DIANA. *The Hills of Faraway: A Guide to Fantasy*. New York: Atheneum, pp. 34–35, 223–227.
    "Lewis alone among the mythopoeic fantasists convinces the reader of the vibrant reality of religious experiences, while conveying the mystical, supra-rational, ecstatic, entranced qualities that we think characteristic of them." Waggoner provides a summary of each book in the Ransom Trilogy and the Chronicles of Narnia and includes a brief bibliography of works about Lewis.

46 WALKER, JEANNE MURRAY. "Science Fiction: A Commentary on Itself as Lies." *Modern Language Studies* 8 (Fall):29–37.
    Good fiction, whether it rebels against or conforms to conventions, comments on the nature of literature. In *Perelandra* "Lewis defines the human imagination as the least trustworthy of man's mental faculties." The Green Lady's temptations come via her imagination; the Un-man uses stories to produce in her "the capacity to imagine herself something she is not." *Perelandra* shows the imagination being tainted by literary art; the implication is that stories create confusion in their readers, "that the *suspension of disbelief* necessary to the art of reading may rapidly turn into *belief* and trap the reader."

47 WALSH, CHAD. "The Spirit of C. S. Lewis." *Book World (Washington Post)*, 26 February, p. E1+.
    In his review of *The Joyful Christian: 127 Readings from C. S. Lewis*, Walsh finds that the sudden insights of Lewis's works lend themselves to the type of "wit and wisdom" anthology that this is. He considers the book useful as a good introduction to Lewis's religious and philosophic thoughts, as a reference work, and for daily meditations.

48 WARD, PATRICIA A. "Great Spiritual Autobiographies and the Modern Reader." *Christianity Today* 22 (8 September):22–27.
    Augustine's *Confessions*, St. Teresa of Avila's *Life*, John Woolman's journal, and Lewis's *Surprised by Joy* are truth "cast in the language and form of literature." They draw from the archetypes and images of the Bible, especially from the biblical doctrines of "redemption, grace, providence and the sovereignty of God." Each of the writers refuses to claim "he is different from any other Christian touched by grace even as he describes his unique experience." The stories end when the writer "comes to terms with God, with himself, with his purpose in life, or with a higher and fuller level of living."

49 WATKINS, DUFF. "*The Screwtape Letters* and Process Theism." *Process Studies* 8 (Summer):114–118.

Lewis's portrait of God in *The Screwtape Letters* functions well in terms of process theology. As in process thought, "Screwtape implies that the world is in a process of becoming in which transience and activity are fundamental." The use of reason and science, which Screwtape opposes as being on the Enemy's ground, are basic to process theology. Screwtape admits Christ's full understanding of real life, due to his former existence in the human world; process theology believes that Christ's participation in human selfhood is proof of a higher metaphysical reality. Screwtape encourages the quest for the historical Jesus; however, process theology asserts that historical biblical criticism is essential to prevent Christianity from distorting historical facts. Humankind's struggle is to align itself with God's will while retaining individuality; Screwtape recognizes that God wants us united with him but still distinct.

50 WILLIAMS, TERRI. "CSL, Scripture, and Inerrancy." *Chronicle of the Portland C. S. Lewis Society* 7, no. 1 (January–March):3–12.

Lewis believes that the writers of Scripture "were guided by God to communicate God's word" but that human qualities of the writer have not been corrected in this process. He believes Scripture progresses from myth to fact and so thinks the New Testament more factually true than the Old Testament. He feels that the lack of systematic truth in the Bible forces the whole person to understand it. Lewis's principles for scriptural interpretation are that one part of the Bible should not be read to contradict another: one must not assume that the Bible is in error but rather that one has missed the point. One should not read it for facts but for its overall message, and since the Bible communicates difficult truths, one should not be surprised that it is difficult to understand. Tools for interpreting Scripture are one's intellect under Divine grace and literary analysis, which enables one to discern the form of literature used. While Lewis saw gradual revelation as moving from imperfect to perfect, it could also mean a completion or fullness; thus one should be cautious in asserting a qualitative difference between the Old and New Testaments. Lewis "did not come to grips with the philosophical issue of how one combines that which is authoritative with error."

51 ———. "C. S. Lewis on Equality." *Chronicle of the Portland C. S. Lewis Society* 7, no. 3 (July–September):5–10.

Lewis felt that equality is a necessary legal fiction to protect against the abuse of power, but that it is not the basis for relationships or a goal to strive for. He believed man has a natural craving for hierarchy, which if denied leads to danger. He argued that there should not be equality in marriage because hierarchy is necessary for sex and there is a need for a final decision maker. He denied ecclesiastical equality because it negates love. He believed "that

1979

equality is artificial and deadening and willing acceptance of hierarchy and differences [is] both realistic and life giving."

1979

1   ADEY, LIONEL. "CSL—The Man and What He Stood For." *Canadian C. S. Lewis Journal* no. 7 (July):3–10.
     Reprint of 1977.1.

2   ARLTON, BEVERLY. "Lewis on Prayer." *CSL: The Bulletin of the New York C. S. Lewis Society* 10 (April):1–6.
     Lewis felt prayer was an act of relating to God; each person matters integrally in God's scheme and prayer has a central place in the flow of that activity. Lewis kept the mechanics of prayer in the background; although he appreciated words, he saw their limitations in prayer. Our temporal sequence versus God's Eternal Now, foreknowledge and predetermination, proof of God's response to prayer, and God's overall purpose are all issues that contribute to the misunderstanding of petitionary prayer. Lewis felt that the faith needed to pray for and receive a specific thing was a special gift from God given to only a few.

3   BAKER, LEO. "Near the Beginning." In *C. S. Lewis at the Breakfast Table and Other Reminiscences*. Edited by James T. Como. New York: Macmillan, pp. 3–10.
     Baker met and became friends with Lewis in 1919 at Oxford; their initial link was poetry. Lewis "lived in an enclosed world, with rigid walls built by his logic and intelligence, and trespassers would be prosecuted. Within these walls were his ambition and single-minded determination." The death of his mother, the estrangement from his father, his stay at boarding school, and his experiences in the army during World War I taught him that in order to escape from personal suffering, "he must hedge himself round, keep apart from emotional contacts, and live the life of a very private man."

4   BARFIELD, OWEN. "The Sound of Friendship." *CSL: The Bulletin of the New York C. S. Lewis Society* 10 (May):5–6.
     In this review of *They Stand Together: The Letters of C. S. Lewis to Arthur Greeves (1914–1963)*, Barfield says the letters provide a "new and privileged intimacy with the lovable, warm-hearted, richly and hungrily fanciful, supremely intelligent and thoroughly good human being." The introduction, annotations, and index make this almost a Lewis encyclopedia. Reprinted: 1980.1.

5   BARFIELD, OWEN, McGOVERN, EUGENE, and MARCHINGTON, ANTHONY F. "Dialogue." *Christianity and Literature*. 28 (Winter):9–13.
    The authors respond to Lindskoog's article "Some Problems in C. S. Lewis Scholarship" [see 1978.23]. See 1979.67 for Lindskoog's reply.

6   BAYLEY, PETER. "From Master to Colleague." *In C. S. Lewis at the Breakfast Table and Other Reminiscences*. Edited by James T. Como. New York: Macmillan, pp. 77–86.
    Bayley was Lewis's pupil in 1940 and later a fellow don. Lewis adopted a boisterous bluffness and geniality to cover his shyness and uncertainty in social relations and to preserve impersonality. "His greatness lay in extraordinary powers of clarification and illumination. His weakness lay in this very strength: he could not resist oversimplification and beautifully neat conclusions." His work *The Allegory of Love* in its discussion of Spenser's *The Faerie Queene* demonstrates both these strengths and weaknesses.

7   BERNHARD, WENDY. "Personhood in Narnia." *The Lamp-Post of the Southern California C. S. Lewis Society* 3, no. 1 (January):3–6.
    Themes in the Narnia Chronicles that demonstrate Lewis's theology of Personhood are "creation and election (including the providence of God); being, non-being and fallen being; enchantment (the power of sin over the human person); and, finally, the longing for ultimate fulfillment in the Eschaton." The Chronicles show us what it really means to be a Person, how to transcend our creatureliness and how to "fulfill both the twin ontological motives: *Eros* through knowing that, as individuals, we have a unique gift and calling, and *Agape*, the confidence and assurance that we are part of something greater than ourselves."

8   "Beyond Screwtape." *Economist* 271 (5 May):133.
    Review of *They Stand Together: The Letters of C.S. Lewis to Arthur Greeves (1914–1963)*. Lewis writes of things that "really mattered to him, other people's books and his quest for religion, which are curiously interwoven." Greeves served as a sounding board; these letters show Lewis in a new light.

9   *Bibliography of the Works of C. S. Lewis*. New York: New York C. S. Lewis Society, 10 pp.
    This bibliography covers Lewis's writings that have appeared in book form, including books edited or with prefaces by Lewis. Only first editions, both British and American, are listed. Listed separately are the "Contents of Books that are Collections," including references to other collections in which the individual item appears. Also included is a brief chronology of Lewis's life and a list of a few selected books about Lewis's life and works.

1979

10   BISENIEKS, DAINIS. "Children, Magic, and Choices." *Mythlore* 6
      (Winter):13–16.
          The child characters of Ursula LeGuin's Earthsea trilogy, Lloyd
      Alexander's Prydain books, and Alan Garner's works have true-to-life charac-
      terization. Those of Susan Cooper and C. S. Lewis do not. Lewis moralizes in
      the Chronicles of Narnia. He softens the effect of pain and death on his char-
      acters and thereby for the reader. He depicts best the magic in his tales.
      Lewis's style is marred by auctorial intrusions into the stories.

11   BRADSHAW, NORMAN. "Impressions of a Pupil." *Canadian C. S. Lewis
      Journal*, no. 11 (November):3–5; no. 15 (March 1980):1–5.
          Lewis used "his pupils as a whetstone on which to sharpen his own
      powers of dialectic argument, rather than, as I had hoped, helping us in a
      search for truth." He was unpopular at Oxford because he had a tendency to
      destroy other people's arguments, making them feel inferior; he believed in
      the supernatural, he had no time for small talk; he allowed his name to
      become a household word; and he was a conservative. Lewis was an enigma, a
      paradox, a contradictory human being. Reprinted: 1983.6.

12   ———. "Notes of a 'Learned Pupil.'" *Canadian C. S. Lewis Journal* no. 12
      (December):9–10.
          Bradshaw claims that the book *C. S. Lewis at the Breakfast Table* [see
      1979.24] is the "fairest, least one-sided, least uncritically adulatory book I've
      read on CSL." Lewis had a strange and sinister attitude toward sex in litera-
      ture, he was obsessed with sin, and he ignored the modern world, which was a
      great weakness. He was frightened "that pride and fleshly desire would pull
      him to Hell."

13   BREWER, DEREK. "The Tutor: A Portrait." *In C. S. Lewis at the Breakfast
      Table and Other Reminiscences*. Edited by James T. Como. New York:
      Macmillan, pp. 41–67.
          Brewer, as an undergraduate at Oxford in 1941–1942 and 1945–1947,
      had Lewis as his tutor. For Lewis and his colleagues, learning was conceived
      as a way of life exemplified by bachelor fellows who lived in the college;
      "their reading, thinking and writing were a part of a unified life, neither 'job,'
      nor 'recreation,' because they were both." This world of masculine comrade-
      ship "was not exactly an equalitarian society, but there was a sense of funda-
      mental equality and unity, divided into rank and stage." Lewis's primary
      energy went into tutorial teaching. Although "few other Oxford tutors were as
      thorough, conscientious, learned or perceptive as Lewis," he despised tutor-
      ing. Lewis, with his breadth of interest, concern with language, magnanimity,
      tolerance of others, empiricism, historical sense and sympathy, and humor, is
      representative of the best of the Oxford tradition as it was at that time.

14 BRIDGES, LINDA. "A First Look at *Selected Literary Criticism*." *CSL: The Bulletin of the New York C. S. Lewis Society* 10 (January):1–7.

Lewis, unlike other professional students of literature, did not succumb to the temptation of defining his specialized period or genre by attacking others. He writes with evident pleasure in these essays of Addison, Scott, Austen, William Morris, Chaucer, Chapman, Marlowe, Milton, Donne, Bunyan, and Shakespeare. He enjoyed or disliked "these authors on his own terms, not in terms of some grand theory of literature." He looked for the "quiddity," the "whichness," of everything he read.

15 BROWN, CAROL ANN. "Mirrors of Ourselves: Reflections from the Psalms." *CSL: The Bulletin of the New York C. S. Lewis Society* 10 (June):1–5.

"The Psalms are omnipresent and inescapable in the thread of Judaeo-Christian civilization." *Reflections on the Psalms* will satisfy the general reader because it concentrates on the difficulties in reading the Psalms as a devotional aid and in noting and explaining the differences between ancient Hebraic attitudes and our own. However, Lewis should have explained that in a "language with few adjectives and adverbs, one in which it is necessary to use the concreteness of nouns and the drive of verbs," the ancient poets had no effective alternative to the "hot breathing intimacy" of the Psalms. Lewis also says too little about the resentment, which is both a temptation and a torture, evident in the cursing psalms.

16 "C. S. Lewis Goes Marching On." *Canadian C. S. Lewis Journal*, no. 12 (December):11.

Reprint of 1977.12.

17 "C. S. Lewis's Letters to Arthur Greeves." *Canadian C. S. Lewis Journal*, no. 8 (August):1, 12.

This article compares three reviews of *They Stand Together: The Letters of C. S. Lewis to Arthur Greeves*. The book is a "monument to Lewis's concept of friendship." An honest and immediate, unconscious autobiography, "the present collection is important as writing and as biography at once." Reprinted from 1979.62.

18 CECIL, DAVID. "C. S. Lewis Unmasked." *Books and Bookmen* 24 (July):11–12.

Review of *They Stand Together: The Letters of C. S. Lewis to Arthur Greeves, (1914–1963)*. "Lewis was by nature a mixture, half stern intellectual, half boyish romantic." In his public writings he adopted a mask, partly due to his pleasure in hard-hitting argument but also out of "a desire to protect his vulnerable spirit from what he felt to be a hostile world." The real Lewis,

1979

"gentler, subtler, more spontaneous, reflective, tentative and unexpected," is revealed through these letters.

19 CHAPMAN, EDGAR L. "Anima Figures in a Demonic Comedy in the Lewis Tradition: E. E. Y. Hales's *Chariot of Fire*." *Mythlore* 6 (Summer):19–23.
    E[dward] E[lton] Y[oung] Hales's *Chariot of Fire* (Garden City, N.Y.: Doubleday, 1977) is in the tradition of Lewis's *The Great Divorce* and the Ransom Trilogy. Like Lewis's novels, Hales's novel modernizes "theological allegory in sardonic twentieth century imagery"; it is pervaded by satiric irony, it emphasizes making the proper choice, its characters struggle with a passion that enslaves them, and it shows that great romantic lovers are egoists.

20 CHRISTENSEN, MICHAEL J. *C. S. Lewis on Scripture: His Thoughts on the Nature of Biblical Inspiration, the Role of Revelation and the Question of Inerrancy*. Waco, Texas: Word Books, 120 pp. Reprint. London: Hodder and Stoughton, 1979.
    While he "addressed countless theological subjects, Lewis never offered a systematic appraisal of the nature of Scripture." He defies classification as either a liberal or a conservative because he did not attempt to construct a logical system of thought that account for all the evidence. Lewis approached the Bible as a literary scholar, not as a theologian. His approach to literature consists of four essential parts: "(1) the characteristics of the good reader, (2) the nature of the true poet, (3) the role of the imagination, and (4) the relationship between language and Ultimate Reality." Lewis's view of Scripture is that it is to be approached as inspired literature. "Its literary elements—images, symbols, myths and metaphors—are actual *embodiments* of spiritual reality, *vehicles* of divine revelation." Lewis's unique contribution "is in helping us view the Bible as human literature carrying a divine message."

21 COLBERT, JAMES G., Jr. "A Note on *The Abolition of Man*." *CSL: The Bulletin of the New York C. S. Lewis Society* 10 (August):4–5.
    "Subjectivism" was a live issue in philosophy when Lewis wrote *The Abolition of Man* and also appeared in a disguised version in works "not about pure speculative philosophy but about language and logic." In order to combat this theory, Lewis chose to write a popular polemic rather than a scholarly work.

22 COLLINGS, MICHAEL [R.]. "C. S. Lewis and the Music of Creation." *The Lamp-Post of the Southern California C. S. Lewis Society* 3, nos. 3–4 (July–October):1–3.
    Lewis treats music as a mode of creation in *The Magician's Nephew*. The humans who are present and witness the creation react to the music according to their natures: the children and the cabby listen in rapt wonder,

Uncle Andrew convinces himself the song is only ungovernable noise, and the Witch responds "with violence and pain, recognizing [the celestial music] and hating it."

23   COMO, JAMES T. "Introduction, within the Realm of Plenitude." In *C. S. Lewis at the Breakfast Table and Other Reminiscences*. Edited by James T. Como. New York: Macmillan, pp. xxi–xxxiv.

Lewis and his work are an organic whole. The features that constitute his life, faith, thought, and literature are Joy or *Sehnsucht*; "the validity of reason and the objectivity of the natural moral order"; quiddity, the essence of things, expressed as concreteness, the reason Lewis avoided theories; imagination as a source of knowledge; myth, which is best suited to arousing Joy; attacks on chronological snobbery, the myth of progress; the need to disregard the self; the belief in a supernatural that "is solid and impinges on us imminently."

24   ——, ed. *C. S. Lewis at the Breakfast Table and Other Reminiscences*. New York: Macmillan, 299 pp. Reprint. London: Collins, 1980.

Essays written by people who knew Lewis (with two exceptions) offer perceptions and impressions that allow the reader to meet him. These perspectives vary by "the length of time and the stage of life during which Lewis was known, the degree of intimacy to which he was known, the 'angle' of friendship that was shared and the depth of familiarity with his work." The list of contributors includes brief biographical information about their education, career, works, and acquaintance with Lewis. Essays are listed individually in this bibliography.

*25 ——. "The Militant Intellect: The Conditions and Elements of the Rhetoric of C.S. Lewis." DAI 42 (1981):4972A. Columbia University, 155 pp.

Lewis's life was a relentless struggle to derive meaning from experience. This hermeneutic effort led to a rhetoric that attempted to establish the coherence of Christianity rather than to prove its tenets. A pre-rhetorical analysis of his world reveals it to be variegated but organic and whole. "Lewis uses the lessons he learned—experiential, epistemological, and literary—to equip his reader with his own hermeneutic armaments." Basic to this equipping is the idea that each person must take the road out of self to become the self God intends. "A taxonomy of Lewis's world of discourse reveals a heavy reliance on obliqueness, even to the point of literary genres being contrived (conventions feigned) and a persona projected in what a reader would take to be a literal setting." Lewis is a literary figure, a thinker, and a religious writer. His world is trustworthy.

26   COWAN, ROSAMUND. "Women as Pupils." *Canadian C. S. Lewis Journal* no. 4 (April):4–10.

Lewis was a joy to have as a tutor. He wanted his students to express their own opinions clearly and honestly. His lectures were marvelous. Reprinted: 1983.12.

27 DANA, MARGARET [E.]. "The Tao of Space Travel." *The Lamp-Post of the Southern California C. S. Lewis Society* 3, nos. 3–4 (July–October):4–8.
Lewis sees the Tao as the ground of all human values—a process that is capable of evolving, of being transcended as man learns more. There are several instances in *Out of the Silent Planet* and *Perelandra* where the Tao is transcended; "though 'there are different laws in different worlds' . . . there is an underlying unity inhering in them all, through their common source, which makes transition possible for the man who is not too culturally bound." Through following the Tao and finding it can sometimes be transcended, Ransom is progressively strengthened, purified, and sensitized to the point that he recognizes God, "the creator and sustainer of the *Tao*, the spirit behind the law."

28 DART, JOHN. "Questions Raised on C. S. Lewis Lore." *Los Angeles Times* 24 March, Part 1, pp. 30–31.
The questions involve a controversy that had developed over the biographical details of Walter Hooper, "who is well established as a gatekeeper for much of the Lewis lore and literature." Kathryn Lindskoog has questioned the length and quality of his association with Lewis [see 1978.23]. Most Lewis admirers "believe such attention is irrelevant and unfair." Some critics think "the problem is one of exaggerations and omissions." Reprinted: 1979.29.

29 ———. "Questions Raised on C. S. Lewis Lore." *Canadian C. S. Lewis Journal* no. 9 (September):1–4.
Reprint of 1979.28.

30 DeCAMARA, RICHARD D. "*The New York Times* versus C. S. Lewis." *National Review* 31 (12 October):1306–1309.
"Lewis' magnetism, which so strongly attracts some necessarily repels others whose views are antipathetical to Christianity." John Leonard ("Books of the Times," *New York Times*, 29 March 1979, p. C20), Christopher Ricks ("Dabblers in Ink and Self-Admiration," *New York Times Book Review*, 8 April 1979, pp. 3, 33), and Samuel Hynes [1979.52], in their reviews of books about Lewis, have attacked him on the basis of his marriage, his views on politics and science, the type of people who read his works, and his Christianity. Reprinted: 1980.13.

31   DEL MASTRO, M. L. Review of *They Stand Together: The Letters of C. S. Lewis to Arthur Greeves (1914–1963)*. *Library Journal* 104 (1 December):2572.

"Control, urbanity, polished wit, and a gentlemanly reticence mark the letters from the start, eliminating idle gossip and filtering out raw emotions, while revealing Lewis' responsible concern and zest for living. Since the friends' most private communications took place in conversation, the letters hold no wild revelations. But they show Lewis as a loving Christian and a steadfast, honest friend. Hooper provides narrative links, explanatory notes, and full identifications of people and places mentioned."

32   "Did Christianity Corrupt Lewis?" *Christianity Today* 23 (21 December):9.

Three reviews in the *New York Times* in 1979 have criticized Lewis himself rather than books about Lewis. Samuel Hynes [1979.52], in particular, has attacked Lewis's fantasy and his Christianity. These reviews "don't share Lewis's Christian faith, and . . . Lewis's understanding of Christianity defies their stereotypic categories." By branding Lewis an oddball, they "can avoid having to consider the truly biblical Christianity he sets forth." Yet, ultimately they are not denouncing Lewis but Jesus Christ.

33   DOUGLASS, JANE. "An Enduring Friendship." In *C. S. Lewis at the Breakfast Table and Other Reminiscences*. Edited by James T. Como. New York: Macmillan, pp. 115–119.

Douglass became acquainted with Lewis in 1954 when she was thinking of adapting *The Lion, the Witch and the Wardrobe* for radio. Lewis had a "dread of such things as radio and television apparatus and expressed his dislike of talking films." The project was abandoned when Lewis disliked the treatment given the story. The friendship and correspondence continued.

34   DUNDAS-GRANT, JAMES. "From an 'Outsider.'" In *C. S. Lewis at the Breakfast Table and Other Reminiscences*. Edited by James T. Como. New York: Macmillan, pp. 229–233.

Dundas-Grant met regularly with the Inklings. Lewis was an essentially kind man who had a plenitude of charity; "the essential teacher in him always came out but so effortlessly that one didn't realize that one was being fed."

35   EDWARDS, BRUCE [LEE], Jr. "Overdoing a Good Thing? Soon It Will Become Fashionable to Criticize Lewis." *Christianity Today* 23 (2 November):40.

So much has been written about Lewis himself, "whether or which of his books 'will endure,' his exact relationships with the Inklings, or just how many people were converted through his letters," that there is now a glut.

1979

People will start dismissing this glut as "much ado about nothing" and will dismiss Lewis as well. "A moratorium would be restful." Reprinted: 1980.14.

36   ELLWOOD, GRACIA FAY. "Of Creation and Love." *Mythlore* 6 (Fall):19.
       The article contains a reprint of the letter Lewis sent the author in response to the question "can we accurately say . . . that God has anger"? For Lewis, answering letters was a matter of love; for him, " 'there are no ordinary people.' " His reply said " 'I hear you. You exist. Your question deserves the best answers I can give.' " His response was "like an act of new creation" for the author.

37   FARRER, AUSTIN. "In His Image." In *C. S. Lewis at the Breakfast Table and Other Reminiscences*. Edited by James T. Como. New York: Macmillan, pp. 242–244.
       Lewis "took in more, he felt more, he remembered more, he invented more" than the common breed of man. His feeling intellect and his intellectual imagination gave strength to his religious writings. He had fundamental sympathy, consideration, and respect for people.

38   FITTON, TOBY. Review of *They Stand Together: The Letters of C. S. Lewis to Arthur Greeves (1914–1963)*. *TLS: Times Literary Supplement*, 7 December, p. 102.
       The volume is an epistolary counterpart to *Surprised by Joy*. Early letters reflect interest in Norse mythology and MacDonald; later letters are personally reticent but interesting for their informal literary judgments.

39   GEBBERT, VERA M. "Warm Briar & Cold Teak." *Canadian C. S. Lewis Journal*, no. 3 (March):6.
       After Lewis's death, his teakwood box containing three of his pipes was sent to Gebbert who had corresponded with him for twenty-three years. The pipes were warm as if recently in someone's hands. Also after Lewis's death, Gebbert received a letter from Warren carrying the initials CSL in dark blue ink, which Gebbert thinks was "one last greeting from the affectionate and dear old friend."

40   GILMORE, CHARLES. "To the RAF." In *C. S. Lewis at the Breakfast Table and Other Reminiscences*. Edited by James T. Como. New York: Macmillan, pp. 186–191.
       Gilmore was commandant of the Royal Air Force Chaplain's School during 1941 when Lewis gave lectures to the chaplains and members of the RAF. "As a result of hearing Lewis, there were handfuls of young people all gaining new concepts of how they fitted into the life that immediately lay before them." Lewis spoke on wondrously varied subjects with grace and clar-

ity and gave his audience "a sterling and direct purpose, where before they had found only the confusion of a whirlpool."

41   GREEN, ROGER LANCELYN. "In the Evening." In *C. S. Lewis at the Breakfast Table and Other Reminiscences*. Edited by James T. Como. New York: Macmillan, pp. 210–214.

Green was Lewis's student and friend. Lewis loved bawdy stories, which are outrageous and extravagant but not cruel or pornographic. When Lewis speaks of his sins of the flesh before his conversion, he is exaggerating; readers should not be too ready to read "sex" for "sin." Lewis often had nightmares and used them and other mental pictures in his works.

42   GRIFFITHS, ALAN BEBE. "The Adventure of Faith." In *C. S. Lewis at the Breakfast Table and Other Reminiscences*. Edited by James T. Como. New York: Macmillan, pp. 11–24.

Griffiths was Lewis's pupil and friend from 1929 to 1932; they engaged in the venture of faith that was to lead to their becoming convinced Christians. Lewis reacted too strongly against the transpersonal absolute Godhead in favor of a Personal God. He did not care about the Church as an institution and found the externals of church worship unattractive; he did not see "ritual as the dramatization of myth," or the "church as a worshipping community and of cult as something 'sacred,' a reflection on earth of a heavenly reality." Lewis did not understand "the place of mystical experience in religious life."

43   HARWOOD, A. C. "About Anthroposophy." In *C. S. Lewis at the Breakfast Table and Other Reminiscences*. Edited by James T. Como. New York: Macmillan, pp. 25–30.

Reprint of 1974.17.

44   ———. "A Toast to His Memory." In *C. S. Lewis at the Breakfast Table and Other Reminiscences*. Edited by James T. Como. New York: Macmillan, pp. 237–241.

Reprint of 1975.22; 1976.17.

45   HAVARD, ROBERT E. "Philia: Jack at Ease." In *C. S. Lewis at the Breakfast Table and Other Reminiscences*. Edited by James T. Como. New York: Macmillan, pp. 215–228.

Havard was the Lewis brothers' physician and friend. The talk when the Inklings met was "good, witty, learned, high hearted, and very stimulating"; Lewis was the link that bound them together. He felt the first duty of a writer was to entertain. He enjoyed the physical act of writing; his major works grew from a painful gestation period and the process of actual writing was "akin to parturition—painful but enlivening." Lewis was "magnanimous," yet he could be intolerant and abusive; he made enemies; he was a staunch Conservative; "he was most at ease among a few friends, acquaintances, or admirers in informal surroundings"; he enjoyed holidays like a schoolboy.

46 HEIDELBERGER, PATRICIA. "With Girls and Women." *Canadian C. S. Lewis Journal*, no. 4 (April):3–4.

Heidelberger stayed at the Kilns during World War II. Mrs. Moore was "kind, solicitous, and indeed most forbearing." Lewis was tolerant and generous, helping to pay for Heidelberger's school tuition. Reprinted: 1983.31.

47 HODGENS, RICHARD [M.]. "Some Aspects of *Perelandra*." *CSL: The Bulletin of the New York C. S. Lewis Society* 10 (March):1–6.

The description of Venus is "traditional" in astronomy and "conventional" in science fiction. The "explicit assumption of orthodox Christian doctrine" sets the trilogy apart from other science fiction and its science sets it apart from other religious fiction. Manlove's criticism [see 1975.31] is not valid since he objects to Lewis's beliefs rather than *Perelandra*'s construction.

48 HOOPER, WALTER. "A Bibliography of the Writings of C. S. Lewis." Revised and enlarged. In *C. S. Lewis at the Breakfast Table and Other Reminiscences*. Edited by James T. Como. New York: Macmillan, pp. 245–288.

This bibliography is a definitive list of Lewis's writings, originally published in *Light on C. S. Lewis* (Edited by Jocelyn Gibb. London: Geoffrey Bles, 1965, pp. 117–160.) It is divided by form: books; short stories; books edited or with prefaces by Lewis; essays, pamphlets, and miscellaneous items; single short poems; and book reviews by Lewis; published letters; books containing numerous small extracts from Lewis's unpublished writings. Within each section items are listed chronologically and are individually numbered. Only the original edition of each item is listed; both British and American publishers are included. The contents of collections of essays are analyzed. One single alphabetical title index refers to section and item number.

49 ———. "Oxford's Bonny Fighter." In *C. S. Lewis at the Breakfast Table and Other Reminiscences*. Edited by James T. Como. New York: Macmillan, pp. 137–185.

The Oxford Socratic Club, the idea of Monica Shorten and Stella Aldwinckle, was founded in 1942 to discuss the pros and cons of the Christian religion. Lewis was president from 1942 until 1954. The practice was to have two speakers, a Christian and an atheist, one to read a paper and the other to open the discussion. The *Socratic Digest*, published from 1942 to 1954, contains the club's minutes and recollections of those present. Through the *Digest* Hooper summarizes Lewis's contributions to the discussion, including his famous debate with G. E. M. Anscombe on naturalism. Hooper's chapter also contains a list of topics and speakers at each meeting from 1942 to 1954.

50   ———. *Past Watchful Dragons: The Narnian Chronicles of C. S. Lewis*. New York: Collier, 140 pp. Reprint. London: Front Paperbacks, 1980.

The book is a revision and expansion of Hooper's two essays, "Past Watchful Dragons," published in *Imagination and the Spirit*, edited by Charles A. Huttar (Grand Rapids, Mich.: Eerdmans, 1971) and "Narnia: The Author, the Critics and the Tale" [1974.21]. "Dressed animals," mythology, and Joy were important elements in Lewis's youth and contributed in various ways and degrees to his conversion to Christianity. These elements "appear transformed and regenerated in the world of Narnia." Lewis's "outline of Narnian history so far as it is known," written after the tales were completed, and several fragments of the few surviving Narnian manuscripts are included. Religious elements vested in Aslan are "the experience of the numinous," "the consciousness of a moral law," and the obligation felt toward the numinous power that is the guardian of morality. The analogy of Aslan to Christ must not be pressed too closely: there is not "an exact, geometrically perfect equivalent of Christ's Incarnation, Passion, Crucifixion and Ascension in the Narnian stories." Lewis's goal was to recast Christianity in an imaginary world in order to steal past the watchful dragons of inhibition.

51   ———. Speech before the Portland C. S. Lewis Society, March 8, 1979. *Chronicle of the Portland C. S. Lewis Society* 8, no. 2 (April–June):9–19.

Hooper's speech covered a wide range of topics about Lewis. The editing of Lewis's letters to Arthur Greeves was complicated because Lewis never dated them. Greeves wanted the letters to go to the Bodleian Library, but Warren Lewis sent them to the Wade Center. Warren's alcoholism is treated in *They Stand Together* as well as in the film about Lewis, *Through Joy and Beyond*, co-written by Hooper and Anthony F. Marchington, because "it was a problem of very considerable significance to both brothers." Another problem with *They Stand Together* was whether to reinstate passages Greeves had obliterated dealing with sexual fantasies. Lewis's most perfected virtue was his obedience to God, which was supported by his belief in an objective moral law and his denunciation of feelings. Although the friendship between Lewis and Tolkien cooled, they owed a great debt to and retained a deep affection for each other. Lewis was careful about how his works were translated into other media.

52   HYNES, SAMUEL. "Guardian of the Old Ways." *New York Times Book Review*, 8 July, pp. 3, 26.

Hynes sees Lewis's readers, like Lewis himself, as either children or Christians. They share a "willingness to extend reality beyond the visible, and to accept myths of that other reality as a form of truth telling"; they see moral issues in dramatic terms, as actual combat between good and evil. Lewis was estranged from his own time, probably as a result of his unhappy childhood; this estrangement is the "source of his strength, both as a polemicist and as a novelist." He wrote social and political novels while appearing to write religious ones; he wrote rapidly and carelessly. He seemed to dislike children and women; "evil is whatever irritates him." See responses 1979.30, 32.

53 JANSEN, JOHN F. Review of *The Joyful Christian: 127 Readings from C. S. Lewis*. *Theology Today* 35 (January):523–524.

   The Joyful Christian provides an introduction to and sampling of Lewis's lively apologetic. The selections have limitations but these readings do include many of Lewis's keenest observations and can lead readers to the works in their entirety as well as to an appreciation of these excerpts.

54 KARKAINEN, PAUL A. *Narnia Explored*. Old Tappan, N.J.: Fleming H. Revell, 192 pp.

   Karkainan explores the themes, symbols, characters, and biblical parallels in each of the seven stories. "Lewis filled his books with characters and events which portray a variety of Christian truths"; "by making his stories parallel to the biblical account, without following it exactly, he invites comparison without causing confusion." One of the basic concepts in Lewis's philosophy is that what is inside is bigger than the outside. He illuminates the nature of the soul by putting souls into animals. Each book offers a different perspective on evil.

55 KAWANO, ROLAND M. "C. S. Lewis and the Transcendence of Irony." *Mythlore* 6 (Spring):17–20.

   Irony occurs because the image and the idea, imagination and reason, have become separated. Lewis transcended irony through his doctrine of "stock responses," fixed conventional responses to life. He reacted against the theory of the unchanging human heart, which implies that an individual cannot transcend his own perspective in order to give himself to and understand other perspectives. Lewis also transcended irony through his impersonal theory, which states that one should be concerned with the work of art and not the artist, and his method of reading literature receptively. "We transcend our own selves, our own ironies, and those in literature, when we read receptively. And yet we find that in doing so, we remain distinctively ourselves."

56 KIRKPATRICK, HOPE. "Was Lewis Consistent on Punishment and Purgatory?" *CSL: The Bulletin of the New York C. S. Lewis Society* 11 (December):9–10.

   Lewis deplored the humanitarian theory of punishment that treats prisoners as patients to be cured, yet he believed in purgatory where God corrects us through pain and transforms us into creatures worthy of heaven. "The clarity for which Lewis is so justly prized requires focusing on that point which he is explaining." Yet truth is multifaceted and can be approached from many different sides. Lewis is human and has "the limitations that all who must function through the brain have to accept."

57 KIRKPATRICK, JOHN. "Fresh Views of Humankind in Lewis's Poems." *CSL: The Bulletin of the New York C. S. Lewis Society* 10 (September):1–7.
     Lewis's poems can be grouped by "their differences of approach: humankind in relation 1) to other kinds, 2) to other humans, 3) to the divine, within us or outside us."

58 KOLLMANN, JUDITH J. "C. S. Lewis as Medievalist." *CSL: The Bulletin of the New York C. S. Lewis Society* 10 (May):1–5.
     Lewis's scholarly method was historical, dealing with ideas; his goal was to reconstruct the state of mind at a particular point in time in order to understand the literature produced. *The Allegory of Love* is his most specialized study and traces the development of the idea of courtly love and its usual literary vehicle, allegory, from *The Romance of the Rose* through Chaucer's *Troilus and Criseyde* to Spenser's *Faerie Queene*, where adulterous courtly love became reconciled with the European concept of marriage. Lewis believed that the Middle Ages had understood, more accurately than any other age, man and man's place in the universe; the distinguishing factor is Christianity.

59 KOTZIN, MICHAEL [C.]. "Mrs. Moore as the Queen of Underland." *Mythlore* 6 (Summer):46.
     Like Mrs. Jane King Moore, the Queen of Underland in *The Silver Chair* "gains control of a motherless young man . . . separating him from his father." She is domineering and possessive. Like Lewis, the Queen's victim "lives under 'stifling tyranny,' in 'servitude,' as his actions are controlled and limited by the exploitative queen."

60 LADBOROUGH, RICHARD W. "In Cambridge." In *C. S. Lewis at the Breakfast Table and Other Reminiscences*. Edited by James T. Como. New York: Macmillan, pp. 98–104.
     Reprint of 1975.27.

61 "Lewis, C(live) S(taples) 1898–1963." In *Contemporary Authors: A Bio-Bibliographical Guide to Current Writers in Fiction, General Nonfiction, Poetry, Journalism, Drama, Motion Pictures, Television, and Other Fields*. Vol. 81–84. Edited by Frances Carol Locher. Detroit: Gale Research Company, pp. 328–331.
     The interplay of imagination and reason characterized the body of

1979

Lewis's works. He translated Christian dogma into fresh terms. The tributes to Lewis's works far outweigh the assaults upon it.

62   LEWIS, NAOMI. "Dear Galahad, Yours Jack." *Observer* (London), 20 May, p. 37.
Lewis reviews *They Stand Together: The Letters of C. S. Lewis to Arthur Greeves (1914–1963)*. This book is open about matters such as Lewis's adolescent sexual fantasies and his brother's alcoholism. The counterattack to Christianity by the young "unsaved" Lewis is contained in these letters. Reprinted: 1979.17.

63   LEYERLE, JOHN. "No Glory, Please, I'm Cringing." *Canadian C. S. Lewis Journal*, no. 3 (March):12.
Lewis had an extraordinary memory and could cite little-known poems by heart. He "would cringe at the developing level of hagiographical material about him."

64   LINDSKOOG, KATHRYN [ANN]. "C. S. Lewis the Dreamer." In *The Gift of Dreams: A Christian View*. San Francisco: Harper & Row, pp. 154–158.
Lewis likened the "polishing of creative ideas from his unconscious to the clear-headed waking evaluation of dream material." He confided his dreams to his friends and used his dreams in his fiction. Reprinted: 1980.31.

65   ———. "C. S. Lewis's Search for Joy." *Radix* 10, no. 6 (May–June):6–11.
Lewis had several childhood experiences in which he "was overwhelmed with an enormous bliss beyond description" that he later called Joy. When he read MacDonald's Phantastes, Joy took on a holy quality. After he came to believe in Christianity, he never took as great an interest in Joy again. Reprinted: 1979.66.

66   ———. "C. S. Lewis's Search for Joy." *Canadian C. S. Lewis Journal* no. 12 (December):3–7.
Reprint of 1979.65.

67   ———. "Dialogue." *Christianity and Literature* 28 (Winter):13–14.
Here Lindskoog responds to criticism of her article "Some Problems in C. S. Lewis Scholarship" See 1979.5 for criticism; see 1978.23 for original article.

68   ———. "Getting It Together: Lewis and the Two Hemispheres of Knowing." *Mythlore* 6 (Winter):43–45.
Reprint of 1975.29.

69 ———. "RSV: Revised Screwtape Version." *Christian Century* 96, no. 18 (16 May):568–569.

The new edition of *The Screwtape Letters* published by Revell contains alterations in the text, including a change of setting from England to the United States, and illustrations by Wayland Moore that are execrable. Walter Hooper in the preface greatly exaggerates his relationship to Lewis. Reprinted: 1979.70.

70 ———. "RSV: Revised Screwtape Version." *Canadian C. S. Lewis Journal,* no. 7 (July):10–11.

Reprint of 1979.69.

71 McCASLIN, SUSAN. "A Critical Study of C. S. Lewis' *Till We Have Faces.*" *Crux* 15, no. 3:3–8.

Lewis approaches the problem of human identity relative to the identity of God in the novel and explores how humans resist the divine. Orual ultimately experiences the divine presence directly and comes to self-awareness. The lives of Orual and Psyche can be seen in terms of spiritual rebirth analogous to the Christian experience. "Psyche, acting as the redeemed soul, takes up and regathers the body, or Orual." In this the novel is particularly Christian because it concerns the regeneration of both body and soul at a spiritual level of consciousness.

72 McGOVERN, EUGENE. "Last Wine: The Letters to Arthur Greeves." *CSL: The Bulletin of the New York C. S. Lewis Society* 11 (December):1–8.

Some of the letters provide new information about Lewis's personal relationships: he became infatuated with Mrs. Moore soon after he met her and never grumbled about her domestic demands; Lewis was never close to his father and the evidence is that Lewis was mostly at fault for this estrangement; some of the remarks in these letters about his father are vicious and cruel. His brother Warren's alcoholism and selfishness put restrictions on his activities. Lewis's views on Christian marriage suggest that his marriage to Joy Davidman, a divorcee, was never consummated. If this is the case, *A Grief Observed* should not be regarded as a psychological history but as "a great piece of Christian prose."

73 ———. "Our Need for Such a Guide." In *C. S. Lewis at the Breakfast Table and Other Reminiscences.* Edited by James T. Como. New York: Macmillan, pp. 126–134.

Lewis was an intelligent modern man who found Christianity. He had the ability to dissect the various enthusiasms and follies of the twentieth century. He "convinces his readers that he is the most reliable guide they have found on the subjects that matter most": God, spiritual reality, epistemology,

1979

morality. Enthusiasm for Lewis often includes a strong desire to learn about his life; the New York C. S. Lewis Society fosters this interest. This concern with Lewis himself is not cultish—readers find that reading Lewis's works expands and widens their interests rather than narrows them. Curiosity about the man is a natural outgrowth of interest in his work, and his example helps us in living as Christians.

74 MARTIN, JOHN. "C. S. Lewis and 'The Foolish Things of the World.'" *CSL: The Bulletin of the New York C. S. Lewis Society* 10 (February):1–8.

The supreme question of wisdom and foolishness is "choosing between the Cross and its ten thousand fascinating alternatives." In *The Pilgrim's Regress* Lewis pointedly combats all that the world calls wisdom but is not. One thing considered foolish by the world, which we associate with Lewis, is the desire he called Joy. Joy can either make us think our wisdom is incomplete and thereby help grace penetrate our natural armor or it can make us think our wisdom, though incomplete, is so poignant and impressive that we need no spirit greater than our own.

75 MATHEW, GERVISE. "Orator." In *C. S. Lewis at the Breakfast Table and Other Reminiscences*. Edited by James T. Como. New York: Macmillan, pp. 96–97.

A strange popular image of Lewis is developing: he is supposed to have regarded lectures and tutorials as a waste of his time and to have held undergraduates in contempt. Nothing could be further from the truth. His audiences could not have "enjoyed his lectures so much if he had not been so obviously enjoying them himself." He always forged a personal link with his audience.

76 MORRIS, CLIFFORD. "A Christian Gentlemen." In *C. S. Lewis at the Breakfast Table and Other Reminiscences*. Edited by James T. Como. New York: Macmillan, pp. 192–201.

Reprint of 1973.29.

77 MORRISON, JOHN. "The Idea of Covenant in Narnia." *CSL: The Bulletin of the New York C. S. Lewis Society* 10 (October):1–7.

Scripture illuminates Narnia and vice versa; a Christology cannot be developed from it, but Aslan implies Christ and the Narnians us. Narnia has meaning, historical significance, and purpose only through Aslan. His covenant with Narnia is a "gift freely given and available to all who choose to respond to it." Because of the entrance of evil into their world, Narnians cannot keep the covenant perfectly; they must rely on faith working through love to justify it. Aslan is personally involved in the world and man's struggle. The security of the Narnians is based in the person of Aslan; their hope is grounded in his undeviating reliability and their relationship to him is one of communion, praise, and obedience in love. See Huttar's response, 1980.30.

*78 NAKAO, SETSUKO. "Salvation Theme in C. S. Lewis's *That Hideous Strength.*" *Bulletin of Seisen Women's College* 27:1–16.
Source of citation: *MLA Bibliography* 1979.

79 NARDO, A. K. "Decorum in the Fields of Arbol: Interplanetary Genres in C. S. Lewis's Space Trilogy." *Extrapolation* 20 (Summer):118–128.
Lewis uses epic to characterize Malacandra (Mars), and pastoral and lyric to characterize Perelandra (Venus). To characterize earth he uses satire and farce to laugh at evil, gothic novel to feel the terror of evil, and medieval romance to portray the quest for the ideal by the redeemed man in an all-too-real world. Paradoxically, these genres are both partial and central; the festive conclusion of each novel, where all merges in the harmony and rejoicing of a dance, is the genre of comedy.

80 NOLAN, CHARLES J., Jr. "Lewis's Objective Room: Key to Aesthetics." *CSL: The Bulletin of the New York C. S. Lewis Society* 10 (August):5–6.
The section of *That Hideous Strength* in which Frost, by use of the "Objective Room," hopes to rid Mark of all human reactions provides a key to understanding Lewis's sense of the beautiful. Man has an innate predilection for beauty; beauty possesses total congruity, is pleasantly colorful, and conveys emotional warmth; "beauty involves an exact sense of symmetry and proportion"; regularity is essential because it creates pattern, which once recognized, satisfies the perceiver's desires; beauty requires an exact correlation of parts; there is an inextricable link between beauty and morality.

81 O'HARE, COLMAN. "The Hero in C. S. Lewis's Space Novels." *Renascence* 31 (Spring):142–154.
Lewis wrote himself and his friends into the Trilogy. Ransom, it is stressed in *Out of the Silent Planet* and *Perelandra*, is a philologist and Oxford don as was J. R. R. Tolkien. Echoes of Tolkien's work abound in the Trilogy and much of his thought informs the theme of Lewis's novels. In *That Hideous Strength* Ransom has changed his name and his status, and he has delegated much of his heroic action to others; here he more closely resembles Charles Williams. "The friends are not 'immortalized' so much as used to flesh out the author's creations, color his 'portraits' and make them more 'real.'"

82 PATTERSON, NANCY-LOU. "*Guardaci Ben*: The Visionary Woman in C. S. Lewis' Chronicles of Narnia and *That Hideous Strength.*" *Mythlore* 6 (Summer):6–10; 6 (Fall):20–24.
Jane Studdock, discussed in the summer issue, Lucy, Jill, Aravis, and Polly, discussed in the fall issue, play roles, in these fantasies based on seeing, as seers and guides. These women "find the ultimate source and goal of all vision and lead others to Him. He whom they envision is Himself the light."

1979

83   PAYNE, LEANNE. *Real Presence: The Holy Spirit in the Works of C. S. Lewis.* Westchester, Ill.: Good News, Cornerstone Books, 198 pp. Revised and reprinted. Westchester, Ill.: Crossway Books, 1988. Reprint. London: Monarch, 1989.

Lewis's experience and understanding of the reality of God, incarnational reality, "informs his vision of man's relationship to God, in which God redeems man from his fragmented and alienated condition." He restores to Christianity "the knowledge and the *vocabulary* with which to speak of the supernatural and of the Absolute." God's Real Presence is manifested in our world through a "mediated" or "transposed" form; this sacramental view of reality, "that Spirit can be and is encountered in and through material forms," is central to Lewis's thought. He constantly points out the danger of dwelling on the subjective—our sensations and feelings about reality—at the expense of the objective reality itself. Our two minds, imaginative and rational, work in different, incomparable ways. Lewis is one of the few great bulwarks against the attempt to combine good and evil.

84   REDMANN, ESTHER. "From Mere Christian to *Alter Christus.*" *The Lamp-Post of the Southern California C. S. Lewis Society* 3, no. 2 (April):3–5.

The story movement in the Ransom Trilogy is a downward progression from heaven on Malacandra to purgatory on Perelandra to the hell of earth; Ransom's inner journey is an upward progression from tutelage to trial to triumph.

85   RIGBY, LUKE. "The Solid Man." In *C. S. Lewis at the Breakfast Table and Other Reminiscences.* Edited by James T. Como. New York: Macmillan, pp. 38–40.

Reprint of 1974.42.

86   ROGERS, MARY. "Jane McNeill and C. S. Lewis." *Chronicle of the Portland C. S. Lewis Society* 8, no. 1 (January–March):9–12.

Rogers knew McNeill from 1931 till her death in 1959 and also heard Lewis lecture at Oxford. McNeill was nine years older than Lewis and was the Lewis brothers' "dear friend Janie M." She never married, cared devotedly for her mother, never wavered in her Christian faith, had a glorious sense of fun, and had "kindness and wit" and a nonacademic appreciation of literature. She felt Lewis spent too much time on his novels and apologetic works and should have devoted more time to his profession of literary criticism. She hated *That Hideous Strength* and wished Lewis had dedicated any other work to her. Reprinted: 1979.87.

87   ———. "Jane McNeill and C. S. Lewis." *CSL: The Bulletin of the New York C. S. Lewis Society* 10 (August):1–4.

Reprint of 1979.86.

88 ROOK, ALAN. "The Butcher." *Canadian C. S. Lewis Journal* no. 10 (October):1–4.

Rook, a pupil of Lewis's for six months, found Lewis's ineluctable logic chilling. He felt there was no real human contact or warmth with Lewis. Lewis, he said, would "demolish an argument like a butcher bringing down a meat cleaver—almost to the point of rudeness." He was not a good lecturer; he read word for word from his text. In Rook's view, Lewis never illuminated anything. Reprinted: 1980.50; 1983.61.

89 ROUTLEY, ERIK. "A Prophet." In *C. S. Lewis at the Breakfast Table and Other Reminiscences*. Edited by James T. Como. New York: Macmillan, pp. 33–37.

Reprint of 1973.37. Reprinted: 1979.90; 1983.64.

90 ———. "Stunning Effect." *Canadian C. S. Lewis Journal,* no. 5 (May):1–6.

Reprint of 1973.37; 1979.89. Reprinted: 1983.64.

91 SAMMONS, MARTHA C. *A Guide through Narnia.* Wheaton, Ill.: Harold Shaw, 164 pp. Reprint. London: Hodder and Stoughton, 1979. Reprint. Westchester, Ill.: Cornerstone Books, 1980.

The *Guide* is a comprehensive companion to the tales. In it Sammons provides a brief sketch of Lewis's life and discusses how he came to write the stories; she summarizes the plot of the individual tales, the history, and the geography of Narnia. She discusses the role and nature of Aslan as well as the other characters, human and animal, and analyzes the Christian concepts in the tales. Also provided is an index to the names and places that appear in the stories.

92 SAYER, GEORGE. "Jack on Holiday." In *C. S. Lewis at the Breakfast Table and Other Reminiscences*. Edited by James T. Como. New York: Macmillan, pp. 202–209.

Sayer describes the ordinary routine of Lewis's visits to him and his wife: their walks, talks, Lewis's habits, likes, dislikes, jokes, and imagination.

93 SCHAKEL, PETER J. *Reading with the Heart: The Way into Narnia.* Grand Rapids, Mich.: Eerdmans, 154 pp.

Schakel sees myth and allegory as being on a continuum of imagination and intellect. The Chronicles of Narnia lie "slightly to the myth side of the dividing line, so that their primary and most profitable appeal is to the imagination, not to the intellect." By the use of archetypes, the Chronicles "communicate directly to the imagination and the emotions a sizable share of the central element of the Christian faith." Following are some of the archetypes or themes in the individual stories—*The Lion, the Witch and the Wardrobe*: the deep magic of the law of human nature and the deeper magic

1979

of God's love and grace; *Prince Caspian*: the debate between belief and disbelief, and the theme of faith; *The Voyage of the "Dawn Treader"*: a spiritual journey or progress, a longing for spiritual fulfillment; *The Silver Chair*: movements of descent and ascent that give structure to the story; *The Horse and His Boy*: the loss and regaining of identity; *The Magician's Nephew*: archetypes of autumn and spring, a shift from tragedy to comedy; *The Last Battle*: archetypes of winter and summer, "out of a tone of fear, [creating and building] a tone of longing, which . . . becomes the unifying quality of the story."

94   SCHOFIELD, STEPHEN. "'Congratulations—You Have Done It.'" *Canadian C. S. Lewis Journal,* no. 9 (September):5–6.
      James Forsyth dramatized *The Screwtape Letters* and met with Lewis to discuss the project. Lewis wrote "'I was uneasy about the conversion of Wormwood, but I found myself very moved when it happened.'" Reprinted: 1983.67.

95   ———. "Impact." *Canadian C. S. Lewis Journal,* no. 6 (June):1–5
      Lewis irked some people. Tolkien did not like the theological allegory in his fiction, Alistair Cooke thinks his arguments are too simplistic, and Victor Yarros calls Lewis a "paradox-monger and word-juggler." Nevertheless, his work has had far-reaching effect, including its impact on Charles Colson, who was converted through *Mere Christianity*. Reprinted: 1983.67.

96   ———. "The Joke about the Inklings." *Canadian C. S. Lewis Journal*, no. 3 (March):3–5.
      The best collection about the Inklings is in an American college, not a British one. "It is a curious thing that Lewis is a subject of serious study much more in the US than in Britain."

97   ———. "A Knife Is Quiet." *Canadian C. S. Lewis Journal*, no. 5 (May):7–8
      Lewis believed it was right for a Christian soldier to kill an enemy.

98   ———. "Letter to Walter Hooper No. 1." *Canadian C. S. Lewis Journal*, no. 9 (September):7–9.
      No one denies that Hooper has been a careful and dedicated trustee of the Lewis estate, but he has impeded other Lewis scholars by denying them permission to quote from Lewis's materials.

99   ———. "Letter to Walter Hooper (No. 2)." *Canadian C. S. Lewis Journal*, no. 10 (October):5.
      Hooper has "a pronounced inclination to slant" the work of others.

100 ———. "Letter to Walter Hooper (No. 3)." *Canadian C. S. Lewis Journal*, no. 11 (November):6–10.

      Hooper has lied on the cover of his book *Past Watchful Dragons* by representing himself as Lewis's sole biographer, forgetting to mention his co-author, Roger Lancelyn Green. Also, as an editor, Hooper has left out important passages from Lewis's work. Hooper has also misrepresented the length of his relationship with Lewis. See retraction 1980.56.

101 ———. "Lewis in French." *Canadian C. S. Lewis Journal*, no. 1 (January):9–11.

      A dozen books by Lewis have been translated into French, a remarkable occurrence for a British writer. His Narnia series is the most popular. Reprinted: 1983.67.

102 ———. "Lewis on the Prairies: No Slackers Allowed." *Canadian C. S. Lewis Journal*, no. 10 (October):6–7.

      At St. John's Cathedral Boys' School in Selkirk, Manitoba, the works of Lewis are used for teaching religion. Reprinted: 1983.67.

103 ———. "Lunch with Lewis." *Canadian C. S. Lewis Journal*, no. 1 (January):1, 3.

      Lewis "gave me his entire attention such as I had never received from anyone. . . . His presence stimulated me." Reprinted: 1983.70.

104 ———. "Who Was Lewis?" *Canadian C. S. Lewis Journal*, no. 1 (January):4.

      "He had whipped his mind to produce 49 books, mostly in spare time—a magnificent achievement."

105 ———. "Why the Impact?" *Canadian C. S. Lewis Journal*, no. 3 (March):7.

      Lewis had such a great impact because he was a genius, was dead accurate as far as possible, and was not distracted by the events of his own era. His works reveal "an astonishing breadth of thoroughly assimilated ancient literature," and his reasoning is as hard as flint.

106 SHENKER, ISRAEL. "Faithful Gather to Recall a Dinosaur: C. S. Lewis (1898-1963)." *Canadian C. S. Lewis Journal*, no. 3 (March):8–9.

      Reprint of 1976.39.

107 SHOEMAKER, STEVEN ROBERT. "Beyond the Walls of the World: Practical Theology in the Fantasy Novels of C. S. Lewis." Ph.D. dissertation, Duke University, 179 pp.

      Lewis opposed the ideas of subjectivism, naturalism, and the myth of progress he saw in the world. So, in response to this "misleading, inadequate view of human beings and the natural world, [Lewis] did not criticize, he cre-

ated. . . . He imagined Another World." Lewis believed the world to be characterized by objective value, God in and beyond nature, and self-intoxication
and sin. In his fantasy novels, the Ransom Trilogy, the Chronicles of Narnia,
and *The Screwtape Letters*, Lewis preached the Christian virtues of hope,
which he considered the "desire for the real good and true and beautiful";
love, which is "affection and acceptance, and sacrifice and commitment"; and
faith, or "courage in the face of doubt and fear." Lewis wrote fantasy because
"the world of the imagination is nearer to the truth than the world of the senses." Lewis, "provoked by modern people's nonworship of anything, begins by
proclaiming to us of a world where gods and awe and miracles and goodness
and courage are at least possibilities."

108 SULLIVAN, RACHEL. "'On the Reading of Old Books.'" *Chronicle of the
Portland C. S. Lewis Society* 8, no. 1 (January–March):3–8.
     Lewis identifies the reasons old books are not read: false humility, lazi-
ness, or inertia on the part of the reader. Old books are forbidding and
unpredigested; they have to be sought out, and there are few people to share
them with. He feels it is important to read old books because they allow the
reader to test the current controversies against the standard of central
Christianity, they help guard against the development of a combat mentality,
they provide nurturing and knowledge, and they expose the spirit of the age
and correct its fallacies.

109 SWINDALL, WAYNE. "The Cool, Mellow Flavor of Adam Fox." *The Lamp-
Post of the Southern California C. S. Lewis Society* 3, no. 1 (January):1–2.
     Swindall recounts a meeting around 1955 with Adam Fox, Dean of
Divinity at Magdalen College and referred to by Lewis as the "Chaplain" of
the Inklings.

110 TAYLOR, A. J. P. "Intellectual Gaiety." *Canadian C. S. Lewis Journal*, no. 2
(February):3–8.
     Taylor and Lewis were Fellows together at Magdalen College. Lewis
never talked of religion there because no one wanted to hear it. He talked
about literature and "had adolescent tastes and adult gifts of appreciation." He
loved playing with ideas. He could not resist an argument, not because he
wanted to score but because of the fun of the thing. Reprinted: 1983.74.

111 TOLLEFSEN, OLAF. "C. S. Lewis on Evaluative Judgments of Literature."
Modern Schoolman 56, no. 4 (May):356–363.
     A good theory of aesthetic merit would include the intuition both that
literary judgments are based on actual responses to works of art and that these
judgments are somewhat objective. Lewis, in *An Experiment in Criticism*, dif-
ferentiates between good and bad reading based on overt behavior; good liter-

ature promotes good reading and communicates concrete qualitative informa-tion about experience. He sets sharp limits on applying negative judgments of literary merit. "Lewis seems to have sketched out a coherent and potentially workable method of identifying objectively reliable judgments of aesthetic merit without recourse to any prior theory of the nature of beauty, aesthetic value and so forth."

112 TYNAN, KENNETH. "Exhilaration." *Canadian C. S. Lewis Journal*, no. 1 (January):5–9.
Tynan was pupil of Lewis who found him to be a powerful and forma-tive influence. Lewis was invigorating, stimulating, and inspiring. He had an astonishing memory. He could take one into the mind of medieval and classi-cal writers. He was incomparable as a teacher. Reprinted: 1979.113; 1983.79; 1988.77.

113 ———. "My Tutor, C. S. Lewis." *Third Way* 3, no. 6 (June):15–16.
Reprint of 1979.112. Reprinted: 1983.79; 1988.77.

114 WALSH, CHAD. *The Literary Legacy of C. S. Lewis*. New York: Harcourt Brace Jovanovich, 269 pp. Reprint. London: Sheldon Press, 1979.
Walsh examines the strengths and weaknesses of each of Lewis's indi-vidual works in depth and concludes that his poetry, though uneven, is "strongly visual, turned outward, [and] objective," qualities that are handi-caps today when poetry is confessional and subjective. As a literary scholar he is an "appreciative critic" who whets "the reader's appetite for a particu-lar book" and gives practical guidance to its reading. Lewis's apologetics direct the reader to the concepts and ideas that lie beyond their language. But his greatest achievement lies in "those imaginative and mythological books in which his ability as a writer and his sensibility as a Christian are fruitfully wedded": the Ransom Trilogy, the Chronicles of Narnia, *The Screwtape Letters*, *The Pilgrim's Regress*, *The Great Divorce*, and *Till We Have Faces*.

115 ———. "The Literary Stature of C. S. Lewis." *Christianity Today* 23 (8 June):20–23.
Summary of *The Literary Legacy of C. S. Lewis*, 1979.114.

116 WEAVER, MARY JO. "Creative Teaching: Hellfire and Damnation: An Approach to Religion and Literature." *Horizons* 6 (Fall):241–255.
Weaver, in a university religious studies class, used Lewis's *The Great Divorce*, along with other literary works, to explore the concept of hell and damnation. "This little book had the advantage of taking the notion of choice

1979

and dramatizing it against the background of modern, relatable examples of wrong choices."

117 WILLIAMS, DONALD T. "A Closer Look at the 'Unorthodox' Lewis." *Christianity Today* 23 (21 December):24–27.

Liberal critics tend to separate "Lewis the rational defender of a stubbornly conservative orthodoxy and Lewis the poet and myth-maker," thus protecting themselves against the gospel in Lewis and enabling themselves to praise his stories for their "'competence' rather than for their truth." Conservatives tend to overlook Lewis's doctrinal deficiencies because he was a European who came to orthodoxy from atheism and because his heart is "so obviously in the right place." But it is Lewis's opposition to relativism, his "absolute refusal to compromise or accommodate the truth that finally aligns C. S. Lewis with fundamental, evangelical, orthodox Christianity against the modern world."

118 WOLFE, GARY K. "The Rocket and the Hearth." In *Selected Proceedings of the 1978 Science Fiction Research Association National Conference*. Edited by Thomas J. Remington. Cedar Falls: University of Northern Iowa, pp. 22–29.

Wolfe discusses the images of the spaceship in science fiction and briefly mentions this image in Lewis's *Out of the Silent Planet*. The spaceship has a social rather than a technological image and is a place of security and comfort.

119 WRONG, CHARLES. "A Chance Meeting." In *C. S. Lewis at the Breakfast Table and Other Reminiscences*. Edited by James T. Como. New York: Macmillan, pp. 107–114.

Reprint of 1973.45.

120 YORK, THOMAS. "Jack." *Christian Century* 96 (5 December):1220.

In this review of *They Stand Together: The Letters of C. S. Lewis to Arthur Greeves (1914–1963)*, York finds that the work "supplements, and to some extent balances, the view we already had of Lewis."

121 ZITZMAN, SUSAN. "Lewis, Tolkien, Kilby & Co." *The Lamp-Post of the Southern California C. S. Lewis Society* 3, no. 2 (April):1–3.

Clyde S. Kilby has studied Lewis, Tolkien, and the other Oxford Christians for more than thirty years and "has had much behind-the-scenes influence on all levels of study of these popular Christian authors" through his writings, his teaching, and the development of the Marion E. Wade Collection at Wheaton College.

1980

1   BARFIELD, OWEN. Review of *They Stand Together: The Letters of C. S. Lewis to Arthur Greeves*. *Seven: An Anglo-American Literary Review* 1 (March):128–129.
    Reprint of 1979.4.

2   BELL, ALBERT A., Jr. "Origin of the Name 'Narnia.'" *Mythlore* 7 (Summer):29.
    "Narnia" is mentioned by classic Latin writers Martial, Pliny the Elder, Pliny the Young, Tacitus, and Livy. The modern Narni is about fifty miles north of Rome.

3   BLECHNER, MICHAEL HARRY. "Tristan in Letters: Malory, C. S. Lewis, Updike." *Tristania: A Journal Devoted to Tristan Studies* 6 (Autumn):30–37.
    "Mark vs. Tristram" by Lewis and Owen Barfield is based on Malory's Tristram and "starts out with the protagonists appealing to law, but ends with law overpowered by force."

4   BOENIG, ROBERT E. "Lewis' Time Machine and His Trip to the Moon." *Mythlore* 7 (Summer):6–9.
    Lewis's *Out of the Silent Planet* and "The Dark Tower" correspond to H. G. Wells's *The First Men in the Moon* (London: G. Newnes, 1901) and *The Time Machine* (London: W. Heinemann, 1895), respectively. Where Wells's voyage to the moon is one of neurotic fear and violence, Lewis's journey to Malacandra is "a journey away from fear towards final understanding of the order and peace behind the cosmos." Based on this inversion, Lewis, had he completed "The Dark Tower," would have made his time travel move from hell to Eden, in the opposite direction of Wells's.

5   BROWN, CAROL ANN. "Die Engel." *CSL: The Bulletin of the New York C. S. Lewis Society* 11 (August):1–3.
    Lewis depicts angels, especially in the Space Trilogy, as "dynamic, radiant, masculine entities . . . who are unanswerable in their authority and numinous splendor."

6   BRUGALETTA, JOHN J. "Lewis on Storge: A Rejoinder." *CSL: The Bulletin of the New York C. S. Lewis Society* 11 (September):8–10.
    Brugaletta here responds to the McGovern article on Lewis's insufficient treatment of affection between parents and children. [See 1980.33.] He claims that Lewis would not ignore something so apparent and so spiritually important. Lewis felt affection of this type should not be displayed in public and, since fiction is public, did not include it in his works. Lewis's personal

life should not be used to explain the absence of parental affection in his fiction.

7 CHANG, H. C. "Memories." *Canadian C. S. Lewis Journal*, no. 24 (December):1–3.
   Chang, who met Lewis in 1952, sees a vein of chivalry underlying Lewis's writings and explaining the style and verve of his literary criticism. Chang thought Lewis had "a great deal of learning and insight, and a real sense of obligation towards his subject, his readers and himself." Reprinted: 1983.9.

8 CHRISTENSEN, MIKE [MICHAEL J.]. "C. S. Lewis on Scripture." *CSL: The Bulletin of the New York C. S. Lewis Society* 11 (May):1–5.
   Lewis's views on biblical inspiration and inerrancy are contained in a chapter on Scripture in *Reflections on the Psalms*. He acknowledges Scripture as inspired of God and believes Scripture is literature as a vehicle of God's word. He finds human qualities of naivete, error, contradiction, and wickedness present in Scripture but believes Scripture "carries" the word of God. Lewis finds that truth in Scripture is not systematic but rather is presented in images and in a Person. He feels one should steep oneself in the tone and temper of the Bible to learn its message.

9 CHRISTOPHER, JOE R. "Letters from C. S. Lewis in the Humanities Research Center, the University of Texas at Austin: A Checklist." *CSL: The Bulletin of the New York C. S. Lewis Society* 12 (November):1–7.
   Christopher describes the physical format of the letters as well as their contents. He provides notes to explain the references in the letters.

10 COLLINGS, MICHAEL R. "The Mechanisms of Fantasy." *Lamp-Post of the Southern California C. S. Lewis Society* 4, nos. 3–4 (August–November): 13–14, 16.
   Most fantasies have a division between the real universe and the fantasy universe. In some this gap is not bridged; in others the author provides interactions between worlds but these are controlled by the fantasy universe and the worlds remain separate, totally different realities. In the Chronicles of Narnia and the Ransom Trilogy, Lewis has no actual barriers between worlds; the worlds coexist on the same plane, and interactions between them are free flowing and accomplished by mechanisms created by humans. He visualizes the universe as a unity presided over by God.

11 COMO, JAMES T. "*The Screwtape Letters*: A Description of the Manuscript in the Berg Collection of the New York Public Library." *CSL: The Bulletin of the New York C. S. Lewis Society* 11 (October):2–8.

Como provides a detailed description of the manuscript, including the differences between it and the first edition as well as between it and the text as first published in the *Guardian*. He describes the physical characteristics of the manuscript (type of paper, margins, number of leaves per chapter, etc.). The article contains a detailed chart of each emendation Lewis made, with the location in the first edition and in the manuscript, type of emendation, original text, and emendation.

12 DANIEL, JERRY [L.]. "The Taste of the Pineapple: A Basis for Literary Criticism." *CSL: The Bulletin of the New York C. S. Lewis Society* 11 (June):1–10.
    Lewis by nature had an appreciation of the essence of things, sharpened by the influence of Arthur Greeves and A. K. Hamilton Jenkin. Lewis "read the works of others with a view to the inherent *quality* of the work." For him, "unless stylistic shortcomings are so bad as to destroy the feeling, stylistic shortcomings are unimportant." As a literary critic, his method is based largely on his reading method. Lewis deplored several trends in modern criticism, including the anthropological approach, personal heresy, character criticism, source criticism, motif criticism, and authorship criticism. He felt all of these techniques diverted attention from the text itself. Lewis also wrote his imaginative works based on the essence of things.

13 DeCAMARA, ROBERT C. "*The New York Times* versus C. S. Lewis." *Canadian C. S. Lewis Journal*, no. 14 (February):1–4.
    Reprint of 1979.30.

14 EDWARDS, BRUCE [LEE], Jr. "On the Excesses of Appreciation." *CSL: The Bulletin of the New York C. S. Lewis Society* 11 (January):3–4.
    Reprint of 1979.35.

15 FISCHER, PHILIP C. Review of *They Stand Together: The Letters of C. S. Lewis to Arthur Greeves*. *Review for Religious* 39, no. 4 (July):638–639.
    "The letters reflect intimately the integrity of the man and of his previously published literary and religious works. A few things revealed within this epistolary privacy have the astringent taste of an unripe persimmon, but usually there is the homely taste of especially good apples, and sometimes the taste of a Perelandrian fruit."

16 FITZGERALD, DOROTHY HOBSON. "C. S. Lewis and Charles Williams: Differences and Similarities in the Shape of Their Thought." *CSL: The Bulletin of the New York C. S. Lewis Society* 11 (March):1–11.
    In this article Fitzgerald provides a biography of Williams. She claims that Lewis's philosophy of love was broadened and mellowed by Williams's deep understanding of human love. Lewis was also influenced

1980

by Williams's concept of substituted love, "the coinherence of all human beings with each other."

17   FORD, PAUL F[RANCES]. *Companion to Narnia.* Illustrated by Lorinda Bryan Cauley. San Francisco,: Harper & Row, 313 pp.

In an encyclopedia format, Ford lists characters, places, objects, and themes from the Chronicles of Narnia; also listed are the book(s) and the page(s) where the referenced material may be found as well as cross references to other entries. The work is designed to "help you explore the various strands that Lewis weaves into the fabric of the Chronicles—literary, religious, philosophical, mythological, homely, and personal images."

18   FREUD, JILL. "Lewis Teaches the Retarded." *Canadian C. S. Lewis Journal,* no. 16 (April):3–5.

Freud stayed at the Kilns from 1943 to 1945. During this time she found that Lewis had a great understanding of human nature. "The day-to-day conversation of a man with a first class brain and a tremendous education" was an education in itself. He built her confidence and self-esteem by making her believe she was an intelligent human being. Freud observed the great loving care Lewis displayed toward Mrs. Moore whose whole life centered around him; she absolutely adored him. Reprinted: 1983.23.

19   FRYER, W. R. "Disappointment at Cambridge?" *Canadian C. S. Lewis Journal,* no. 20 (August):1–5.

Lewis "was superhuman in the range of his knowledge and in the height of his intellectual vision . . . he was not only friendly and encouraging, but super-hospitable, gentle, ever tender." There is a suggestion in his writings of a dark, terrifying imagination, which is a weakness in his character. Also Fryer thinks Lewis had too strong a belief in the devil. It irked Lewis that his colleagues did not think enough of his scholarship and of what he had come to stand for in life for him to be given a professorship at Oxford. He probably found Cambridge disappointing also because there was too little stress on the philological and early elements in which he specialized and the university's academic policy was moving away from what he valued. Reprinted: 1983.25.

20   FUTCH, KEN. "How His World Went On: A Review Essay." *Lamp-Post of the Southern California C. S. Lewis Society* 4, no. 1 (February):1–4.

In his review of *They Stand Together: The Letters of C. S. Lewis to Arthur Greeves*, Futch considers this epistolary autobiography a delight—difficult to put down. The editing makes it more than a collection of letters: "the footnotes identify and explain, the insertions fill in gaps and discuss." In the letters one finds Jack, the inner man, speaking intimately, rather than C. S. Lewis, the public man.

21 GEIGER, WILLIAM A., Jr. "C. S. Lewis Interprets I. A. Richards." *Lamp-Post of the Southern California C. S. Lewis Society* 4, nos. 3–4 (August–November):7–12.

Lewis frequently misinterpreted Ivor Armstrong Richards because of aesthetic, personal, and philosophic differences. Lewis treated Richards's ideas negatively, quoted him in headnotes to try to transfer Richards's authority to his work, and objected to Richards's naturalism and use of literature for its therapeutic value. Lewis also "frequently misquoted Richards to further his own arguments." Lewis saw Richards as an enemy because Richards used psychology to discuss literature, while Lewis applied historical and moral approaches; Richards emphasized modern works, especially poetry, which Lewis disliked; and Lewis "saw the close reading of literary texts and the discipline required for practical criticism as a modern substitute for theological exegesis and moral discipline."

22 GIBSON, EVAN K. *C. S. Lewis, Spinner of Tales: A Guide to His Fiction.* Washington, D.C.: Christian University Press, 284 pp.

Gibson's book is intended for the ordinary reader who wants to understand the ethical and theological implications of Lewis's fiction. Gibson summarizes each work of fiction and explains Lewis's technique, the structure of the work, and the ethical and theological ideas present. He describes elements of Lewis's style such as the use of personal narrative, concrete images, vivid characterization, and logical structure. He details the recurrent ideas in Lewis's fiction: the nature of divinity—God's incomprehensible yet self-revealing and approachable nature; and man's relationship to God—man must develop the virtues of obedience, hope, and love to carry out God's purpose.

23 GRIFFIN, EMILIE. "C. S. Lewis on Conversion." *CSL: The Bulletin of the New York C. S. Lewis Society* 11 (April):1–8.

The principal books that contain Lewis's thoughts on conversion are *Surprised by Joy, The Pilgrim's Regress,* and *Mere Christianity.* He sees the conversion process involving two phases: the emotional and spiritual and the intellectual. Lewis's rational mind led him to a point where he knew a good case could be made both for and against the existence of God. His experiences of Joy and kinship with "the minds and hearts of writers and poets of every age," especially Arthur Greeves and George MacDonald, challenged his unbelief. Lewis depicts conversion as a homecoming, a transformation, a spiritual evolution, a good inflection, and an invasion.

24 ———. *Turning: Reflections on the Experience of Conversion.* Garden City, N.Y.: Doubleday, 189 pp. passim.

Lewis, Bede Griffiths, and Thomas Merton's stories of personal encounters with God influenced Griffin's own conversion. They showed it was possible to be a Christian and an intellectual at the same time as all the writers had vigorous imaginations and metaphorical styles of thought. The stages in the conversion experience are desire, dialectic, struggle, and surrender. Lewis lived out an ontological proof of desire by testing earthly pleasures to see whether they would satisfy the longing he felt. The central dialectic issue for him was not God's existence but "the question of what kind of force one might be called upon to deal with if one entertained the possibility of the invisible universe." During the struggle phase Lewis felt surrounded; God, through Lewis's believing friends, began to close in. After his surrender, Lewis experienced a complete sense of freedom. Lewis's life of charity is an example of how Christianity should become inward, deep, and real.

25 HALLAN, LEILA. "The Problem of Pain and Pleasure: A Look at *The Problem of Pain* by C. S. Lewis." *Chronicle of the Portland C. S. Lewis Society* 9, no. 3 (July–September):2–5.

Three themes in the book are the glory of God, the sinfulness of man, and man's rightful place. Lewis's description of God's glory is reverent and awe inspired. He says that sin is man choosing himself over God. Although man is sinful, he was created to adore and enjoy God, acts that lead to Joy. The doctrine that God perfects us through suffering is credible although not necessarily palatable.

26 HELFRICH, JOHN [W.]. "Inner Rings and C. S. Lewis." *CSL: The Bulletin of the New York C. S. Lewis Society* 11 (July):1–3.

Lewis's warnings against inner rings are found in the essay "The Inner Ring" published in *The Weight of Glory*.

27 HOLLWITZ, JOHN CHARLES. "The Mythopoeic Art of C. S. Lewis." Ph.D dissertation, Northwestern University, 225 pp.

Jung's technique of amplification is used to follow images in the Ransom Trilogy to gain access to their numinous meaning. Lewis uses transformation images from alchemy and initiation rituals as well as the mythology of Hermes, Perseus, Dionysos, and Demeter. In *Out of the Silent Planet* he creates a masculine world and explores its elemental *phallos*. The purpose of Ransom's journey is "to be transformed, made wholly masculine within the world of Mars." In *Perelandra* the symbolism indicates a redemption of the feminine, represented by the Green Lady and the planet itself, and an acceptance of the feminine within Lewis's masculine Christianity. The Trilogy shows a reversal of Lewis's theological position with the glorification of the feminine and the subservience of men. Jung felt the image of the Trinity was distorted because it left out a fourth element, *eros* (nature and sexuality). In *Perelandra* "Ransom unites the two sides of the Christian spirit, *logos* and *eros*, masculine and feminine." In *That Hideous Strength* Lewis further modifies his view of the feminine by incorporating the sexual element of *eros*. In the novel, Jane "is equivalent to Perceval, and the Grail that she attains is the vessel of her own femininity in both its maternal and erotic aspects."

28   HOWARD, THOMAS. *The Achievement of C. S. Lewis*. Wheaton, Ill.: Harold Shaw, 193 pp.

The themes of the Chronicles of Narnia are women as receptive to the divine; the sheer pleasure of the senses; great things hanging on seemingly insignificant decisions; and duty requiring daunting tasks to be done. *Out of the Silent Planet* displays themes of decency and duty; moral questions; charity enabling one to greet other selves; and pleasure as complete only when it is remembered. In *Perelandra* the following themes occur: "acceptance of the given, and submission to it, is the key to contentment"; obedience is synonymous with freedom and maturity; "the distinction between flesh and spirit, nature and supernature, history and myth, is only a provisional and contingent one." *That Hideous Strength* depicts the themes of marriage as central; diabolical horrors and chaos result from the disjuncture of mind and body; human flesh is the focal point because humans have a shared nature of animality and rationality and because "the Incarnation focused the drama forever in this human flesh." The central idea of *Till We Have Faces* is that the only way to freedom is to surrender to the love of the gods. Themes depicted in the novel are the intrusion of the gods into the self; Orual's missing all the signs; love turning into tyranny and hate; "the pellucid wisdom of the Greeks versus the dark and bloody wisdom of the barbarian cult"; the transfiguring process; and *Sehnsucht*. Reprinted in part: 1981.30.

29   HUGHES, LARRY RAYMOND. "The World View of C. S. Lewis Implicit in His Religious Writings." Ph.D. dissertation, Oklahoma State University, 143 pp.

Lewis felt that religious language ranged between the ordinary and the poetical and had significance, meaning, and truth. He felt that the laws of nature, man's rationality, and the moral law indicate an ultimate objective reality in the universe: God. He stated that God is above space–time, is the core of all existence, and is a person. Lewis believed that the desire for knowledge is implanted in man by God and points to God. Man gains knowledge through reason, experience, and authority. Man fulfills his God capacity by self-surrender, which is aided by the presence and persistence of pain, and then by becoming a unique person in the proper setting of community. He emphasizes the objective reality of Christianity as well as its practical applications. Lewis's worldview has four key thoughts: (1) religious language must be flexible; (2) religious truth must be accepted first in order to be understood and proved; (3) there are two levels of reality, supernature and nature, and communication between the two comes from higher to lower (transposition); and (4) experience and thinking are viable means of understanding reality. These four principles are methodological rather than metaphysical in nature and are

1980

defensive, or apologetic, in tone. While Lewis's writings are helpful in pointing toward truth and furnish creative explanations of accepted truth, they do not provide proofs for foundational truths.

30 HUTTAR, CHARLES A. "The Heresy of Allegorizing Narnia: A Rejoinder." *CSL: The Bulletin of the New York C. S. Lewis Society* 11 (January):1–3.

In this response to Morrison's article [1979.77], Huttar presents three propositions regarding allegory. One may read allegory into a work even though the work is more than an allegory. Allegory is used by an author to point to something else, while myth cannot be decoded. Allegory is ideologically neutral, while myth affirms a reality beyond the physical world and reason. With this understanding, the Chronicles of Narnia should not be considered allegorical. Aslan is not Christ, the redeemer, but rather the Son of God in an "other world."

31 LINDSKOOG, KATHRYN [ANN]. "The Gift of Dreams." *Canadian C. S. Lewis Journal*, no. 20 (August):6–7.

Reprint of 1979.64.

32 LINDVALL, TERRENCE ROY. "C.S. Lewis' Theory of Communication." Ph.D. dissertation, University of Southern California, 598 pp.

Lewis's writings "offer the basis for a reasonable and ethical theory of human discourse." His philosophy of communication is founded on his views of God as the one true Fact, humans as rational creatures, the reality of the supernatural world revealed through the natural world, and knowledge as acquired through experience, authority, reason, and imagination. Basic concepts in Lewis's theory of communication are the dialogical relationship between author and audience, lucidity and clarity of expression, a phenomenological hermeneutic with humility and receptivity, the centrality of language, and a system of shared values. His apologetic communications adhere to these principles; they are clear and compelling and "defend fundamental principles of belief and morality." In his fictive communication, he addresses the imagination that he felt gave impetus to move the will. *That Hideous Strength* illustrates Lewis's communication theory by showing readers a true vision through mythopoeic and metaphorical elements; by challenging the reader through the use of satire, hyperbole, irony, humor, and the numinous; by expressing in a fictional form two hermeneutic modes of receiving the other in communication; by demonstrating "the role of language as the primary mode of reasonable life"; and by depicting the axiological dimension of human behavior.

33 McGOVERN, EUGENE. "An Objection to Lewis's Treatment of *Storge*." *CSL: The Bulletin of the New York C. S. Lewis Society* 11 (July):3–5.

Lewis does not pay enough attention to the love between parents and children, both in his apologetic works and in his fiction. This is due to Lewis's lack of a strong relationship with his own parents and his not having children. See response, 1980.6.

34 MICHAEL, SISTER BRENDA. "C. S. Lewis in the Company of All the Saints." *CSL: The Bulletin of the New York C. S. Lewis Society* 12 (December):3–4.

Lewis is included in the Martyrology for November 22nd because he is an ordinary person who was able to write about Christianity with openness in communicating his experiences and with reticence so as not to impose his own pattern of development on others.

35 MILWARD, PETER. "A Judgment Judged—C. S. Lewis on the More-Tyndale Controversy." *Moreana* 64:28–36.

Lewis's critique of the More–Tyndale controversy in *English Literature of the Sixteenth Century Excluding Drama* is one-sided. He overlooks More's development of rational arguments and concentrates on More's style. More was in deadly earnest, trying to "prove his opponents are both heretics (in faith) and fools (in reason)," while Lewis sees only a lack of "'the joyous, lyric quality'" discernible in Tyndale. More did not misunderstand his opponents' position as Lewis states; rather, More's aim is to show that their view is a travesty of the reality he perceives.

36 MUSACCHIO, GEORGE. "Courting Mnemosyne: Lewis' Reading Practices in His Letters to Greeves." *Lamp-Post of the Southern California C. S. Lewis Society* 4, no. 2 (May):5–6.

They Stand Together shows how Lewis developed his reading program. He read widely, he discriminated between causal reading and serious literature, he developed different categories of literature for different reading occasions, he reread books many times, and he made extensive annotations and indexes in his books.

37 NEULEIB, JANICE [WITHERSPOON]. "Love's Alchemy: Jane in *That Hideous Strength*." *Mythlore* 7 (March):16–17,19.

Jane and Mark represent what Lewis saw as the chief ills of fallen human nature: "the first, a desire for independence at all costs, including one's relationship with God; the second, a will to power which ignores all morality." At the end of the novel both find Charitas; Jane submits to Mark only because he has humbled himself. "Jane relinquishes selfishness, not self."

38 NOLAN, CHARLES J., JR. "*That Hideous Strength*: Antidote to Modernism." *CSL: The Bulletin of the New York C. S. Lewis Society* 11 (July):5–6.

Lewis's traditional views oppose modernism. He sees man as a social

1980

animal, with marriage as the focal point. He believes man is created by God, in order to please Him. He "affirms his belief in an historical and cultural past by using English legend."

39 PATTERSON, NANCY-LOU. "An Appreciation of Pauline Baynes." *Mythlore* 7 (Autumn):3–5.
Patterson describes Baynes's illustrations for the Chronicles of Narnia, some of Tolkien's work, and other fiction.

40 ———. "The Host of Heaven: Astrological and Other Images of Divinity in the Fantasies of C. S. Lewis." *Mythlore* 7 (Autumn):19–29; (Winter 1981):13–21.
Lewis uses Mesopotamian, Greek, Roman, and Norse mythology, filtered through the medieval Christian culture, in his fiction. The article presents Lewis's description of the medieval model of the planets from *The Discarded Image*, along with his treatment of planetary symbolism in his interplanetary trilogy. It describes the mythological motifs in the Trilogy and the divine personalities with which the planets are associated. Patterson discusses the images of stars, Dionysus/Bacchus, and Longaevi in the Chronicles of Narnia and describes the character of Cupid in *Till We Have Faces*.

41 PHELPS, RUSS A. "*Mother Hubberds Tale* and *The Last Battle*." *CSL: The Bulletin of the New York C. S. Lewis Society* 11 (April):9–10.
Aesop and Spenser were the sources for Lewis's *The Last Battle*. Aesop has two stories in which an ass wears a lion skin. Spenser in *Mother Hubberds Tale* has an ape, wearing a lion skin, and a fox, who is the brains behind him, taking over the kingdom from the true ruler, the lion. "Lewis took the ass from Aesop, the ape from Spenser, altered their characters, and came up with the anti-Aslan and the false prophet who announces him."

42 PHILIP, PETER. "South African View." *Canadian C. S. Lewis Journal*, no. 17 (May):5–7.
Philip was a pupil of Lewis. Lewis was jovial and in good humor most of the time. "I cannot say that I ever got close to him or that I ever felt relaxed in his company. I was too immature to meet him on his own ground, and he was too cultivated to be able to come down to mine." Lewis's most impressive quality was his lucidity. He could be very helpful and understanding. Reprinted: 1983.52.

43 PIEPER, JOSEF. "On the Use of Plain Language in Philosophy." *Lamp-Post of the Southern California C. S. Lewis Society* 4, no. 2 (May):2–4.
Lewis's writing in *The Problem of Pain* is a graphic example of the use of plain language in philosophy. Plain language guarantees the speaker's cred-

ibility, gives objective meaning, respects the reader as a partner in dialogue, and does not disguise the unfathomable meaning of reality.

44   PILE, JOAN B. "The Dangling Slipper." *Canadian C. S. Lewis Journal*, no. 23 (November):1–3.

Lewis was kind to Pile at a difficult time in her life. Reprinted: 1983.53.

45   PITTER, RUTH. "Poet to Poet." *Canadian C. S. Lewis Journal*, no. 18 (June):3–7.

Lewis was a good poet-craftsman and word master rather than an inspired poet. In his lectures and broadcast talks "it was a pleasure to hear his splendid voice, never a dull phrase, and hardly any notes, and he looked straight at you the whole time." Personally, Lewis "was very touching . . . very simple and useful." Reprinted: 1983.54.

46   RAMSHAW, WALTER. "Reflections on *Reflections on the Psalms*." *CSL: The Bulletin of the New York C. S. Lewis Society* 11 (September):1–7.

In the first three-quarters of the work Lewis explains recurrent themes in the Psalms, explores the cultural differences between us and the Israelites, and reconciles us to much in the Psalms that is strange. In the last quarter, he explains the way in which Christians use the Psalms. Lewis identifies the double meanings behind Psalm 110. Many examples of Lewis's piety show through in this work.

47   REDDY, ALBERT F. "*Till We Have Faces*: 'An Epistle to the Greeks.'" *Mosaic* 13, no. 3–4 (Summer):153–164.

Till We Have Faces is a story about a love that becomes a complicated form of hatred through jealousy. Lewis re-creates an intellectual climate to dramatize "the recurring conflict between the spirit of rationalism and traditional belief." He presents a defense of primitive religion, emphasizes the limits of reason, and shows the validity of romantic longing. His "purpose is to present an imaginative demonstration of the validity of myth."

48   Review of *They Stand Together: The Letters of C. S. Lewis to Arthur Greeves*. *Choice* 16 (February):1585.

The letters reveal much of Lewis's personal life, including his reading, and demonstrate his love of nature and Ireland.

49   Review of *They Stand Together: The Letters of C. S. Lewis to Arthur Greeves*. *New Yorker* 56 (5 May):174–175.

"Lewis wrote letters as well as he wrote everything else, and was never condescending."

1980

50 ROOK, ALAN. "The Butcher." *Canadian C. S. Lewis Journal* no. 14 (February):6–7.
    Reprint of 1979.88. Reprinted: 1983.61.

51 SAMMONS, MARTHA C. "Christian Doctrines 'Transposed' in C. S. Lewis' *Till We Have Faces*." *Mythlore* 7 (March):31–35.
    Lewis takes key biblical doctrines of the Fall, redemption, the relationship between man and God, and man's glorious potential and restates them in new terms.

52 ———. *A Guide through C. S. Lewis' Space Trilogy*. Westchester, Ill.: Cornerstone Books, 189 pp.
    Sammons examines Lewis's sources for the Space Trilogy; she details the types of science fiction he liked and that influenced him as well as the types he disliked. She summarizes the myths told in the Trilogy and compares these with detailed descriptions of Lewis's sources—the medieval model of the universe, the Arthurian legend, and the Bible. Scientism, the idea that science or technology can solve all man's problems, and myth, which Lewis said conveys realities that cannot be known in any other way, are thematic elements in the Trilogy. Sammons details Lewis's view of the individual and his or her relationship to God and purpose in the universe. The appendixes provide a summary of the plot of each book in the Trilogy; a description of the languages Lewis invented along with definitions of various words; and "A Dictionary of Deep Heaven," listing characters and terms used in the Trilogy, including the book where the name or term appears.

53 SAYER, GEORGE. "C. S. Lewis's *Dymer*." *Seven: An Anglo-American Literary Review* 1:94–116.
    When Lewis wrote *Dymer* he was "in full flight from his romantic sensibility." The main subject of *Dymer* is the temptation of fantasies of love, lust, and power. Lewis contended that "the love dream made a man incapable of real love; the hero dream made him a coward."

54 SCAER, DAVID P. "C. S. Lewis on Women Priests." *Concordia Theological Quarterly* 44 (January):55–59.
    Hoffecker and Timmerman's article [1978.16] analyzes Lewis's opposition to women priests. Lewis held that a woman cannot represent God to the people since God has taught us to refer to Him in the male gender. He argues that God is masculine in His relationship to the church, which is feminine. Lutherans have little difficulty in agreeing with his liturgical posture and in accepting the masculine–feminine relationship of God to the church. Lewis provides a satisfactory rationale for the prohibitions against women clergy.

55 SCHAKEL, PETER J. "A Retelling within a Myth Retold: The Priest of Essur and Lewisian Mythopoetics." *Mythlore* 9, no. 4 (Winter):10–12.

 Lewis felt compelled to retell the Cupid and Psyche myth in *Till We Have Faces* because Apuleius's tale fails to imbue it with the imaginative and numinous qualities essential to myth. The story told by the Priest of Essur to Orual is the middle step between Apuleius and Lewis. The Priest's tale emphasizes the theme of sacrifice, which Apuleius missed. In the novel, Lewis "points beyond pagan sacrifice to what it prefigures, the full embodiment of this theme in Christianity." The novel is lifted above Apuleius's and the Priest's tales because it unites the theme of sacrifice with the theme of love; the sacrifice in the novel is the unselfish giving of individuals for others.

56 SCHOFIELD, STEPHEN. "Corrections." *Canadian C. S. Lewis Journal*, no. 13 (January):6.

 The blurb on Hooper's book *Past Watchful Dragons* declaring him the sole biographer of Lewis, was written by the publisher, Macmillan, and not by Hooper as was alleged in 1979.100.

57 ———. "Lewis and (North) Americans." *Canadian C. S. Lewis Journal*, no. 22 (October):7.

 Lewis was prejudiced against Americans because, while he believed in democracy, he felt the monarchy provides nourishment to the human spirit. Americans, without a monarchy, honor millionaires, movie stars, and gangsters. Reprinted in part: 1983.68; 1984.60.

58 ———. "Lewis Asked Hooper to Sign." *Canadian C. S. Lewis Journal*, no. 16 (April):8–9.

 Walter Hooper's handwriting is similar to Lewis's. Hooper says Lewis noticed this fact and asked him to sign Lewis's name to his letters. This is noteworthy because for all the years Warren was his brother's secretary he always submitted letters to Lewis for his signature.

59 ———. "Where?" *Canadian C. S. Lewis Journal,* no. 20 (August):9.

 Hooper says he and Lewis corresponded for ten years but he has not deposited any of his letters from Lewis with the Bodleian Library, as he has urged others to do.

60 SHAW, MARK. "Is There Salvation Outside the Christian Faith?" *East Africa Journal of Evangelical Theology* 2, no. 2:42–62.

 Lewis believed in the possibility of salvation outside the Christian faith. He felt that honest rejection of Christ would be forgiven. He felt the experience of Joy was God's way of drawing people to Himself. He believed in pur-

1980

gatory as preparation for entrance into God's presence. The arguments for salvation outside the Christian faith offered by Lewis and others, since they are made outside of Scripture, are not convincing.

61   SLACK, MICHAEL D. "Sehnsucht and the Platonic Eros in *Dymer*." *CSL: The Bulletin of the New York C. S. Lewis Society* 11 (August):3–7.
     Sehnsucht in *Dymer* is eros, explained by Plato as the desire for the beautiful or the good, through which man attempts to obtain immortality. Dymer pursues lesser reflections of beauty and goodness until, governed by the rational, he undergoes a four-stage transformation and finally unites with the Form Beauty in the eternal world.

62   STEWART, D[AVID] H. "What Lewis Really Did in *That Hideous Strength*." *Modern Fiction Studies* 26, no. 2 (Summer):248–254.
     The structure of the novel "resolves the issues that the action and characters raise." The parallel settings of the brainwashing room at Belbury and the marriage chamber at St. Anne's, both works of art, convey Lewis's message that life is preferred to art. The parallels and symmetry between the chapters, Lewis's use of the terms *elasticity* and *inflexibility*, and the time frame of the novel are all ways he criticizes modernism and offers an alternative to it. Lewis's answers to modernism, "his theories of obedience, decorum, and formal order," are liberating.

63   STOCK, R. D. "The Tao and the Objective Room: A Pattern in C. S. Lewis's Novels." *Christian Scholar's Review* 9:256–260.
     Lewis's chief antagonists are the objectivists who repudiate the natural law and view man as an object to be manipulated. The Ransom Trilogy and *Till We Have Faces* show the difference between the Tao and objectivism. Some of Lewis's characters know the natural law and have appropriate, stock responses. Some characters, like Ransom and the Lady in *Perelandra*, have superficial responses because they do not fully understand their experiences but yield better responses when they grasp their situation more intelligently. Some characters, like Weston and Frost, have sophistical responses related to objectivism, which are the consequence of a twisted code of values. And some characters, like Jane and Mark in *That Hideous Strength* and Orual in *Till We Have Faces*, come to the Straight Path.

64   THOMSON, PATRICIA. "The Academic Influence of C. S. Lewis." *Canadian C. S. Lewis Society*, no. 21 (September):1–4.
     Thomson, a pupil of Lewis, saw him as a man of formidable learning who "possessed a Johnsonian power of turning knowledge into wisdom." He encouraged students to form their own opinions. Reprinted: 1983.2. 65

65   WAIN, JOHN. "C. S. Lewis." *American Scholar* 50 (Winter):73–80.
     Lewis lived by the values and customs of Edwardian England and
defended these values. In "Our English Syllabus" Lewis's "main argument is
that studying a literature is like working over a piece of natural woodland and
seeing what actually grows there." Lewis believed learning needed to start
with a broad base to prevent parochiality, faddishness, and loss of perspective.
He worked hardest to instill intellectual integrity in his pupils. His teaching
method was forensic and disputatious, and in his lectures he set out to impart
information. Reprinted: 1981.72, 73.

66   WERTZ, SHARON. "C. S. Lewis—Down South: Hattiesburg Festival."
     Canadian C. S. Lewis Journal, no. 17 (May):1–4.
     Brooks Wester and Charles Moorman say Lewis loved argument. His
appeal is due to the clarity with which he explained complex theological ideas.

67   WILLIS, JOHN [RANDOLPH]. "The Eldila in the Space Trilogy." *CSL: The
     Bulletin of the New York C. S. Lewis Society* 11 (February):1–5.
     Lewis's principal point in the Trilogy is that outer space is not a vacuum
but "that it is better described as Deep Heaven which is populated by innu-
merable benign beings, utterly devoted to Maleldil and deeply concerned
about the fate of human beings on this planet."

68   WISSLER, STEVEN PAUL. "C. S. Lewis on Work." *Lamp-Post of the
     Southern California C. S. Lewis Society* 4, nos. 3–4 (August–November):2–6.
     Lewis hated idleness and had an ordered pattern of existence. He was
pushed on by his intellectual vigor, ambition, sense of duty, and desire for aesthetic experience. Lewis felt "the ultimate value of work is measured by God
and His purposes for man." He viewed human action as "'divinely guaranteed,
and therefore, ruthless.'" He believed that the work process itself is a reflection of preexisting eternal beauty and wisdom. He saw a healthy synthesis
between work and leisure. He felt that work is proper to man's physical nature
in the same way contemplation is proper to our rational nature. See second
part of the article 1981.78.

1981

1   ANDERSON, KATHERINE. "Christianity, a Personal Religion: C. S. Lewis."
     In "Christian Concepts and Doctrine in Selected Works of Science Fiction."
     Ph.D. dissertation, University of Denver, pp. 155–284.
     The Space Trilogy is "united by the character of Ransom, with the
themes of moral reeducation, the quest, and Lewis's 'silent planet' myth." The
purpose of *Out of the Silent Planet* is to warn against the evils represented by
Weston, to familiarize readers with ideas represented by the *hnau* societies on

1981

Malacandra, and to change the conceptions of space to that of heaven. In *Perelandra* Lewis stresses the need for obedience to God. In both these novels, Ransom's development is presented as a model of the way Christians need to develop. *That Hideous Strength* is filled with Arthurian, the silent planet, and Christian myths. Lewis also includes "his ideas of the proper attitude towards animals, the role of women in marriage, and the ideal community." This novel focuses on the reeducation of Mark and Jane rather than of Ransom.

2   BECKER, JOAN QUALL. "Patterns of Guilt and Grace in the Development and Function of Character in C. S. Lewis's Romances." Ph.D. dissertation, University of Washington, 275 pp.
     Lewis uses his protagonist to illustrate patterns of guilt and grace. His "protagonists, through their respective quests, grow to discover what it means to sin, to repent verbally and/or behaviorally, and to receive a better or redeemed identity as a result of obeying powers of grace." He also uses them to demonstrate "the compelling nature of grace by showing its desirability." In the Chronicles of Narnia "Lewis's close adherence to the romance form keeps characterization intimately bound" to the descent pattern of the protagonists' guilt and the ascent pattern of Aslan's grace. The characters are illustrative and serve the plot, but are highly realistic in their childlike responses. Aslan is the most complex character, mainly because Lewis "uses him as the main carrier of the ascent pattern, [and] imbues him with paradoxes and powers." Ransom is depicted in highly realistic terms in *Perelandra* but in *That Hideous Strength* realism is suggested more than realized. In the Space Trilogy as a whole, complexity is derived from the tension between the nature of guilt and grace rather than from characterization. "In emphasizing aspects of the numinous Lewis places the availability of grace and its powers of restoration in the central position structurally so far as theme and form are concerned." In *Till We Have Faces* Orual "is both an exception to, as well as a culmination of, Lewis's development of character." Her complexity results from the disparity between her self-understanding and her intelligence. Others in the novel have greater complexity than Lewis's earlier characters but still fulfill mythic, romantic, or realistic functions. "Lewis selected a form in which he could explore particular ideas associated with universal verities about human beings and supernatural reality rather than the particular idiosyncrasies of an individual."

3   BELA, TERESA. "The Critical Principles of C. S. Lewis." *Prace Historycznoliterackie Z. 42*, no. 575:69–84.
     Lewis's critical creed has two seemingly contradictory characteristics— classical and romantic. He is classical in his view of literature as communicating true reality that should delight and teach the reader. He viewed the critic's role as that of "removing obstacles to an appreciation and understanding of the text" by attending to both the meaning and the form of the work. He

is romantic in his "predilection for the marvelous, the magic, for fairy tales, adventures, chivalry" in subject matter and in the metaphysical dimensions of his criticism.

4   BOARDMAN, PHILLIP C. "Lewis, Tolkien and Williams in the Modern Authors Collection at the University of Nevada, Reno Campus." *Christianity and Literature* 30, no. 2 (Winter):110–112.

The collection holds about 225 items of Lewis's works, including many successive editions of his books. Also included are items available in reprint locations other than those listed in Hooper's bibliography and unusual items such as signed copies, first editions, Braille editions, and audio cassettes.

5   BUDZIEN, GREGORY. "An Un-Christian Aspect of *Mere Christianity.*" *Canadian C. S. Lewis Journal*, no. 35–36 (November–December):1, 3–9.

Lewis says it is " 'perfectly right for a Christian judge to sentence a man to death or a Christian soldier to kill an enemy.' " Budzien believes Lewis is wrong to justify killing simply because Christ never told soldiers not to do so; rather we should follow Christ's example—He never killed. For Lewis to say a Christian soldier can kill is heinous and results in the sacrifice of an individual to society. "Lewis' ideas on 'justifiable killing' are not only incorrect in themselves, but are easily misapplied or distorted, giving us the ever-vengeful world we live in today." See response, 1981.63.

6   CARNELL, CORBIN S[COTT]. "Ransom in Perelandra: Jungian Hero?" *Mythlore* 8 (Summer):9–10.

Lewis's fiction reflects certain Jungian categories. Ransom undergoes "a process of individuation which includes initiation, trials, suffering, and other aspects of the psychoanalytic 'monomyth.' " Also, Lewis depicts in his fiction Jung's theory of personality, which emphasizes interdependence and mutual giving by the exchange of unlike gifts. Jung's theory of synchronicity helps illuminate the significance of miracles in Lewis's fiction. Reprinted: 1981.7.

7   ———. "Ransom in C. S. Lewis' *Perelandra* as Hero in Transformation: Notes toward a Jungian Reading of the Novel." *Studies in the Literary Imagination* 14, no. 2 (Fall):67–71.

Reprint of 1981.6.

8   CHRISTENSEN, MICHAEL [J.]. "On Lizards and Stallions." *CSL: The Bulletin of the New York C. S. Lewis Society* 12 (February):1–5.

The Great Divorce is a mythological fantasy in which there are no simple one-to-one correspondences between symbols and meanings. The passage in the novel in which the red lizard of lust is killed and becomes the beautiful white stallion means one must give up a false old self to gain a true new self fit for heaven.

1981

9   CLASPER, PAUL. "C. S. Lewis's Contribution to a 'Missionary Theology':
An Asian Perspective." *Ching Feng* 24, no. 4 (December):203–214.
Reprint of 1981.10. Reprinted: 1982.9.

10   ———. "C. S. Lewis's Contribution to a 'Missionary Theology': An Asian
Perspective." *CSL: The Bulletin of the New York C. S. Lewis Society* 12
(July):1–6.
Lewis's work is a constructive help to people in Asia concerned with
missionary theology. Lewis helps one see that Christianity leads to an appreciation of the universal mythical heritage. His emphasis on the common elements in Christianity shows how the Church can allow diversity of expression.
His insights into the temptations of the devil clarify the inner and outer power
struggles of the times. Lewis's reading of the Bible avoids the extremes of literalism and of demythologization and shows the Bible to be the source of
truth for the Christian community. His life is a model of the spiritual director
who gives guidance through conversation, with special attention to prayer. His
life also shows an "unfrantic learning-listening, relational-availability" that is
important for those in Asia who want to work in the mode of missionary theology. Reprinted: 1981.9; 1982.9.

11   COMO, JAMES [T.]. "Broadening the Lewisian Context: Some Suggestions."
CSL: The Bulletin of the New York C. S. Lewis Society 12 (January):11–15.
The community of Lewis scholars, both professional and amateur, fre-
quently fail to read Lewis in the spirit in which he wrote and therefore invite
the rational opposition to reject him. Some lines of Lewis scholarship that
should be developed are the influence on him of Rudolf Otto's *The Idea of the
Holy* (London: Oxford University Press, 1923) and Samuel Alexander's
Space, Time and Deity (The Gifford Lectures at Glasgow 1916–1918.
London: Macmillan, 1920), his similarities with other authors, and the effect
of odd elements in his life and mind on his writings.

12   COVINGTON, MICHAEL A. "C. S. Lewis as a Semanticist." *CSL: The
Bulletin of the New York C. S. Lewis Society* 13 (November):1–6.
In *Studies in Words* Lewis induced two major principles. The principle
of the insulating power of the context is the ability to sort through the many
senses attached to a sound or spelling and choose the appropriate one. The
second principle is the necessity of the distinction between the speaker's
meaning and the word's meaning to determine the particular meaning of a
word at a particular time. Lewis observes that when an author has to explain
what a word means, he or she is not using it in its most common sense and
that status words have become moralized.

140

13 CUNNINGHAM, VALENTINE. "Lewis, Clive Staples 1898–1963." In *Makers of Modern Culture*. Edited by Justin Winthe. New York: Facts on File, pp. 306–307.

"Lewis's forte was expository prose." He favored modes of persuasion for a mass audience. In his apologetics he proved little because illustrations masqueraded as evidence. Of his theological arguments, only transposition, "that 'higher' systems sometimes have to use 'lower' systems for their expression," has worn well. His allegorical fictions are his most successful works.

14 DANIEL, JERRY [L.]. "Lewis and Chesterton: The Smell of Dew and Thunder." *CSL: The Bulletin of the New York C. S. Lewis Society* 12 (September):1–16.

Lewis and Chesterton both saw life as a mystery and they evoke a sense of wonder for which the modern world has lost its capacity. Both find that "the real beauty of this world is the fact that there is something more than this world." They use the image of the dance to describe the world because it expresses joy and involves order and a plan. Chesterton communicates his enthusiasm more explicitly than Lewis. Lewis is more restrained; his mental and emotional power is carefully directed and controlled. The emphasis on wonder leads to the great moral truth of gratitude. Both men wrote works of gratitude, not works of despair. The laughter and sense of fun that pervade their works are a natural outgrowth of their relationship with God.

15 DERRICK, CHRISTOPHER. *C. S. Lewis and the Church of Rome: A Study in Proto-Ecumenism*. San Francisco: Ignatius Press, 225 pp.

"Why didn't Lewis become a Roman Catholic?" While he had an emotional and imaginative sympathy toward Catholicism, especially toward its liturgical paganism and the literature of Catholic centuries, he also had a sharp emotional revulsion from it, stemming from his Ulster-Protestant background. Lewis implied that Catholicism "exaggerates by pressing the principle of incarnation or actuality too far." In his own Christology, he emphasized Christ's deity rather than humanity. He "circled cautiously round two critical and Catholic concepts, not fully accepting and not fully rejecting either of them": the development of doctrine and the concept of the teaching Church. He came close to Catholicism in seeing the need for orthodoxy and for distinguishing true doctrines from learned opinions and heresy. Lewis saw denominational divisions as a great moral evil but he evaded the question of how they came into existence. He had a pioneering commitment to ecumenism, especially in the sense of not engaging in denominational controversy, with his concept of "mere Christianity." However, in generalizing from the denominations to their Highest Common Factor, Lewis is guilty of a way of thinking he repudiated elsewhere when he stated that prescinding differences between particulars would lead not to a more universal truth but to unreality. Derrick

1981

believes that by becoming a Catholic, Lewis would have resolved his inner conflicts and would have been an even stronger and more influential writer. See response, 1982.13.

16   EDMONDS, E. L. "'Don't Call Me Sir, Edmonds, I'm Not a Sir.'" *Canadian C. S. Lewis Journal*, no. 29–30 (May–June):1–9.
      Edmonds was a pupil of Lewis. Lewis was critical but never cynical or sarcastic. "His own frequent change of intellectual stance taught me one very valuable lesson, namely that no one should be regarded as an absolute authority." His lectures were a joy. Lewis's and Tolkien's common public school background gave them a boyish loyalty to each other, is one reason Lewis was attracted to the knights of King Arthur and Tolkien to the heroes of the saga, and explains why both were predisposed to the art of fabling, "where good and evil can always be suitably anthropomorphized." Reprinted: 1983.17.

17   EDWARDS, BRUCE LEE, Jr. "A Rhetoric of Reading: A Study of C. S. Lewis's Approach to the Written Text." Ph.D. dissertation, University of Texas at Austin, 226 pp.
      Contemporary literary criticism—New Criticism, deconstruction, reader-response criticism, and dialectical criticism—tends to emphasize one component of the reading/writing process (author, text, reader) over the others. Lewis felt the purpose of literature was to take the reader outside him- or herself, and to do so it must have an objective textual status. He believed that the most appropriate way of reading was to study things outside the text, compare the text to other works, and to immerse oneself in its period; thereby one can reenter the text with eyes more like a native. Lewis also stated that to treat a text with integrity, one must first determine the author's intention through his or her own testimony, the comparative study of his or her work, and its historical context, rather than psychoanalyzing the author or trying to reconstruct his or her creative process. Lewis "saw the reader as a willing participant in the literary process, one who 'makes meaning' by confronting a text which an author has intended; the interaction of the reader with the text . . . yields a particular aesthetic experience." Lewis's own critical stance is rehabilitative; his strategy is to keep current critical dogma at arm's length, to identify prevailing orthodoxy that causes an author to be ignored, and then to provide an alternative paradigm to account for the author's achievement. His understanding of literacy is helpful for the teaching of composition; the beginning writer must acknowledge the objective status of his or her text and must have an intention and make it real in the text for others to perceive and understand. Lewis provides a legitimate rhetoric of literacy because he maintains a balance between the components of discourse and takes into account their grammatical, psychological, and sociological dimensions. Revised for publication: 1986.13.

18 ELGIN, DON D. "C. S. Lewis and the Romantic Novel." *CSL: The Bulletin of the New York C. S. Lewis Society* 12 (April):1–5.

Lewis created a new literary form, the romantic novel, that "violated the tradition of formal realism which had been the basis for the growth of the novel." He sees myth as an element of humankind that contains universal truth and aids reality by picture making. His theory of literature evolves from this idea of myth and is basically romantic; he sees reality as supra-rational, eternal, and ineffably good. Lewis replaced realism and science, which is the myth embodying realism, with an orthodox Christianity and sought to create "an inner truth which was often strange and fanciful but which was also inherently more faithful to reality than objective reality had ever been."

19 ———. "True and False Myth in C. S. Lewis' *Till We Have Faces.*" *South Central Bulletin* 41, no. 4 (Winter):98–101.

Lewis portrays Orual, Fox, and Bardia as attractively rational and Ungit as repulsively mystical. When the characters reveal, in the stunning conclusion, that Ungit's way represents true myth and Orual's false, Lewis establishes the nature and demands of the Christian God.

20 FITZGERALD, DOROTHY HOBSON. "Themes of Joy and Substitution in the Works of C. S. Lewis and Charles Williams." *CSL: The Bulletin of the New York C. S. Lewis Society* 12 (January):1–9.

The theme of Williams's *Descent into Hell* (London: Faber & Faber, 1937) is substitution, in which someone takes on another person's burden and by doing so finds joy. Lewis, in *Till We Have Faces*, has a more complex use of this theme, involving a double act of exchange between Orual and Psyche.

21 FITZPATRICK, JOHN. "Lewis and Wagner." *CSL: The Bulletin of the New York C. S. Lewis Society* 12 (October):1–9.

Lewis saw Richard Wagner as an incomparable mythopoeic poet. Lewis's experience of Wagner is tied up with *Sehnsucht*; future Lewis biographers should investigate the roots of this phenomenon in Wagner and in German Romanticism. Wagner's music influenced Lewis's imaginative works, including those written when Lewis was a teenager, *Dymer*, *Perelandra*, *The Pilgrim's Regress*, and *The Voyage of the "Dawn Treader."* Fitzpatrick includes an appendix on Arthur Rackham, the illustrator of *The Ring of the Neibelung,* Lewis's favorite work of Wagner. He also provides an appendix on approaches to Wagner and includes a brief bibliography.

22 GLOVER, DONALD E. *C. S. Lewis: The Art of Enchantment.* Athens: Ohio University Press, 235 pp.

Lewis's correspondence traces his reactions to the literature he was reading and his criticism shows his theories regarding literature. He stated that the "good reader" was central to the literary experience; the reader should be receptive to all experiences the work offers. The work read is of secondary importance; it "should have structure, artistry of presentation, unity and coherence, selectivity of material for an effect, and, by whatever magic of creativity, it offers the experience which draws us out of ourselves and enlarges our being." Glover uses Lewis's standards and methods of criticism to evaluate his fiction. For each work he gives the general meaning, examines the techniques used, and assesses the form's suitability for conveying the theme. Lewis had one message: "the search for truth begins with a longing to recapture an impression which has tantalized our senses and our minds." We must clear the obstacles of contemporary life from our path to find the spiritual truth that is the satisfaction of that longing, what Lewis calls "Joy."

23 HANNAY, MARGARET PATTERSON. *C. S. Lewis*. New York: Frederick Ungar, 299 pp.

Hannay provides detailed summaries of each of Lewis's works, including fiction, literary criticism, apologetics, poetry, uncompleted stories, and letters, and discusses the themes that bind his works together. Two interesting patterns in Lewis's works are "a correspondence among his literary scholarship, his fiction and his apologetics; and a progression from dogmatism to gentleness in all his works." The book includes a biographical sketch and a chronology of Lewis's life and career.

24 HARTT, WALTER F. "Godly Influences: The Theology of J. R. R. Tolkien and C. S. Lewis." *Studies in the Literary Imagination* 14, no. 2 (Fall):21–29.

Lewis felt that "art is subcreation when it is both good art and thematically Christian," while Tolkien felt that "art is subcreation when it is good art, regardless of whether or not it is thematically Christian." Because Lewis conformed to a predetermined order, his art has a constricted cast, his world is closed off. Tolkien's work, on the other hand, is more open and free.

25 HELMS, RANDEL. "All Tales Need Not Come True." *Studies in the Literary Imagination* 14, no. 2:31–45.

Tolkien, a Roman Catholic, felt a rich aesthetic response to the Scriptures, while Lewis, an Evangelical Protestant, was unable to find aesthetic pleasure in Scripture. Tolkien felt that mythology and religion could be fused in literature and the Gospels themselves were true fairy tales. Lewis, on the other hand, "cannot allow the Bible to be literature; to lower it to that status will in his view necessarily be to deny its sacred character." Lewis also fails to see modern critical theory as coming from the Bible by way of Romantic theory: human creativity is equivalent to divine creativity. As an artist, Lewis could only find one use for the Bible, as a source for his Christian apologetic. The Ransom Trilogy is more interested in showing biblical mythology as true and universally valid than in telling a story.

26   HOOPER, WALTER. "Observations of a Trustee." *CSL: The Bulletin of the New York C. S. Lewis Society* 12 (August):1–6.

One should not read criticism of Lewis in place of reading Lewis's works themselves. The differences between England and the United States, namely a national church and a monarchy, have not been adequately recognized in Lewis scholarship. The trustees of Lewis's literary estate are inundated by manuscripts of plays about Lewis that contain many inaccuracies. Lewis's publishers are considering suspending quotation rights to Lewis's works for fear books about Lewis will smother his own works. Much written about him is replete with extreme literalness and humorlessness.

27   HORSMAN, GAIL. "C. S. Lewis and George MacDonald: A Comparison of Styles." *CSL: The Bulletin of the New York C. S. Lewis Society* 13 (December):1–5.

Lewis's comments in the Preface to *George MacDonald: An Anthology* and in the essay "On Three Ways of Writing for Children" show why he held so much reverence for a bad writer. Lewis was able to overlook MacDonald's poor writing style for the great mythopoeic art in which he excelled. Passages from MacDonald illustrate his difficult vocabulary, his going off onto tangents, and his moral sermons. Passages on similar subjects from Lewis illustrate his simpler vocabulary, use of dialogue to explain the plot, and lack of moralizing.

28   HOUTMAN, MARCIA K. "Maleldil: C. S. Lewis's Vision of God." *Lamp-Post of the Southern California C. S. Lewis Society* 5, no. 3 (July):1–4.

Out of the Silent Planet and *Perelandra* reflect the nature of Lewis's God as expressed in his theological works. He believed in a Triune God; the novels identify Maleldil the Old One, Maleldil the Young, and the Third One. The Christian finds comfort in knowing himself to be a small reflection of God, as the Oyarsa tells Ransom that we are copies of Maleldil. God's omnipresence is explained through the Green Lady's replies to Weston's temptation and evident when Ransom recognizes the fullness of "Deep Heaven." Other facts about God revealed in the novels are that He takes the initiative in our knowing Him; He is the Maker of all; all power, especially to fight evil, comes from Him.

29   ———. "Science Fiction and Christianity in the Ransom Trilogy." *Lamp-Post of the Southern California C. S. Lewis Society* 5, no. 1 (January):5–6.

Lewis's Trilogy is an effective blending of entertaining science fiction and edifying theology. By bringing together two physical worlds in the Trilogy, he shows how the physical and spiritual worlds work together to provide a complete life for the individual. He uses strange adventures to illustrate his "orthodox theories about God, Satan, good and evil, heaven and hell, and the Christian community."

1981

30   HOWARD, THOMAS. "The Peal of a Thousand Bells." *Canadian C. S. Lewis Journal*, no. 27–28 (March–April):1–3.

Underlying Lewis's works is a fixed moral order that guarantees liberty. This idea is evident in *That Hideous Strength*. The word "Joy" "rings like a peal of a thousand bells from Lewis's country." Reprinted from 1980.28.

31   JANSSEN, GUTHRIE E. "The Doctrine of Glory in Lewis and Charles Williams." *Chronicle of the Portland C. S. Lewis Society* 10, no. 2 (April–June):2–6.

Both Lewis and Williams saw glory as a central Christian doctrine and commented upon it in artful, imaginative, and convincing ways. The meaning of glory we are concerned with is an attribute of God and His kingdom, whose "connotations are excellence, an aura, splendor, beauty, majesty, effulgence, numinosity, transformation, transfiguration, transcendence, and so on." In "The Weight of Glory" Lewis points out that God promises us approval for obeying and pleasing Him. Williams in *He Came Down from Heaven* (London: W. Heinemann, 1938) sees glory as a web or pattern of the knowledge of good. Lewis's fiction, especially *That Hideous Strength* and *Perelandra*, "are suffused with the doctrine of divine glory." Williams deals with an aspect of glory on earth—romantic love.

32   JONES, ALAN, and FULLER, EDMUND. "An Affectionate and Muted Exchange Anent Lewis." *Studies in the Literary Imagination* 14, no. 2 (Fall):3–11.

In a series of letters between Jones and Fuller, Jones expresses his belief that Lewis "enables many Christians to hang onto a world-view (a view of themselves and their religion) which a more rigorous honesty would oblige them to abandon." He feels that Lewis's greatest limitation was his attitude toward women and finds no fully developed female characters in his fiction. Jones does not find much joy in Lewis. Fuller replies that Lewis would be appalled at those who seek to "cult-ivate" him. He finds several fully developed women characters in Lewis's work: the Green Lady, Jane Studdock, and Orual. Fuller finds an austere joy in Lewis's work. He feels that Lewis's prolific and inventive fiction keeps alive his didactic apologetical works. Reprinted: 1984.35.

33   KEEBLE, N. H. "C. S. Lewis, Richard Baxter, and 'Mere Christianity.'" *Christianity and Literature* 30 (Spring):27–44.

Baxter was a seventeenth-century Puritan divine. Lewis not only uses Baxter's phrase "mere Christianity," meaning the features of Christianity common to all Christians, but he also uses the principle as a touchstone, a way to organize his apologetic writings, and "a rallying cry in meeting the challenge of his time." Both men concentrate on the practice of Christianity rather than on the theology. "Lewis' responsiveness to Baxter's insight . . . proves him not so much old-fashioned as immune to the fashions of any age."

34   KILBY, CLYDE S. "A Note on the Wade Collection." *Studies in the Literary Imagination* 14, no. 2:117–119.
      Kilby believes that the Marion E. Wade Collection at Wheaton College holds the best collection anywhere of materials on Lewis, Charles Williams, Dorothy L. Sayers, and Owen Barfield.

35   KOLBE, MARTHA EMILY. "Three Oxford Dons as Creators of Other Worlds for Children: Lewis Carroll, C. S. Lewis, and J. R. R. Tolkien." Ph.D. dissertation, University of Virginia, 274 pp.
      Examines Carroll's, Lewis's, and Tolkien's family backgrounds; environment; personality traits; historical, religious, and literary influences; perceptions of their writings; and uniqueness of their writings. Commonalities of background include a relative known for storytelling ability, fathers who used words to persuade people, and mothers who nurtured freedom and individuality in their children. Similarities in their environments include a high degree of adult attention, access to books, siblings who provided support, early schooling at home, being read to as children, a love of drawing, the death of mother during childhood or adolescence, happy experiences as an undergraduate at Oxford, and a secluded adulthood with few interruptions. Some shared personality traits include being bookish; living in the imagination; being systematizers, artists, and nature lovers; being shy; having a disciplined life; holding "a romantic, idealistic view of life and a deep belief in the realm of faerie"; and being secure in their own scholarship. They had commonality in religious outlook, a sincere dedication to Christianity, and a deep spirituality. Common literary influences include wide reading and a love of words. Their perceptions of their works have in common the desire to tell a good story, being unable to identify the exact origin of the idea for the story, and actual children having a part in the creation of the story.

36   KOTZIN, MICHAEL C. "C. S. Lewis and George MacDonald: *The Silver Chair* and The Princess Books." *Mythlore* 8 (Spring):5–15.
      Lewis's *The Silver Chair* and MacDonald's *The Princess and the Goblin* (London: Blackie & Son, 1871) and *The Princess and Curdie* (London: Blackie & Son, 1883) have action set in an underground world, have young heroes going on a quest, echo folk fairy tales, and depict holy characters. While MacDonald's images are from nature, Lewis's are objects in modern everyday life. MacDonald's supernatural character is human and feminine whereas Lewis's is animal and masculine. Lewis's novel is more explicitly Christian than MacDonald's.

1981

37 LINDSKOOG, KATHRYN ANN. *C. S. Lewis, Mere Christian*. Revised and expanded. Downers Grove, Ill.: InterVarsity Press, 258 pp. Reprint. Wheaton, Ill.: Harold Shaw, 1987.

An expanded version of 1973.23, the book includes Lewis's views on science, the arts, and education. It provides a one-year Lewis reading schedule.

38 LLOYD, CHARLES E. "In the Great Cloud of Witnesses." *Sewanee Review* 89 (Spring):281–287.

Lloyd reviews *They Stand Together: The Letters of C. S. Lewis to Arthur Greeves* and nine other books on Lewis and Tolkien. Lloyd observes that Lewis treasured his friendship with Greeves, who never accomplished much of anything, and never makes Greeves feel diminished.

39 MACKY, PETER W. "The Human and the Divine in the Bible: Some Interesting Metaphors from C. S. Lewis." *Lamp-Post of the Southern California C. S. Lewis Society* 5, no. 2 (April):1–7.

Lewis believed that the Bible provides a variety of metaphors to express the divine-human relationship. Macky has isolated a number of Lewis's central insights: words are not always identical with meaning; talk about supersensible realities must be through metaphor; the relationship between God and the writers of the Bible is a deep, hidden reality that must be expressed through metaphor; since metaphors are only partially adequate, if a single metaphor is developed into a theory, that theory will be less adequate than the original metaphor; theologies provide metaphors by which the divine-human relationship is pictured; a variety of metaphors is needed to do justice to the complexity of reality. Lewis himself offers a variety of metaphors to describe the relationship of God to the Bible: the word of God being carried in the Bible as a passenger in a leaky boat; God's voice coming through a human instrument that distorts it like a voice over shortwave radio; God as a noble master taking a peasant into his service and elevating him or her; the transposition of a richer medium to a poorer one, as in drawing; God as the fountain of life, and the Bible as a map.

40 ———. "The Role of Metaphor in Christian Thought and Experience as Understood by Gordon Clark and C. S. Lewis." *Evangelical Theological Society* 24, no. 3:239–250.

Clark believes that geometry is the standard for all thought whereas Lewis sees a spectrum of language running from poetic to scientific. Clark feels all knowledge is verbal and propositional but Lewis believes some knowledge cannot be expressed in words. Clark limits "true" only to propositions that are perfectly, absolutely true while Lewis thinks true statements are those that adequately reflect reality. For Clark reality and truth are identical whereas Lewis believes truth is a linguistic reflection of reality not to be confused with reality itself. Clark believes metaphor is fancy packaging for the real thing while Lewis feels masters use metaphor to communicate something they know directly to someone who does not know it directly. Clark believes the meaning of a metaphor can be expressed in literal speech. Although Lewis agrees this is true for metaphors about observables, he thinks metaphors about supersensibles can only be expressed in other metaphors. Clark believes biblical metaphors are only surrogates, with the real thing being an abstract interpretation. However, Lewis thinks biblical metaphors are the best means to come into personal contact with God.

41 MARTIN, J. H. "Wain's Theories Challenged." *Canadian C. S. Lewis Journal,* no. 29–30 (May–June):12–14.
      John Wain ["C. S. Lewis." *Encounter* 22, no. 5 (May 1964):51–53, 56] is wrong when he states that Lewis's account of his conversion in *Surprised by Joy* is "'lame and unconvincing.'" "If there are omissions, diminutions or de-emphasis in the tale, then they are likely to have been deliberately chosen, and not to conceal but to avoid being misleading."

42 MEDCALF, STEPHEN. "The Coincidence of Myth and Fact." In *Ways of Reading the Bible*. Edited by Michael Wadsworth. Totowa, N.J.: Barnes & Noble, pp. 55–78.
      Lewis believed myth was the closest we come to experiencing as concrete what otherwise is only an abstraction. The story of Christ's death and resurrection is the only myth that is identical with truth and fact. The main defect in Lewis's theology and ethics is "a taint of the idealist instinct to maintain the independence of the mental subject from the bodily world." *Perelandra* succeeds because it is a fictional world in which myth, truth, and fact are not detached. In the Gospel of Mark, the myth was condensed into fact from the very event. Lewis pointed out that myth and fact father innumerable abstract truths; we might add that the Gospels also father innumerable myths. Christ deliberately made myth of fact, using symbols not for self-expression but to comfort. Imagination has some advantages over myth to describe the patterning of the gospels because it suggests creative action and it comes closer to the image of the Word.

43 MEILAENDER, GILBERT. "Theology in Stories: C. S. Lewis and the Narrative Quality of Experience." *Word & World* 1 (Summer):222–229.
      Lewis searched for a way, besides abstract thought, which cuts us off from experience, to transcend the limitations of space and time and rest in God. Myth is more concrete than abstract but the truth given in myth is not a truth to live by, so Lewis looks to story. Story "unites the temporal and eternal as intimately as plot and theme." Escaping from narrative by abstraction and accepting our finite condition as the whole meaning of life are two erroneous ways to escape the temporality of existence and find a false infinite. Certain

features of Christian life cannot be conveyed adequately by theology. "Lewis offers not abstract propositions for belief but the quality, the feel, of living in the world narrated by the biblical story." Reprinted: 1983.46.

44   MERCHANT, ROBERT. "The Conscience and Moral Reasoning." *CSL: The Bulletin of the New York C. S. Lewis Society* 12 (March):1–7.
      In his essay "Why I Am Not a Pacifist," Lewis synthesizes the extreme positions that regard the conscience as either an act of the emotions or an act of reason. Lewis sees two meanings in conscience. The first, the pressure a person feels to do what is right, should always be obeyed. The second, a person's judgment as to right and wrong, may be mistaken. "Lewis offers two courses of action to bring peace to a troubled conscience: Argument or Authority." Argument involves facts, intuition, and arranging the facts to prove something. A person's facts and arrangement may be corrected but "'faulty intuition is incorrigible.'" Therefore an appeal to authority, in matters of conscience, supersedes reason.

45   MERRITT, JAMES D. "'She Pluk'd, She Eat.'" In *Future Females: A Critical Anthology*. Edited by Marleen S. Barr. Bowling Green, Ohio: Bowling Green State University Popular Press, pp. 37–41.
      The image of Eve, the "archetypal myth of the Western world . . . the woman who brings suffering, death and pain into the world," is evident in Lewis's *Perelandra*, H. P. Lovecraft's *The Dunwich Horror* (New York: Editions for the Armed Services, 1939), and Carolyn Neeper's *A Place Beyond Man* (New York: Scribner, 1975). Lewis's Green Lady lacks the intellect to protect herself against devilish arguments; the male strength of Ransom and the King is required to prevent the fall of Perelandra.

46   MUGGERIDGE, MALCOLM. "The Mystery." *Canadian C. S. Lewis Journal*, no. 26 (February):1–4.
      There is an element of mystery in Lewis's life concerning his attitude toward women and sex. "I think he was probably a very deeply sensual man, and he fought to put it away from him." Stephen Schofield believes Lewis's prejudice against women is the result of the death of his mother when he was nine, his difficult father, the lack of female companionship in his youth, and his lack of good looks and athletic ability making him unattractive to girls his age. Muggeridge is overwhelmed by the clarity of Lewis's mind and the total sincerity and honesty of his beliefs. Reprinted: 1983.48. See response, 1981.71.

47   NEULEIB, JANICE WITHERSPOON. "Comic Grotesques: The Means of Revelation in *Wise Blood* and *That Hideous Strength*." *Christianity and Literature* 30, no. 4 (Summer):27–36.

Lewis's *That Hideous Strength* and Flannery O'Connor's *Wise Blood* (New York: Harcourt, Brace, 1952) both use grotesque characters to force an awareness of the healthy norm. O'Connor chooses to chill the reader by depicting only the fallen side of man while Lewis offers three views of humanity and depicts characters choosing between good and evil. O'Connor renders grotesques to force the reader to search for the brightness of reality whereas Lewis uses "the shining brilliance of goodness to show his grotesques for the parody of fallen humanity that they are."

48 NOEL, HENRY. "Skeptic Turned Apostle." *National Catholic Reporter* 17 (6 March):92.
    In his review of *A Mind Awake: An Anthology of C. S. Lewis*, Noel calls the book a treasure trove of excerpts. All Lewis's books are represented as well as previously unpublished material. "For Lewis lovers, this book of gleanings—and sheaves—will be precious."

49 PAULINE, SISTER, CSM. "Secondary Worlds: Lewis and Tolkien." *CSL: The Bulletin of the New York C. S. Lewis Society* 12 (May):1–8.
    Lewis, who had the clear purpose of writing about "various aspects of the truth that is in Christ Jesus" in his novels, kept setting and detail subordinate to the story. Tolkien, who had no clear aim in writing other than for fun, delights in describing the settings themselves. Although Tolkien did not write deliberately Christian works, "so deeply did that Truth underlie his thought that his stories also show it forth."

50 PATTERSON, NANCY-LOU. "Banquet at Belbury: Festival and Horror in *That Hideous Strength*." *Mythlore* 8 (Autumn):7–14, 42.
    There are common elements in Lewis's description of the banquet where N.I.C.E. is destroyed and Lewis Carroll's description of the nightmare tea party in *Through the Looking Glass*. Northrop Frye's depiction in *The Secular Scripture: A Study of the Structure of Romance* (Cambridge, Mass.: Harvard University Press, 1976) of the contrast between festival and horror applies here. The characteristics of Lewis's animals are similar to the animals in Rudyard Kipling's The Jungle Book. The first appearance and the death of the characters killed at the banquet show how each is accorded justice.

51 PITTENGER, NORMAN. "C. S. Lewis: Combative in Defense." *Studies in the Literary Imagination* 14, no. 2 (Fall):13–20.
    Pittenger finds too much dogmatism in Lewis's apologetic works; "there is an irritating certainty which allows of no—or to be more just, very little—questioning about some of the affirmations of the Christian tradition as Lewis accepted it." His apologetic works are unsatisfactory because they are not centered on eucharistic observance. However, Lewis did a valuable job.

1981

52   PRICE, STEVEN. "Freedom and Nature in Perelandra." *Mythlore* 8 (Autumn):38–40, 42.
     Lewis reveals in *Perelandra* his belief that humanity is only achieved by spontaneous, free-will choices based on "an acceptance of change as the essential nature of life and reality." He sees God as the origin of change and human acceptance of change as an existential affirmation of faith in God. The Green Lady, by not accepting the tempter's suggestion to stop change and movement, asserts her freedom and becomes a completely integrated individual.

53   PURTILL, RICHARD L. *C. S. Lewis's Case for the Christian Faith*. San Francisco: Harper & Row , 146 pp.
     Lewis is successful as an apologist because of his intellectual abilities, his imaginative power, and his moral qualities. His arguments for believing in God were the existence of moral law, the longing he called Joy, and the existence of reason. He emphasized the personality of God; he believed that our sufferings contribute to the redemption of others, and that because God wants our freely given love He permits sin. He thought of miracles as "interventions in the normal course of nature by a higher power outside of nature." Lewis felt that faith should be based on evidence; he recommended a certain discounting of seemingly contrary evidence since faith is also based on a personal relationship to God that includes complete trust. He thought that "all religions except Christianity are partial truths masquerading as the whole truth and drawing their power from their element of truth." He believed that moral law was God's instructions to enable humans to live in harmony and to develop fully. He wrote about how God answers prayer, about petitionary prayer, and the relationship of feelings to prayer. Lewis saw the promise of heaven not as a bribe for belief in God but as the fulfillment of the desire of believers to enjoy God forever.

54   REDDY, ALBERT F. " 'The Inklings.' " *America* 144 (21 February):142–143.
     Lewis, Tolkien, and Williams were all dedicated Christians with similar literary tastes but also significant differences. Lewis's friendship united the Inklings. Tolkien was a perfectionist, deeply pessimistic, and jealous of Lewis. Williams was charismatic and more catholic in his literary tastes. Lewis delighted in male companionship; he was intellectually brilliant, prone to bullying, and quick to generalize but had a large and generous heart.

55   Review of *The Visionary Christian: 131 Readings from C. S. Lewis*. *Booklist* 78 (15 September):87.
     These "significant passages from Lewis' fiction and poetry . . . speak strongly of his Christian ideals."

56 Review of *The Visionary Christian: 131 Readings from C. S. Lewis. Library Journal* 106 (15 September):1742.

"Lewis buffs will delight in sampling from this smorgasbord. . . . [but] so much context is missing that readers unfamiliar with the original may be frustrated."

57 Review of *The Visionary Christian: 131 Readings from C. S. Lewis. Publishers Weekly* 220 (18 September):149.

This volume contains "representative selections of Lewis's fiction, fantasies and poems that dramatize in unique ways the major themes of life, death, sin and redemption."

58 ROSE, MARY CARMAN. "The Christian Platonism of C. S. Lewis, J. R. R. Tolkien, and Charles Williams." In *Neoplatonism and Christian Thought.* Edited by Dominic J. O'Meara. Norfolk, Va.: International Society for Neoplatonic Studies, pp. 203–212.

Lewis, Tolkien, and Williams were orthodox Christians and deliberately choose "Platonist concepts and beliefs for the development and illumination of Christian beliefs." Three Christian Platonist elements in the fiction of the writers are the reality of suprasensory aspects of the universe; how these aspects are known; and the presence of truth, beauty, and goodness in creation. Christian Platonism has had a resurgence because it has "proved capable of harmonious synthesis of diverse philosophical views."

59 SAN JOSE, PILAR, and STARKEY, GREGORY. "Tolkien Influence on C. S. Lewis." *Mallorn,* no. 17 (October):23–28.

Tolkien was first in chronological order of composition and therefore influenced Lewis rather than vice versa. Tolkien's influence is seen in Lewis's vocabulary, symbolic techniques to express ideas such as language, evil expressed as destruction of nature, and the use of riddles to construct plot and anticipate the future. Ransom is a new Frodo: both are involved in their adventures without their consent, are not exceptionally intelligent, suffer injuries, are not affected by the passage of time, and receive everlasting life. In both authors music is related to creation and discord to evil. See also Yates's article, 1982.70.

60 SAYER, GEORGE. "Two Guests." *Canadian C. S. Lewis Journal,* no. 33–34 (September–October):1–6.

Sayer reveals personal details of Lewis's visits to Sayer's house, including his shaving habits, the kind of underwear he wore, what he liked to eat and drink, and his daily activities. Reprinted: 1983.65.

61 SCHOFIELD, STEPHEN. "'The Awful Chatty Example of C. S. Lewis.'" *Canadian C. S. Lewis Journal,* no. 35–36 (November–December):19.

Anthony Burgess refers to Lewis's style as "awful chatty." Lewis, like

1981

Winston Churchill and Franklin Roosevelt, used prosaic and unliterary language to give an appearance of casualness, one of the rhetorician's weapons.

62   ———. "Oxford Loses a Genius." *Canadian C. S. Lewis Journal*, no. 31–32 (July–August):1–11.
      The chief reason Lewis was hated in Oxford was his popularity outside Oxford. "The key to England is the desire that knowledge and power should be sustained at the top. What really riled these Oxonians was that when Lewis acquired a vast following they saw power slipping through their fingers which loved to hold the reins. Lewis was gaining power; they were losing it." According to his brother, Warren, and friend Adam Fox, Lewis felt more in his proper element and was happier at Cambridge. Reprinted: 1983.69. See response, 1982.19.

63   ———. "Personified Finger." *Canadian C. S. Lewis Journal,* no. 35-36 (November–December):11–18.
      In Schofield's response to Buzien's article [1981.5], he claims that greed and lust for power are the source of war. Soldiers are needed to prevent the unscrupulous from getting out of hand on a national scale. Lewis felt that the work of a good soldier was less evil than letting an aggressor have his way.

64   ———. "Warrior in a Wilderness." *Canadian C. S. Lewis Society*, no. 26 (February):6–7.
      Lewis felt temperance applied not only to liquor but to all pleasures and "'meant not abstaining, but going the right length and no further.'"

65   SMITH, ROBERT HOUSTON. *Patches of Godlight: The Pattern of Thought of C. S. Lewis*. Athens: University of Georgia Press, 275 pp.
      Lewis's philosophy of religion can best be described as Christian objectivism; he found the most definitive explanation of this view of reality in Plato. While Plato emphasized the transcendent view of the absolute as having no personality, Christianity stresses the immanence of God. Lewis himself generally stressed the transcendence of God. His cosmology is the Old Western World model, a hierarchical universe where every creature has its proper place and every aspect of existence has absolute objective meaning. Lewis believed that the absolute impinged upon the natural world through reason, universal moral principles, and mythology. He felt the function of the imagination was to guide the mind toward higher truths; his richest imaginative thought describes the mystical ascent of the self toward God. Lewis adapted the Platonic model of the self as having three aspects—rational, spiritual, and appetitive—and gave considerable attention to the disorder resulting when the rational element is unable to control the appetitive.

He reconciled the contradictory concepts of the soul's longing for merging itself with God and the soul's desire for self-fulfillment by postulating that in the denial of self there is fulfillment of self. His concept of evil as a corruption of goodness is also Platonic; he saw evil as a stance of mind, an individual choice made when there is disharmony among the three elements of the soul. Lewis's philosophical problems result from intrinsic conflicts between Christianity and Platonism or from unresolved problems each has separately. His achievement was in formulating a comprehensive objectivist worldview that brought together these two great supernaturalist positions. Throughout the book Smith uses Lewis's fiction, especially the Ransom Trilogy and the Narnia Chronicles, to illustrate concepts of Lewis's philosophy of religion.

66 SOBRAN, JOSEPH. "Happy at Home." *Human Life Review* 7:44–78.
    Lewis believed that politics should be based on the Christian view of humanity, but since this view has been discarded the proper basis of politics has been undermined. *The Abolition of Man* shows "Lewis's apprehension of the social and political order of the post–Christian era." He regarded collectivism as an evil and mistrusted material progress because he thought it would lead to totalitarianism. He held that the natural law was unalterable and opposed the modern theory that states are free to make whatever laws they please. Lewis felt the State was destroying individual privacy and that by ceasing to protect the rights of individuals the State was destroying its legitimacy. He recognized that leftism results not from a hunger for justice but from envy. Lewis believed that the cure for collectivism was not individualism but membership in the Mystical Body and that this membership belongs to private life. For responses, see 1984.2, 71.

67 SUNOHARA, MASAHIKO. "*King Lear* as a Tragedy of Love—With Special Regard to Passive Love." *Shakespeare Studies* 20:59–89.
    Lewis's distinctions between Gift-Love and Need-Love, as set forth in *The Four Loves*, is used to analyze "how Shakespeare explores the tragic nature of human love" in *King Lear*.

68 SWETNAM, JAMES. "Three Englishmen Recollected in Tranquility." *America* 145 (5 December):358–360.
    Lewis, Gerard Manley Hopkins, and G. K. Chesterton each caught the romance of being Christian, had a common instinct for the role of the transcendent, and had an imaginative grasp of faith.

69 "Thomas Howard Visits Lewis." *Canadian C. S. Lewis Journal*, no. 27–28 (March–April):15.
    Impressions of Lewis that Howard retains from their meeting are clarity, agility, merriment, toughness, and candor.

1981

70   THORSON, STEPHEN. "Thematic Implications of C. S. Lewis' *Spirits in Bondage*." *Mythlore* 8 (Summer):26–30.
      Part I, The Prison House, presents tension between bitter reality and more hopeful fantasy. Part I ends with the possibility of a good, though ineffectual, God and the narrator turning from "despair and anger (alone) in response to pain and evil and Satan" to a fighting stance. In Part II, Hesitation, the poet is "brooding, full of fear and 'fretted by desire.'" In Part III, The Escape, the poet is "free from dark thoughts and free to search for the meaning of his experience of Joy."

71   VANAUKEN, SHELDON. "The Muggeridge Interview." *Canadian C. S. Lewis Journal*, no. 26 (February):5.
      The issues cited in the Muggeridge interview [see 1981.46] are taken out of context and do not prove that Lewis was prejudiced against women.

72   WAIN, JOHN. "C. S. Lewis." *Canadian C. S. Lewis Journal*, no. 25 (January):1–10.
      Reprint of 1980.65.

73   ———. "C. S. Lewis as a Teacher." In *Masters: Portraits of Great Teachers*. Edited by Joseph Epstein. New York: Basic Books, pp. 236–252.
      Reprint of 1980.65.

74   WALSH, CHAD. "C. S. Lewis: Critic, Creator and Cult Figure." *Seven: An Anglo-American Literary Review* 2 (March):66–80.
      Lewis's enduring popularity is based on many attributes. Since he was not interested in current events or modern ways of thinking, he saved his work from being outdated. He brought to his writings a keen intellect and an immense knowledge of the classics, mythology, and the Bible. Lewis's freedom in using legends, myths, and archetypes is a major reason for the resonance of his works. His favorite form of argument, the either–or, "often carries along the reader who is not completely convinced but lacks . . . words to express his misgivings." His powerful imagination coupled with "unrivalled powers of descriptive writing" allows him to invent new worlds.

75   WATSON, JAMES D. "A Reader's Guide to C. S. Lewis: His Fiction." Ph.D. dissertation, East Texas State University, 119 pp.
      Lewis's fiction—the Ransom Trilogy, the Chronicles of Narnia, *Till We Have Faces*, *The Screwtape Letters*, and *The Great Divorce*—depicts external evil as concrete, embodied in actual devils who possess individuals and whose dominant trait is their desire to consume. Evil characters such as witches and black dwarfs, as well as evil situations such as enslavement, are evident. The effects of evil are to displace order with disorder and destruction. Evil employs deception and fear. Lewis also portrays internal evil in his characters

by showing the problem of self-deception, especially in Orual's case, and the bondage that results from it. All characters need deliverance and only a few are without hope. "The reality of supernatural evil in his fiction allows Lewis to introduce supernatural deliverances." He identifies two kinds of salvation: the corporate deliverance of a group, nation or world, and the deliverance of individuals. God directly brings about salvation and also uses agents such as spirits, human beings, and the Christian Church. The means of salvation Lewis depicts are external circumstances such as fear and revelations of the supernatural, a sense of personal need through self-knowledge and guilt, and personal response requiring a leap of faith. "While the Lewis canon is unified around the themes of supernatural evil and deliverance, the variety of the author's characters and settings prevent such unity from producing a monotony of theme."

76 WILLIAMS, JAN. "Letters to an American Lady or Portrait of the Artist as an Old Man." *Lamp-Post of the Southern California C. S. Lewis Society* 5, no. 4 (October):3–5.

Lewis answered his letters faithfully because he felt people were "'in great need of help and often in great misery.'" We have little sympathy for the Lady because references to her family problems have been excised but also because she is a pest, takes offense where none was intended, and is not concerned for Lewis's health. He shares much of his personal life with her to provide an example for her. The letters cover the topics of materialism; spiritual elements such as forgiveness, humility, holiness, prayer, and the love of God; mutability and mortality; and such miscellanea as the weather, daily routine, letter writing, and differences between men and women.

77 WILLIAMS, TERRI. "C. S. Lewis on Friendship." *Chronicle of the Portland C. S. Lewis Society* 10, no. 4 (October–December):1–5.

In *The Four Loves* Lewis characterizes friendship as arising out of a common goal or interest as well as a liking for the other person, as being better in groups than in pairs, and as not being intrusive about personal matters. His friendship with Arthur Greeves, revealed in *They Stand Together*, is more personal and intimate than this general description. The two men shared their personal lives, emotions, joys, and temptations. The letters reveal "that friendship takes work and commitment."

78 WISSLER, STEVEN PAUL. "C. S. Lewis on Work (Part 2)." *Lamp-Post of the Southern California C. S. Lewis Society* 5, no. 1 (January):1–4.

Lewis saw the proper ends of work as friendship, domestic happiness, and cultural enjoyment. He considered the greatest pleasure of money as giving one freedom from thinking about it and its greatest danger as making one independent of God. He believed that ambition was inherently evil and that the key to good work was to apply oneself humbly to the task rather than to strive for success. Lewis saw the ultimate end of work as the glory of God, achieved by applying one's abilities and intending to serve God. He offered some ideas on how to survive today's "fatal economy": recognize the insanity of a system where obsolescence is built into products; look for ways to escape by choosing inherently useful jobs; remember that friends, family, hobbies, and cultural enjoyments offer happiness; one cannot demand happiness and can achieve it only when one ceases trying to gain it; there is more to life than work as one's life should be a sharing of Christ's life. See 1980.68.

1982

1   BLATTNER, PAUL [F., Jr.]. "*Perelandra*, The Practical Fantasy." *Chronicle of the Portland C. S. Lewis Society* 11, no. 3 (July–September):3–8.

Perelandra is a study of innocence in Tinidril and Tor, a study of evil and temptation in Weston, and a study of man's duty to God in Ransom. Innocence is not fragile or weak; Tinidril's obedience makes her a ruler, not a slave. On Perelandra, clinging to an old good is the root of evil because it means one does not trust God. Weston is evil itself and his temptation techniques introduce self-consciousness, vanity, and pride. Ransom is full of fears and doubts but through grace he acts, saving Tinidril from falling into sin. Practical lessons from the novel are that children are not innocent; faith and obedience are strong; evil has sophistication; we need to detect lies that are almost true; when exposing anti-Christian positions we should not do it by stating their opposites; and sometimes Christians need to say stop.

2   BORKLUND, ELMER. "Lewis, C(live) S(taples)." In *Contemporary Literary Critics*. 2d ed. Detroit: Gale Research Company, pp. 368–377.
Reprint of 1977.5.

3   BRIDGES, LINDA. Review of *They Stand Together: The Letters of C. S. Lewis to Arthur Greeves*. *National Review* 34 (22 January):65.
This "correspondence gives us an oddly binocular view, with the Lewis his readers are familiar with fading in and out of focus with a rather different person."

4   BROWN, CAROL ANN. "Who is Ungit?" *CSL: The Bulletin of the New York C. S. Lewis Society* 13 (April):1–5.
Orual in *Till We Have Faces* echoes Hamlet: she does evil things while groping toward self-knowledge. Lewis's use of a pagan past to probe current religious questions is controversial because it promotes ambiguity. Another controversial element is the depiction of Orual as morally virtuous and sensitive, yet blind to her own jealousy and possessiveness.

5   CARTER, M[ARGARET] L. "The Cosmic Gospel: Lewis and L'Engle." *Mythlore* 8 (Winter):10–12.

Madeleine L'Engle's trilogy of *A Wrinkle in Time* (New York: Farrar, Straus and Giroux, 1962), *A Wind in the Door* (New York: Farrar, Straus and Giroux, 1973), and *A Swiftly Tilting Planet* (New York: Farrar, Straus and Giroux, 1978) and Lewis's Space Trilogy use similar images to describe evil and to represent angels; they both emphasize that ordinary people can do God's work. Both present good as positive, bright, and strong, and evil as a mere negation.

6   CHRISTOPHER, JOE R. "C. S. Lewis Dances among the Elves: A Dull and Scholarly Survey of *Spirits in Bondage* and 'The Queen of Drum.'" *Mythlore* 9 (Spring):11–17, 47.

In *Spirits in Bondage* fairies are psychological symbols of "the mysterious, the Romantic, the dream of escape." In "The Queen of Drum," when the queen rejects God in favor of the fairy ideal, Lewis projects "what he had felt during his years of atheistic romanticism" against his newfound Christianity.

7   ———. "Concerning the Inklings . . ." *Niekas* 30 (May):57–58.

Humphrey Carpenter [1978.4] sees the Inklings as a circle of Lewis's friends. John Wain says the Inklings were "incendiaries, meeting to urge one another on in the task of redirecting the whole current of contemporary art and life." The truth lies somewhere between these two views. The Inklings were conservative romantics.

8   CLARK, DAVID G. "C. S. Lewis as a Yapping Old Woman." *Lamp-Post of the Southern California C. S. Lewis Society* 6, no. 2 (April):9–12.

Vivisection is a central theme of the Ransom Trilogy. In *Out of the Silent Planet* Lewis argues that vivisection leads to a disregard for human life. In *Perelandra* he presents a positive relationship with animals by showing the Green Lady's love of them; he presents a negative relationship by depicting Weston dissecting a frog-like creature. In *That Hideous Strength* Lewis shows the animals kept for experimentation at Belbury having their revenge.

9   CLASPER, PAUL. "C. S. Lewis's Contribution to a 'Missionary Theology': An Asian Perspective." *The South East Asia Journal of Theology* 23, no. 1:75–82.

Reprint of 1981.9, 10.

10 CLUTE, JOHN. "C. S. Lewis 1898–1963." In *Science Fiction Writers: Critical Studies of the Major Authors from the Early Nineteenth Century to the Present Day*. Edited by E[verett] F[ranklin] Bleiler. New York: Scribner, pp. 243–248.

Lewis's science fiction is "at heart exercises in Christian apologetics"

1982

and "is an assault upon the genre whose plots and concerns it seems superficially to share." In *Out of the Silent Planet* Lewis's use of science is inaccurate and his universe "can only be understood as an intense, intricate testimony of the abiding and fully active existence of God." *That Hideous Strength* is lightweight satire. The heart of the Trilogy is *Perelandra*; "it is in this superb vision that Lewis reaches his peak as a writer of fiction."

11 COLLINGS, MICHAEL R. "'To Be Still a Man': Abstraction and Concretion in C. S. Lewis." *Lamp-Post of the Southern California C. S. Lewis Society* 6, no. 1 (January):1–6.

Lewis uses concrete statement and images as structures for his arguments. In his characterization, he has single individuals function as representatives of entire races while maintaining their concreteness. Lewis also uses the differences between abstraction and concretion to deliver moral judgments: his Christian viewpoint is expressed concretely while statements with which he disagreed are communicated by abstractions.

12 COMO, JAMES [T.]. "Routes of Regression: Brothers and Friends, Then and Always." *CSL: The Bulletin of the New York C. S. Lewis Society* 14 (December):1–6.

Como recounts Warren's life, as found in *Brothers and Friends: The Diaries of Major Warren Hamilton Lewis* [1982.28]. There are two important weaknesses in the work: distracting footnotes, some of which explain obvious things while others are unconvincing, and inconsistency in treating Warren's alcoholism.

13 CORKERY, TIM. "Lewis, Roman Catholicism, and Christopher Derrick." *CSL: The Bulletin of the New York C. S. Lewis Society* 13 (July):1–3.

Derrick attempts to answer the question of why Lewis did not become a Roman Catholic [1981.15]. He says the primary obstacle was Lewis's upbringing as an Ulster Protestant, which resulted in prejudice against Catholics. Derrick suggests that Lewis would have converted if he had traveled more and had seen a broader style of Roman Catholicism. Also, Lewis in this matter alone displayed the English temperament of not wanting to engage in rigorous abstract argument. Derrick faults Lewis for not involving himself in religious controversies. Corkery finds that Lewis "attempts to cool down the religious controversy by finding common and substantive ground."

14 CRAWFORD, FRED D. "Charles Williams and C. S. Lewis: Unreal City." In *Mixing Memory and Desire: "The Waste Land" and British Novels*. University Park: Pennsylvania State University Press, pp. 90–102.

Both Williams and Lewis borrowed from T. S. Eliot's "poem to present the modern Waste Land in a theological perspective." Williams willingly borrowed from Eliot's work—his novels contain Eliot's imagery and apply myth in the same manner. Lewis disapproved of Eliot's high-brow approach to theology, distrusted his literary criticism, and rejected what he considered the negative and despairing tone of Eliot's poetry. The resemblances between *The Waste Land* and Lewis's novels may result from their having common sources rather than from direct borrowing by Lewis. Instead of focusing on the bleakness of modern life as Eliot did, Lewis emphasized the solution.

15 CREGIER, SHARON E. "An Ethologist Looks at the *Deeper Magic.*" *Canadian C. S. Lewis Journal*, no. 39 (Summer):9–12.

In this response to Yagyu [1982.69], Cregier says that the natural environment of animals must be preserved so they can exercise their responsibility to us, a responsibility that, contrary to what Lewis and Yagyu say, is treated in the Bible. When the natural drives of animals are frustrated through human interference or misunderstanding, the animals will degenerate.

16 DERRICK, CHRISTOPHER. "C. S. Lewis and the Church of Rome." *Canadian C. S. Lewis Journal*, no. 37 (Winter):14–16.

Excerpts from Derrick's book, 1981.15.

17 EDWARDS, BRUCE L[EE]., Jr. "Deconstruction and Rehabilitation: C. S. Lewis and Critical Theory." *CSL: The Bulletin of the New York C. S. Lewis Society* 13 (September):1–7.

Lewis's literary criticism was rehabilitative; he rejuvenated authors and genres of literature that had been ignored by a generation of critics and readers. Deconstruction, the contemporary nihilism in literary criticism, "reduces each text to the basic message that there is and can be no message: all texts consist of an infinite play of meanings, turning all reading into misreading." Lewis saw literature as a means to transcend oneself, which means the text must have an objective status. He distinguished between reading and the examination of what reading is. Lewis would state "that by confusing the contemplation of the text with the contemplation of reading, deconstructive critics lose the text." Reprinted: 1985.20; 1986.12.

18 FERNANDEZ, IRENE. "C. S. Lewis on Joy." Translated by John S. Maddux. *International Catholic Review: Communio* 9 (Fall):247–257.

Lewis's "entire corpus is an attempt to explain, celebrate, and also situate properly what he himself called the central experience of his life," Joy. The dialectic of desire starts us off on the path we must follow; it does not illuminate it. Lewis considered pleasure as coming from God. He also had a profound vision of the tragic and a strong sense of the seriousness of Christian life, hence the moral analysis of his work. There are two ways to avoid the dialectic of desire: lack of attention and moral rigor.

1982

19 FRYER, W. R. "Power in Oxford." *Canadian C. S. Lewis Journal*, no. 37 (Winter):7–9.

Responding to Schofield [1981.62], Fryer notes that many dons at Oxford viewed a fellowship as a career in itself, so Lewis was not alone in not having a professorship. The fellows of each college had little power and were courteous, hospitable, and encouraging to students. See Schofield's reply, 1982.49.

20 HAJJAR, JACQUELINE ACCAD. "Spiritual Quest in French and English Post–War Novels." Ph.D. dissertation, University of Illinois at Urbana–Champaign, pp. 114–157, 193–232.

Lewis believed in a hierarchy in which individuals have responsibilities that impose limits on their freedom but help them fit into their proper place. In *That Hideous Strength* he "describes the epitome of evil within the context of freedom without limits of any kind." Mark and Jane eventually find freedom in marriage after they learn that "true freedom implies the limits of a hierarchy which imposes set rules upon the individuals." In *Till We Have Faces* the discovery of truth is correlated to the discovery about the self and others. Orual finally finds true faith when she achieves "a perfect balance between the cognitive and the volitional aspects."

21 HODGENS, RICHARD M. "C. S. Lewis Considered as a Surrealist." *CSL: The Bulletin of the New York C. S. Lewis Society* 13 (June):1–6.

Lewis's inspiration for his fiction is consistent with surrealist theory and is an important part of the appeal of his fiction. His inspirations were automatic, visual, and singular, not sequential or narrative. Lewis was able to rework the material supplied by his imagination into "more-than-adequate representations of 'the real world.'"

22 HOOPER, WALTER. *Through Joy and Beyond: A Pictorial Biography of C. S. Lewis*. New York: Macmillan, 176 pp.

Hooper provides a brief biography that quotes liberally from Lewis's autobiography and letters, provides reminiscences by Lewis's friends, and gives Hooper's personal account of the last months of Lewis's life. The book includes over 150 photographs of Lewis, his family and friends, and places associated with him.

23 HOUTMAN, MARCIA K. "The Bent One: C. S. Lewis' Vision of the Devil." *Lamp-Post of the Southern California C. S. Lewis Society* 6, no. 4 (October):9–13.

In the Ransom Trilogy "the Devil is a definite, concrete, and unavoidable reality." In *Out of the Silent Planet* Lewis depicts the basic characteristics of Satan as being bent and not equal to God. In *Perelandra* he shows the ultimate conclusion of allegiance to the devil in Weston's possession by Satan.

The Bent One "is capable of making his corrupt thought sound very convincing and thus presents a very real and great danger." In *That Hideous Strength* the devil is not personified but his presence comes through archetypal symbols. Lewis presents "the Devil as a formidable enemy, a most concrete threat which each individual must be prepared to meet."

24 IRWIN, MARK T. "Puddleglum: The Figure of the Comic Hero in C. S. Lewis' *The Silver Chair*." *Lamp-Post of the Southern California C. S. Lewis Society* 6, no. 4 (October):1–5.

Puddleglum provides a healthy balance between sentimentalism and nihilistic despair. He is a comic hero who reminds us of our finitude and physical condition. The comic vision restores confidence in the physical world and convinces us that our lives will lead to the ultimate significance. The name Puddleglum suggests a clown's name; he is both happy and silly, and sad and melancholy. Puddleglum's faith in Aslan gives him grounds for optimism; it is based on discipline, the conviction that there are no accidents, and a Platonic notion of essence preceding existence.

25 KAWANO, ROLAND M. "C. S. Lewis: The Public Poet." *Mythlore* 9 (Autumn):20–21.

Two events in Lewis's life helped to make him a public poet, interested in the public character and traditional conventions of poetry rather than in personal and private modern poetry. The first was his conversion to Christianity, after which he turned his attention away from himself to the world outside. The second was Lewis's development of the syllabus for the Final Honour School of English at Oxford, in which he emphasized unity and continuity.

26 KIRKPATRICK, HOPE. "Lewis as Communicator." *CSL: The Bulletin of the New York C. S. Lewis Society* 13 (March):1–7.

Lewis needed to share and to interact with others. He was concerned with words, their meanings and implications. He adjusted his vocabulary for his audience, using plain talk in his apologetics and more sophisticated language in his criticism. Lewis is noted for his clarity, knowing what he wants to communicate and saying exactly that. He knew he worked best using an intellectual approach rather than one based on emotions. "He was a nourisher as well as a communicator"; he wanted his audience to grow in understanding, in wisdom, and in joy. Lewis's major characteristics are imagination, objectivity, originality, and humility.

27 KREEFT, PETER. *Between Heaven and Hell: A Dialogue Somewhere beyond Death with John F. Kennedy, C. S. Lewis and Aldous Huxley*. Downers Grove, Ill.: InterVarsity Press, 115 pp.

Kreeft has created an imaginary dialogue between Lewis (representing traditional orthodox Christianity), Kennedy (modern humanistic Christianity),

1982

and Huxley (Orientalized or mystical Christianity), focusing on the divinity of Christ. The dialogue also covers such topics as the nature of heaven, hell, and purgatory; literal versus poetic interpretation of the Bible; the roles of faith, reason, and authority; and the reliability of the Gospel texts.

28   LEWIS, W[ARREN] H[AMILTON]. *Brothers and Friends: The Diaries of Major Warren Hamilton Lewis.* Edited by Clyde S. Kilby and Marjorie Lamp Mead. San Francisco: Harper & Row, 308 pp.

Abridged diaries of C. S. Lewis's elder brother, covering the period from 1912 to his death in 1973. The writings emphasize the character of Warren, his relationship with his brother, and the Inklings. The editors have included notes explaining gaps in entries and detailing important events in C. S. Lewis's life not recorded by Warren, as well as footnotes explaining references to people, places, and books. The volume also contains a chronology, family genealogies, and photographs.

29   LOGAN, DARLENE. "Battle Strategy in *Perelandra*: *Beowulf* Revisited." *Mythlore* 9 (Autumn):19, 21.

Lewis echoes the battle strategy found in the first part of *Beowulf*. In both works the villains are referred to as outcasts, the combatants are evenly matched, the heroes are possessed of a righteous anger toward the villains, the heroes are weaponless, and they must follow the villains through the sea to finish the fight.

30   LUTTON, JEANETTE HUME. " 'Fit Vessel': Devil Possession in *Paradise Lost* and *Perelandra*." *Lamp-Post of the Southern California C. S. Lewis Society* 6, no. 2 (April):2–8.

Weston is a recasting of *Paradise Lost*'s serpent. Both creatures suffer disastrous consequences of the demonic possession: the serpent is judged and sentenced by God while Weston's soul is lost to the devil. Lewis's use of Weston as the devil's receptacle avoids two errors Milton made: Weston is liable for punishment because he has the reason and will to make moral choices, which the serpent did not, and the grandeur and high poetry found in Milton's Satan is absent in Lewis's depiction of evil.

31   McCARTHY, PATRICK A. *Olaf Stapledon*. Boston: Twayne, pp. 136–140.

Lewis attacks Stapledon and scientific humanism in the form of the character Weston in the first two novels of the Ransom Trilogy. Lewis misconstrued Stapledon's beliefs; Stapledon agreed with Lewis that intelligence may exist in many forms and other species may be more spiritually developed than mankind. Both authors asserted the importance of human life and insisted that real spiritual advancement is based on the need of the individual to develop in his or her own way.

32 McGOVERN, EUGENE. "Reflections Provoked by *On Stories*." *CSL: The Bulletin of the New York C. S. Lewis Society* 13 (July):3–6.

McGovern's observations concerning *On Stories* include the following: Lewis emphasized authors' strengths and said no more than had to be said about their weaknesses; he defended G. K. Chesterton against James Stephens's criticism that his work was dated; although George Orwell soundly criticized Lewis's apologetic works, Lewis praised *Animal Farm* as almost perfect; Tolkien, whom Lewis encouraged, befriended, and praised, found little pleasure in books, including those of Lewis.

33 MACKY, PETER W. "Myth as the Way We Can Taste Reality: An Analysis of C. S. Lewis's Theory." *Lamp-Post of the Southern California C. S. Lewis Society* 6, no. 3 (July):1–7.

For Lewis, myth "is concerned with participant knowing, which mainly involves the imagination; it is composed of quite concrete language used metaphorically; it is at the literary end of the spectrum but is even more imaginative and fantastic than ordinary literature; it provides us with the taste of reality itself rather than with a statement about reality we should label 'truth.'" Lewis thought the most important characteristic of myth was its effect on the imagination. He perceived that myth transcends both abstract generalizations and concrete experience. He believed pagan myths were real reflections of divine reality and that these myths became fact in Christ, thus emphasizing the dual nature of the Gospel as both myth and history. To read modern readers Lewis created myths, especially the descent and ascent stories in *The Pilgrim's Regress*, *Till We Have Faces*, *Perelandra*, and *The Silver Chair*.

34 MARTIN, JOHN. "A Lewis Capriccio." *CSL: The Bulletin of the New York C. S. Lewis Society* 13 (August):1–7.

Martin extracts quotations from Lewis's works, grouped by the following subjects: echoes (of other authors in Lewis), drolleries, scintillations (his ability to pinpoint in a phrase an elusive evil), deflations (Lewis's assault against the modern chronological snobbery), exaltations, and friendship.

35 ———. "Voices of Fire: Eliot, Lewis, Sayers, Chesterton." *CSL: The Bulletin of the New York C. S. Lewis Society* 13 (May):1–16.

Martin provides a brief biography of Lewis and longer biographies for T. S. Eliot, Dorothy L. Sayers, and G. K. Chesterton. He describes each author's strengths and quotes samples from each one's works. Martin finds Lewis most valuable when he reasons together with the audience to find the truth; Lewis fights with fixed bayonet "to root out every fallacy and defeat every objection." Sayers's writing is "as disciplined as Euclidean geometry"; she emphasizes "getting things straight intellectually." Chesterton has a great variety of weapons: "irony, ingenuity, sense of proportion, ability to make surprising

1982

connections, memory for specifics, and a talent for generalizing convincing-
ly"—and his supreme weapon, analogy. Eliot writes poetry best and has a talent for the unforgettable declarative. Reprinted: 1988.48.

36 MIEHLS, DON G. "The Giant Killer." In "The Self in History: A
Contemporary View." Ph.D. dissertation, Texas Christian University, pp.
134–151.
      In his inaugural lecture at Cambridge Lewis argued that there was no
great divide between the medieval and Renaissance periods. He maintained
that later scholars liked the sixteenth-century ideas of humanism, protes-
tantism, and science, and decided they were of a piece. Lewis did not agree
with Max Weber that there was an intrinsic connection between capitalization
and Puritanism.

37 MORRISON, JOHN. "God Means What He Says: C. S. Lewis on
Forgiveness." *CSL: The Bulletin of the New York C. S. Lewis Society* 13
(January):1–7.
      Lewis agrees with Doland Baillie that one cannot deal with one's moral
failures without a belief in God. Edmund, in *The Lion, the Witch and the
Wardrobe*, is an illustration of forgiveness. Lewis stated that one must forgive
the inexcusable because God has forgiven the inexcusable in us.

38 MURRIN, MICHAEL. "The Dialectic of Multiple Worlds: An Analysis of C.
S. Lewis's Narnia Stories." *Seven: An Anglo-American Literary Review*
3:92–112.
      Lewis describes four methods of transit between England and Narnia:
the door, the picture, a railroad station, and the rings taking the characters to
the Wood between the Worlds. His literal use of the door forces the reader to
reflect on his art. The door also points to the ladder of imitation: the historical
Narnia is only a shadow of the "real" Narnia. The children's adventures force
them to think dialectically, "finding more than one Narnia, [they] must simultaneously see that one differs from another because it is better." Use of the
picture indicates that Lewis prefers the narrative to the dramatic. The railroad
station is associated with separation and death. The Wood between the Worlds
is outside time and therefore has eschatological implications; its labyrinthine
character "creates a set of comparisons which in turn encourage an ethical
analysis."

39 PITTS, MARY ELLEN. "The Motif of the Garden in the Novels of J. R. R.
Tolkien, Charles Williams, and C. S. Lewis." *Mythlore* 8 (Winter):3–6, 42.
      The garden is paradise in Tolkien's ring trilogy, a place of temptation in
Williams's *Descent into Hell* (London: Faber & Faber, 1937), and both par-
adise and a place of temptation in Lewis's Space Trilogy.

40 PRICE, MEREDITH. "'All Shall Love Me and Despair': The Figure of Lilith in Tolkien, Lewis, Williams, and Sayers." *Mythlore* 9 (Spring):3–7, 26.

The archetype of Lilith is present in Tolkien's *Fellowship of the Ring* (London: G. Allen & Unwin, 1954), Williams's *Descent into Hell* (London: Faber & Faber, 1937), Sayers's *The Devil to Pay* (London: Gollancz, 1939), and Lewis's characters of Jadis and the Emerald Witch in the Chronicles of Narnia. The common attributes in the authors' depiction of Lilith are "1) association with the garden motif, 2) great beauty (or at least, allure), 3) immortality, 4) association with the cold or with darkness, 5) dominion over (or at least truck with) a host of hideous creatures."

41 QUIGLEY, E. MICHAEL. "Reflections on C. S. Lewis' *The Abolition of Man*." *Homiletic & Pastoral Review* 83 (November):60–65.

Lewis discusses in *The Abolition of Man* the misuse of language and the relationship between language and the preservation of social values. Western society, with subjective social values and greed for material possessions, reigns over mankind through the use of technology. Lewis focuses on genetic engineering, which offers the prospect of power over life itself and tempts man to claim equality with God. The rejection of the divine will leaves a void filled by an assertive human will. Lewis sees in Christianity the only solution to the modern dilemma.

42 REICHENBACH, BRUCE R. "C. S. Lewis on the Desolation of De-Valued Science." *Christian Scholar's Review* 11, no. 2:99–111.

Lewis sees modern science as reducing nature to the mechanical; science becomes devalued by reducing reasoning to a by-product of nonrational nature, a course that makes any thinking, even moral reasoning, invalid. He deplores the tendency to justify the use of technology simply because it is possible, rather than using an objective set of values to determine whether such use is desirable. Lewis is also concerned about experimentation because it is subject to abuse when not guided by objective values. He objects to the temptation of science to go beyond experimentation into metaphysics when science treats experimental hypotheses as fact. In *That Hideous Strength* Lewis depicts a world run by devalued science, a confusion between means and ends, and the barrenness of nature, human lives and souls, and humanistic institutions. Reprinted: 1983.58.

43 Review of *On Stories: And Other Essays on Literature*. *Kirkus Reviews* 50 (15 February):257.

The review calls the book "a minor but occasionally stimulating collection." Some items look like filler and none is truly memorable. "But Lewis' wide reading and sturdy common sense . . . make him a rewarding, if not illuminating, critic."

1982

44 Review of *On Stories: And Other Essays on Literature. Publishers Weekly* 221 (12 March):80.

"A reading of these pieces leaves one in total agreement with Lewis's belief that literature should not be read, but reread. This volume certainly deserves to be reread, and savored."

45 RIBE, NEIL. "That Glorious Strength: Lewis on Male and Female." *CSL: The Bulletin of the New York C. S. Lewis Society* 14 (November):1–9.

Lewis, as presented in *That Hideous Strength*, believed that the proper sphere of man's activities is intellectual and political, but from this activity arise the sins that beset men: the tendency to substitute abstract concepts for reality, to treat people as objects to be manipulated, and to compromise moral principles. According to Lewis, a woman's role is to nurture children and preserve the values of the home. He views haughtiness as a temptation of the female. Lewis believes that discovering the true nature of male and female results in discovering the nature of God.

46 RITCHIE, DAN. Review of *On Stories: And Other Essays on Literature. National Review* 34 (1 October):1236.

In these essays Lewis tries to explain his love of writers who make myths. "The book is radiant with those short flashes of brilliance which are so characteristic of Lewis."

47 SALE, ROGER. "The Audience in Children's Literature." In *Bridges to Fantasy*. Edited by George E. Slusser, Eric S. Rabkin, and Robert Scholes. Carbondale: Southern Illinois University Press, pp. 78–89 passim.

Rhetoric is the enemy of imagination, as evident in *The Lion, the Witch and the Wardrobe*. "Lewis as a writer of books explicitly written for children is a writer of self-imposed manacles, false rhetoric." The best children's literature results when a writer writes out of an individually felt need. Critics of children's literature should deal with their individual response to the work rather than repressing these experiences in order to appear professional.

48 SCHOFIELD, STEPHEN. "Il Fait le Beau Temps." *Canadian C. S. Lewis Journal*, no. 38 (Spring):23–26.

Some of Schofield's observations about Lewis include the following: Lewis illustrated *la politesse du coeur*, warmheartedness. Walking was his hobby. Laval University in Quebec awarded him an honorary degree. He read the magazine *Punch* at breakfast because silence was the rule. In "one way or another all his books bring light and sunshine."

49 ———. "When CSL's *Pilgrim's Regress* Appeared in 1933 the British People Had No Daily Newspaper." *Canadian C. S. Lewis Journal*, no. 37 (Winter): 10–11.

Here Schofield responds to Fryer [1982.19], claiming that the influence of the fellows at Oxford was local only, while Lewis's influence extended beyond Oxford.

50 SAYER, GEORGE. "Why Not Roman Catholic?" *Canadian C. S. Lewis Journal,* no. 37 (Winter):17.
    The Catholic Church was repugnant to Lewis because of his childhood in Belfast. Because he was a member of a very broad church he was able to state doctrines common to all Christians in a masterly way.

51 SELLIN, BERNARD. "Lewisian Progenitor." *Canadian C. S. Lewis Journal,* no. 40 (Autumn):8–13.
    David Lindsay's *A Voyage to Arcturus* (London: Methuen, 1920) is the father of Lewis's Space Trilogy. Lewis had this description of Lindsay's novel: "'scientifically it's nonsense, the style is appalling, and yet this ghastly vision comes through.'" The two writers had much in common: they resented the evolution of the modern world and felt out of joint with the times, they looked for answers in religious or spiritual experiences, they shared the same taste for fantasy, and because of their sensitivity, they feared emotion. In their works "both writers [excelled] in their presentation of unearthliness," they limited their narratives to a few characters who embody moral values, and they ignored analysis of society. The essential differences between the two writers is that Lewis's Perelandra is an innocent world whereas Lindsay's Tormance is evil; while on Lewis's Malacandra and Perelandra life is pleasant and attractive, Lindsay's theme is that one must reject beauty to attain God.

*52 SMITH, KAREN PATRICIA. "The Keys to the Kingdom: From Didacticism to Dynamism in British Children's Fantasy, 1780-1979." *DAI* 43 (1983): 3327A. Columbia University, 459 pp.
    Four stages of British fantasy writing are identified. Didactic fantasy (1780–1840) is characterized by "the key concepts of structure, social order and pedagogical concerns." In the Enlightenment stage (1841–1899), fantasy is written for pleasure, contains colorful story lines, and has realistic children in fanciful adventures. Diversionary fantasy is distinguished by pleasure and a lighthearted mood. The Dynamic stage, exemplified by Lewis, among others, has vigorous story lines, authors who have confidence in their audience's sophistication, and strong mythical elements. British fantasy evolved from an instructive form to one of great imagination and creativity.

53 SPRAYCAR, RUDY S. "C. S. Lewis's Mechanical Fiends in *That Hideous Strength.*" In *The Mechanical God: Machines in Science Fiction.* Edited by Thomas P. Dunn and Richard D. Erlich. Westport, Conn.: Greenwood Press, pp. 19–26.
    The novel is replete with images of the mechanization of man, his

institutions, and his environment. Lewis was not satirizing science but the bureaucracy that tries to control man and science. His images are based on various traditions—science fiction, classical, medieval, Renaissance, and romantic.

54 STARR, NATHAN COMFORT. "C. S. Lewis' *Till We Have Faces*: Introduction and Commentary." In *Religious Dimensions in Literature*. Edited by Lee A. Belford. New York: Seabury Press, pp. 28–48.

The novel "is an extraordinarily subtle tale of a person's lifelong attempt to achieve release from the burden of sin." It is a poetic fusion of the religious and the marvelous. Lewis explores the difference between devoted love and possessive love, the mysterious beauty and terror of the divine, the symbolic death as an awakening to truth, and the Christian longing for heaven. *Till We Have Faces* is the most concentrated and powerful expression of Lewis's religious belief.

55 STEWART, J. I. M. "Floating Islands." *London Review of Books* 4 (21 October–3 November):17–18.

Stewart reviews *Of This and Other Worlds*, noting that Lewis maintained he always started off with pictures swimming in his mind when writing fiction, but it is hard to reconcile this with what he had to say about the character and purpose of his fiction. His doctrine of *docere et delectare* does not help us understand why he wrote what he did.

56 STEWART, MARY ZEISS. "The Procession of the Time-Bearing Gods: Soul-History in Autobiography." Ph.D. dissertation, Syracuse University, pp. 245–255.

Central to *Surprised by Joy* and *The Autobiography of Malcolm X* (New York: Grove Press, 1965) is the experience of being fundamentally at odds with the world. Lewis's life story reflects the development of religion from polytheism to Christian monotheism. Both Lewis's and Malcolm X's "story became truly 'his own' only when he realized it was the story of the Other acting through him."

57 STURM, RITA L. Review of *On Stories: And Other Essays on Literature. Science Fiction & Fantasy Book Review* September, p. 4.

The collection reveals a few of Lewis's minor faults, but these flaws are overshadowed by his virtues.

58 SWETCHARNIK, WILLIAM. "C. S. Lewis and Visual Art." *CSL: The Bulletin of the New York C. S. Lewis Society* 13 (February):1–7.

Lewis's appreciation of visual arts derived from literary associations. In his youth, "illustration exercised a tremendous influence on his artistic tastes, and on his visual imagination." Lewis wanted art to awaken Joy in the viewer.

59 THIENES, JOHN. "Lewis on Heaven." *Chronicle of the Portland C. S. Lewis Society* 11, no. 4 (October–December):5–7.

Lewis believes in heaven as an integral part of the New Testament. He feels it is a place where our deepest desires for fulfillment will be satisfied. Heaven is not a state of mind like hell, but reality itself. Heaven is a reward promised to Christians. Lewis argues that heaven and hell are destinations made by individual choice. He says a Christian is supposed to look forward to heaven.

60 TRAVIS, BYRON M. "The Imbedded Bible in *Till We Have Faces*." *Lamp-Post of the Southern California C. S. Lewis Society* 6, no. 3 (July):11–14.

In *Till We Have Faces* Lewis echoes scriptural themes through the use of imbedded quotations, biblical words and phrases, situations that evoke biblical images, and biblical allusions. Many of the more important parallels make Psyche a Christ figure. Lewis's biblical allusions "set tone, add connotations and give a flavor of authenticity."

61 TURNEY, AUSTIN, and TURNEY, RUTH. "*English Literature in the Sixteenth Century (Excluding Drama)*." *CSL: The Bulletin of the New York C. S. Lewis Society* 13 (October):1–7.

The Turneys find *English Literature in the Sixteenth Century* to be "fresh, slightly crotchety and stimulating throughout, largely because Lewis is so frank in his likes and dislikes when appraising a host of writers." Three reasons for the bad press the work has received are that some critics find it too idiosyncratic; Lewis divided the century into three periods, using descriptive tags that distract and irritate some critics; Lewis's attitude toward the Renaissance and humanism is seen as bitterness by some critics. In the chapter, "Religious Controversy and Translation," Lewis goes beyond his role as literary critic and provides "exegesis, theology, and church history."

62 VISWANATHAM, K. "C. S. Lewis the Literary Critic." In *The Laurel Bough: Essays presented in Honour of Professor M. V. Rama Sarma, Vice-Chancellor, Sri Venkateswara University*, Tirupati. Edited by G. Nageswara Rao. Bombay: Blackie, pp. 130–137.

The author provides a brief overview of Lewis's works of literary criticism, including Lewis's dicta on literature.

63 VOGELPOHL, JAN. "*The Horse and His Boy*—Lessons in God's Guidance." *Chronicle of the Portland C. S. Lewis Society* 11, no. 4 (October–December):10–14.

The magic in the novel is from Aslan's guiding and comforting his people as a natural part of their world. Aslan's taking control of situations in the novel shows how God works in our lives: by keeping us on His road, by caring for even the little things in life, by keeping devils at bay, by shocking us into making greater efforts, by revealing Himself when we are ready to receive Him, by providing a fresh outlook, by teaching us through firsthand experience, by proving there is no escaping His will, and by having purposes within purposes.

64 WATSON, GEORGE. "From Fiction to Faith." *Times Literary Supplement* 24 September, p. 1024.

In his review of *Of This and Other Worlds*, Watson finds that the collection of essays "bristles with sharp argumentative points, combatively offered, and comes close to offering a convincing aesthetic of story as a literary art. . . . Lewis now looks like the finest British polemicist of the mid-century. . . . The real substance of the books lies in its grasp of the relation between fiction and faith."

66 WILCOX, STEVEN MICHAEL. "Reality, Romanticism and Reason: Perspectives on a C. S. Lewis Pedagogy." Ph.D. dissertation, University of Colorado at Boulder, 180 pp.

The two poles of Lewis's thought, reason and romanticism, found meaning in Christianity. He was a Platonist who felt the reality of this world was but a reflection of the ultimate reality of God. Lewis felt the main objective of humanity was to achieve godhood and to help others do so. But before a person could reach this destiny he or she needed to remake the self through a complete surrender to Christ. Lewis felt Joy was "the one trustworthy link with Reality" and that myth "was God's way of allowing humanity to sense Reality." Reason also indicated that there was something "other and outer." Elements of modernism that Lewis saw rivaling his concept of reality were materialism, inner rings, scientism, and self-blindness. He thought the purpose of education was to conserve the traditional values of Western culture. He was a perennialist—believing in the wisdom of the past, stressing reason, viewing humanity unchanged from culture to culture, and aiming at the development of the rational person. "Lewis's Pedagogy was his theology." His educational objectives "can be summarized in three overriding goals: 1) the destruction of the Self, 2) the re-establishment of Christian Values and 3) the unification of the individual with Reality." His curriculum would be his concept of reality, with its central premise of the immortality of the individual, including all truth in the universe, containing all religious and moral systems, and art and literature. Lewis's methodology would be to use reason and romanticism to infuse reality into the present and to bring the individual in contact with reality.

66 WILKINSON, ROBIN. "Evil and Ignorance in *The Magician's Nephew*." *Lamp-Post of the Southern California C. S. Lewis Society* 6, no. 1 (January):11–12.

In *The Magician's Nephew* Lewis shows that ignorance leads to misconduct and evil, and evil causes ignorance. Ignorance also makes characters think they know more than they do. "It does not necessarily follow that wisdom always leads to goodness, but it may prevent evil."

67 WILSON, A. N. "Lewis's Waste-paper Basket." *Spectator* 11 September, pp. 20–21.

In his review of *Of This and Other Worlds* Wilson finds "it is an extraordinary tribute to the greatness of C. S. Lewis that his genius shines out of the most trivial things he wrote and said."

68 WRIGHT, JOHN L. "C. S. Lewis on Sexuality." *Canadian C. S. Lewis Journal*, no. 40 (Autumn):16–20.

Lewis wrote that the sexual act was justified by prosaic criteria: by charity or selfishness, by obedience or disobedience. He felt that the human sexual instinct had gone wrong, that the Christian rule of chastity was to be followed. He believed that pleasure is a matter of obedience and seeking God's will. He warned that eros can become a demon if followed unconditionally and that it waxes and wanes. He argued that one cannot have sexual happiness at the expense of all other moral considerations. He felt the carnal element of sexuality should be play but believed sexuality was important because theologically it is the image of the union between God and man, it represents our participation in the forces of nature, it results in the incalculable momentousness of being a parent, and it has great emotional seriousness for the participants.

69 YAGYU, NAOYUKI. "Animals and Heaven." *Canadian C. S. Lewis Journal*, no. 39 (Summer):3–8.

Lewis believed that pets would be raised from the dead along with their human masters. He based this theory on Romans 8:19 and felt that when Christianity remakes nature it will not stop at man. "Lewis repeatedly underscores the God-ward rather than Man-ward movement of the Incarnation." With MacDonald, he believed some lower animals would be moved God-ward because of their association with man. Wild animals are outside this context. See response 1982.15.

70 YATES, JESSICA. "Tolkien's Influence on the Chronicles of Narnia." *Mallorn* 18 (June):31–33.

There are other parallels between Tolkien and Lewis in addition to the ones mentioned in San Jose and Starkey's article [see 1981.59]. Lewis's borrowing of the words "troll-fells" and "giant-country" is an affectionate tribute

1983

to Tolkien. Some of Tolkien's ideas reflected in the Chronicles are a secondary world with British topography, trees cut down as a sign of evil, and characters conveyed to heaven by a sea voyage.

71   YOST, CARLSON WARD. "The Researched Novel: Definition, Explication of Five Examples, and Theoretical Discussion of Research in Fiction." Ph.D. dissertation, Texas A & M University, pp. 205–207.

A model of reading can be inferred from the discussion of the Tao in *The Abolition of Man*. Tao reading is challenging, where "one moves understandings from higher levels to lower ones." Researched novels are excellent for converting readers into Tao readers because they demonstrate the multidimensional nature of reading.

72   ZOGBY, EDWARD G. "'A Place of Light, of Liberty and of Learning.'" *America* 146 (10 April):281–282.

Zorby's review of *The Visionary Christian: 131 Readings from C. S. Lewis* finds the mythopoetic Lewis is represented in this anthology.

1983

1   AESCHLIMAN, MICHAEL D. *The Restitution of Man: C. S. Lewis and the Case against Scientism*. Grand Rapids, Mich.: Eerdmans, pp. 94.

Lewis appealed to the common sense of mankind and the traditional values and intellectual assumptions of Western culture to make his case against scientism and naturalism. The debate between scientism and *sapientia*, metaphysical wisdom, has raged since the seventeenth century. Scientism, since it is divorced from value and reduces people to objects, has malignant effects. Scientism also contains an internal contraction—regarding man as part of nature like an animal or inanimate object denies his rationality; but "the scientific method derives from the rational method, and not vice versa." Lewis's contribution to this debate, found in *The Abolition of Man*, is that he addressed his arguments to ordinary people, appealing to their common sense. He believed that good was objective and could be apprehended through reason. Love, virtue, the pursuit of knowledge, the reception of the arts, and worship are the means by which the individual can transcend himself and achieve *sapientia*. "Without a doctrine of objective validity, only individual desire remains as a standard to determine action" resulting in "the lust for sensation, the destructive lust for knowledge, and the will to power." See Price's commentary 1986.48.

2   BERRY, PATRICIA (THOMSON). "Part B: With Women at College." In *The Search for C. S. Lewis*. Edited by Stephen Schofield. South Plainfield, N.J.: Bridge Publishing, pp. 67–70.

Reprint of 1980.64.

1983

3   BLATTNER, PAUL [F., Jr.]. *"Out of the Silent Planet*: An Introduction of C. S. Lewis' Space Trilogy." *Chronicle of the Portland C. S. Lewis Society* 12, no. 2 (April–June):1–4.

Lewis's magnificent ability to create stages from which to speak outweighs the fact that *Out of the Silent Planet* is bad science fiction. One of the main themes developed in *Perelandra* "is that every part of God's creation has its own purpose sufficient for itself and does not depend on man for its meaning." Each novel in the Trilogy shows how the characters, through their decisions, are either becoming like God or like hideous monsters. *Out of the Silent Planet* introduces the themes of "the importance of each part of creation, the nature of choices, the nature of humility, [and] the nature of good and evil" which are fully explored in the other novels of the trilogy.

4   BOENIG, ROBERT [E.]. "C. S. Lewis' *The Great Divorce* and the Medieval Dream Vision." *Mythlore* 10 (Summer):31–35.

There were several influential medieval Dream Visions, including *The Romance of the Rose*, Chaucer's works, and John Lydgate's works. In the typical plot of a Dream Vision, "a first-person narrator falls asleep and finds himself in a springtime garden where he meets a guide who points out the garden's wonders and reveals, often through allegory, some kind of wisdom, usually somehow associated with love." Similarities between *The Great Divorce* and the typical Dream Vision include the first-person narrative, the garden setting, the guide, and the descriptions of nature and people. A significant difference in the two is Lewis's emphasis on time not moving.

5   BRADSHAW, NORMAN. "The Extraordinary Being." *Canadian C. S. Lewis Journal*, no. 42 (Spring):1–16.

The good things Lewis did for Bradshaw include teaching him how to think, teaching him to test the exact meaning of words, showing him how to clarify ambiguous meanings of a word, challenging his immature foundations of thought, and clarifying his concept of the laws of nature. The bad things about having Lewis as a tutor were being treated " 'merely as a controversialist who demand[ed]' " an answer, being subjected to a limited range of enthusiasms, being undermined in one's own critical values and taste, and becoming lost in chop-logic dialectic where reason had become an idol. Lewis overrated the value of morality as the foundation of religious faith. His ability to be a good teacher was impaired by his lack of interest in the major social and political problems of the times. He produced his own "Impersonal Heresy," teaching that literature should be objective and impersonal. His military-club life-style tended to treat love as sex and a biological joke. Lewis was shortsighted to condemn psychology. He overstressed pride and came close to dualism or Manichaeism. See Kreeft's commentary 1983.38 and Bradshaw's reply 1984.9. See Fryer's commentary 1984.26 and Griffiths's response 1984.28.

1983

6 ———. "Impressions of a Pupil." In *The Search for C. S. Lewis*. Edited by Stephen Schofield. South Plainfield, N.J.: Bridge Publishing, pp. 17–27. Reprint of 1979.11.

7 ———. "Some Strange Gulfs between Lewis and An Early Pupil." *Canadian C. S. Lewis Journal*, no. 41 (Winter):1–4.

For all his passion for myth, Lewis never had any interest in Irish mythology, perhaps because it places too much emphasis on the beauty and grace of women compared to the Norse and Teutonic myths, which he favored. He delighted "in chopping and slashing his way to victory in argument, when tutoring, rather than encouraging the diffident and over-awed youth." He disliked "culture" and did not consider it civilizing or helpful in furthering the cause of Christianity. For him, literature was first a good yarn. He treated sexuality with a good deal of broad humor so as not to idealize it. He "underestimated the effect on conduct of the beauty of language." Bradshaw felt there was "as well as a 'beauty of holiness,' also a 'holiness of beauty,' a view that [Lewis] regarded as idolatry."

8 BROWN, CHRISTOPHER C., and THESING, WILLIAM B. "C. S. Lewis (1898–1963)." In *English Prose and Criticism, 1900–1950: A Guide to Information Sources*. Detroit: Gale Research Company, pp. 300–313.

This article provides a brief annotated bibliography listing Lewis's non-fictional prose, his works in collections edited by others, and bibliographies, biographies, and criticism about Lewis.

9 CHANG, H. C. "Memories." In *The Search for C. S. Lewis*. Edited by Stephen Schofield. South Plainfield, N.J.: Bridge Publishing, pp. 103–106. Reprint of 1980.7.

10 CHRISTOPHER, JOE R. "The World of Narnia." *Niekas* 32 (Winter):46–57.

Lewis and Tolkien shared a medieval culture, a Christian worldview, and a love of the genre of romance; their worlds of Narnia and Middle-earth reflect these similarities. Both authors show their worlds created through music, they depict the Fall and evil, their stories have either quest or battle plots, they use similar vocabulary, they connect magic with royalty, and they have characters who undergo death and resurrection. Both include poems in their stories; they use the interlace method of narration, which involves shifting back and forth between different groups of characters; they are inventive in creating names; they portray similar mythological figures such as dragons, dwarfs, giants, and stars or planets that are people; and they describe the last battle and Judgment Day.

11 COLLINGS, MICHAEL R. "Of Lions and Lamp-Posts: C. S. Lewis' *The Lion, the Witch and the Wardrobe* as Response to Olaf Stapledon's *Sirius*." *Christianity & Literature* 32, no. 4 (Summer):33–38.

 Lewis responded to the scientism in Stapledon's *Sirius* (London: Secker & Warburg, 1944) by pitting his own Christian ethics, images, and views against Stapledon's scientific ones. Lewis uses images and events similar to Stapledon's but he inverts them, arguing the opposite side of the same issues.

12 COWAN, ROSAMUND. "Part A: With Women at College." In *The Search for C. S. Lewis*. Edited by Stephen Schofield. South Plainfield, N.J.: Bridge Publishing, pp. 61–66.

 Reprint of 1979.26.

13 D'ADAMO, AMADEO. "Science and Technology in the World of C. S. Lewis." *CSL: The Bulletin of the New York C. S. Lewis Society* 14 (May):1–6

 Lewis argues that the intent behind scientific discoveries makes them good or evil and opposes a materialism that says these discoveries lead to a better world. The effects of science and technology are to change nature and to achieve a sense of empowerment. This course is dangerous since the outcome of a specific scientific application cannot always be predicted. Lewis warns that the sense of empowerment is illusionary: "each new power won by man is a power *over* man as well." His solution to these problems is to integrate science with other fields of knowledge. Lewis sees no relationship between science and understanding the ultimate ends of existence. Lewis feels Christianity teaches the right use of science.

14 DANA, MARGARET E. "Metaphor in *The Great Divorce*." *Lamp-Post of the Southern California C. S. Lewis Society* 7, no. 1 (January):1–9.

 Lewis uses metaphors of "darkness as opposed to substance, and diminution as opposed to expansion" to describe hell and heaven. He depicts man as freely choosing damnation or salvation. He develops the metaphor of clinging as a form of pride, the individual's desire to control his life rather than trusting God. His concept of good is exciting, and dynamic, calling for risk and growth. Lewis shows in the episode of the ghost with the lizard on his shoulder that sensual pleasure is not wrong but can be a powerful impulse toward good if used correctly. In the episode of the Dwarf and the Tragedian, he explains that the damned do not impose tyranny on the good through their self-imprisonment. Lewis throws as much light on the problem of freedom within time as he can and ultimately leaves it a mystery.

15 DORSETT, LYLE [W.]. *And God Came In.* New York: MacMillan, 167 pp.

 This biography of Joy Davidman covers her childhood, writing career, conversion to Christianity, and marriage to Lewis.

1983

16 ———. "The Search for Joy Davidman." *CSL: The Bulletin of the New York C. S. Lewis Society* 14 (October):1–7.

Dorsett describes how he came to write a biography of Davidman. Since she was an American, a Jewess, a divorcee, and an ex-Communist, the tendency of Lewis fans is to ignore her or belittle her marriage to Lewis. Davidman was not well known for either her poetry or her Christian writings because "she cut off her first career herself, and death cut off her second one."

17 EDMONDS, E. L. "C. S. Lewis, the Teacher." In *The Search for C. S. Lewis.* Edited by Stephen Schofield. South Plainfield, N.J.: Bridge Publishing, pp. 37–51.

Reprint of 1981.16.

18 EDWARDS, BRUCE L[EE], Jr. "Toward a Rhetoric of Fantasy Criticism: C. S. Lewis's Reading of MacDonald and Morris." *Literature and Belief* 3:63–73.

Lewis's criticism of George MacDonald and William Morris rehabilitates them by concentrating on *Sehnsucht* in their works. Lewis's strategy for reclaiming these authors is by disregarding current critical dogma, by sketching an alternative paradigm for receiving them, and by being an eclectic critic. His critical mode is "reverse deconstruction," identifying the central myth in the text that appeals to the imagination of the reader.

19 FISHER, JUDITH L. "Trouble in Paradise: The Twentieth-Century Utopian Ideal." *Extrapolation* 24, no. 4 (Winter):329–339.

The combination of urban and pastoral utopias lets technology create freedom instead of slavery. Lewis's *Out of the Silent Planet* and *Perelandra,* Isaac Asimov's *Second Foundation* (New York: Gnome Press, 1953), Robert Heinlein's *The Moon Is a Harsh Mistress* (New York: Putnam, 1966), and Ursula Le Guin's *The Dispossessed* (New York: Avon, 1974) all treat the problem of reconciling the individual to the state and man to machine. Lewis emphasizes the transcendence of the individual over limits. He rejects science and replaces it with communication. Technology on Malacandra is directed toward aesthetic ends and each species' work is also their play. Ransom progresses toward salvation by ridding himself of unnatural desire for complete possession.

20 FITZGERALD, DOROTHY HOBSON. "C. S. Lewis's Images." *CSL: The Bulletin of the New York C. S. Lewis Society* 14 (September):1–7.

Outstanding images from Lewis's apologetic works include his illustrations of the universal moral law, his use of everyday things, and his tender and human images of God's help. The images in *Out of the Silent Planet* are shaped by Lewis's intellect rather than by feeling, but those in *Perelandra* arise from his deeper self. His poetry seems to be drawn from his vast reading rather than from his personal life. His poems illustrate his "brilliant flashes of image." The imagery in *A Grief Observed* conveys in a masterly fashion "the anger, the despair, the bitterness, the emptiness, the helplessness" of grief. The Chronicles of Narnia are the pinnacle of Lewis's imaginative output, especially the creation of Aslan.

21 FITZPATRICK, JOHN. "The Short Stories: A Critical Introduction." *CSL: The Bulletin of the New York C. S. Lewis Society* 14 (April):1–5; (June):1–4; (July):1–5.

The April issue of the *Bulletin* states that Lewis's short stories have been ignored by readers and critics, who have found them to be uninteresting or repellent. These stories "offer grounds for psychoanalytic interpretations of Lewis that may take a hostile turn." "The Man Born Blind" was written in response to the idealism–realism conflict of Lewis's "Great War" with Owen Barfield, illustrates "the delusory nature of idealism," and is "part of a realist attack on Barfield's position." Sammons's Christian reading of the story [1977.56] is out of touch with Lewis's beliefs during the late 1920s. The June issue has an examination of "The Shoddy Lands," in which Lewis is concerned with the nature of consciousness. He tells the story through the first person, using his own persona. "The latent prejudices in Lewis's intellect enable him to produce such a devastating portrayal of a shallow mind." In the July issue Lewis's last two short stories are examined. "Ministering Angels" satirizes a spaceborne brothel proposed by Robert S. Richardson. The story is fatally weak; Lewis showers on a single female character all his invectives. "Form of Things Unknown" is "lifeless at its core. It is as if the author had glanced too long at the stony brilliance of his central conceit and found himself paralyzed in his efforts to manipulate the material." The story "suggests unconscious misogynist tendencies at work yet again in Lewis's fiction."

22 FORD, PAUL F[RANCES]. "The Day After 'The Day After' and the Day Before an Anniversary." *Lamp-Post of the Southern California C. S. Lewis Society* 7, nos. 3–4 (December):15–17.

Lewis's points in his sermon "Learning in War-time" can be adapted to deal with the threat of nuclear war. His basic conclusion is that we should not let our emotions lead us to think the current situation is abnormal. He warns against the enemies of excitement, frustration, and fear. He argues that the best defense is to live in the present moment, including working for justice and peace. He identifies our real fear as the fear of death.

23 FREUD, JILL. "Part B: With Girls at Home." In *The Search for C. S. Lewis.* Edited by Stephen Schofield. South Plainfield, N.J.: Bridge Publishing, pp. 55–59.

Reprinted from 1980.18.

1983

24 FRIESEN, GARRY L. "Scripture in the Writings of C. S. Lewis." *Evangelical Journal* 1, no. 1:17–27.

Lewis sees Scripture as only one means of God's revelation. He feels that the Bible contains degrees of inspiration, depending on the writers' closeness to God. Lewis sees a hierarchy of authority consisting of Scripture, the Creeds, and tradition. His high view of Scripture is "supported by his willingness to accept difficult doctrines on the authority of Scripture." Lewis's weaknesses on the doctrine of Scripture are his ignoring claims the Bible makes for itself, his concept of myth, his not recognizing the special revelation of the Old Testament, and his views of inspiration and authority. He leaves us with an errant Bible from which to find absolute truth.

25 FRYER, W. R. "Disappointment at Cambridge?" In *The Search for C. S. Lewis*. Edited by Stephen Schofield. South Plainfield, N.J.: Bridge Publishing, pp. 29–35.

Reprint of 1980.19.

26 FULLER, EDMUND. "'Help Yourself to Scotch.'" *Canadian C. S. Lewis Journal*, no. 42 (Spring):20.

"I have never felt myself in the presence of such depth and breadth of humane learning" as in Lewis's company.

27 GEISLER, NORMAN L. "Christian Humanism." In *Is Man the Measure? An Evaluation of Contemporary Humanism*. Grand Rapids, Mich.: Baker Book House, pp. 95–107.

The writings of Lewis are a primary example of Christian humanism. He attacks secular humanism because of its view of God, miracles, morals, education, and justice; its frightening political potential; and its attempt to control nature through science. From Lewis's critique of secular humanism one can see the form of his Christian humanism: he affirms mankind's powers, rationality, morality, aesthetic nature, eternal value, and dignity. The crucial difference is that secular humanism believes humans are the measure of all things, while Christian humanism believes they are made and measured by God. A problem with Lewis's Christian humanism is that he sometimes fell into the secular humanism he attacked, especially in his naturalistic interpretation of Old Testament miracles and negative criticism of Old Testament events and writings.

28 GLUSMAN, JOHN A. Review of *On Stories: And Other Essays on Literature*. *Sewanee Review* 91 (Winter):R20.

"A selection of Lewis's least polemical and most enjoyable prose writings."

29 GURNEY, STEPHEN. "The 'Dialectic of Desire' in *Madame Bovary* and *Le Grand Meaulnes*." *Romanticism Past and Present* 7, no. 1:37–62.

Gustave Flaubert's *Madame Bovary* and Alain Fournier's *Le Grand Meaulnes* can be seen as "though they were expressly written to illustrate the psychology of Lewis' dialectic in its several moral, social, and spiritual ramifications."

30 HANGER, NANCY C. "The Excellent Absurdity: Substitution and Co-Inherence in C. S. Lewis and Charles Williams." *Mythlore* 9 (Winter):14–18.

Substitution, "the act of putting oneself in another's place," becomes co-inherence, "the state of giving and taking, holding and being held," in the fiction of Lewis and Williams. The "excellent absurdity" in *Perelandra* is that Ransom is needed but is also superfluous, because if he did not succeed, another would. The community of St. Anne's in *That Hideous Strength* has an atmosphere of substitution and co-inherence that brings absolute freedom from absolute obedience. In *Till We Have Faces*, "exchange upon exchange is made, the sacrificer becomes the sacrifice and co-inherence reigns."

31 HEIDELBERGER, PATRICIA. "Part A: With Girls at Home." In *The Search for C. S. Lewis*. Edited by Stephen Schofield. South Plainfield, N.J.: Bridge Publishing, pp. 53–54.

Reprint of 1979.46.

32 HOUSTON, JAMES [M.]. "Reminiscences of the Oxford Lewis." *Lamp-Post of the Southern California C. S. Lewis Society* 7, no. 2 (August):6–12.

Houston and Lewis belonged to a group that met regularly on Wednesday nights to discuss literature. Lewis was thought by people at Oxford, especially the philosophers, to cheat at debating because he would create an incongruent analogy and under the roar of laughter would dash off in another direction. He had an intense shyness in personal matters, especially about his own religious experiences. His scholarship tended to be overlooked because he was too popular as a religious writer. Lewis was not a good tutor as he did not have enough patience with his students. His skill in writing comes from a university system that demands writing and from polishing his works by sharing them with friends. Losing his mother at an early age and spending so many years in the misogynistic tradition at Oxford, "Lewis was himself a bit gauche about his personal life."

33 HUNT, DAVID. "Observations of a Magdalen Don." In *The Search for C. S. Lewis*. Edited by Stephen Schofield. South Plainfield, N.J.: Bridge Publishing, pp. 123–125.

Lewis's love for classical literature was strong. He would encourage people to talk on their own subjects. He was good-natured, affable, and never patronizing.

1983

34   JONES, MURIEL. "Part D: With Women at College." In *The Search for C. S. Lewis*. Edited by Stephen Schofield. South Plainfield, N.J.: Bridge Publishing, pp. 74–75.

    Lewis quotes Jones (née Bentley) in *A Preface to Paradise Lost*. Jones remembers him as "an extremely good teacher. He made you want to read whatever books he mentioned. He taught that the text of anything you are reading is to be taken seriously."

35   KESSLER, DAVID NATHAN. "Design Arguments: A Re-Evaluation." Ph.D. dissertation, University of Notre Dame, 331 pp.

    Design arguments are "intended to show that human beings have not acquired the form they have due to accident or to unguided causal forces." David Paley and R. G. Swinburne advanced versions of the argument that are ultimately unsuccessful. Richard Taylor's argument, derived from Lewis's version, also fails. Lewis's argument in the revised edition of *Miracles* has an important problem in "supposing the utter distinctness of Ground–Consequent (GC) relations from Cause–Effect (CE) ones." His argument fails because he tries "to prove too strong a thesis: that the naturalist's view is inconsistent with the trustworthiness of thinking." While Lewis's version of the argument in the first edition of *Miracles* is also unsuccessful, its basic principle can be developed into a successful design argument that shows "the human ability to think is to be found in the intentions of at least one intelligent being."

36   KEGLEY, CHARLES W. "Lewis, C(live) S(taples)." In *Thinkers of the Twentieth Century: A Biographical, Bibliographical and Critical Dictionary*. Edited by Elizabeth Devine, Michael Held, James Vinson, and George Walsh. Detroit: Gale Research Company, pp. 331–333.

    Lewis merits the adjective *genius*. He avoided extremes and was conservative in his religion, his politics, and his personal life. He was a deeply Christian humanist. "Lewis's international fame was based on his witty, brilliant, highly imaginative yet common sense discussion of basic Christian belief and practices." Kegley includes a brief biography and bibliography.

37   KNIGHT, BETTIE JO. "Paradise Retained: *Perelandra* as Epic." Ph.D. dissertation, Oklahoma State University, 175 pp.

    To be an epic a work must satisfy the following criteria: it must be a long narrative poem with a serious subject written in an elevated style; it must have a hero of imposing stature who embodies the ideal of the culture; it must have a vast setting; its action will involve a battle requiring superhuman courage; and the hero must be aided or hindered by supernatural forces. Science fiction is the successor to the epic genre because it is vast in scope, allows for heroic deeds in battle, retains the supernatural element, and often balances the fate of an entire planet or universe on the hero's actions. *Perelandra* employs the devices and conventions of Western epic and echoes and parallels other epics. It is a long narrative, depicts the struggle between good and evil in biblical terms, and has passages of elevated style. Although Lewis's hero is an ordinary person, the author's point is that each individual person is of immense value because he or she is a child of God. *Perelandra* follows the conventions of epic: statement of argument or theme, long catalogs of animals and supernatural beings, descriptions of weapons (Lewis transposes this convention by listing Ransom's fists and teeth as his weapons), use of similes with biblical and mythological references, stock epithets, and descent into the underworld. Lewis follows Milton and Dante in putting God at the center. "It is a mark of the genus of Lewis's schemata that he combines within the framework of a science fiction novel the epic tradition, Greek mythology, and Biblical references."

38 KREEFT, PETER. "A Thin Slice of the Genuine Article." *Canadian C. S. Lewis Journal*, no. 44 (Autumn):1–5.

Bradshaw's [1983.5] "essay seems like an adolescent's desperate attempt to declare his independence from a formidable and domineering father." The Lewis he met is only one facet of the whole. Contrary to Bradshaw's claim, after Lewis's conversion there was a synthesis between the logical and imaginative. "Bradshaw does not explore the most serious personal deficiency in Lewis, his tendency to sadism." To say that greed, not pride, is the primal sin is to call for another gospel. "Lewis was not the mere moralist Bradshaw depicts." Bradshaw looks at Lewis's diagnosis of sin without Lewis's cure of salvation. See Bradshaw's reply 1984.9.

39 LEOPOLD, PAUL. The Writings of Joy Davidman Lewis (1915–1950)." *CSL: The Bulletin of the New York C. S. Lewis Society* 14 (February):1–10; (March):1–9.

Leopold provides a biography of Helen Joy Davidman and an analysis of her writings, including novels, poems, propaganda for the Communist party, and Christian writings. Her writing was limited by bonds of fashion and politics. Her novels are strong in construction and scene painting but weak in character depiction; her expository writing is vivid and imaginative, with her later works having great power. She "was clearly a writer of considerable talent."

40 LINDSKOOG, KATHRYN [ANN]. "C. S. Lewis on Christmas." *Christianity Today* 27 (16 December):24–26.

Lewis's 1954 story "Xmas and Christmas" shows his loathing for the commercialization of Christmas. In his 1957 essay "What Christmas Means to Me" he condemns the commercialization of Christmas because it causes more pain than pleasure, is a trap of obligations, results in the purchase of rubbish, and is exhausting. In his poem "Nativity" Lewis "shows what the nativity scene meant in his own prayer life" and wishes for the ox's strength, the ass's patience, and the sheep's innocence. Reprinted: 1985.43.

1983

41 ———. "Reactions from Other Women." *Canadian C. S. Lewis Journal*, no. 43 (Summer):1–11.
   Reprint of 1976.27. Reprinted: 1983.42.

42 ———. "Reactions from Other Women." In *The Search for C. S. Lewis*. Edited by Stephen Schofield. South Plainfield, N.J.: Bridge Publishing, pp. 77–88.
   Reprint of 1983.41.

43 LONEY, JOHN DOUGLAS. "Reality, Truth and Perspective in the Fiction of C. S. Lewis." Ph.D. dissertation, McMaster University, 263 pp.
   Three tenets of his Christianity dominate Lewis's fiction: objective reality can be known by man and depends on the fundamental reality of God; objective truth can be discovered by reason and by acceptance of the universal moral law, the Tao; "man's perception dictates his experience of reality, the operation of his reason, and his response to the Tao, and so is of crucial importance in the matter of establishing his relationship to the central Reality, the person of God." In *Out of the Silent Planet* Lewis depicts the reordering of Ransom's perception as he learns that the reality of the universe is dependent on the person of Maleldil. In *Perelandra* Ransom acts in a manner ordinate to that reality; the novel also deals with the themes of "the interpretation of truth, myth and fact, and [the] dismantling of the Empirical Bogey of space and time." In *That Hideous Strength* Mark and Jane are reconciled to each other by their individual reconciliation to reality. In the Chronicles of Narnia the children learn they must establish a responsible relationship to the central reality, Aslan. In *Till We Have Faces*, Orual endures a violent contest between two beliefs—rationalism and a fertility cult—until she accepts the greater reality that neither had been adequate to describe.

44 McGOVERN, EUGENE. "C. S. Lewis." In *British Novelists, 1930–1959*. Part 1: A–L. Edited by Bernard Oldsey. *Dictionary of Literary Biography*, vol. 15. Detroit: Gale Research Company, pp. 298–305.
   Lewis had several reputations: critic and literary scholar, expositor and defender of Christian beliefs, and novelist. Some critics fault Lewis for his inattention to scientific hardware and his antiscientific streak in the Space Trilogy, but he would respond that he was not interested in hardware and treated the "real" scientists in the Trilogy with respect. Lewis hoped the Chronicles of Narnia would prepare the imagination to receive Christianity, but they are not simply a retelling of the Gospels. In *Till We Have Faces* he depicts three complete and convincing characters. Although Lewis's novels have received respect and admiration they have "not often attracted the attention of the most celebrated critics" because they are science fiction and fairy tales, they are not experimental, and they are accessible to the general reader.

45 MATTHEWS, KENNETH ERNEST. "C. S. Lewis and the Modern World." Ph.D. dissertation, University of California, Los Angeles, 177 pp.

Lewis's hyperbolic style is to blame for the widespread view that he was antimodern or neomedieval. His "Great War" with Owen Barfield taught him the importance of the growth of human self-consciousness, and he was interested in literature of the medieval/Renaissance period because this sort of self-consciousness first presented itself in writers of this period. Lewis's real genius lies in using the past to understand the present. While "his views on the self and the relation between consciousness and time closely parallel those of contemporaries like Proust and Bergson and Jung," his insistence that enrichment of self means to go out of self is not part of the modern temperament. Lewis believed that progress demanded an unchanging element; his psyche demanded something permanent to allow growth. In *Mere Christianity* Lewis identified a Protestant interpretation of Pauline soteriology as the central and permanent element in Christianity. His poetry argues for a return to classical values and stands as evidence of his belief in the value of this earlier vision of the world and its importance to the wholeness of the human self. In his fiction, Lewis attempts "to pass on to the future a 'poetic symbol' of the past." His characters are always modern people who confront the past, learn from it, and become better modern people. The hierarchical model and medieval cosmology provide the philosophical basis of the Space Trilogy. "The Dark Tower" develops the themes of inner versus outer reality and a modern, Bergsonian, view of time. The Chronicles of Narnia are dominated by the "there and back" pattern and develop the theme of hierarchy. In *Till We Have Faces* Orual goes on a journey through her own past to achieve a wholly renovated self who is able to face the wasteland of the present and to face eternity. Lewis agreed with modern authors that aloneness and alienation are the watchwords of the age but he disagreed with them that there is no escape; he finds the means to escape is to go out of ourselves by experiencing other selves in the literature of the past.

46 MEILAENDER, GILBERT. "Theology in Stories: C. S. Lewis and the Narrative Quality of Experience." *Chronicle of the Portland C. S. Lewis Society* 12, no. 1 (January–March):7–14.

Reprint of 1981.43.

47 MITCHELL, L. J. "Miracles, Natural Laws, and Christian Theology." *Theologia Evangelica* 16, no. 3 (September):51–58.

David Hume's definition of miracles as a transgression of an absolute universal law of nature is a logical contradiction. The problem with the traditional understanding of miracles is that although science cannot now explain certain phenomena, this does not mean the phenomena are ultimately inexplicable or that they must be attributed to supernatural agents. Lewis contends that "a critique of miracles which confines itself to the uniformity of natural

1983

laws withholds from argument the very central issue at stake, this interference or intervention factor." He emphasizes that all Christian miracles either prepare for, exhibit, or result from the Incarnation. Lewis believes that miracles are not arbitrary violations of natural laws but are a "retelling of the story nature has already told and is still telling." He also says that nature cannot be explained in terms of itself, that God is beyond and yet in control of nature. The theological approach to miracles is grounded in the "actual, spacio-temporal revelation of an eternal, omnipotent and sovereign God."

48   MUGGERIDGE, MALCOLM. "The Mystery." In *The Search for C. S. Lewis*. Edited by Stephen Schofield. South Plainfield, N.J.: Bridge Publishing, pp. 127–130.
      Reprint of 1981.46.

49   MURPHY, BRIAN. *C. S. Lewis*. Mercer Island, Wash.: Starmont House, 95 pp.
      Lewis's fiction examines the whole question of value, is concerned with the freeing of the spirit, and "treats the relationship between the soul and the self in a unique way." The real accomplishment of *Out of the Silent Planet* is the working out of a coherent philosophy against the backdrop of the Christian cosmology. Ransom's progress through the Trilogy is an entire life-as-learning cycle; "he understands himself more fully because he sees the relationship between the self and the rest of Reality more accurately." In *Perelandra* Lewis opposes fear and pleasure: "Fear leads to despair, a refusal to live or see any longer. Pleasure leads to Joy, and ultimately to God who is Reality itself." The main theme of the novel is the dilemma between destiny and free will. *That Hideous Strength* dramatizes a main theme of *The Abolition of Man*, that "the use of power must not be separated from a prior consideration of the value of that power." In the last decade of his life, "Lewis seems to have seen God less clearly, perhaps even less surely, but more profoundly, more passionately." In the Chronicles of Narnia and *Till We Have Faces* the main theme is the search for the real, hidden God. Lewis's most impressive virtue as an artist is his courage; he "argues for the assertion of the whole human being—head, heart and gut; and, indeed sees the heart as the crucial link between the other two."

50   MUSACCHIO, GEORGE. "Foreign Words in *The Discarded Image*." *CSL: The Bulletin of the New York C. S. Lewis Society* 14 (July):5–7.
      Musacchio provides translations for unexplained Greek, Latin, Italian, French, and Middle English words in Lewis's book and gives the page number on which the term appears in the text.

51 PATTERSON, NANCY-LOU. "Bright-Eyed Beauty: Celtic Elements in Charles Williams, J. R. R. Tolkien, and C. S. Lewis." *Mythlore* 10 (Spring):5–10.

Celtic literature has "astonishing vigour and brilliance of detail." Lewis points out how Williams used Celtic elements in his recreation of the Arthurian story. Lewis describes Celtic myth as sensuous, "'all transparent and full of nuances"—evanescent—but very bright.'" Lewis's fiction is a "true continuation of the Celtic tradition."

52 PHILIP, PETER. "South African View." In *The Search for C. S. Lewis*. Edited by Stephen Schofield. South Plainfield, N.J.: Bridge Publishing, pp. 93–96.

Reprint of 1980.42.

53 PILE, JOAN B. "Part C: With Women at College." In *The Search for C. S. Lewis*. Edited by Stephen Schofield. South Plainfield, N.J.: Bridge Publishing, pp. 71–73.

Reprinted from 1980.44.

54 PITTER, RUTH. "Poet to Poet." In *The Search for C. S. Lewis*. Edited by Stephen Schofield. South Plainfield, N.J.: Bridge Publishing, pp. 111–115.

Reprint of 1980.45.

55 "A Previously Unpublished Lewis Letter." *CSL: The Bulletin of the New York C. S. Lewis Society* 15 (November):10.

Lewis highlights in his letter his journey from baptism in the Church, through atheism to conversion.

56 PYLES, FRANKLIN ARTHUR. "The Language Theory of C. S. Lewis." *Trinity Journal* 4, no. 2:82–91.

Lewis followed F. H. Bradley in believing that "imagination is one way the mind grasps meaning from the external world; and, along with language, imagination manifests meaning into consciousness." Lewis thought that scientific-philosophical language is concerned with the abstract while poetic language pertains to the concrete. Lewis believed that the activity of analyzing and making distinctions about reality makes new metaphors that carry meaning into language. Lewis sees three ways symbol may function as a mediator of meaning: symbols may have a sacramental character; the ability of the symbol to perform this sacramental task depends on the similarity between the material element and spiritual reality; and capturing the soul of a work of art hinges on participating in the aesthetic experience of the artist. He believed that when religion speaks about that which is most concrete, God, it speaks in poetic language.

1983

57 RAWSON, ELLEN. "The Fisher-King in *That Hideous Strength.*" *Mythlore* 9 (Winter):30–32.

   The conflict in the novel is between Logres, representing the spiritual England of King Arthur, and modern Britain, representing evil. Ransom, acting as the Fisher-King, is wounded, unable to walk. Jane, acting as Perceval, becomes a Christian through her encounter with Ransom and will bear the heir to the Fisher-King.

58 REICHENBACH, BRUCE R. "C. S. Lewis on the Desolation of Devalued Science." *Seven: An Anglo-American Literary Review* 4:14–26.
   Reprint of 1982.42.

59 Review of *On Stories: And Other Essays on Literature. Science Fiction Review* 12 (February):42.

   Lewis "was one of the most lucid, sensible critics ever to enter the fray. He was more interested in providing understanding than building up his reputation, which is a large part of why he was so good."

60 RIGSBEE, SALLY ADAIR. "Fantasy Places and Imaginative Belief: *The Lion, the Witch and the Wardrobe* and *The Princess and the Goblin.*" *Children's Literature Association Quarterly* 8, no. 1 (Spring):10–11.

   Both *The Lion, the Witch and the Wardrobe* and George MacDonald's *The Princess and the Goblin* (London: Blackie & Son, 1871) are "versions of the archetypal plot of initiation and maturation," where "belief in the reality of a fantasy place is a crucial issue in the developmental process of a child." In both novels setting represents different states of the psyche, the plot is the struggle between good and evil, and the issue of belief in the imaginative other world is the main concern.

61 ROOK, ALAN. "The Butcher." In *The Search for C. S. Lewis.* Edited by Stephen Schofield. South Plainfield, N.J.: Bridge Publishing, pp. 11–15.
   Reprint of 1979.88; 1980.50.

62 ROSENBAUM, STANLEY N. "Our Own Silly Faces: C. S. Lewis on Psalms." *Christian Century* 100 (18 May):486–489.

   Reflections on the Psalms is detrimental to the Christian's understanding of Judaism. Lewis did not know Hebrew, shows no understanding of Hebrew poetry, and suffers under the "misapprehension that Judaism is runaway 'legalism.'" "If one doesn't know Hebrew Scripture in Hebrew, one does not know it." The Torah states that the highest human task is to establish justice and doing justice requires exacting precision. Lewis's attitude that no Jew knows God in the way Christians do prevents serious discussion between Jews and Christians.

63 ROSSOW, FRANCIS C. "Echoes of the Gospel-event in Literature and Elsewhere." *Concordia Journal* 9 (March):50–58.

Echoes of Christ's incarnation, life, death, and resurrection can be found in the Gregorian calendar, the process of plant growth, the metamorphosis of the caterpillar into the butterfly, the analogy between the womb and the tomb, a multiple-phase rocket, the vicariousness in nature, paganism, mythology, and literature. *The Lion, the Witch and the Wardrobe* is an example of an intentional Gospel pattern. The Witch is associated with Satan, Aslan with Christ; Aslan undergoes a Passion suffering, is killed and rises from the dead, and appears before his disciples. Shakespeare's *All's Well That Ends Well* is an example of a probable Gospel pattern and Oscar Wilde's *The Picture of Dorian Gray* is an example of an unintentional Gospel pattern.

64 ROUTLEY, ERIK. "Stunning Effect." In *The Search for C. S. Lewis*. Edited by Stephen Schofield. South Plainfield, N.J.: Bridge Publishing, pp. 97–101.

Reprint of 1973.37; 1979.89, 90.

65 SAYER, GEORGE. "A Guest in the House." In *The Search for C. S. Lewis*. Edited by Stephen Schofield. South Plainfield, N.J.: Bridge Publishing, pp. 89–92.

Reprinted from 1981.60.

66 SCHAKEL, PETER J. "Seeing and Knowing: The Epistemology of C. S. Lewis's *Till We Have Faces*." *Seven: An Anglo-American Literary Review* 4:84–97.

In his early fiction and apologetic works, Lewis holds that knowledge comes through the senses and is the result of reasoning. He "regarded Christianity as something to be accepted with the intellect rather than arrived at by a leap of faith." Lewis believed that imagination was important as a way to create mental images of things not accessible to sensual experience. In the 1950s, Lewis's confidence in rationalism lessened considerably. He broadened his views to a reliance on individual imagination as the only source of knowledge. Through the character of Fox in *Till We Have Faces*, who moves away from his philosophy of objective rationalism and admits its inadequacy, "Lewis acknowledges his own realization of the limitations of rationalism and of the need to be open to the mythical and the imaginative as avenues to Truth."

67 SCHOFIELD, STEPHEN. "Impact." In *The Search for C. S. Lewis*. Edited by Stephen Schofield. South Plainfield, N.J.: Bridge Publishing, pp. 131–146.

Reprint of 1979.94, 95, 101, 102.

68 ———. "Letters to an Editor." In *The Search for C. S. Lewis*. Edited by Stephen Schofield. South Plainfield, N.J.: Bridge Publishing, pp. 163–199.

This chapter reprints letters received by the *Canadian C. S. Lewis*

1983

Journal regarding chapters in this collection that first appeared in the journal. Also included are letters Lewis and his brother, Warren, wrote to Schofield. Reprinted from 1980.57. Reprinted in part: 1984.60.

69 ———. "Oxford Loses a Genius." In *The Search for C. S. Lewis*. Edited by Stephen Schofield. South Plainfield, N.J.: Bridge Publishing, pp. 147–155. Reprint of 1981.62.

70 ———. "Part A: Lunch with Lewis." In *The Search for C. S. Lewis*. Edited by Stephen Schofield. South Plainfield, N.J.: Bridge Publishing, pp. 1–2. Reprint of 1979.103.

71 SCHULMAN, J. NEIL. "An Escape to Narnia: *The Silver Chair. Lamp-Post of the Southern California C. S. Lewis Society* 7, nos. 3–4 (December):6–14.

Reading *The Silver Chair* as a young boy, Schulman felt Lewis understood how rotten school can be and was an ally in the war against bullies. The opening chapters of *The Silver Chair* provide exciting adventure. The novel provides marvelous bits of satire—for example, on education and the theory of management. Puddleglum is the funniest conceit. The Chronicles of Narnia do not contain blatant Christianity. The novel taught Schulman that imagination might be a path to truth.

72 STEIGENGA, J. JOHN, "Through a Veil of Tears: Reflections on C. S. Lewis' *Till We Have Faces*." *Lamp-Post of the Southern California C. S. Lewis Society* 7, no. 2 (August):13–15, 25.

The theme of the novel is "the purification of its characters through suffering and misfortune while they were yet wrestling with the most powerful force in the universe—love." In terms of developmental psychology Orual was deprived of parental affection and was constantly degraded in her early life. Her ego development was slowed and her superego grew rigidly proper. In her complaint against the gods she comes to understand why things happened the way they did. As Orual's self-perception begins to change, the Ungit part of her wavers and the Psyche part gains ground. The veil she wears is a symbol of the defenses she uses to ignore her pain and tension. The message Lewis gives us as the culmination of his exploration of Orual's development is "the forgiveness of past transgressions, making intercession for another, and subsequent sanctification." The novel integrates individual psychology with theological truth.

73 TANDY, GARY LYNN. "The Non-Fiction Prose of C. S. Lewis: A Rhetorical Analysis." Ph.D. dissertation, University of Tulsa, 177 pp.

Lewis adopted the rhetorical stance of an old Western man "in order to communicate effectively his religious and literary ideas in the modern world."

His approach to language was functional and practical; he "was careful to maintain a balance between style and content, form and matter." Lewis's rhetorical theory was to translate technical theological language into every-day English. Much of his success as an apologist is due to his ability to imagine an audience and address it. The rational appeal predominates in Lewis's works, with four categories of arguments being used: deductive, inductive, argument by definition, and either–or arguments. At times he used nonlogical techniques, including logical fallacies, satire, and personification. Several personae are displayed in his works, including amateur theologian, literary historian, and writer of certitude. Lewis's common structural pattern is that of problem–solution, with frequent interruptions to answer possible objections. His style is "an unusual blend of literary flavor and logical clari-ty." His tone is informal, with frequent use of colloquial phrases, and with humorous witticisms, analogies, or similes. He uses inverted sentences, negation, and word repetition for variety and emphasis. The dominant quali-ty of Lewis's nonfiction prose style is the rhetoric of certitude. He chooses words and phrases to "create the impression of certainty for the concepts which he is discussing." He makes frequent use of series, asyndeton, and polysyndeton creating "'an aura of certainty, confidence, didacticism, and dogmatism.'" These characteristics "create a style which is clear, vigorous, and memorable."

74   TAYLOR, A. J. P. "The Fun of the Thing." In *The Search for C. S. Lewis*. Edited by Stephen Schofield. South Plainfield, N.J.: Bridge Publishing, pp. 117–121.
        Reprint of 1979.110.

75   THORSON, STEPHEN. "Knowing and Being in C. S. Lewis's 'Great War' with Owen Barfield." *CSL: The Bulletin of the New York C. S. Lewis Society* 15 (November):1–8.
        Lewis thought the soul emerges from the spirit; one cannot enjoy and contemplate at the same time, "for the Spirit *is* the contemplating self and the soul *is* the enjoying self." By imagination we see things as spirit sees; "since we cannot both enjoy Imagination and contemplate whether it is true at the same time, knowledge of truth must be objectively demonstrated"; therefore, we cannot find truth through imagination. Barfield thought seeing things as spirit means ascending from contemplation to "con-enjoyment." "Enjoyment and contemplation are not mutually exclusive"; therefore, truth and knowledge come from imagination. Lewis's metaphysics changed after his conversion. The short story "A Man Born Blind," written during the "Great War," is a warning against taking idealism too far. "Lewis wrote this story to show the grave danger of trying to *see* what is there to see *by*." See Adey's response 1984.1 and Thorson's reply 1984.69.

1983

76 THORSON, STEPHEN, and DANIEL, JERRY [L.]. "Bibliographic Notes." *CSL: The Bulletin of the New York C. S. Lewis Society* 14 (June):6–7.
   The authors provide a supplement to Walter Hooper's bibliography of Lewis's works [1979.48], listing published drawings by Lewis.

77 THORSON, STEPHEN. "Bibliographic Notes." *CSL: The Bulletin of the New York C. S. Lewis Society* 14 (August):6–7.
   The author lists published holographs. See also his later "Bibliographic Notes," 1986.58–61 and 1987.57.

78 TREASE, GEOFFREY. Review of *Of This and Other Worlds*. *British Book News* February, p. 123.
   Most of these pieces are on the types of storytelling in which Lewis excelled: children's books and science fiction. "To these matters Lewis brings a deeply thoughtful, responsible and disarmingly modest mind."

79 TYNAN, KENNETH. "Part B: Exhilaration." In *The Search for C. S. Lewis*. Edited by Stephen Schofield. South Plainfield, N.J.: Bridge Publishing, pp. 3–9.
   Reprint of 1979.112–113. Reprinted: 1988.77.

80 ULREICH, JOHN C. "Prophets, Priests, and Poets: Toward a Definition of Religious Fiction." *Cithara* 22, no. 2 (May):3–31.
   Religious fiction may be either iconic (mythic, hierarchical, and hieratic) or iconoclastic (antagonistic toward myth, anarchic, and prophetic). "The religious poet is either a priest or a prophet, either a maker or a breaker of mythic images." Spenser is the archetypal English maker of myth while Milton is the greatest iconoclast. Lewis's fiction, like Spenser's, is hierarchical and sacramental; the sacramental perception is reinforced by his archetypal structure. A comparison of *The Pilgrim's Regress* with its model, Bunyan's *Pilgrim's Progress*, shows the sacramental quality of Lewis's universe. *Till We Have Faces* reveals that Lewis only appears to be like Spenser but is in truth an iconoclast like Milton because he knows fiction is only images, not sacraments. Orual's self-discovery "represents Lewis's reflection on the nature of his own imaginative life."

81 WALL, ROBERT WALTER. "The Problem of Observed Pain: A Study of C. S. Lewis on Suffering." *Journal of the Evangelical Theological Society* 26 no. 4:443–451.
   A Grief Observed calls into question the logical theological and philosophical conclusions of *The Problem of Pain* and finally extends them. *Grief* is authorized by a Mosaic theology—in the midst of the total disarray of Lewis's life and anger, God finds him and frees him to regain his faith. In *Pain*

Lewis states that pain, through humility and dependency, makes humankind more lovable to God. The structure of *Grief* is a pilgrimage toward faith recovered, conducted in four stages: questioning, rejecting the traditional forms of comfort, making sense of the present through the past, and recognizing "the tension and ambiguity between earthly reality and transcendent trust." The problem of pain is not the silence of God but our own wailing that needs to be silenced. What counts is knowing that God's goodness is present and that He is with us in power.

82   WILLIS, JOHN RANDOLPH. *Pleasures Forevermore: The Theology of C. S. Lewis*. Chicago: Loyola University Press, 157 pp.

Willis evaluates Lewis's theology from a Roman Catholic viewpoint. He summarizes Lewis's views on God, angels, temptation, evil, Jesus Christ, redemption, the Church, sacraments, Scripture, prayer, ethics, hell, heaven, and the end times, as presented in his theological works and fiction. "From the logical point of view, Lewis's foundations for *Mere Christianity* must collapse, because the very topics he attempted to avoid—pope, magisterium, sacraments—are essential ingredients to the theological whole."

83   WOLFE, GREGORY. "C. S. Lewis's Debt to George MacDonald." *CSL: The Bulletin of the New York C. S. Lewis Society* 15 (December):1–7.

Lewis was influenced by MacDonald's dealing with the philosophical and social consequences of the Romantic movement, which he saw as a conflict between love and power; MacDonald saw that the "effort to force joy into being ends in a 'will to power.'" Lewis was enchanted by the way MacDonald "took the ordinary materials of life and transfigured them into symbols of God's immanent presence in the world, and of the way man relates spiritually to God and the world." MacDonald manipulates archetypal images to write mythopoetic works while Lewis reworked and gave new meaning to biblical and classical stories. A theme the two have in common is the "doctrine of Becoming," that human life is in "motion either towards fullness of being through holy action, or negation through the assertion of self."

84   WUNDER, DICK. "C. S. Lewis and Nuclear Weapons." *Lamp-Post of the Southern California C. S. Lewis Society* 7, no. 2 (August):16–17, 25.

Lewis says in *God in the Dock* that "the Bomb" won't kill all of humanity and even if it did Christians know that human history must end someday. He argues that scientists should not be the authority on what is good for mankind, a position implying that arms control should not be left to the specialists. He says that Christians should refuse to bomb civilians thus calling into question the whole deterrence theory of nuclear weapons. He calls Dachau and Hiroshima recent advances of the "'ruthless, non-moral utilitarianism over the old world of ethical law.'"

1984

85 YAGYU, NAOYUKI. "My Encounter with Lewis." *Canadian C. S. Lewis Society*, no. 41 (Winter):9–11.

Yagyu first became aware of Lewis by reading his literary criticism but after reading Lewis's popular books he came to regard Lewis as his spiritual mentor. "To me, his magnetism still resides in his style. . . . his way of saying things is as delightful as the things themselves." Reprinted: 1983.86.

86 ———. "Surprise Encounter." In *In Search of C. S. Lewis*. Edited by Stephen Schofield. South Plainfield, N.J.: Bridge Publishing, pp. 107–110.

Reprint of 1983.85.

1984

1 ADEY, LIONEL. "A Response to Dr. Thorson." *CSL: The Bulletin of the New York C. S. Lewis Society* 15 (March):6–10.

Adey responds to Thorson's article on Lewis's "Great War" with Owen Barfield [1983.75]. Comments written in pencil on the manuscript of *Summae Metaphysices Contra Anthroposophos* were written by Lewis himself, between 1930 and 1950. Thorson's claim that Barfield's criticism of Lewis is "unanswerable from within his own and Lewis's system" is not clear since Lewis did not subscribe to anthroposophy. Adey states he is not unsympathetic to Lewis and therefore not prone to error in interpreting the *Summa*. Thorson is less than generous in failing to acknowledge Adey's explanation of the contemplation/enjoyment antithesis and in quoting out of context. Lewis was wrong in his "refusal to entertain the literature and thought of his own time" and in his "notion of continuing revelation beyond Biblical times." See Thorson's reply 1984.69.

2 ADKISON, DANNY M. "The Politics of C. S. Lewis Reconsidered." *CSL: The Bulletin of the New York C. S. Lewis Society* 15 (June):4–6.

Sobran's [1981.66] labeling of Lewis as conservative is wrong. The same reasons Sobran uses to give him the conservative label—Lewis's emphasis on government leaving people alone and providing only minimum services—could just as easily be used to call him a moderate or a liberal. "Lewis's remarks concerning politics are inconclusive in terms of expressing a particular ideology." See response 1984.71.

3 AESCHLIMAN, M[ICHAEL] D. "C. S. Lewis and the Case against Scientism." *CSL: The Bulletin of the New York C. S. Lewis Society* 15 (February):1–5.

The fallacy of scientism is the belief that scientific observation is the only way we can find out about nature. Aeschliman examines current arguments and relates them to Lewis's case against scientism as presented in *The Abolition of Man.*

4   AVELING, HELEN A. "The Need for Belief in the 'Narnian Chronicles.'" *CSL: The Bulletin of the New York C. S. Lewis Society* 15 (September):16–17.
    Belief in Aslan and Narnia is the cornerstone of the Chronicles. Aveling discusses Lucy's, Susan's, and the animals' belief in Aslan.

5   BERGVALL, AKE. "A Myth Retold: C. S. Lewis' *Till We Have Faces.*" *Mythlore* 11 (Summer):5–12, 22.
    The novel is a myth working on various levels, even though the characters are realistically portrayed and the story is psychologically profound. The novel is about the dangers of love; it is a quest for true love and self-knowledge. The second part of the work is a true answer to Orual's accusation against the gods in the first part. "The answer to Orual's charges lies within herself. The moment she sees what she has been—jealous and possessive— she is also freed to see the gods."

6   BERMAN, RUTH. "Dragons for Tolkien and Lewis." *Mythlore* 11 (Summer):53–58.
    Dragons were used to represent the devil in Spenser's *Faerie Queene* and Milton's *Paradise Lost.* Because of this "too rigid identification of the dragon with the dragon of the Book of Revelations, that is, Satan," there was a reluctance to depict dragons in the eighteenth and nineteenth centuries. At the end of the nineteenth century dragons began to appear again, due to the discovery of dinosaurs and the study of folktales, but mostly in the form of the comic dragon. Tolkien portrayed dragons as noncomic evil. Lewis used a dragon as a symbol of redeemable evil in *The Voyage of the "Dawn Treader."* In *The Pilgrim's Regress* he used dragons allegorically as images of the excesses of North and South. Tolkien, and Lewis to a lesser extent, "were important in bringing the non-comically evil side of dragon nature back into use."

7   BESTON, ROSE MARIE. "C. S. Lewis's Theory of Romance." *Ariel* 15, no. 1 (January):3–16.
    According to Lewis, the principal characteristics of romance are the quest of fulfillment of *Sehnsucht* in the realm of the numinous and the quality of imaginative freedom. He used these principles of romance in his criticism of Damon's *Brut,* Malory's *Morte d'Arthur* and Spenser's *Faerie Queene.* Lewis's view of romance is limited in its applicability because it emphasizes only those elements that interest him and neglects elements that link romance to the real world, including the longing for love, the psychological aspects of life, the noncourtly aspects of life, and humor.

1984

8   BLATTNER, PAUL F., Jr. "An Analysis and Application of C. S. Lewis' 'The Humanitarian Theory of Punishment.'" *Chronicle of the Portland C. S. Lewis Society* 13, no. 2 (April–June):1–4.
   According to the Bible, man is responsible for his choices. Humanists view man not as a responsible moral agent but as a conditioned animal. Only the retributive theory contains hope for the criminal to truly change, "since one who is not responsible for his actions cannot change his own behavior." The rehabilitation approach says that people are sick and must be treated until they are well and can function in society. This view puts justice in the hands of experts who determine when the patient is well and whose decisions are not open to criticism by the public. The deterrence approach is even more dehumanizing, turning the criminal into an object lesson. Biblical law prescribes either restitution to the victim or death as the penalty for crime.

9   BRADSHAW, NORMAN. "Humble Contributions." *Canadian C. S. Lewis Journal*, no. 45 (Winter):13–15.
   Here Bradshaw responds to Kreeft [1983.38]. Bradshaw admired Lewis greatly but was disappointed by his lack of interest in his pupils, a reaction also described by Alan Rook and John Wain. Bradshaw was also troubled by Lewis's dark imagination by which he means Lewis's obsession with pride, the horror and loathsomeness of hell, and the temptation of devils.

10   BREWER, DEREK. "Living in the Imagination." *Times Higher Education Supplement* 601 (11 May):15.
   Lewis was Brewer's tutor at Magdalen College shortly before and after World War II. Lewis had a magnetic personality without being an attractive person. He had a "passionate attention to the nature of experience." He was the perfect Christian humanist in his literalism, "his love of idealized beauty and noble ideals, both in life and literature," and his desire for those things he studied to be important for human destiny.

11   BROWN, ROBERT F. "Temptation and Freedom in Perelandra." *Renascence: Essays on Value in Literature* 31, no. 1 (Autumn):52–68.
   Through the Green Lady's interaction with Ransom, Lewis develops the theme of maturation and the emergence of self-consciousness. Through Weston's temptation of the Green Lady, he provides a vivid portrait of the adoption of a dramatic conception of the self, which is a precondition of pride, but avoids the theological pitfall of "treating actual pride, which is already a sin, as though it were the cause of falling." Lewis's theological and philosophical achievement in Perelandra lies in how he "preserves the freedom of the Green Lady uncompromised, and at the same time gives us a psychologically plausible and theologically orthodox narrative of her temptation."

12 BUCKLEY, JEROME HAMILTON. *The Turning Key: Autobiography and the Subjective Impulse since 1800.* Cambridge, Mass.: Harvard University Press, pp. 91–92.

   Surprised by Joy "places its spiritual affirmation in a closely observed ordinary world." Lewis describes Joy as the longing "for a dimension of life beyond our commonplace routine" and comes to consider it "the evidence of a deeper subjective need."

13 COATS, DAN. "An Eternal Debt to C. S. Lewis." *Christianity Today* 28 (6 April):38.

   "No writer or single book . . . has had more influence on my life or drawn me closer to Christ than the C. S. Lewis masterpiece *Mere Christianity.*"

14 COBB, LAWRENCE [W.]. "An Interview with C. S. Lewis and Meister Eckhart." *CSL: The Bulletin of the New York C. S. Lewis Society* 15 (January):1–6.

   Cobb compares the views of Lewis and Johannes Eckhart, a Dominican theologian of the early fourteenth century, through use of a fictional "interview" with both. Both value conviviality but put it in its proper place, and both wrote on the experience of Joy.

15 COCKSHUT, A. O. J. *The Art of Autobiography in 19th and 20th Century England.* New Haven: Yale University Press, pp. 203–209.

   Lewis records in *Surprised by Joy* his rebellion against life. "Not only was he uninterested in society, but he was in revolt against his own being and the very laws of nature under which he held it." But the longing he experienced, Joy, was "so dominating that he had to change his view of life to fit it." Lewis's autobiography is interesting for its depiction of the gradual convergence of joy and reason.

16 COMO, JAMES [T.]. "A Look into Narnia." *CSL: The Bulletin of the New York C. S. Lewis Society* 15 (July):1–6.

   The Chronicles of Narnia "*educe*: 'draw out, elicit,' . . . the inner, unique, individual child." They are the stuff of theogony; they depict the appearance of God in the world. The Chronicles work because Lewis portrays his world so vitally readers cannot help believing in it. The Narnia books are a means of inviting readers to see the next world in this one.

17 DAIGLE, MARSHA ANN. "Dante's Divine Comedy and the Fiction of C. S. Lewis." Ph.D. dissertation, University of Michigan, 226 pp.

   "The *Commedia* is nothing less than a paradigm for Lewis's fiction, i.e., both a model and a source for Lewis." Lewis uses Dante's strategies for translating spiritual truths into fiction, and he uses Dante's characters, settings, and plots as archetypes in his fiction. Lewis's literary theory and his understanding of the relationship between an author's originality and his predecessor shed light on his own relationship to Dante. In *The Pilgrim's Regress* Lewis uses Dante's principles to construct the geography of an imaginary universe; like Dante's, the design of the world carries spiritual significance, and the pattern of the journey recalls elements from the *Inferno* and the *Purgatorio*. In the Ransom Trilogy he relies on Dante's structure and methodology to construct a Christian cosmos; the journey evokes the journey in the *Commedia*. In *The Screwtape Letters* Lewis uses spiritual concepts prominent in the *Commedia*, and the development of the protagonist is reminiscent of Dante's pilgrim. In *The Great Divorce* Lewis draws on the *Purgatorio* for the narrative sequence and setting; he "also makes use of the *Commedia* as a whole for his characters and for the presentation of his contrast between Heaven and Hell." *The Silver Chair* alludes to the journey through Dante's hell, and *The Voyage of the "Dawn Treader"* has material from the *Purgatorio* and the *Paradiso*. The main parallel between the Narnia Chronicles and the *Commedia* lies in similar handling of biblical material. "The variety of ways in which the *Commedia* is evoked in Lewis's several novels is a tribute not only to the wealth of material that can be tapped in Dante's poem but also to Lewis's keen insight into Dante's art and methodology and to the synthesizing power of his own imagination."

18 DONALDSON, MARA ELIZABETH. "Narratives of Transformation: C. S. Lewis's *Till We Have Faces* and Paul Ricoeur's Theory of Metaphor (Temporality)." Ph.D. dissertation, Emory University, 231 pp.

Traditional interpretations of *Till We Have Faces* find it consistent with Lewis's other work, dealing with such themes as spiritual and personal quests. However, a metaphorical reading shows the discontinuities between this novel and Lewis's other fiction. Paul Ricoeur's philosophy provides a critical model for understanding fictional narratives, especially narratives of transformation in which characters come to understand themselves differently. Ricoeur's theory of metaphor and metaphorical logic provides a model for showing how the two metaphors in the novel—"You also are Psyche" and "Holy places are dark places"—are related. The first is a metaphor for Orual's personal transformation and the second for her spiritual transformation. This metaphorical analysis of *Till We Have Faces* raises the question of the relationship between temporality and the logic of metaphor. Ricoeur's work on the problem of temporality is helpful but ultimately inconclusive concerning the interaction between metaphor and narrative temporality. In *Till We Have Faces*, "the temporal context of the narrative provides sequential specificity to the metaphors while the logic of metaphor lends significance to certain events in that sequence." Revised for publication: 1988.17.

19 FILMER, KATH. "Speaking in Parables." *Mythlore* 11 (Autumn):15–20.

Lewis used mythic characters, British cultural traditions, and biblical symbolism in *The Lion, the Witch and the Wardrobe* to create different levels of meaning. He maintains a close relationship between these elements and the traditional form of the fairy tale throughout the book. Lewis's characters fulfill the traditional roles of the genre, as heroes, donors, and a supernatural helper. Lewis uses British cultural traditions to define good and evil. He uses biblical symbolism with a sense of mystery and adventure that does not hinder the story. "Lewis has imbued the Biblical elements with new potency by virtue of their contextual link with the fairy tale."

20 FISHER, ROBERT. "Lewis's Acceptance of Paganism." *CSL: The Bulletin of the New York C. S. Lewis Society* 15 (September):15–16.

In *The Pilgrim's Regress* "Lewis says the Holy Spirit creates pagan imagery so it may be eventually schooled by the Law." This principle may be illustrated by using Plato's theory on the entrapment of the soul within the body. Paul, in 2 Corinthians, corrected Plato by portraying the body as a sacred temple.

21 FITZGERALD, DOROTHY HOBSON. "Arthurian Torso: Lewis's Commentary on Williams's Arthuriad." *CSL: The Bulletin of the New York C. S. Lewis Society* 15 (September):1–11.

In his commentary on Charles Williams's prose work *The Figure of Arthur* (London: Oxford University Press, 1948), "Lewis explores Williams's concepts of a basic orderly universe, the origins of good and evil, Dantean love, the doctrine of substitution, and the action of the Holy Spirit in time, space and eternity." Fitzgerald summarizes Williams's work and quotes Lewis's explanations.

22 FOREMAN, FRANK. "C. S. Lewis on the Christian and the State." *Chronicle of the Portland C. S. Lewis Society* 13, no. 1 (January–March):9–18.

Lewis felt Christianity should not have a political program because of the divisions among Christians and his fear that personal opinions would be claimed as authoritative. He believed Christians could do most for this world by concentrating their thinking on the next. Lewis thought the true basis of democracy was that fallen man was so wicked he could not be trusted with power over his fellow men. Lewis believed that "God created an ordered, hierarchical world and that political egalitarianism is very useful but notwithstanding remains a legal fiction." He argued that government's purpose was "'to promote and to protect the ordinary happiness of human beings in this life.'" He believed that the natural law is the basis of all law and government. He saw two threats to the future of mankind: an increasing application of science and governments treating people like children.

1984

23 ———. "C. S. Lewis' View of War and the Christian's Responsibility." *Chronicle of the Portland C. S. Lewis Society* 13, no. 1 (January–March): 18–28.

Lewis believed that all politics, including war, was important only in how it affected the immortal souls of individuals. While Scripture is very warlike, the early Church was pacifist. When Church and State merged under Constantine, Christian soldiers became commonplace. St. Augustine developed a "just war" thesis that allowed Christians to participate in war. During the Crusades the concepts of violence and holiness merged. Modern warfare is conducted by the "total war" theory: "war is to be fought 'to the utmost bounds of violence in order to win.'" There are four basic Christian views towards war: "biblical nonresistance," which allows Christians to be noncombatants only; "Christian Pacifism," which declares war and violence wrong for everyone; "just war," whose advocates apply Christian principles to warfare; and "preventive war," which allows Christians to support wars to stop injustice. Lewis belonged to the last group. He believed the timing or form of death is unimportant, and that only the inner state of the soul mattered. Because of this belief he argued that it is permissible for Christians to kill if there is no other way to restrain someone from doing evil. He warned that pacifism leads to a "coterie" mentality. He said "we must make 'every effort to ensure a good government and to influence public opinion,' but in the end we must obey." He offered the practical suggestion that Christians become soldiers but refuse to obey anti-Christian orders. He took it for granted that human history would end one day and so was not concerned about a nuclear holocaust.

24 FOREMAN, LELIA. "A Short Look At C. S. Lewis' Short Science Fiction." *Chronicle of the Portland C. S. Lewis Society* 13, no. 1 (January–March):1–7.

Lewis's works and symbols are easy and comforting for a Christian to read, but non-Christians are totally confounded by them. In "The Man Born Blind" he has the correct science and the right feeling of a blind person finding his sight. When Lewis created a dull woman in "The Shody Lands" he was not being misogynistic but was merely depicting a human trait. This story arouses such ire because it hurts; it makes us examine ourselves, and, while we have all met and despised women like this, "Lewis saw a women that God cares about very much." "Ministering Angels" is tremendously funny. LeGuin [1977.37] found it to be horrible because the female university lecturer is not saved, saying there is a lot of hatred in Lewis. Lewis only hates evil and "has enough examples of all sorts of people converting in his stories that it should be obvious he considered conversion possible for anyone." "Form of Things Unknown" is a chilling story.

25 FORD, PAUL F[RANCIS]. "The Sweet Prose and the Honeyed and Floral Christianity of François de Sales: A Note on His Influence Upon C. S. Lewis."

Lamp-Post of the Southern California C. S. Lewis Society 8, no. 1 (January):6–12.

Lewis in "Two Ways with the Self" quotes de Sales's advice that we must not fret over our imperfections. In *Letters to Malcolm* he uses de Sales's method of meditation, placing oneself in the presence of God, to counteract the Puritan tradition of attending to the inner self. He recommended reading de Sales in *Letters to an American Lady* and used de Sales's insight that anxiety is a temptation in *The Screwtape Letters*. Lewis "esteemed highly and learned much from François de Sales."

26 FRYER, W. R. "This Journal's 'Most Valuable Piece.'" *Canadian C. S. Lewis Journal*, no. 45 (Winter):3–9, 12.

Here Fryer comments on Norman Bradshaw's articles on Lewis [1979.11; 1983.5, 7]. Bradshaw knew Lewis intimately and such personal knowledge yields unique insights. Lewis's interpretation of the faith makes Fryer uneasy; his characterization of God as judge is intolerable. In this, Lewis seems to have been superficial and did not agonize or read enough. B. F. Westcott, in *The Historic Faith* (London: Macmillan, 1882), achieves a deeper level of analysis than Lewis.

27 GOODKNIGHT, GLEN [H.]. "20 and 10 Years." *Mythlore* 37 (Winter):3.

"1983 was the tenth anniversary of the passing of J. R. R. Tolkien, and the twentieth anniversary of the death of C. S. Lewis." Their impact reverberates in countless people and will continue to do so.

28 GRIFFITHS, [ALAN] BEDE. "The Unexpected Controversy." *Canadian C. S. Lewis Journal*, no. 47 (Summer):1–2.

In this response to Bradshaw's article [1983.5], Griffiths claims that Lewis was not aloof in his attitude during tutorials but would discuss everything under the sun. "His understanding of the nature of God was extremely balanced. He never lost sight of the 'terrible aspect of God' . . . but he was no less firmly convinced of the infinity of love and grace."

29 HART, DABNEY A. "Through the Open Door." *CSL: The Bulletin of the New York C. S. Lewis Society* 16 (November):1–5.

Hart reminisces about her visit with Lewis when she was working on her Ph.D. dissertation about him. She quotes several of Lewis's poems. "Lewis's wide range of books and wide range of readers inevitably create some problems of interpretation." His increasing popularity has caused people to concentrate on his life and to read his books as clues to biography, a course of action he called the personal heresy.

30 ———. *Through the Open Door: A New Look at C. S. Lewis*. University: University of Alabama Press, 164 pp.

The theme of the open door, "the opportunity for new perspectives, new views, free movement of the mind and spirit," unifies and dominates Lewis's works of literary criticism and fiction. Lewis believed that the concept of myth is the basis of literature and that myth embodies universal truth. He was interested in the origins of human language and its development from concrete metaphor to abstraction. The power of language is a theme in all his fiction and also operates in his literary criticism. "One of his most consistent aims was to distinguish between the meanings that words have accrued over the centuries and to strip them back to the native grain of their meaning for the original audience." Lewis argued that what makes literature great is the imagination's response to myth, a response that enabled him to transcend many academic and popular generalizations about literature. He used his pedagogical skills to challenge students to think for themselves.

31 HAWKINS, PETER. "Lewis as a Writer of Letters." *CSL: The Bulletin of the New York C. S. Lewis Society* 15 (June):1–3.

Lewis's letters reveal his "extraordinary capacity to take other persons' religious life seriously." Many of his letters to admirers contain warnings about the primacy of emotion in religion. His letters to Arthur Greeves offer rich examples of intelligence, humor, and affection. The Greeves letters display his vulnerability, the struggles he had with his faith, and how well he knew himself.

32 HELFRICH, JOHN W. "A Letter from Malcolm." *CSL: The Bulletin of the New York C. S. Lewis Society* 15 (April):5–7.

Lewis's means of communication in *Letters to Malcolm* was chosen to force readers to think about his ideas. There are over 400 separate items in the work for "meaty discussion," but answers cannot always be found since these subjects deal with the divine and eternal.

33 IMBELLI, ROBERT. "Screwtape Revisited." *America* 151 (17 November):324.

Screwtape furthers the goals of his Infernal Majesty by substituting cause for Christianity, by restricting church to sect, by removing humans from concreteness and replacing this solidity with ideal images, and by destroying the devotional life of believers.

34 JENKINS, SUE. "Love, Loss, and Seeking: Maternal Deprivation and the Quest." *Children's Literature in Education* 15, no. 2 (Summer):73–83.

Lewis, George MacDonald, and J. R. R. Tolkien all lost their mothers during childhood or adolescence, events that had an effect on their fiction. The most direct reference Lewis makes to his mother's death is in *The Magician's Nephew*, where Digory calls his mother back to life by means of Aslan's gift of the Apple of Life.

35 JONES, ALAN, and FULLER, EDMUND. "An Affectionate and Muted Exchange Anent Lewis." *Lamp-Post of the Southern California C. S. Lewis Society* 8, nos. 2–3 (November):3–10, 26.
   Reprint of 1981.32.

36 KAWANO, ROLAND M. "C. S. Lewis and 'The Nameless Isle': A Metaphor of a Major Change." *CSL: The Bulletin of the New York C. S. Lewis Society* 15 (March):1–4.
   Lewis's poem "The Nameless Isle" reflects the pilgrimage that brought him into Christian orthodoxy. The poem contains his first use of the image of the dance. The air of the poem is different from the atmosphere of his other narrative poems, a difference that comes from his "desire to create a sense of enchantment." The overall structure of the poem—showing reconciliation between the Lord and the Lady and thus with the rest of creation, a sense of being released from bondage and homecoming—flows from a poet struggling "intellectually and imaginatively with the whole problem of religion, and Christian orthodoxy in particular."

37 KENNEY, ALICE P. "Mistress of Creation." *Mythlore* 11 (Summer):18–20, 45.
   Images of women as creators occurs in the works of Charles Williams, Dorothy L. Sayers, Lewis, and Iris Murdoch. Lewis, in *A Preface to Paradise Lost*, sees Eve as a primeval mistress and mother of creation, infinitely superior to us in wisdom and grace. In *Perelandra* the Green Lady "uses her intelligence to learn from her mistakes, and acquires the discrimination necessary to choose the good by her own will rather than blind obedience." In *Till We Have Faces* Orual develops intellectual, military, and political skills, but her creative accomplishments fail to bring her satisfaction." The four authors show that women are "quite as capable as men of experiencing creative insights, acquiring the skills of craftsmanship, and embodying their conceptions in significant works of art."

38 KING, DON. "Narnia and the Seven Deadly Sins." *Mythlore* 10 (Spring): 14–19.
   Each book of the Chronicles of Narnia highlights a different deadly sin. Lewis shows sin's destructive power and gives examples to avoid. In *The Lion, the Witch and the Wardrobe* Edmund personifies gluttony and shows how people can become slaves to their own desires. In *Prince Caspian* Lewis shows that lust for power, when embodied in a society's rulers, has a negative effect on the society. *The Voyage of the "Dawn Treader"* shows how Eustace, consumed by greed, is useless to society and to himself. *The Silver Chair* shows the dangers of sloth; Jill becomes susceptible to the dull repetition of routine and slides "into self-fulfillment at the cost of spirituality." In *The Horse and His Boy* Lewis shows how pride goes before destruction. In *The Magician's Nephew* Jadis's devilish temper leads toward egotism and turns her away from

the truth. In *The Last Battle* Shift's envy of Aslan's power is catastrophic to Narnia both socially and spiritually.

39 KIRKPATRICK, JOHN. "A Lewis Pupil, Richard Selig, 1929–57." *CSL: The Bulletin of the New York C. S. Lewis Society* 15 (October):1–7.
     Kirkpatrick provides a brief biography of Selig, whom Lewis tutored at Oxford from 1953 to 1954. He compares Lewis's poem "*Vitrea Circe*" and Selig's poem "The Island: November 1953." Lewis's poem has short lines and fancy rhymes. Selig's has long lines and subtle rhymes. The article includes a reprint of Lewis's letter to Selig commenting on Selig's poetry and recounts an incident between them regarding Lewis's phenomenal memory for everything he had read. Lewis influenced a new clarity in Selig's work.

40 KOCH, KATHLEEN. "*Till We Have Faces*, An Overview." *Chronicle of the Portland C. S. Lewis Society* 13, no. 3 (July–September):2–7.
     In the novel, Lewis changes the plot of the Cupid and Psyche myth and adopts it for the doctrine of transference where Orual sees herself united with everyone. The novel demonstrates Lewis's changing attitude toward women: Orual is a strong woman who makes her country prosper. Lewis places the story in an unusual setting, a totally barbarian culture, and shows that God is present outside the Judaeo-Christian development. Orual does not accept the vision of the palace because it interferes with her plan to be in control of her sister. She wants the gods to be horrible so she will be justified in controlling Psyche; if the gods are beautiful, they will represent competition with Orual for her sister's love.

41 KREEFT, PETER. "C. S. Lewis and the Case For Christianity." In *The Intellectuals Speak Out about God: A Handbook for the Christian Student in a Secular Society*. Edited by Roy Abraham Varghese. Chicago: Regnery Gateway, pp. 223–229.
     The qualities that make Lewis a great apologist are humility, understanding of the human soul, imagination, Christian faith, clarity, and joy. Besides the argument from desire for the existence of God, what Lewis called Joy, two others in his apologetics are distinctive: that Christ must have either been God or a lunatic, and there are contradictions in naturalism that "if nothing, not even human reasoning, is more than a natural process of material objects moving in space . . . then no one thought can be said to be more true or valid than any other." Other areas of excellence in Lewis's apologetics are his Christian fiction, his studies about the problems of pain and miracles, *Mere Christianity*, his clear and pointed essays, his profound religious and ethical psychology, *Reflection on the Psalms*, "The Weight of Glory," and *George MacDonald, An Anthology*.

42 ———. "C. S. Lewis and the Future of the World." *CSL: The Bulletin of the New York C. S. Lewis Society* 15 (May):1–13.

Lewis's philosophy of history has five principles: (1) disbelief in the philosophy of history because it assumes "an unproven parallel between the development of the human race and that of an individual"; (2) antihistoricism where "truths about our accidental qualities may change through history but never the laws of our essence"; (3) denial of universal evolutionism, accidental change for the better; (4) negation of chronological snobbery; and (5) the doctrine of original sin. Medieval Christendom had a unified cosmos but now technology has replaced religion. The result is naturalism, the belief that moral values are manmade, replacing supernaturalism. Lewis sees this shift leading to eductionism, the movement of internalization and "aggrandizement of man and dissection of the outer universe." Lewis's philosophy of history has three principles: (1) the Principle of First and Second Things—"when one of two values is really greater than another, for man to upset this order is to lose both"; (2) the demon of collectivism; and (3) man's natural tendency to seek God—when derived of spiritual joy he turns to carnal pleasures. When applying these principles to the future (1) we must think of ourselves as being in enemy territory; (2) we must be honest and realistic; (3) we should live in the peace of Christ; (4) we should accept God's grace and avoid determinism; and (5) we can work for peace in any political and social ways that are effective.

43 LAMBERT, BYRON C. "Unfinished Business: Reflections on One Aspect of the Lewis Legacy." *CSL: The Bulletin of the New York C. S. Lewis Society* 15 (August):1–5.

In Lewis's debate with Gertrude Anscombe over his thesis that naturalism is self-refuting, Anscombe's arguments were not as strong as Lewis seemed to think and his subsequent revision of *Miracles* was unnecessary. Anscombe's attack on Lewis's logic "evacuates his metaphysics and poetic vision." See response 1985.61, reply 1985.41, and response 1986.51.

44 LINDSKOOG, KATHRYN [ANN], and ELLWOOD, GRACIA FAY. "C. S. Lewis: Natural Law, the Law in Our Hearts." *Christian Century* 101 (14 November):1059–1062.

The Being behind the natural law is interested in fair play, unselfishness, honesty, and truthfulness but is not soft or indulgent. Christianity "explains how God can be the impersonal mind behind the Natural Law and also be a person." In *The Lion, the Witch and the Wardrobe* and *The Last Battle* Lewis illustrated his concern that many people are losing their belief in the natural law. Only those who live by this law can interpret it successfully and those who do not have no grounds for criticizing it. Reprinted: 1988.41.

1984

45 McGOVERN, EUGENE. "The Characteristic Blindness of an Age." *CSL: The Bulletin of the New York C. S. Lewis Society* 15 (April):1–5.

Lewis thought every age believes certain things that future generations will find unacceptable. Examples he identified in his works are the ideals of romantic love, inequality, and hierarchy. Lewis enumerated four major differences between the modern age and the past: "the amount of attention given to political affairs, the novelty of modern painting and poetry, the decline in the importance of Christianity, and the effect of the proliferation of machines."

46 MACKY, PETER W. "Malacandra as the Ideal: Social Criticism in C. S. Lewis' *Out of the Silent Planet.*" *Topic*, no. 38 (Fall):46–50.

Malacandra has no inherent social evil and the different rational species live in harmony with each other. At the heart of this society is the authority of Oyarsa, the ruler of Malacandra. In contrast there is no chief eldil ruling earth so humans "set themselves up as their own ultimate authorities, resulting in constant conflict between individuals and groups." Other sources of evil on earth are moral collectivism versus the individualism of the Malacandrians and the fear of death versus seeing death as part of the natural order. Lewis succeeds in effectively presenting these major criticisms of earth by drawing a detailed picture of the harmonious life on Malacandra.

47 MEYERS, D. E. "The Complete Anglican: Spiritual Style in the Chronicles of Narnia." *Anglican Theological Review* 66, no. 2:148–160.

The Chronicles of Narnia develop the unified theme of "the emotional climate of Christian commitment at various age levels" and follow the Anglican style of spirituality of Lewis's time with its emphasis on the individual's gradual growth in faith. *The Lion, the Witch and the Wardrobe* depicts children's first awareness of Christianity through Christmas and Easter. *Prince Caspian* represents the second stage of spiritual development, doubt, and disillusionment associated with early adolescence. *The Voyage of the "Dawn Treader"* explores membership in the church, especially participation in communion and baptism, and ethical behavior. *The Silver Chair* and *The Horse and His Boy* depict "the mundane problems of living according to Christian values in a hostile environment." *Chair* focuses on intellectual maturation and *Horse* on social maturation. *The Magician's Nephew* shows Christian middle age concerned with nurturing the new generation and aging parents and has the prevailing tone of sober realism. *The Last Battle* explores the feelings of the elderly Christian in his last days.

48 MORRISON, JOHN. "A Pleasure Is Full Grown Only When It Is Remembered: The First British C. S. Lewis Conference." *CSL: The Bulletin of the New York C. S. Lewis Society* 16 (December):1–7.

Morrison reports on the conference held at Saint Deniniol's Library, Hawarden, Deeside, Clwyd, Wales, United Kingdom. He recounts Walter

Hooper's reminiscences and Roger Lancelyn Green's congenial conversation about Lewis and he summarizes Harry Blamires's views on Lewis's theology and John Lawlor's comments on each volume of the Narnia Chronicles and several of Lewis's scholarly works.

49 MOYNIHAN, MARTIN. "C. S. Lewis and T. D. Weldon." *Seven: An Anglo-American Literary Review* 5:101–105.
     Moynihan was a pupil of both Lewis and Weldon in the 1930s. Although he studied Kant and was a Freemason, Weldon was not an atheist as Lewis believed but rather an agnostic deist.

50 NUTTALL, A. D. "Jack the Giant-Killer." *Seven: An Anglo-American Literary Review* 5:84–100.
     Lewis defended objective value in *The Abolition of Man* and killed the giant of subjectivism. He sought to "reawaken the sense of moral substance by showing what we actually do when we admire, approve, love." His questions are "what is presupposed?" and "what do we actually do?" The all-or-nothing character of Lewis's philosophy of the Tao is fatal to his strategy. The thesis that everyone else accepts the Tao exerts no compulsive force and is simply false. Despite this strategic flaw, Lewis performed a great feat: he has established that "when we value things we refer outside ourselves." See response 1988.75.

51 OVERBY, CHARLES. "A Smorgasbord of Christian Insight." *Christianity Today* 28 (6 April):35, 49.
     God in the Dock is Lewis's most practical and far-ranging book. Lewis's strengths are simplicity of style, anticipation of questions that nag believers, and refusal to water down the supernatural underpinnings of Christianity.

52 PATTERSON, NANCY-LOU. "Halfe Like a Serpent: The Green Witch in *The Silver Chair*." *Mythlore* 11 (Autumn):37–47.
     The archetypal images of the feminine in the novel are found in the characters of the Star's daughter (the Queen of Heaven), Jill Pole (the heroine on a descent-quest), and the Green Witch (the Queen of the Nether World). Possible sources for the Green Witch include Circe, Lilith, Morgan Le Fay, Spenser's monster Error, Proserpina, the false sorceress Duess, Hel the goddess who is the northern ruler of night, and the Reparent Tiamat. The central symbol is the feminine as vessel.

53 ———. "Ransoming the Wasteland: Arthurian Themes in C. S. Lewis's Interplanetary Trilogy." *Lamp-Post of the Southern California C. S. Lewis Society* 8, nos. 2–3 (November):16–26; 8, no. 4 (December 1985):3–15.
     The central mythological motif of *That Hideous Strength* and the theme

integral to the structure of the entire Trilogy is the wasteland. "The 'Arthurian material' is part of a complete *schema* around which all three novels are organized and hence neither an afterthought nor a case of mismanagement." Two interrelated themes in the trilogy, Arthurian in form, are the concept of the knightly quest as accepting a challenge, and the role of substitute or sacrifice as an exchange. In *Out of the Silent Planet* Ransom is a sacrifice, in *Perelandra* he mediates between Tinidril and the Tempter, and in *That Hideous Strength* he is a wounded king who must be saved by Merlin through exchange. Both Mark and Jane succumb to temptation by not taking the adventures God sends them and therefore not trusting in His support. They are called upon to exchange each other. Their salvation is embodied in the symbol of a picnic, a figure of the Eucharist, and their physical rescue is through a stranger offering them a ride in an automobile. The myth of the wasteland is a land that lies infertile "because its king, the 'Fisher King,' has been wounded." Ransom's sister in India, who gives him the name Mr. Fisher-King, is related to this same tradition. In Malory, Sir Perceval's sister "sacrifices herself in exchange for the other, offering her example to her brother." The wasteland situation of the Trilogy is the work of the Bent One and marked by death and pollution. "The richly sensual passages with which [*That Hideous Strength*] concludes are prefigurations of a restored world of prelapsarian perfection."

54 PRESLEY, HORTON. "C. S. Lewis: Mythmaker." In *Voices for the Future*, vol. 3. Edited by Thomas D. Clareson and Thomas L. Wymer. Bowling Green, Ohio: Bowling Green University Popular Press, pp. 127–150.

Lewis considered the Ransom Trilogy and the Chronicles of Narnia to be primarily mythic. He chose science fiction because it excited his imagination, and he thought literature needed new sources of unknown worlds to populate. Lewis's approach to science fiction is "the creation of the Marvelous as a means of adding a new dimension to life." He clearly attempts to create a new mythology, that "presents a highly imaginative, pleasurable experience that reaches truth by indirect means." Lewis treats the subjects of religious truth, education and teachers, science, and scientism.

55 PURTILL, RICHARD L. "Mind, Matter, and Magic in Fantasy and Science Fiction." In *The Transcendent Adventure: Studies of Religion in Science Fiction/Fantasy*. Edited by Robert Reilly. Westport, Conn.: Greenwood Press, pp. 27–35.

Lewis's work is fantasy rather than science fiction because it assumes the animistic view that nonmaterial minds or spirits can directly affect matter and embody minds.

56 QUINN, DENNIS B. "The Narnia Books of C. S. Lewis: Fantastic or Wonderful?" *Children's Literature: An International Journal* 12:105–121.

The fantastic is unreal while the wonderful is "real but strange, mysterious, unexplained." Lewis writes in the neo-Platonic tradition that denies "the reality of the sensible world and substitutes for it a world that exists only in the mind." The Narnia stories lack merit as literature since they present images and scenes to convey ideas rather than action, and the characters fail to come alive because they fail to act. Fantasy is harmful because it encourages "the reader to turn inward and to distrust if not despise reality."

57 QUINN, WILLIAM A. "Science Fiction's Harrowing of the Heavens." In *The Transcendent Adventure: Studies of Religion in Science Fiction/Fantasy.* Edited by Robert Reilly. Westport, Conn.: Greenwood Press, pp. 37–54.

In *Perelandra* the Un-man argues deism, that God exists but is indifferent to the universe. Ransom, according to the rules of theological logic, rejects this as a false First Principle. Lewis clarifies the end that awaits the occupants of both Perelandra and Thulcandra as a gift of sanctifying grace.

58 ROSSI, LEE D[ONALD]. *The Politics of Fantasy: C. S. Lewis and J. R. R. Tolkien.* Ann Arbor, Mich.: UMI Research Press, pp. 1–87.

Lewis and Tolkien are apolitical; for both "the motive for fantasy is essentially an attempt to liberate themselves from the ugliness and moral impasse of the modern world." Besides Lewis's attempts to escape into an imaginary world, his love of inanimate nature and reliance on a small circle of friends are other touchstones of his imagination. The dual aspects to Lewis's personality and his works are romanticism and logic. "Romanticism is the more important of the two and represents an imaginative response of escape to certain threatening realities. . . . [Logic] sees in romanticism the dangers of narcissism and anarchy, the threat of being totally cut off from the human community. Lewis tried to reconcile these two imperatives by becoming a Christian. Christianity embodied a similar project of escape, but offered Lewis an historical and social sanction for his escape from society." His earliest fiction has a basic artistic problem: he chooses to stress the Christian polemics of his writing rather than concerning himself primarily with realizing his fictional world. In his later fiction, he "develops a confidence that men's natural desires will eventually lead them to Christ [which] allows him to eschew the dogmatism which had previously weighed his work down." Because of his lack of politics Lewis fails to deal ethically with major concerns of adults in modern society: problems of social organization, property, and status.

59 SCHAKEL, PETER J. *Reason and Imagination in C. S. Lewis: A Study of 'Till We Have Faces'.* Grand Rapids, Mich.: Eerdmans, 208 pp.

Part I provides a detailed summary of each chapter of *Till We Have Faces*, explaining the tone and language of the novel, the structure and plot, and the issues, ideas, and themes that underlie each section. Part II gives a decade-by-decade survey of Lewis's thought, focusing on key works that in theme or method are useful for explaining the novel. Schakel traces the ongoing tension Lewis experienced between reason and imagination. *Till We Have Faces* "is the culmination of efforts Lewis made in a number of works throughout his life to use similar images and imaginative structures to resolve that tension." See response 1988.75.

60   SCHOFIELD, STEPHEN. "Why Was Lewis Prejudiced Against Americans?" *Canadian C. S. Lewis Journal*, no. 46 (Spring):7–13.
     Reprint of 1980.57. Reprinted from 1983.68.

61   SHARISHAW. "Proud Characters in the Chronicles of Narnia." *Lamp-Post of the Southern California C. S. Lewis Society* 8, no. 1 (January):13–19.
     In the Chronicles of Narnia, Lewis portrays several "proud characters who exempt themselves from the moral law. Uncle Andrew, Jadis, and Shift free themselves from the common law, and their actions result in social discord and destruction. Edmund Pevensie, Eustace Scrubb, and Aravis Tarkheena also exhibit pride. But through their difficult experiences they realize their pride and become humble."

62   SHARPE, JACK. "A Look at C. S. Lewis' *Miracles*." *Chronicle of the Portland C. S. Lewis Society* 13, no. 4 (October–December):1–3.
     Miracles is a lucid, well-reasoned, thumbnail sketch of several modern philosophies and "a lengthy description of the Christian philosophy behind a belief in miracles." Lewis shows that naturalistic and materialistic worldviews cannot account for reason, which he argues is fundamentally supernatural. Every time God performs a miracle He affirms the "creatureness" of nature, trusting her with interferences. Although in *Miracles* Lewis uses precise, logical reasoning, he also lets his imagination roam free.

63   SHUTTE, AUGUSTINE. "The Refutation of Determinism." *Philosophy* 52 (October):481–489.
     Lewis argues that naturalism is self-contradictory because "if it were true then no process of thought could claim to be rational since it, like everything else, would have been produced by mechanical causes." G. E. M. Anscombe contends that "the validity of a piece of reasoning has nothing to do with what happened to cause it to take place." However, Lewis correctly "claims that if the causes of a person's holding a belief do not include the actual grasping of the logical link between premise and conclusion as holding between that belief and another then his holding of the belief will be unreasonable." His argument prevents the determinist from claiming to know truth but the theory itself is not refuted. E. L. Mascall points out that if determinism is true "then there could be no reason why one should recognize the normative

force of rules of logic." Lewis and Mascall claim that the process of thought provides us with the experience of reason and it is this experience that is the foundation of the laws of logic as well as the basis of the argument against determinism. Therefore, Lewis's argument against naturalism has been vindicated.

64   SPRINGER, KEVIN. "In Search of Joy." *New Covenant* 14 (September): 21–23.
       For the first thirty-two years of his life Lewis was a seeker of Joy, a search that led him to God. For the last thirty-two years he lived as a thoroughly convinced Christian. The key to his success is his humility, a virtue that comes through in all his works. His clarity of language and precision of logic have helped millions to understand more clearly the message of the Gospel.

65   STARR, NATHAN C[OMFORT]. "Eschatology in C. S. Lewis's *The Last Battle*." *Lamp-Post of the Southern California C. S. Lewis Society* 8, nos. 2–3 (November):11–15, 26.
       Lewis was deeply concerned with life after death; the most original aspect of his belief of heaven is its reality. He gives a vivid description of heaven in *The Great Divorce*, provides glimpses of heaven in *The Screwtape Letters*, and emphasizes the solidity of heaven in *Letters to Malcolm: Chiefly on Prayer* and *A Grief Observed*. *The Last Battle* is Lewis's most explicit transmigration to heaven. In the novel he makes credible the vast difference between life on earth and life after death, and he develops powerfully the concept that earth is enemy-occupied territory. He maintains we must die to the world, "makes the most of the apotheosis of the serene soul," and depicts a new Narnia that has been "idealized and made *real* in the clarity and beauty of detail."

66   STURCH, RICHARD L. "Fantasy and Apologetics." *Vox Evangelica* 14:65–84.
       Fantasy serves apologetics by remythologizing and by stretching the imagination. Lewis uses satire to deal with prejudices against Christianity but satire is rarely accepted by those who do not believe in Christianity. He also tries to change the psychological factors that prevent modern readers from believing in the supernatural by appealing to reason and overcoming modern biases. MacDonald and Tolkien make no attempt to have readers believe in their worlds while Williams and Lewis wrote stories that never lose touch with the real world. Lewis and Williams are no longer the effective apologists they once were because intellectual fashions have changed. Tolkien's works have eclipsed Lewis's and Williams's in popularity because they are not theoretical, abstract, or rationalistic but full of action.

1984

67 SWINFEN, ANN. *In Defense of Fantasy: A Study of the Genre in English and American Literature since 1945*. London: Routledge and Kegan Paul, pp. 75–99, 147–159.

In the Chronicles of Narnia Lewis is interested in ultimate beginnings and ending but shows little concern with the history and development of the inhabitants of the mythical land. He uses varying styles of speech for the different races and his principal element of humor is linguistic. He makes greater use of the marvelous than do other authors, but this is acceptable because his creatures are well known from traditional literature. The central theme of the Chronicles is the battle between good and evil. Lewis's interest in metaphor and analogy focuses attention on the narrative structure and imagery while characterization is less important. Some questionable elements in Lewis's ethics are the code of vengeance by which enemies are ruthlessly hunted down and destroyed, the treatment of the nontalking animals as having no chance for salvation, and the position of Susan, which indicates his dislike of women. Lewis's strengths are "his ability as a picture-maker and the creator of an imaginatively tangible otherworld with its own distinct 'sensation,' and his quite definite and avowed moral purpose."

68 TEICHERT, MARILYN CHANDLER. "A Healing Art: Autobiography and the Poetics of Crisis." Ph.D. dissertation, Princeton University, 289 pp. passim.

A Grief Observed is both a quarrel with God and an apologia. Lewis's attempt to understand grief reveals a deep fear of being crippled or diminished by it. Naming the dangers to which he is vulnerable—sentimentality and the tendency to make himself into a tragic hero—is his way of gaining control over them. Lewis finds that Christian rhetoric has failed him in the face of despair. Grief shakes him out of "'merely verbal thinking' and 'merely rational beliefs.'" He uses a pseudonym so that he will not scandalize those who revere him as a model of strong faith. He uses Job as a model, casting God as the antagonist, presenting a case against Him. For Lewis the writing process is a drug to dull the pain of grief and a way to objectify his suffering. His crisis of faith causes him to make a conscious decision to validate Christianity rather than his own perceptions when the two conflict. The emotional honesty of *A Grief Observed* makes it unique in Lewis's canon.

69 THORSON, STEPHEN. "A Reply." *CSL: The Bulletin of the New York C. S. Lewis Society* 15 (March):1–11.

Thorson responds to Adey's reply [1984.1] to his article on Lewis's "Great War" with Owen Barfield [1983.75]. Lewis held entirely different post–conversion views of the arguments contained in the *Summa*. Adey's theory that Lewis wrote the *Summa* from the position of his opponent is wrong. The system Lewis and Barfield had in common was not anthroposophy as assumed by Adey but idealism. Lewis's penciled comments on the *Summa* may have been written during the process of his conversion to Christianity. He needed the doctrine of creation to "support the Enjoyment/Contemplation distinction and the doctrine of the Incarnation to overcome it." "Adey cannot be blamed for what he dislikes, but neither can I be blamed for warning others to be careful when reading a book by a writer whose opinions differ greatly from those of the subject's."

70   TRICKETT, RACHEL. "Uncrowned King of Oxford." *Canadian C. S. Lewis Journal*, no. 46 (Spring):16.

When Trickett was at Oxford between 1942 and 1945, Lewis was the uncrowned king of the university. His manner was no-nonsense and his method of argument was Chestertonian. The triumph of *The Allegory of Love* was his ability to get people to read Gower and to take Spenser seriously. *The Preface to Paradise Lost* forced critics to take Milton's theology seriously. *English Literature in the Sixteenth Century* is full of paradox and prejudice. Lewis retained a child's vision of life.

71   WOLFE, GREGORY. "Lewis on the Nature of Politics: A Reply to Danny Adkison." *CSL: The Bulletin of the New York C. S. Lewis Society* 16 (November):6–7.

Adkison [1984.2] confuses some distinctions crucial to understanding Lewis's approach to politics. Lewis did not participate in issue-oriented politics, but held, with Aristotle, that man is a political animal. While Sobran [1981.66] is "guilty of looking for a party 'line' in Lewis's thought," his insights on Lewis's political thought are sound. Lewis feared the natural law would be replaced by arbitrary rules imposed by the State unrestrained by moral values. He did not ignore politics because it was unimportant but he felt "most of what was humanly valuable (worship, study, work, family) took place in the private sphere."

72   YANCY, PHILIP. "How Dirty Jokes and the Fear of Death Prove There Is a Heaven." *Christianity Today* 28 (2 March):78.

Lewis said that natural theology could be proved from the human phenomena of dirty jokes and the fear of death. These phenomena confirm the biblical view of humanity as spiritual beings trapped in matter.

73   YOUNG, ROBERT L. "The Anglicanism of C. S. Lewis." *Chronicle of the Portland C. S. Lewis Society* 13, no. 2 (April–June):5–12.

Richard Hooker, who influenced Lewis's thinking, saw Anglicanism as a middle way "because it retained the essentials of the Catholic religion and yet remained open to the reforming insights of the Continental Protestants." Lewis upheld Hooker's view that Christian authority depended on Scripture, tradition, and reason. A controversy within Anglicanism to which Lewis alludes is the divisions between High Church, emphasizing the Catholic heritage, Low Church, emphasizing the biblical Protestant heritage, and Broad

1985

Church, emphasizing social concerns, new theology, and human reason. Lewis started out as a Low Churchman, with his Ulster background, but had some Anglo-Catholic preferences later in his life, with his belief in purgatory, going to Mass, and use of a confessor; he never had any use for the Broad or Liberal Church faction. Lewis shared Anglicanism's uniquely liturgical piety, parochial system, and view of priests as representatives of us to God and God to us.

1985

1   ARMSTRONG, ROBERT L. "Friendship." *The Journal of Value Inquiry* 19, no. 3:211–216.
    For Lewis friendship arises out of companionship and requires common interests. He maintains that friendship is only possible between people of the same sex. Friendship should be based on honesty, trust, and loyalty, and not on usefulness.

2   BENESTAD, JANET. Review of *C. S. Lewis Letters to Children*. *Best Sellers* 45 (September):237–238.
    "This volume is a wonderful collection that provides a glimpse into the heart and mind of a prolific and profound writer, who is at one and the same time grown-up and child-like."

3   BEVERSLUIS, JOHN. "Beyond the Double Bolted Door." *Christian History* 4, no. 3:28–31.
    In his apologetics of the 1940s, Lewis placed reason squarely on the side of faith. However, his arguments for the existence of God are seriously flawed and he attacks opposing positions based on misunderstandings. *A Grief Observed* reveals that Lewis "was ultimately undone by the problem of contrary evidence and left with a deity of dubious moral character. After reading it, we can no longer read Lewis's earlier books as we once read them."

4   ———. *C. S. Lewis and the Search for Rational Religion*. Grand Rapids, Mich.: Eerdmans, 182 pp.
    Lewis has three arguments for the existence of God: desire, morality, and reason. His argument from desire uses a metaphysical theory of desire and therefore cannot be proved on empirical grounds; also, it is derived from Plato and contradicted by biblical texts. His moral argument also fails on logical and theological grounds: he does not prove there is a power behind the moral law and even if he had, it follows that if "the Power *cannot* reveal itself publicly within the universe, then Jesus cannot have been God incarnate." His argument from reason, which holds that reason must have a supernatural

source, fails to acknowledge experience, not reason, as providing human beings with truths about the world. Lewis's "tendency is to rush into battle, misrepresent the opposition, and then demolish it." He also uses the false dilemma by habitually confronting "his readers with the alleged necessity of choosing between two alternatives when there are in fact other options to be considered." He is not fair—his apologetic writings characterize the unbeliever as a fool. His explanation of the existence of evil is unconvincing. "Why would a good and omnipotent God create free creatures with real alternatives from which to choose and then by the infliction of pain and suffering systematically attempt to nullify their options in the hope of restricting them to the one desired?" *A Grief Observed* demonstrates Lewis's shift "from the Platonic view that God says things are good because they are good to the Ockhamist view that things are good simply because God says they are." However, he "never succeeds in making the Ockhamist conception of God his own. The rediscovered faith lacks . . . the conviction of his earlier writings." See responses 1985.46; 1987.56; 1988.31, 55.

5 BLAMIRES, HARRY. "C. S. Lewis." In *Chosen Vessels: Portraits of Ten Outstanding Christian Men.* Edited by Charles Turner. Ann Arbor, Mich.: Servant Publications, pp. 1–19.
   As a tutor, Lewis was meticulously conscientious. He carefully considered the effect his words would have on others; he was a model of charity and sympathy. He was hurt by the negative criticism of his apologetic works at Oxford. His enjoyment of puncturing pretentiousness, "his polemical combativeness, his irony, and his rich imaginative power" are evidence of his Irishness. His lectures were clear, orderly, and meaty; "he was a lucid, entertaining, and highly instructive lecturer."

6 BORDEN, MATTHEW. "Lewis and Friendship." *CSL: The Bulletin of the New York C. S. Lewis Society* 16 (January):7.
   Borden discusses Lewis's comments on friendship as found in the question "Do you care about the same truth?"

7 BROWN, GEOFFREY. "Praying About The Past." *Philosophical Quarterly* 35, no. 138 (January):83–86.
   Lewis thought prayer about a past event was possible because it is one of the causes of the event. Peter T. Geach's essay "Praying for Things to Happen" in *God and the Soul* (London: Routledge and Kegan Paul, 1969, ch. 7) rejects petitionary prayer about the past. Geach states that nothing can be done in the present to form part of the causal nexus of a past event, "a mere unsupported contradiction" of Lewis's thesis. He insists on treating Lewis's thesis as assuming the past can be altered by prayer. Lewis is not saying that prayers rewrite the past but the prayer "*will have been* taken into consideration already: it is God's ability to know the future, not His ability to alter the past . . . that is

being invoked." Geach is mistaken in not thinking God's omniscience and omnipotence are central issues.

8   BRUGALETTA, JOHN J. "How Nice Was Lewis?" *Lamp-Post of the Southern California C. S. Lewis Society* 8, no. 4 (December):16–22.
    There is a tendency to think that all opinions are equally valid, that there is no independent standard of truth. Lewis feels it is his duty to show people how to reexamine their opinions, which some people consider "not being nice."

9   BURGESS, ANDREW J. "The Concept of Eden." In *The Transcendent Adventure: Studies of Religion in Science Fiction/Fantasy*. Edited by Robert Reilly. Westport, Conn.: Greenwood Press, pp. 73–81.
    The Eden motif is treated in both Lewis's *Perelandra* and James Blish's *A Case of Conscience* (New York: Ballantine, 1958). Blish's hero "struggles with the possible threat to faith on earth because of the discovery of a distant planet" while Lewis's hero tries to prevent the temptation of a new and innocent race. Lewis's novel, with its depiction of the innocence and childlikeness of the Green Lady, allows the reader to see her moral battle as one in which they are also involved.

10 CARNELL, CORBIN S[COTT]. "The Friendship of C. S. Lewis and Charles Williams." *CSL: The Bulletin of the New York C. S. Lewis Society* 16 (May):1–9.
    Similarities between Lewis and Williams include "the theory of Platonic forms as a basis for thought, art, and language"; belief in classical Christianity; being theological about romance—Williams's Beatrician Moment and Lewis's *Sensucht*. Lewis is indebted to Williams for the idea of co-inherence, which was not just a literary idea to Lewis but a practice. Among their differences was Williams's wider range of interests. Also, Williams was a mystic while Lewis was not at home with ritual; Williams's vision was darker than Lewis's; Williams's works are often obscure where Lewis's are lucid. Without Williams's influence Lewis would have been a narrower thinker.

11 CLUTE, JOHN. "C. S. Lewis 1898-1963." In *Supernatural Fiction Writers: Fantasy and Horror*. Edited by E[verett] F[ranklin] Bleiler. Vol. 2, A. E. Coppard to Roger Zelazny. New York: Scribner, pp. 661–666.
    Lewis's works "share common doctrinal, literary, social, and sexual prejudices."

12 COBB, LAWRENCE [W.]. "A Gift from the Sky: The Creative Process in Lewis and Sayers." *CSL: The Bulletin of the New York C. S. Lewis Society* 16 (February):1–5.

Dorothy L. Sayers's theory of the trinity of creation consisted of the Creative Idea (the Father), the Creative Energy (Christ), and the Creative Power (Holy Spirit). Lewis fulfills all three modes of this creative trinity.

13 COLSON, CHARLES. "'Men without Chests.'" *Christianity Today* 29 (22 November):72.
    Lewis argued that the knowledge of right and wrong is powerless against man's appetites and that "reason must rule the appetites by means of the 'spirited element'—learned desired for the good, or 'trained emotions.'" Today's spy cases are the consequence of the nation's loss of its spirited element.

14 CORE, E. L. "On the Obstetrical Interpretation of *Perelandra*." *CSL: The Bulletin of the New York C. S. Lewis Society* 16 (March):1–3.
    Core disagrees with Hinman's [1985.33] interpretation of the novel. "What to Mrs. Hinman is obstetrical symbolism is to me just reasonable writing and good fiction in a well-crafted story." People who hunt for "real" meanings in fiction are "trying to be more profound and sophisticated than the rest of us."

15 COTTLE, BASIL. *The Language of Literature*. New York: St. Martin's, pp. 133–134.
    In *The Screwtape Letters*, Lewis writes with a clear, fastidious style, with wit and neatness; "no phrase is illogical or obscure, or awkward to hear aloud."

16 DAIGLE, MARSHA ANN. "Dante's *Divine Comedy* and C. S. Lewis's *Narnia Chronicles*." *Christianity & Literature* 34, no. 4 (Summer):41–58
    The Divine Comedy is both a source and a model for the Narnia Chronicles. Lewis uses Dante's technique of biblical typology, using the history of another universe to tell "the story of a fresh instance of God's saving action in history." *The Silver Chair* contains allusions to the journey in Dante's *Inferno* and *The Voyage of the "Dawn Treader"* transposes metaphoric elements in the *Purgatorio* and the *Paradiso* onto a literal level.

17 DIRDA, MICHAEL. "Cutting Literary Teeth." *Book World (Washington Post)* 15 (14 April):10.
    In his review of *C. S. Lewis Letters to Children*, Dirda says the letters are a delight, offering good advice on writing and literature.

18 DORSETT, LYLE [W]. "C. S. Lewis: A Profile of His Life." *Christian History* 4, no. 3:6–11.
    Biography of Lewis.

1985

19 DORSETT, LYLE [W], and MEAD, MARJORIE LAMP, ed. *C. S. Lewis Letters to Children*. New York: Macmillan, 120 pp.
    Lewis personally responded to thousands of fan letters from the young readers of the Chronicles of Narnia. In this volume a representative sample of Lewis's letters to children are arranged chronologically. Most address questions about the Narnia tales, "the spiritual reality within these stories, and the craft of writing itself." The book includes a short sketch of Lewis's childhood and an annotated children's bibliography of Lewis's works.

20 EDWARDS, BRUCE L[EE], Jr. "C. S. Lewis and the Deconstructionists." *This World*, no. 10:88–98.
    Reprint of 1982.17. Reprinted: 1986.12.

21 ELGIN, DON D. "C. S. Lewis." In *The Comedy of the Fantastic: Ecological Perspectives on the Fantasy Novel*. Contributions to the Study of Science Fiction and Fantasy, no. 15. Westport, Conn.: Greenwood Press, pp. 60–96.
    Lewis is a clear example of "how fantasy integrates the comic and ecological traditions into a romantic fabric to create a new novel and a new critical perspective." In his concept of myth there is conflict between rationality and intuition. His theory of literature is romantic. Lewis created a new novelistic form that combines myth, romanticism, and Christianity. The Ransom Trilogy and *Till We Have Faces* emphasize experience over abstraction; Lewis rejects abstraction because it leads to environmental catastrophe, physical death, and spiritual desolation. His characters act and believe on the basis of their physical being and experience, and come to salvation or destruction based on their actions. The debate in these novels is between the false myth, scientism, which places humanity at the center while subjecting everything else to humanity's will, and experience. Lewis uses the symbol of the Great Dance to depict the complex interdependence of all things in the universe. Each of these novels affirms experience over abstraction, trust in the emotions and instinct as well as in rationality, and acceptance of all creatures.

22 ESPEY, JOHN. Review of *C. S. Lewis Letters to Children*. *Los Angeles Times* 7 July, p. 4.
    Lewis responds to his fans without condescension and with pleasure at the chance to explain his intentions and to express his opinion on diverse subjects.

23 EVANS, MURRAY J. "C. S. Lewis' Narnia Books: The Reader in the Myth." In *Touchstones: Reflections on the Best in Children's Literature*. Vol. 1. West Lafayette, Ind.: Children's Literature Association, pp. 132–145.
    The Last Battle explores and qualifies the fictive world of the earlier books. The sense of ending pervades the book; it has a lean plot and an intensely narrow scope. There is a rhythm of hope and disappointment until

the story passes through the Stable Door, then there is a sense of longing ful-
filled, a reality that is inexpressible, a suspension of expectations of closure. In
the novel Lewis offers experience of two reading processes: the empirical and
the imaginative.

24 FILMER, KATH. "A Place in Deep Heaven: Figurative Language in C. S.
Lewis's *Out of the Silent Planet.*" *Inklings: Jahrbuch für Literatur und Ästhetik*
3:187–195.
    Lewis creates Malacandra through the use of symbolic and metaphorical
language. He uses Ransom's reactions, especially intense fear and intense
pleasure, to depict the numinous atmosphere of Malacandra. This numinous
atmosphere is also developed with the use of clues such as light, kingship,
jewels, and gold. Lewis's images and metaphors depict the immanence
of God, the reality of human corruption, and the cosmic battle between good
and evil.

25 ———. "That Hideous 1984: The Influence of C. S. Lewis' *That Hideous
Strength* on Orwell's *Nineteen Eighty-Four.*" *Extrapolation* 26, no. 2
(Summer):160–169.
    Lewis's novel has a significant influence on Orwell's, even though
Orwell criticized Lewis's "dependence upon the supernatural as an explanation
for the moral struggle." Both are concerned with the dangers of political
power whose aim is the destruction of human values. While Lewis sees the
human spirit triumphing over intense evil, Orwell is pessimistic and sees no
relief for humanity. In both novels the repressive regime regulates biological
functions by eradicating sexual intercourse, both have cliques that are the
source of the villainy, and both use the motif of perversion of language.

25 FRESHWATER, MARK EDWARDS. "C. S. Lewis and the Quest for the
Historical Jesus." Ph.D. dissertation, Florida State University, 289 pp.
    Lewis's conception of "myth became fact" is a major element in his
defense of Christianity, thereby invoking historical investigation of
Christianity. While he felt the Old Testament contained human qualities of
error and contradiction, he assumed the New Testament must be both mythical
and historical. He was critical of modern New Testament scholarship's tendency to reject elements of Christianity that most clearly signify its nature as
"myth became fact": "the Divinity of Jesus, the concept of the Kingdom of
God, the miraculous, and the historical validity of the Gospel record."
However, his own attempts to explain problems with the New Testament were
simplistic and he failed to prove that the New Testament is completely valid
historically. Perhaps his concern for the historical nature of Christianity is
misplaced. "One could state that Christianity is 'myth become religious fact,'
the fact of a New Testament Church guided by a new vision and understanding of reality. Christianity could then be seen as Lewis saw the Old Testament,

the 'chosen mythology' of God." In his mythic writings, especially the Chronicles of Narnia, he went beyond reason to offer a taste of divine reality, and "it is in this recreation of the Christian story rather than in his logical defense of Christian dogma that Lewis is most successful." He transposed the reality of the Gospel in the fictional world of Narnia without distorting or detracting from the Christian message. "Only in interpreting Christianity as myth does Lewis avoid the problems of the historicity of the Gospels." He has shown how the Christian myth fulfills the basic needs and wants of mankind; he has affirmed the truth of myth and thereby the truth of the Christian faith. Revised for publication: 1988.25.

27 "A Gallery of Thumbnail Sketches of Close and Influential Family and Friends of C. S. Lewis." *Christian History* 4, no. 3:12–15.
      The article provides brief biographies of Albert Lewis, Florence Hamilton Lewis, Warren Hamilton Lewis, Arthur Greeves, Owen Barfield, J. R. R. Tolkien, Charles Williams, R. E. Havard, Dorothy L. Sayers, Joy Davidman, G. K. Chesterton, and George MacDonald.

28 GARDINER, KATHERINE. "C. S. Lewis as a Reader of Edmund Spenser." *CSL: The Bulletin of the New York C. S. Lewis Society* 16 (September):1–10.
      Lewis was one of the first critics to see that "the *Faerie Queene* does have a structure, and that in each book, the particular virtue under study is shown both in its transcendental unity and by contrast with its opposite, or with some variant manifestation of itself." He anticipates later critics by explaining that the *Faerie Queene* cannot be interpreted by reading for plot; he feels the image, the pictorial element of the poem, is all important. The value of Lewis's commentary on the poem is his artistic sympathy with Spenser. Lewis's greatest strength is "his ability to render the inward life of Spenser's allegory in the form of outward story accessible to twentieth century readers."

29 GIBRAN, JEAN. Review of *C. S. Lewis Letters to Children*. *Harvard Educational Review* 55, no. 4 (November):476.
      "These precise lessons in answering young people guilelessly and credibly stand as a model of the best in writer–student interaction."

30 HARDIE, COLIN. "A Colleague's Note on C. S. Lewis." *Inklings: Jahrbuch für Literatur und Ästhetik* 3:177–185.
      Hardie recounts memories of Lewis when both were Fellows at Magdalen College. Lewis was so absorbed in his reading and writing that he had little time for the business of the college. The article summarizes letters Lewis wrote Hardie and his wife.

31 HART, DABNEY [A.]. "Teacher, Historian, Critic, Apologist." *Christian History* 4, no. 3:21–24.

One of the reasons for Lewis's productivity and mastery as a literary historian and critic was the close relationship between his teaching and scholarship. He usually revised his lecture notes for publication so his style is not ponderously academic but rather has a colloquial tone. The key charm of Lewis's scholarly writing is that he writes to share his knowledge rather than to impress. Each of his scholarly books shows how and why a book should be read. "The touchstone of myth is responsible for the apparent eclecticism of Lewis's critical judgments."

32 HENTHORNE, SUSAN CASSANDRA. "The Image of Woman in the Fiction of C. S. Lewis." Ph.D. dissertation, State University of New York at Buffalo, 154 pp.

Lewis advocates that women are naturally subordinate to men and that men should keep women in their place. He also displays a distaste for and fear of female sexuality. Lilith, who represents love of power and is a threat to the hierarchy of Christ as head of the Church and man as head of his wife, is the archetype of womanhood foremost in Lewis's imagination. In *Out of the Silent Planet* women are in the background, subordinate to men, and Lewis indicates disapproval of sexual intercourse for any reason other than reproduction. In *Perelandra*, Tinidril is depicted asexually, treated patronizingly by Ransom, has to be saved by him through physical violence, and in the end slips from her original moral position. Lewis does not allow the equality of women because that would necessitate the "utter degradation of men and the assumption by women of godhead for themselves"; he ignores the possibility of the equality of the sexes. In *That Hideous Strength* he depicts marriage as "a bleak and joyless prospect: a passionless, inequal partnership that is endured out of a sense of obligation and unthinking habit." His repulsive depiction of Fairy Hardcastle indicates his feelings about women who follow masculine pursuits. In the Narnia Chronicles his girl characters are flat, lacking any truly distinctive features, since Lewis molds them into his idea of decorous feminine behavior. The girls are "discouraged from traditional feminine preoccupations such as marriage and motherhood" but must submit to masculine authority and are not allowed to participate in masculine arenas. Jadis is a Lilith character who does not have any power of her own but must usurp power from men. Lewis's "treatment of women in his fiction must ultimately be seen as an attempt to re-institutionalize his own personal prejudice against them in the face of the trend in both Church and secular societies to assume a more liberal and realistic attitude."

33 HINMAN, MYRA. "The Ritual Deaths and Rebirths of Elwin Ransom." *CSL: The Bulletin of the New York C. S. Lewis Society* 16 (January):1–6.

In *Perelandra* Ransom experiences a ritual death, when he is transport-

1985

ed in a coffin to the planet, and a rebirth upon his arrival. After his defeat of the Un-man, Ransom again undergoes a ritual death and rebirth. Distinct personalities, with new consciousness and knowledge, emerge after each transformation. Ransom's lack of a miraculous birth is due to the portrayal of these rebirths. See response 1985.14.

34   HODGENS, RICHARD M. "On the Nature of the Prohibition in Perelandra." *CSL: The Bulletin of the New York C. S. Lewis Society* 16 (July):1–6; (August):1–5.

There is no allegorical or symbolic significance to the prohibition against staying overnight on the fixed island. The prohibition is simply a storytelling device that adds to the reader's suspense beyond wondering what will happen next. The symbolic analysis of Clyde S. Kilby [1978.20] and C. N. Manlove's interpretation [1975.31] are incorrect. *Perelandra* can be compared to *The Amphibians: A Romance of 500,000 Years Hence* by S. Fowler Wright (London: Merton Press, 1925), where a similar prohibition is also a fictional device.

35   HOLLWITZ, JOHN [CHARLES]. "The Wonder of Passage, The Making of Gold: Alchemy and Initiation in *Out of the Silent Planet*." *Mythlore* 11 (Winter-Spring):17–24.

Like rites of initiation, Ransom's journey to Malacandra consists of three stages: his abduction and prescient vision, the journey itself, and a period of instruction in the ways of the inhabitants of the planet. The central moment of Ransom's transformation is his enclosure in the spaceship as in a womb and himself envisioned as the womb. This image of symbolic androgyny is present in both alchemical and initiatory symbolism. Ransom "is seized by a powerful masculine principle" just like the alchemical illustration of a lion biting the sun and spilling blood on the ground, a picture of the "transformation of one masculine principle (the sun) by another (the lion)."

36   KARIMIPOUR, ZAHRA. "A Descriptive Bibliography of C. S. Lewis's Fiction: 1938–1981." Ph.D. dissertation, Oklahoma State University, 218 pp.

The bibliography provides detailed summaries and evaluations of criticism about the Space Trilogy, the Narnia Chronicles, and *Till We Have Faces*. References about these works are arranged chronologically. Lewis's masterful use of Norse, classical, and Arthurian myths, "his undisputable imaginative power that forges these myths into tales of great universal myths of belief and salvation, his ability to treat religious matters in diverse forms of fantasy and fairy tales, his dexterous characterization which reveals the depth of psychological conflicts, and his eloquent style make Lewis known as a competent writer of fiction." *Till We Have Faces* will sustain his reputation as a writer of fiction.

37 KILBY, CLYDE [S.] "Into the Land of the Imagination." *Christian Century* 4, no. 3:16–18.
. Lewis insisted that the Bible is literature, believed that the modern imagination has fostered villainy, and thought that contemporary people have avoided the positive potentials of love and holiness. He argued that a Christian writer should aim at edification so far as it is proper to the type of work. He wanted his creative works to embody myth, "'a gleam of divine truth falling on human imagination.'" He saw imagination as a gift of God and an avenue of spiritual witness. Reprinted: 1986.25.

38 KIRKPATRICK, HOPE. "C. S. Lewis's Studies in Words." *CSL: The Bulletin of the New York C. S. Lewis Society* 16 (October):1–8.
    Lewis aims "to facilitate a more accurate reading of old books" and "to follow parallel developments of meaning in different languages." He identifies a number of complexities in semantic study, including ramification (where a basic meaning branches out into new meanings), the speaker's meaning as opposed to the normal meaning, and the moralization of status words. The article summarizes Lewis's development and transformation of the words *sad*, *simple*, and *free*.

39 KLAUSE, ANNETTE CURTIS. Review of *C. S. Lewis Letters to Children*. *SLJ School Library Journal* 32 (November):98.
    These letters "will enthrall Narnia lovers."

40 KREEFT, PETER. "Western Civilization at the Crossroads." *Christian History* 4, no. 3:25–26.
    Lewis was critical of any philosophy of history. He believed human nature does not change and did not believe in evolutionism, that is, accidental change for the better. The Enlightenment discarded the notion of original sin and moral absolutes, and eliminated the foundations of truth and goodness. Lewis believed that reductionism would continue and was suspicious of collectivism. He offers us a choice between seeking for truth or giving in to nihilism.

41 LAMBERT, BYRON C. Reply. *CSL: The Bulletin of the New York C. S. Lewis Society* 16 (September):11–12.
    In this response to Reppert's [1985.61] reply on Lambert's article about the Lewis–Anscombe debate [1984.43.], Lambert claims that Lewis's priority between reason and nature is essential to his position in *Miracles*. Truth must be rationally derived and not caused. See Reppert's response 1986.51.

42 LINDSKOOG, KATHRYN [ANN]. "From the Child in Him to the Child in Us All." *Books & Religion* 13, no. 4–5 (May–June):12.
    The reviewer of *C. S. Lewis Letters to Children* says the book has a snug

1985

Victorian air. Lewis's letters are "written from the child in him to the child in them, and thus to the child in us all—playfully but respectfully, free of sentimentality."

43 ———. "C. S. Lewis on Christmas." *Canadian C. S. Lewis Journal,* no. 52 (Autumn):4–6.
Reprint of 1983.40.

*44 LOWMAN, P. J. "Supernaturalistic Causality and Christian Theism in the Modern English Novel." Ph.D. dissertation, University of Wales, Cardiff.
Source: *Annual Bibliography of English Literature and Language for 1986,* #11456.

45 MARTIN, JOHN, and DANIEL, JERRY [L.]. "CSL and GKC: A Four Star Conversation." *CSL: The Bulletin of the New York C. S. Lewis Society* 16 (April):1–7.
The authors create a fictional conversation between Lewis and G. K. Chesterton emphasizing the agreements between them and quoting liberally from their works. Topics include their lives, George MacDonald, modern art, truth, modern literature, chronological snobbery, "invisibilism" ("the inability of people to see the assumptions on which their reasoning is based"), biblical criticism, orthodoxy, conversion, and Jesus.

46 MEILAENDER, GILBERT. "C. S. Lewis Reconsidered: Can Christian Apology Withstand Rational Appraisal?" *Cresset* 48, no. 9:6–14.
Beversluis [1985.4] does not pay enough attention to Lewis's imaginative works, especially *Till We Have Faces,* and has the same faults of which he accuses Lewis: writing irresponsibly by not understanding the views he rejects, oversimplifying, and establishing false dilemmas. Although Beversluis is correct that Lewis's moral argument does not bridge the gap from an objective moral law to a Lawgiver, Lewis's argument is still weighty and noteworthy in the way he appeals to a basic religious impulse. Beversluis thinks Lewis's argument from reason is worthless, but Lewis's point that a thought cannot be fully accounted for in terms of nonrational causes helps define the intellect. Beversluis is blinded to the significance of Lewis's argument from desire, which is really an invitation. "Lewis was never either Platonist or Ockhamist in the simple senses used by Beversluis." His position was that God's goodness is not utterly different from our understanding of goodness, but what we think good may not be so in God's eyes. Lewis's later writings depict the struggle to give up possessive love for other things and people as part of the journey toward God.

47 MOEN, PEGGY. "Sage Advice for Young and Old." *Reflections* 4 (Summer):18.
      In this review of *C. S. Lewis Letters to Children,* Moen finds that the letters show "the surprising extent of Lewis' active works of charity, and the depth of his kindliness." They provide an unconscious, undeliberate self-portrait of Lewis.

48 MOYNIHAN, MARTIN. "The Latin Letters, 1974–1961, of C. S. Lewis to Don Giovanni Calabria of Verona (1873–1954) and to Members of His Congregation." *Seven: An Anglo-American Literary Review* 6:7–22.
      Moynihan describes twenty-five letters written by Lewis; the originals are preserved in Italy by the archivist Fra Dall'Ora Elviro, and photocopies are in the Wade Collection at Wheaton College. Although Lewis did not keep the replies, five letters from Don Calabria to Lewis were seen by Moynihan. The keynote of the correspondence is Christian unity. The letters show a heartfelt affection between the writers and a mingling of serious reflection and day-to-day concerns. The letters show Lewis's concern for helping others, the importance of prayer, and changes in Lewis's life. Reprinted: 1987.36.

49 MYERS, DORIS T. "C. S. Lewis's Passages: Chronological Age and Spiritual Development in Narnia." *Mythlore* 11 (Winter–Spring):52–56.
      Lewis, in each story of the Chronicles of Narnia, shows the flexibility of chronological age and succeeds in depicting characters who are simultaneously adultlike and childlike. Each story also "presents a task of spiritual development associated with a particular stage in life."

50 NAIR, DEVAN. "Address by President Devan Nair at the National Council of Churches Convention on the 'Role of the National Council of Churches' at St. Andrew's Cathedral on Saturday, 28 July 84 at 4:30 p.m." *East Asia Journal of Theology* 3, no. 1:31–35.
      Nair "received a rewarding insight into the ecumenical spirit in Christianity" by reading Carpenter's *The Inklings* [1978.4]. Friendship and affection existed between these men, even though they belonged to different denominations.

51 NAKAO, SETSUKO. "Friendship." *Canadian C. S. Lewis Journal,* no. 50 (Spring):1–13.
      Lewis, in *The Four Loves,* states that friendship, *philia,* is the communication of personality through a common object. *Philia* was extremely important to him as his life was directed and supported by his friends. The Inklings demonstrate the elements of companionship Lewis writes about. His friendship with Tolkien was "important for his search for Eternal Truth through literature, especially in the world of fantasy." Their friendship was a functional

1985

bond, with the exchange of ideas to their mutual benefit but "their *Philia* probably did not reach to the deep communication of personality because of their different characters." Arthur Greeves was Lewis's closest friend, sharing many subjects with him. Arthur taught him to feel affection for ordinary people, sensitivity to beauty in the homely, and humility. Lewis's assertions that *philia* does not intrude into a friend's life and that friends have naked personalities are unrealistic and exaggerated.

52 ORMROD, RICHARD. Review of *C. S. Lewis Letters to Children*. *The Times Educational Supplement*, 29 November, p. 24.
    "Lewis clearly respected children as people, accepted their criticism and often asked their advice."

53 OXBURY, HAROLD. "Lewis, Clive Staples." In *Great Britons: Twentieth-Century Lives*. Oxford: Oxford University Press, pp. 211–212.
    Short biography of Lewis.

54 PATRICK, JAMES. *The Magdalen Metaphysicals: Idealism and Orthodoxy at Oxford 1901–1945*. Macon, Ga.: Mercer University Press, 190 pp.
    Clement Charles Julian Webb, John Alexander Smith, Clive Staples Lewis, and Robin George Collingwood renewed classical metaphysics and clarified the relation between theology and philosophy. The philosophy shared by the four developed out of four convictions: an interest in classical sources, "participation in the revival of historical studies," "the belief that philosophy was essentially literary, with affinities to poetry," and the conviction that religion was a matter of truth. Lewis first rebelled against idealism and embraced realism, which satisfied his love for the objective. Beginning in 1925 he abandoned realism and had a gradual transformation from idealism to pantheism to Christianity. *The Pilgrim's Regress* is a "guide to the ideas that made Lewis a Christian." Its major themes are joy, the efficacy of reason, the objectivity of value, and "the unity of history and its importance as *preparatio evangelica*." The power of Lewis's writing comes from his being "perhaps the single most effective spokesman for supernatural religion in England or America after 1940" and the intellectual force of his apology.

55 PATTERSON, NANCY-LOU. "Letters from Hell: The Symbolism of Evil in *The Screwtape Letters*." *Mythlore* 12 (Autumn):47–57.
    The temptation depicted in *The Screwtape Letters* has three phases: by the world, the flesh, and the devil (spiritual means). The devils' names are significant, especially the name Wormwood. The devils are spiritual beings who seek to remain hidden, hell is a bureaucracy and "lowerarchy," and Satan seeks to devour all other beings and to comprehend the purposes of God. In his depiction of evil Lewis uses the classical symbols of Western tradition,

including the insect motif, the fear of being devoured, and the concept of defilement.

56 ———. Review of *Boxen: The Imaginary World of the Young C. S. Lewis.* *Mythlore* 12 (Autumn):39–40.

"This boyish world exerts its own fascination: it is more or less consistent, and creates a strong conviction of its reality. . . . The stab of supernal Joy which greets the reader on every page in Narnia is absent from Boxen."

57 ———. "Thesis, Antithesis, and Synthesis: The Interplanetary Trilogy of C. S. Lewis." *CSL: The Bulletin of the New York C. S. Lewis Society* 16 (June):1–6.

The theme of the Trilogy is the Christian gospel, the theme of salvation and rescue. Three motifs that interlock the novels are the symbol of the wasteland, the recurring villains Weston and Devine, and the complex sequence of substitutions of which the character of Ransom is the central figure. There are two models of the Trilogy's structure; one is a trinity of masculine in *Out of the Silent Planet*, feminine in *Perelandra*, and marriage—one flesh—in *That Hideous Strength*. The second is the Christian narrative of "Creation, as a thesis, [that] goes on to the Fall, an antithesis, and concludes with the Passion and Resurrection, as a synthesis." The Trilogy explores this theme on Malacandra, Perelandra, and Earth.

58 PETERS, JOHN. *C. S. Lewis: The Man and His Achievement.* Exeter, Devon: Paternoster Press, 143 pp.

The Pilgrim's Regress is important because it is the first account of Lewis's conversion and has a detailed analysis of *Sehnsucht. Mere Christianity* is significant for "its stimulating, unfailingly robust and logical defence of historic Christianity." In *The Great Divorce* Lewis presents theological ideas in an imaginative manner. In *The Lion, the Witch and the Wardrobe* "literary felicity and Christian symbolism blend together in a work of considerable charm." Lewis "was the most powerful, persuasive and effective apologist for Christianity in the nineteen forties and fifties." *Out of the Silent Planet* convinces us about life on Mars, has intellectual coherence, reflects Christian standards, and is an impressive and wide-ranging book. *Perelandra* is one of Lewis's finest imaginative works; it has a lightness of touch, ingenuity, and descriptive felicity. *That Hideous Strength* is lengthy and tortuous. The Trilogy is a classic in the science fiction genre. Lewis's letters reveal his private side, are full of common sense, show his sympathy and understanding for people, give glimpses of his academic and literary ventures, and show the reasoning behind his key works. His academic works, especially *The Allegory of Love, A Preface to Paradise Lost,* and *English Literature in the Sixteenth Century, Excluding Drama* will ensure Lewis's lasting fame. He will also be remembered as a defender of the faith.

1985

59 PETERSEN, WILLIAM J. "Meet Jack (C. S.) and Joy Lewis." In *C. S. Lewis Had a Wife*. Wheaton, Ill.: Tyndale House, 176 pp. Reprinted. 1986.
Brief biography of Lewis and Joy Davidman.

60 PHILIP, NEIL. Review of *Boxen: The Imaginary World of the Young C. S. Lewis*. *British Book News* July:437–438.
This book has three interests: it makes available to scholars Lewis's earliest known works; it adds work of particular interest to the ranks of fiction produced by children because the child grew up to be a writer; and for those interested in children's play, it allows admission to an elaborate invented world.

61 REPPERT, VICTOR. Letter. *CSL: The Bulletin of the New York C. S. Lewis Society* 16 (May):12–13.
Here Reppert responds to Lambert's article on the Lewis-Anscombe debate [1984.43]. Reppert claims that Lambert's assertion that Anscombe failed to vitiate Lewis's arguments is not correct. Causal questions about reasoning are asked of people who have not made an error. See Lambert's reply 1985.41 and Reppert's response 1986.51.

62 Review of *Boxen: The Imaginary World of the Young C. S. Lewis*. *Kirkus Review* 53 (15 August):810.
"The charm here lies in the innocence and, in fact, the averageness of the stiff, childish drawings and the predictable roster of kings and heads of state. . . . Flashes of the great fantasist-to-be appear only in the increasingly sure-footed handling of humor and characterization."

63 Review of *Boxen: The Imaginary World of the Young C. S. Lewis*. *Observer*, 3 November, p. 24.
The imaginary land of Boxen has an eerie likeness to the Brontean Angria.

64 Review of *Boxen: The Imaginary World of the Young C. S. Lewis*. *Publishers Weekly* 228 (23 August):60.
This book is a must for Lewis scholars. "The tales are a treat for adults who appreciate Lewis's astonishing imagination and sophisticated wit."

65 Review of *C. S. Lewis Letters to Children*. *Booklist* 81 (1 April):1094.
"The letters offer a fascinating perspective on Lewis' private life and contain valuable insights about the crafting of the Narnia chronicles."

66 Review of *C. S. Lewis Letters to Children*. *People* 23 (22 May):18–19.
Lewis communicated with children in the best way. His letters to children are endearing, especially when urging them to write fiction.

67   RICHARDS, JERALD. "C. S. Lewis, Retributive Punishment, and the Worth of Persons." *Christian Scholar's Review* 14:347–359.

Lewis's ethical theory is deontologist. The rightness of an action is determined "by considering its relationship to a relevant principle of duty," which Lewis considers the "respect of human beings as rational creatures." Robert Wennberg's criticism [1973.43] is that Lewis's retributive theory fails to guard against severe and inhumane penalties. Lewis's theory can be interpreted as calling for "both a 'retributive ceiling' and a 'retributive floor' to punishment"; the maximum penalty would be limited by the fundamental principle of respect for persons as rational beings. Wennberg also says that Lewis's theory does not account for strict liability in the law. "Lewis could have argued that strict liability is morally objectionable and has no justifiable place in criminal law." One could add to Lewis's theory by proposing that criminal sanctions should provide compensation to victims.

68   RIGA, FRANK P. "Augustinian Pride and the Work of C. S. Lewis." *Augustinian Studies* 16:129–136.

Augustine held that pride caused the Fall, as the will of the created being preferred itself to its Creator. Lewis follows Augustine; he holds "that the nature of being is good, that evil is a defect in good, and that this defect is made possible by free will." The temptation of Tinidril in *Perelandra*, where Weston appeals to her pride, develops Augustinian positions.

69   ROGERS, KATHERIN A. "Augustianian Evil in C. S. Lewis's *Perelandra*." In *The Transcendent Adventure: Studies of Religion in Science Fiction/Fantasy*. Edited by Robert Reilly. Westport, Conn.: Greenwood Press, pp. 83–91.

Perelandra illustrates St. Augustine's and St. Anselm of Canterbury's theories of evil. Lewis addresses four main questions about evil in the novel: How can evil be an object of choice? Why would anyone choose evil? What happens to a creature who chooses evil? Why does God permit evil?

70   ROOT, JERRY. "Following That Bright Blur." *Christian History* 4, no. 3:27, 35.

The basis of Lewis's theology is the supernatural, the study of literature that showed him the importance of written texts as authorities, rationalism, and illumined subjectivism or Joy. Two cornerstones of his theological thought are the transcendence and the immanence of God. Because God is transcendent, only poetic language can be used to convey the meaning of propositional statements about Him. "Because God communicated Himself to man, man can know about the immanent God."

71   SAMMONS, MARTHA C. "Lewis's Influence on the New Inklings: *The Chronicles of Narnia* and John White's *Tower of Geburah* and *The Iron Sceptre*." *CSL: The Bulletin of the New York C. S. Lewis Society* 17 (November):1–7.

There are "many technical and thematic similarities between" the

1985

Chronicles of Narnia and White's *Tower of Geburah: A Children's Fantasy* (Downers Grove, Ill.: Inter-Varsity Press, 1978) and *The Iron Sceptre* (Downers Grove, Ill.: Inter-Varsity Press, 1981). Both have secondary worlds and comparable ways for entering them. Both have similar concepts of time, an adult who represents the author, and mythic places in the secondary world. Both authors use biblical images to portray a Christ figure who feels the pain and sorrow of each individual and who romps with the children, illustrating a joyous relationship. Children are the heroes in both series, called to the secondary world to perform specific tasks; the oldest becomes the leader and one of the girls becomes closest to the Christ figure. Both authors have characters who are deceived by evil but become changed; these characters are tempted by power, food, and beauty. In both series blood is used as an image of salvation and resurrection and the theme of reality versus illusion is emphasized.

72 SIBLEY, BRIAN. "C. S. Lewis in Love: Surprised by Joy, Shaken by Grief." *Listener* 114 (19/26 December):33–34.

Lewis avoided all expressions of emotion, but in his relationship with Joy Davidman he experienced happiness as well as pain and grief, and enough doubts to shake the foundation of his faith. However, Lewis emerged from his ordeal a stronger Christian, able to write with renewed certainty about his faith in God.

73 ———. *Shadowlands: The Story of C. S. Lewis and Joy Davidman*. London: Hodder and Stoughton, 176 pp. Reprint. *C. S. Lewis through the Shadowlands*. Old Tappan, N.J.: Fleming H. Revell. Bath: Firecrest, 1987.

Shadowlands tells the story of the relationship between Lewis and Joy Davidman and of their separate lives during the years before they met. It includes a bibliography of works by Lewis, Davidman, William Lindsay Gresham, and W. H. Lewis, as well as a selected list of books about Lewis and Davidman.

74 STOCK, R. D. "Dionysus, Christ, and C. S. Lewis." *Christianity and Literature* 34 (Winter):7–13.

Lewis strives to reconcile Dionysus and Christ in his fiction. He emphasizes, in both the children's books and the adult fiction, "the agony of unmaking that preludes the ecstasy of spiritual joy."

75 SUTHAMCHAI, PHANIDA. "The Fusion of Christian and Fictional Elements in C. S. Lewis's Chronicles of Narnia." Ph.D. dissertation, Oklahoma State University, 159 pp.

Lewis used the Chronicles of Narnia to present Christian truths, "an innovative treatment in the development of the fairy tale." This subtle fusion of Christianity and fiction gives the Chronicles their lasting literary value. Through setting, landscape, and atmosphere, Lewis takes the reader to the otherworld of the spirit, informed by Christian truths. The setting illustrates his concept of nature, the struggle between good and evil, and his themes. Aslan exemplifies his concept of Christ (divinity, omnipotence, and goodness) and embodies four elements of Christianity: the numinous, consciousness of the moral law, the numinous power as guardian of the moral law, and historical event. The major child characters show how one should act according to Christian standards, with "conscience, courage, perseverance, good judgement, and especially love for, faith in, and obedience to Aslan." The plot structure is unified by Aslan, who is the central focus for the other characters. The structure is that of medieval romance, a quest in which the characters undergo tests and trials to strengthen their character and enhance their spirituality. The major themes of the stories are "those of Joy and longing, self-knowledge and self-discovery, faith and obedience, testing and temptation, and salvation." These themes convey the essential Christian concepts of the right relationship between man and God and the progress of man from sin to salvation. Lewis's "skillful presentation of setting, characterization, structure, and themes elevates the chronicles to a high art form."

76 TAYLOR, MAURICE. Review of *Boxen: The Imaginary World of the Young C. S. Lewis*. *Library Journal* 110 (15 October):102.
   The book will delight both young and adult readers of the Narnia Chronicles.

77 THOMPSON, RAYMOND H. *The Return from Avalon: A Study of the Arthurian Legend in Modern Fiction*. Westport, Conn.: Greenwood Press, pp. 95–98.
   In *That Hideous Strength*, "the Arthurian elements serve to evoke the eternal quality of the struggle between good and evil which is being waged at a cosmic level." The Arthurian elements help define the self-discovery and growth of the protagonists, which is achieved only at great personal cost.

78 WALKER, JEANNE MURRAY. "*The Lion, the Witch and the Wardrobe* as Rite of Passage." *Children's Literature in Education* 16, no. 3 (Autumn): 177–188.
   The novel has the conventional images and plot sequence of a rite of passage. Narnia allows the children to refashion themselves for their return to London. The narrator takes over functions of an initiator: he "mediates between the confusing mass of adult society and the initiate." In rites of passage, the hero's task is to decipher symbols and internalize them; the symbols in the novel are the Christian interpretation of reality. In the novel the hero undergoes a change in status from childhood to adulthood.

1985

79 WEBBER, ROBERT E. "Are Evangelicals Becoming Sacramental?" *Ecumenical Trends* 14, no. 3 (March):36–38.

  The reason for the rise of a sacramental consciousness among evangelicals "may be found in the wide readership of C. S. Lewis, the growing interest in the early church fathers and the pursuit after Catholic spirituality."

80 WELL, CALVIN RICHARD. "Perception and Faith: The Integration of Gestalt Psychology and Christian Theology in the Thought of C. S. Lewis." Ph.D. dissertation, Baylor University, 249 pp.

  Lewis was a philosopher-psychologist who derived his thought from Carl Jung, D. S. Alexander, and Edwyn Bevan, among others who were directly or indirectly linked with Gestalt psychology. Lewis's apologetic works are phenomenological and perceptually oriented. His philosophy of perception, that "biological processes can 'represent,' but cannot contain, the whole of perceptual meaning," combines Gestalt and Christian concepts. His arguments for the existence of God are based on psychological grounds (the experience of the numinous, the existence of a moral sense, and the experience of *Sensucht*) and are Gestalt-like. Lewis's theory of religious behavior is consistent with a Gestalt approach because his "theory of myth presupposes an integration of the cerebral hemispheres," and "the polarities which Lewis posited have relation to futility itself." For him, diversity in religions results from perceptual failure and are differences between the whole and the parts. "The thought of C. S. Lewis represents a tacit integration of Gestalt psychology and Christian theology."

81 WIDMER, CYNTHIA. Review of *C. S. Lewis Letters to Children. Library Journal* 110 (15 April):68.

  "Young readers will enjoy these letters not only for their lack of condescension but also for the kindly concern and humor with which Lewis encourages young authors, offers spiritual counsel, and responds to questions about writing, the Chronicles of Narnia, and himself." Adults will also find them engaging.

82 WITCHER, GERALDINE. "Beyond Narnia." *Canadian C. S. Lewis Journal*, no. 52 (Autumn):7–11.

  "The Narnia books are ideal for reading aloud" because of their style, vocabulary, and evocative language. Various themes that run through the books are the complexity of creation, the joy of Christianity, the longing for something "other," and the terrible oppositeness of good and evil. The science fiction trilogy can be read as a good story or with an awareness of its Christianity. "There is an amazing complexity to Lewis' works." Every aspect of story, setting, and language fit together and complete each other. His non-fiction works tackle deep subjects in a profound manner and are clear, logical, and convincing. He uses everyday illustrations to clarify abstract points and employs flashes of humor. *Surprised by Joy* is not autobiography but the story of one man's search for God. There were two sides to Lewis: a jovial fun-loving person and a great teacher with a ruthlessly logical mind. "His work is a marvelous mixture of reason and imagination."

83 YANDELL, STEVEN. "The Trans-cosmic Journeys in *The Chronicles of Narnia.*" *Mythlore* 12 (Autumn):9–23.

The transcosmic journeys (i.e., journeys between worlds) in the Chronicles demonstrate how much attention Lewis put into developing the fantasy element in the stories. "Not only did Lewis construct an entire planar geometry in which to organize his worlds, but he also expanded the theory of non-linear time streams." The article includes drawings of the planar geometry in the Chronicles. It also provides a chart detailing each of the sixty separate transcosmic journeys, in chronological order, listing "the participants, the starting location and time, the ending location and time, the method of transport, and the circumstances surrounding each journey."

1986

1 BARCUS, JAMES E. "Broad Swaths and Deep Cuts: The Autobiographical Impulse in G. K. Chesterton and C. S. Lewis." *Chesterton Review* 12 (August):331–344.

Lewis's *Surprised by Joy* and Chesterton's *Autobiography* (London: Hutchinson, 1936) are examples of the diversity of the group known as the Oxford Christians. Neither man embraced the prevailing modern disdain for the past. Both emphasized similar experiences in their autobiographies. Both men were "intolerant of pacifists, and both exalted death on the battlefield." Both remembered childhood as spreading a glory over experience. On the other hand, Chesterton had a lack of concern for the empirical and demonstrable while Lewis related specific events and documented experiences. Chesterton had a joy in life that Lewis lacked. Paradox characterized Chesterton's prose style while Lewis was compelled to explain paradox away. Chesterton used symbolic images, Lewis allegorical ones.

2 BORDEN, MATTHEW. "Lewis and the Future Tense." *CSL: The Bulletin of the New York C. S. Lewis Society* 17 (August):4.

Letter XV in *The Screwtape Letters* is a discourse on Matthew 6:25–34. For Lewis the present touches on eternity, and the future is the field of the devil's activity. Two future-oriented snares evident in the letter are utopianism and despair. The discussion of lust is unsatisfactory and "the present-versus-future idea doesn't serve well in this example."

1986

3 "C. S. Lewis and the Emancipation of Women." *CSL: The Bulletin of the New York C. S. Lewis Society* 17 (February):4–6.

This article reports a panel discussion on Lewis's essay "God's Design and Man's Witness," in which he identifies the emancipation of women as one area of radical change in recent thought that creates difficulty in communicating Christianity to moderns. Lewis presents three main ideas on this topic: "1) Men like men better than women like women; 2) Mixed society reduces the opportunity for discussion of ultimate issues; 3) By nature, the masculine is drawn to the metaphysical, the feminine to the concrete and practical." The panel agreed, with individual exceptions, that men do prefer the company of men while women prefer mixed company. The panel decided that heretrogeneity in general tends to stultify profound discussions. Lewis's assertion that men tend toward the metaphysical and women toward the practical is not sexist, unless the metaphysical is considered superior to the practical.

4 CASEY, ELLEN MILLER. Review of *Boxen: The Imaginary World of the Young C. S. Lewis. Best Sellers* 45 (February):427.

"Lewis is not great enough nor these stories wonderful enough to warrant their appearance in what is obviously designed to be a general interest format."

5 CHERVIN, RONDA. "Discernment in Decision Making in the Novels of C. S. Lewis." *Lamp-Post of the Southern California C. S. Lewis Society* 10, nos. 2–4 (December):3–13, 32.

In the Chronicles of Narnia, the Ransom Trilogy, *Till We Have Faces*, *The Screwtape Letters*, *The Great Divorce*, and *The Pilgrim's Regress* Lewis depicts three paths taken when a decision is made. A wrong choice is sometimes made in response to temptation, usually the result of pride or concupiscence (an "inordinate craving for pleasurable fulfillment of physical needs"). This value blindness comes from holding false philosophies and giving into cynicism and skepticism. The second response to decision making is making "an immediate right choice based on previous experience, intuition, urging of comrades; or, even more often on virtue, authority, voices, visions and intense feelings, on a correct philosophy of life, or on sheer grace." The third decision-making path is uncertainty; Lewis urges us "to trust that God will bring good out of mistakes if we sincerely wish to do the right thing."

6 CHRISTOPHER, JOE R. "The Natural Law Tradition of C. S. Lewis." *Ring Bearer* 4 (Fall):11–16.

In "Right and Wrong: A Clue to the Meaning of the Universe?," Lewis argues that the moral law behind the universe implies a mental purpose. He appeals to personal experience, his arguments are simple and clear, and he uses many examples and analogies, techniques well suited for the mass audience he was addressing. In *The Abolition of Man*, written for a learned audience, he argues that natural law is a set of fundamental principles, which, if discarded, could lead to people being treated like animals. Lewis "elevates Natural Law not to being *of* God but to *being* God." Reprinted in part: 1987.5.

7   COLE, G. A. "Justice: Retributive or Reformative?" *The Reformed Theological Review* 45, no. 1 (January–April):5–12.
      Lewis argues in "The Humanitarian Theory of Punishment" that the retributive theory of justice alone is appropriate. However, the biblical approach is more complex and includes deterrence along with retribution. Lewis qualified his position during the debate generated by his essay and admitted deterrence into his view of penal justice as long as retribution was retained.

8   COLLINGS, MICHAEL R. "Beyond Deep Heaven: Generic Structure and Christian Message in C. S. Lewis' Ransom Novels." *Lamp-Post of the Southern California C. S. Lewis Society* 10, nos. 2–4 (December):17–22, 33.
      The Ransom novels are so distinct that readers need to develop a different reading protocol for each one. *Out of the Silent Planet* should be regarded as a fantasy, sub-genre Cosmic Voyage. *Perelandra* should be regarded as myth. *That Hideous Strength* creates the most problems; in the novel Lewis inverts science fiction by intruding theological elements. He restructures the genre to appropriate it for his Christian concerns and creates Christian science fiction.

9   ———. Review of *Boxen: The Imaginary World of the Young C. S. Lewis*. *Fantasy Review* 9 (January):21–22.
      "Although not successful in their own right as literature, the Boxen stories do show us C. S. Lewis working through many elements of his private mythology."

10   ———. "Science and Scientism in C. S. Lewis's *That Hideous Strength*." In *Hard Science Fiction*. Edited by George E. Slusser and Eric S. Rabkin. Carbondale: Southern Illinois University Press, pp. 131–140.
      In *That Hideous Strength* Lewis "uses the scientific method as a means of defining and identifying the extrahuman beings functioning" in the Space Trilogy. This use of science is a unifying element in the novel and is a technique that places the novel in the tradition of hard science fiction.

11   DIEKEMA, DOUGLAS S. "Yet Still There Is Hell: Damnation and Hell in C. S. Lewis." *Cresset* 49, no. 3:15–19.
      For Lewis, damnation is "a freely made decision in which the individual chooses to spend eternity in his own mind, thereby creating his own hell, an essential nothingness resulting from the absence of God." He emphasizes that self-surrender and submission to God are necessary to salvation. He explains

1986

these concepts in *Mere Christianity* and *The Problem of Pain*, and illustrates them in *Perelandra, The Great Divorce, The Last Battle,* and *That Hideous Strength.*

12 EDWARDS, BRUCE L[EE], Jr. "Deconstruction and Rehabilitation: C. S. Lewis' Defense of Western Textuality." *Journal of the Evangelical Theological Society* 29, no. 2:205–214.
    Reprint of 1982.17; 1985.20.

13 ———. *A Rhetoric of Reading: C. S. Lewis's Defense of Western Literacy.* Values in Literature Monographs, no. 2. Provo, Utah: Center for the Study of Christian Values in Literature, College of Humanities, Brigham Young University, 128 pp.
    Revision of 1981.17.

14 FARRELL, ELEANOR M. "'An Clove the Wind from Unseen Shores': The Sea Voyage Motif in Imaginative Literature." *Mythlore* 12 (Spring): 43–47, 60.
    Farrell traces the image of the sea voyage from the classical Greek works of Homer's *The Odyssey* and Vergil's *Aeneid*, to the Bible, to the early Middle Ages works *Beowulf* and the Welsh *Mabinogi*, to Malory's *Le Morte d'Arthur*, to Dante's *Divine Comedy*. In Lewis's *The Voyage of the "Dawn Treader"* the voyage represents the spiritual life journey. Farrell discusses sea voyages in Tolkien, Williams, Patricia A. McKillip's *Riddle-Master* trilogy, and Ursula K. LeGuin's *Earthsea* trilogy.

15 FILMER, KATH. "The Polemic Image: The Role of Metaphor and Symbol in the Fiction of C. S. Lewis." *Seven: An Anglo-American Literary Review* 7:61–76.
    Metaphor and symbol require metaphysical interpretation and therefore function persuasively, particularly in Lewis's fiction. "As a rationalist, he emphasized the necessity of the dual operation of the imagination and of reason in the apprehension of truth, and in its expression through metaphor and symbol." Because Lewis uses metaphor and symbol not only to instruct but also to delight the reader, his polemic is enhanced and rendered more acceptable to the reader. Reprinted: 1988.24.

16 FISH, STANLEY. "Transmuting the Lump: *Paradise Lost*, 1942–1982." In *Literature and History: Theoretical Problems and Russian Case Studies.* Edited by Gary Saul Morson. Stanford, Calif.: Stanford University Press, pp. 33–56 passim.
    Lewis, in *A Preface to "Paradise Lost,"* criticizes Books XI and XII of the poem as doctrinal and didactic so he can defend the rest of the poem. In his criticism of the poem, Lewis takes a middle position between F. R.

Leavis's demand for realism and T. S. Eliot's desire for an otherworldly purity. Later critics have rehabilitated Books XI and XII, guided by the terms Lewis established.

17   FLIEGER, VERLYN. "Missing Person." *Mythlore* 12 (Summer):12–15.
       Lewis's fiction is more direct than Tolkien's; he "wanted to put readers in touch with the events of Judeo-Christian mythology." Tolkien is indirect; he wanted readers to find these elements for themselves.

18   GRIFFIN, HENRY WILLIAM. "Beer, Beowulf, and the English Literature Syllabus, 1936." *CSL: The Bulletin of the New York C. S. Lewis Society* 17 (February):1–3.
       In Lewis's "beer and Beowulf" parties the poem was read aloud in Anglo-Saxon. Lewis fought for "the centrality of the work in the English literature syllabus."

19   ———. *Clive Staples Lewis: A Dramatic Life*. San Francisco: Harper & Row, 507 pp.
       Griffin has written a narrative biography of Lewis, designed for an American audience, covering his life from 1925 until his death in 1963. He presents incidents and episodes of Lewis's life in chronological order, detailing "his university career first at Oxford, then at Cambridge; his service in the first war as a second lieutenant and in the second as a lay lecturer; his sermons in pulpits and his addresses at the British Academy; his misogyny as a bachelor and his scandal as a lover; his faithfulness as a friend and his loyalty as a brother; his public frugalities and his hidden charities." Griffin does not attempt to evaluate Lewis's works or his place in history.

20   GUSSMAN, NEIL. "C. S. Lewis on Readers: A Resource for Writers." *CSL: The Bulletin of the New York C. S. Lewis Society* 17 (October):1–7.
       Lewis offers help for writers in three areas: (1) reading his work, which is filled with good, clear writing; (2) following his specific advice on writing, found in four letters; (3) following his implicit advice in *An Experiment in Criticism*, which "differentiates between the 'few' and the 'many' in the appreciation of . . . writing." Lewis's advice in *Experiment* benefits Gussman's writing of advertising copy.

21   HANNAY, MARGARET P[ATTERSON]. "Provocative Generalizations: *The Allegory of Love* in Retrospect." *Seven: An Anglo-American Literary Review* 7:41–60.
       Lewis was the first to apply the art/nature contrast to the Bower and the Garden of Adonis in Spenser's *The Faerie Queene*. Although Lewis overstated this contrast, the critical reaction to his "art/nature distinction has contributed to the current emphasis on the self-reflexive nature of Spenser's

statements about the poet's role within *The Faerie Queene.*" Lewis was wrong when he stated that the opposition of natural and artificial is "another of the great antitheses which run through the poem." He established the contrast between sterility and fertility, which is more valid than the art/nature contrast. He redefined the terms of critical discussion on the Bower and the Garden. His brash generalizations "have incited some of the best subsequent readings of Spenser." Reprinted: 1988.28.

22 HODGENS, RICHARD [M.]. "A Note on the Brown Girl." *CSL: The Bulletin of the New York C. S. Lewis Society* 17 (May):1–3.
    The brown girl in *The Pilgrim's Regress* is borrowed from English ballad literature. She is a figment of John's imagination, not a real person, and represents his lusts. In the work, Lewis uses the traditional contrast of the North and the South and makes both equally appalling.

23 HUTTAR, CHARLES A. "Lewis's Memory: A Further Note on a Source in 'Screwtape Proposes a Toast.'" *CSL: The Bulletin of the New York C. S. Lewis Society* 18 (November):11–12.
    Huttar comments on Landrum's article [1986.28] regarding the source of Screwtape's parable. Herodotus, not Livy, is the source. Herodotus agrees in every point with Lewis where Livy does not.

24 JOHNSON, WILLIAM G., and HOUTMAN, MARCIA K. "Platonic Shadows in C. S. Lewis' Narnia *Chronicles.*" *Modern Fiction Studies* 32, no. 1 (Spring):75–87.
    Lewis's Platonism is selective and diffused—"Plato as his doctrines are filtered through St. Paul, Augustine, the Florentine Neo-Platonists, and the Christian Humanists." Lewis is concerned with Platonic questions about the nature of reality, especially in *The Last Battle* where there are examples of the "mistaken identification of the 'shadows,' or insubstantial, for the Real."

25 KILBY, CLYDE [S.] "Into the Land of the Imagination." *Canadian C. S. Lewis Journal,* no. 54 (Spring):1–3.
    Reprint of 1985.37.

26 ———. "The Joy-Minded Professor." *Christian Herald* 109 (March):45–47.
    Lewis "feelingly stressed the importance of practicing joy" in his works, especially in *The Pilgrim's Regress* and *That Hideous Strength.*

27 KING, DON. "The Childlike in George MacDonald and C. S. Lewis." *Mythlore* 12 (Summer):17–22, 26.
    The basic childlike attitudes of the authors' readers are innocence, awe, and longing. Innocence allows the reader to accept the stories without raising "adult" objections to their improbability. Awe allows the reader to see there is

more to life than physical reality. Longing is the reader's desire for "a deeper, more meaningful experience than is available in the daily march of time." Two types of characters in the authors' work are the childish character who is egocentric, dishonest, spiteful, petty, cruel, and pseudo-sophisticated and the childlike character who experiences innocence, awe, and longing in the story itself. King describes the childlike characters of Lucy in the Chronicles of Narnia and Irene and Curdie in MacDonald's *The Princess and the Goblin* (London: Blackie & Son, 1871).

28   LANDRUM, DAVID W. "A Note on a Source in 'Screwtape Proposes a Toast.'" *CSL: The Bulletin of the New York C. S. Lewis Society* 17 (August):1–2.

    The source of Screwtape's parable of a dictator allowing no preeminence among his subjects is Livy's history of the founding of Rome. Differences between Screwtape's version and the original are a Greek tyrant instead of a Roman king offering advice, another tyrant versus the king's son requesting advice, a field of wheat rather than a garden of poppies being cut down, and a lesson rather than a specific course of action showing principles of government . See 1986.23 for reply.

29   LINDBERG, LOTTIE. "Lewis and 'Xmas.'" *CSL: The Bulletin of the New York C. S. Lewis Society* 18 (December):1–2.

    Lewis in "Xmas and Christmas: A Lost Chapter from Herodotus" attributes the essay to Herodotus and thus has "a wonderful vehicle to write this satirical piece." He contrasts Exmas—the commercial festival, with Crissmas—the spiritual festival and shows that the celebrations, the attitudes, and the feelings involved in each are different.

30   LINDSKOOG, KATHRYN [ANN]. *Around the Year with C. S. Lewis and His Friends: A Book of Days.* Norwalk, Conn.: Gibson Co., 400 pp.

    Lindskoog lists events from the lives of Lewis and people associated with him (Warren, Joy Davidman, J. R. R. Tolkien, George MacDonald, G. K. Chesterton, Charles Williams, etc.). Also included are quotations from Lewis and those associated with him, with space for personal comments.

31   ———. "The First Chronicle of Narnia: The Restoring of Names." *Mythlore* 12 (Summer):43–46, 63.

    In the opening sentences of *The Lion, the Witch and the Wardrobe*, Lewis introduces the characters, establishes a "chummy way of speaking directly to the reader," and introduces evil and the use of homely detail and whimsy. Important elements in the novel are identity, choice, the use of names, and irony. The character of Father Christmas is the Holy Spirit, the giver of spiritual gifts.

1986

32   LOGSDON, MIKE J. "The Necessity of Pain." *Lamp-Post of the Southern California C. S. Lewis Society* 10, nos. 2–4 (December):23–25, 33.
      Lewis in *The Problem of Pain* says God uses pain to wake unbelievers out of their self-indulgent state and to draw believers into closer fellowship with Him. Lewis attempted to show how an evil produces an essentially good effect.

33   LUTTON, JEANETTE HUME. "The Feast of Reason: *Out of the Silent Planet* as The Book of Hnau." *Mythlore* 13 (Autumn):37–41. 50.
      The three rational (*hnau*) species on Malacandra are the *seroni*, the planet's intellectuals; the *horossa*, heroes and bards; and the *pfifltriggi*, artists and craftsmen. The novel can be compared to *Gulliver's Travels*. In both novels a human being meets rational creatures with non-human shapes and comes to realize that humans are only imperfectly rational. The major difference is that Gulliver is never accepted as a rational being by the Houyhnhnms while Ransom is accepted without question as being *hnau*. The novel itself is *hnau*; Lewis did not incorporate overt images of the Christian revelation in the novel. He was following the tradition in which traveling is a symbol of spiritual progress; Malacandra represents the stage of reason in Ransom's journey while Perelandra is the stage of revelation.

34   MACKY, PETER W. "Appeasing the Gods in C. S. Lewis's *Till We Have Faces.*" *Seven: An Anglo-American Literary Review* 7:77–89
      The myth of Psyche as the Great Offering can be found in Greek sources, the Old Testament, and the story of Jesus. The central issues raised in the novel are whether Psyche is guilty of any sinful behavior and who caused the natural disasters that fell on Glome and why. The account we are to accept is that of Fox in the Afterworld: Psyche is innocent of any sinful behavior; the god sent the natural disasters upon Glome "in order to draw Psyche to himself, and then through her to redeem Orual." Psyche gives herself in voluntary sacrifice and the result of her loving attitude and self-giving is unity with God.

35   McLAUGHLIN, SARA PARK. "From A-roving to Zoo: A Look at Lewis's Vocabulary in *Poems, Narrative Poems*, and *Spirits in Bondage.*" *CSL: The Bulletin of the New York C. S. Lewis Society* 17 (May):7–8.
      With Mark Webb, the author has completed a word index to the works of Lewis named above [1988.44]. Some insights into Lewis's poetry that have resulted from this index are his creation of vivid images using hyphenated words, references to other authors, the significant role of insects and animals, the presence of "other-worldly" creatures, and recurrent themes such as nature, truth, and love. Lewis's poetry should be read because it is entertaining and contains many of the religious and fantastic elements found in his popular works.

36   McMILLAN, LEX O. "C. S. Lewis as Spiritual Autobiographer: A Study in the Sacramental Imagination." Ph.D. dissertation, University of Notre Dame, 303 pp.

As an autobiographer, Lewis conveys the objective significance of his subjective religious experience. The foundation of his sacramental imagination is his insight that Christianity is myth become fact. Through his doctrine of transposition, "the higher reproducing itself in the lower," he depicts how his own experiences lead beyond subjectivism to the divine. In *The Pilgrim's Regress*, classified as historical self-realization, Lewis characterizes the moralized landscape and sacramental icons that shaped his imagination. In *Surprised by Joy*, classified as philosophic self-exploration, he develops the persona of Prometheus, who comes to believe in Christianity as the inescapable result of his quest for truth in order to induce doubt among modern skeptics. In *Till We Have Faces*, Lewis's greatest work, classified as poetic self-expression, he combines the moralized landscape and Promethean persona of the two earlier works. In the Cupid and Psyche story he found a myth that carries the burden of his own facts. By making the novel a pseudo-autobiography, he dramatizes his criticism of autobiography. The key to Lewis and the basis of his sacramental imagination is his belief in the inseparability of nature and the supernatural.

37   MERCHANT, ROBERT. "Letters to an American Lady: 'More a Wave of the Hand Than a Letter.'" *CSL: The Bulletin of the New York C. S. Lewis Society* 18 (November):1–9.

The style of the letters, written between 1950 and 1963, is relaxed and folksy. Lewis's letter writing reveals his philosophy—to receive whatever life brings with charity and grace and to serve God in others. The person of Lewis displayed in the letters is open, candid, self-deprecating, courageous, confident, and insistent on frankness. The spiritual advice Lewis gave included the importance of perseverance, of counseling charity and patience, and of meeting death with joy. He also warned against the unhealthy attitude of ignoring death.

38   MILES, VERNON GARTH. "Certainty, Ambiguity, and the Leap of Faith in *That Hideous Strength* and *Giles Goat-Boy.*" *Texas Review* 7, no. 1–2 (Spring–Summer):86–93.

The very different depictions of the Supreme Being highlight the important contrast between certainty in Lewis's novel and ambiguity in John Barth's *Giles Goat-Boy; or, The Revised New Syllabus* (Garden City, N.Y.: Doubleday, 1966). In both novels the main character must acquire self-knowledge and make a leap of faith. In Lewis's novel this leads to Christian optimism, the ability to act consistently. In Barth's novel this leads to existential authenticity, the desire to act consistently without the capacity to do so.

1986

39 MORRIS, DANIEL L. "Encounter in a Two-Bit Pub." *Canadian C. S. Lewis Journal*, no. 56 (Autumn):7, 9–12.

 Morris met Lewis in 1959. They discussed Lewis's wife and her illness, how she had thrown light on the Old Testament for him, machines, mathematics, biochemistry, the fourth dimension, prevision, extrasensory perception, predestination, the differences between mystics and geniuses, and evil.

40 MURDOCH, BRIAN. "C. S. Lewis: The Author of Novels, Children's Books and Religious Works is Now Attracting Interest from Collectors." *Canadian C. S. Lewis Journal*, no. 53 (Winter):5–8.

 One problem collectors have is that Lewis's works are so popular they are readily available. So only selected first editions have any great monetary value. Another problem is that his works appeared in several different forms, in American and British editions, so it is hard to establish what is the first edition and whether there really are several "first" editions. His rarest publications are two books of poetry published under the pseudonym "Clive Hamilton," *Spirits in Bondage* and *Dymer*. Interest in his work is centered on the Space Trilogy, the Chronicles of Narnia, *The Screwtape Letters*, and a few others.

41 MURPHY, PATRICK D. "C. S. Lewis's *Dymer*: Once More with Hesitation." *CSL: The Bulletin of the New York C. S. Lewis Society* 17 (June):1–8.

 The poem begins as a hesitation fantasy and is resolved as a supernatural fantasy. The reader hesitates over the description of nature as alternately sympathetic and hostile and over the reality of Dymer's perception. Dymer's egotism is his downfall; he sees everything as an object of his desires. "He confuses the natural and the supernatural, the human and the superhuman." By choosing life over death he comes "to accept the world as it is, as well as recognizing that the supernatural is beyond human attainment." When Dymer accepts this, his and "the reader's hesitation ends and the hesitation fantasy becomes clearly a supernatural fantasy, a marvelous story." Dymer learns to cease romanticizing or rejecting nature, the supernatural, and death. The hesitation fantasy form allows Lewis to make the reader undergo the same experiences as Dymer.

42 MUSACCHIO, GEORGE. "C. S. Lewis' *A Grief Observed* as Fiction." *Mythlore* 12 (Spring):24–27.

 A Grief Observed is not a personal, autobiographical outpouring of grief; it is written as "a fictional journal intended to help its readers through actual crises of grief and faith." There are four reasons that the book's narrator is an adopted persona. First, the work has nine motifs in common with Tennyson's *In Memoriam*, a traditional poetic elegy. Second, Lewis dealt with an earlier loss, in which his manuscript of *Dymer* had been rejected, by imagining the worst and coming to terms with it in writing. He may have adopted the premise what if life on earth is all there is in *A Grief Observed*. Third, if taken as Lewis's own reaction to his wife's death, "the book does not ring true to modern psychological studies of grief." Fourth, the letters Lewis wrote after Joy's death do not exhibit the extreme grief depicted in *A Grief Observed* but rather a calm acceptance of his loss. Reprinted: 1987.38.

43 PATTERSON, NANCY-LOU. Review of *God in the Dock. Mythlore* 13 (Autumn):45.
    The book reviewed makes available at modest price, small and interesting selections of Lewis's thought.

44 ———. "'Some Kind of Company': The Sacred Community in *That Hideous Strength*." *Mythlore* 13 (Autumn):9–19.
    The article provides a detailed description of each member of the Community of St. Anne's, in order of their joining the company, and discusses the relationships among the characters. The company represents "a paradigm of the Body of Christ." The author also discusses the animal characters that are members of St. Anne's. Ransom's title as Fisher-King means he is "a wounded leader whose environs are threatened with ruin, decay, sterility, and death." Ransom's title as Director of the company passes to Grace Ironwood; Ransom's title as Pendragon passes to Arthur Denniston.

45 ———. "The Unfathomable Feminine Principle: Images of Wholeness in *That Hideous Strength*." *Lamp-Post of the Southern California C. S. Lewis Society* 9, nos. 1–3 (July):3–39.
    Bracton College represents Intellect, Bragdon Wood represents Moral Feeling, the Garden at St. Anne's represents Physical Sensation, and St. Anne's Manor represents Intuition. In the plot of the novel, an outburst of psychic force emerges from Moral Feeling and overthrows the rational Intellect; stability is reestablished by a combination of Sensation and Intuition, "which St. Anne's, a feminine image of wholeness, expresses, and for which the new-made marriage of Mark and Jane is the fulfillment." The images, allusions, and motifs Lewis uses to describe Bracton College, Bragdon Wood, St. Anne's Garden, and St. Anne's Manor are explored in detail. "In *That Hideous Strength* all the power of Lewis's imagination has been poured into creating a sequence of feminine images of divine wholeness: Alma Mater, sacred woodland, enclosed garden, protective house, Earthly Venus, Heavenly Charity."

46 PAXFORD, F. W. "'He Should Have Been a Parson': Observations of His Gardener." *Canadian C. S. Lewis Journal*, no. 55 (Summer):7–13.
    Paxford remembers that Lewis enjoyed watching birds and walking in

the woods. He loved trees and would not allow them to be cut down. He had a soft spot for the swans and would feed them every evening. Lewis and his brother helped do a lot of the sawing of firewood. Paxford thought that Mrs. Moore "was a great lady very fond of Ireland and the Irish and of mothering people." She was like a mother to Lewis. Paxford believes that Lewis should have been a clergyman as he had a clear voice that could be heard all over the church. He brought humor into his sermons, which people liked. Paxford also remembers that Lewis was very fond of jokes, especially country ones. He was fond of animals but had no interest in sports. He had queer tastes in food, did not worry about his clothes, was not particularly fond of children, was interested in astronomy, and liked to have little arguments.

47 PHILIP, NEIL. Review of *C. S. Lewis Letters to Children. British Book News*, January, p. 55.

This volume contains nothing of great consequence. Lewis "does not seem at his ease with his young correspondents: they stimulate him to no flights of fancy, prompt him to no conspiratorial confidences."

48 PRICE, GEOFFREY. "Scientism and the Flight from Reality." *Seven: An Anglo-American Literary Review* 7:117–125.

Price discusses Aeschlimann's [1983.1] examination of Lewis as a critic of reductionist scientism. He claims that the cause of scientism does not lie with the present industrial society but "arises from the disorder of the spiritual experience of the subject." Aeschlimann's argument that scientism can be refuted by "counterpoising Christian and classical morality in conceptualized, doctrinal form" is wrong. Scientism's grip can be broken only by religious experience.

49 RAHN, SUZANNE. "The Expression of Religious and Political Concepts in Fantasy for Children." Ph.D. dissertation, University of Washington, pp. 293–315, 423–454.

The Magician's Nephew combines in a new way "Lewis's speculations on unfallen man, unfallen world, and the proper relation between man and the animals." He shows how undisciplined desire for knowledge leads to pride and lust for power. Digory plays the part of Adam but is given a second chance to provide reparation. *The Voyage of the "Dawn Treader"* is a spiritual journey whose plot and character development promote the theme of progress toward union with God. The novel is modeled on two British medieval examples, *Morte d'Arthur* and *The Voyage of St. Brendan*. The various islands the characters encounter are obstacles to their goal of reaching Aslan's country and represent the sins of greed, egocentricity, avarice, and pride, and the fears of the unconscious and of irrevocable commitment to the unknown. Lewis has given the novel the shape of his own conversion: a journey to an unknown place, motivated by Joy.

50   RAWLS, MELANIE. *"Herland* and *Out of the Silent Planet*: A Comparison of a Feminist Utopia and a Male-charactered Fantasy." *Mythlore* 13 (Winter): 51–54.
      In both Lewis's *Out of the Silent Planet* and Charlotte Perkins Gilman's *Herland* (New York: Pantheon, 1979) males assume that the native population is ignorant, superstitious, and unsophisticated because there are no cities or industry. In both works the male protagonist realizes, while trying to explain his world, that many of its superior advances are the result of great misery or lead to great misery. Herlanders and Malacandrians have similar views on love and sexual continence. However, while Gilman believes humans could be educated to behave continently Lewis believes humans are instinctively incontinent and cannot be educated out of this behavior.

51   REPPERT, VICTOR. "Lewis and Anscombe—Again." *CSL: The Bulletin of the New York C. S. Lewis Society* 17 (July):1–3.
      Reppert discusses the Lewis–Anscombe debate. [See Lambert 1984.43, Reppert 1985.61, and Lambert 1985.41 for previous exchange of views on this topic.] Anscombe is not rejecting Lewis's worldview but his *"argument* that if Reason were a part of Nature it would be discredited." Causal questions are posed when no error has occurred. The priority of reason over cause occurs because "we are more concerned with correcting errors than with explaining a successful process." Anscombe did not think that Lewis successfully showed naturalism as absurd, and Lambert fails to show that Lewis was correct and Anscombe mistaken.

52   Review of *Boxen: The Imaginary World of the Young C. S. Lewis. New Yorker* 62 (31 March):82–83.
      "The Boxen stories undertake large themes—war, party struggles, political corruption—on a small, bright canvas that is, in its way, a portrait of the Edwardian mind or mood."

53   RODGERS, PETER. "Roots and Shoots: C. S. Lewis and the Evangelicals." *CSL: The Bulletin of the New York C. S. Lewis Society* 17 (July):5–6.
      Lewis has exercised great influence "on popular apologetic and evangelistic writing in the Church of England." His works are useful to those writing apologetics, attacking Satan, and engaging in controversy in the Church. Lewis is indebted to Richard Baxter.

54   SAUER, JAMES L. "Lewis on the Light Side." *Christianity Today* 30 (18 April):51.
      In his review of *C. S. Lewis Letters to Children*, Sauer finds the works to

1986

be "a light, readable, selection of Lewis that contains many of the things that make him a great writer: depth of insight, humility of spirit, wry English wit, and a childlike enjoyment of life."

55 ———. Review of *Boxen: The Imaginary World of the Young C. S. Lewis.* *Christianity Today* 30 (5 September):61.

The stories are precocious but tedious and primitive. The book is more autobiography than fiction.

56 SCHAKEL, PETER [J.]. "Dance as Metaphor and Myth in Lewis, Tolkien, and Williams." *Mythlore* 12 (Spring):4–8, 23.

Lewis uses dance as an archetype or idea. Dance has a long history in Western cultural tradition, including use by Plato, Andrew Marvell, and Sir John Davies. This image of dance "assumes that the universe is a *cosmos*, a harmonious system, and that human life, as an integral part of that whole, also has order, unity, and meaning." The various levels in which dance appears in Lewis's work are literal dancing as part of the plot, dance as a spontaneous celebration or ceremony, and use of dance metaphor to clarify key themes, such as marriage in *That Hideous Strength* and the concept of the Trinity in *Mere Christianity*. Lewis emphasizes God as a participant in the cosmic dance and insists that the human response to God must be active. Lewis is indebted to Williams's image of dance in *The Greater Trumps* (London: Gollancz, 1932). "Dance images myth itself."

57 TETREAULT, JAMES. "Parallel Lines: C. S. Lewis and T. S. Eliot." *Renascence: Essays on Value in Literature* 38, no. 4 (Summer):256–269.

Tetreault brings together all Lewis's references to Eliot to describe the history and complexity of his attitude toward Eliot. "Lewis's published references to Eliot were often strikingly hostile, sometimes neutral, upon occasion complimentary, but never warm." From the 1940s on they were less acerbic and more respectful. Eliot was the embodiment of the Modernist movement, which Lewis found to be elitist and undemocratic; Eliot's poetry had a cynical, mocking tone, was joyless, and world weary. Lewis loved romantic and epic poetry; Eliot's poetry was "the embodiment of all he detested in the new literature and the postwar climate."

58 THORSON, STEPHEN, and DANIEL, JERRY [L.]. "Bibliographic Notes." *CSL: The Bulletin of the New York C. S. Lewis Society* 17 (July):5–6.

The notes provide a supplement to Hooper's bibliography of Lewis's works [1979.48]. The authors lists poems not included and provide additional data on poems listed in Hooper's bibliography.

59 ———. "Bibliographic Notes." *CSL: The Bulletin of the New York C. S. Lewis Society* 17 (August):6–8.

The notes list essays, pamphlets, and miscellaneous pieces not included, and provide additional data on these items that were listed in Hooper's bibliography [1979.48].

60 ———. "Bibliographic Notes." *CSL: The Bulletin of the New York C. S. Lewis Society* 18 (November):15–18.

The notes list published letters not included in Hooper's bibliography [1979.48].

61 ———. "Bibliographic Notes." *CSL: The Bulletin of the New York C. S. Lewis Society* 18 (December):6–7.

The article continues the list of published letters not included in Hooper's bibliography [1979.48] and includes additional data about letters that are listed. See Thorson and Daniel's earlier "Bibliographic Notes" 1983.76–77 and later one 1987.57.

62 WARNOCK, MARY. "Religious Imagination." In *Religious Imagination*. Edited by James P. MacKey. Edinburgh: Edinburgh University Press, pp. 142–157 passim.

The experience of imagination is seeing an object as symbolic of something else and holding a meaning apart from itself. These moments of illumination, which have in common "the feeling of infinity, of depth or height without end," are elements in Coleridge, Wordsworth, Lewis's autobiography, *Surprised by Joy*, and Proust. Although Lewis was determined "to separate the non-religious imagination from religious knowledge of the truth," religious imagination is the same as aesthetic imagination, since "all knowledge of God must be symbolic."

63 WOLFE, GREGORY. Review of *Boxen: The Imaginary World of the Young C. S. Lewis*. *Reflections* 5 (Winter):3.

"Half the pleasure of reading the Boxen tales is that they were written by a child trying to be 'grown up.'" The surprise is that the stories have no moral.

64 WOOD, DOREEN ANDERSON. "Of Time and Eternity: C. S. Lewis and Charles Williams." *CSL: The Bulletin of the New York C. S. Lewis Society* 17 (March):1–7.

The concept that time exists simultaneously with eternity makes possible three doctrines: Williams's doctrine of co-inherence, as illustrated in *Descent into Hell* (London: Faber & Faber, 1937); God's prescience not precluding our free will; and the harrowing of hell, the medieval doctrine holding that Christ after the Crucifixion descends to hell and preaches to all departed spirits who ever existed, as illustrated in Lewis's *The Great Divorce.*

1987

1   BAILEY, K. V. "Counter-landscapes of Fantasy: Earthsea/Narnia." *Foundation: The Review of Science Fiction* 40 (Summer):26–36.
    In the Chronicles of Narnia, Lewis's world is magical, dreamlike and unearthly; Ursula LeGuin's world in the *Earthsea* trilogy has a realistic anthropological basis and is ecologically consistent. Lewis writes in the tradition of Wordsworth, a kind of scenery of the mind, in which magic energizes the action and is integral to its symbolism. LeGuin writes in the tradition of Coleridge, in which "the scenery is that of cosmos as organism" where "various evolutionary modes operate, including the spiritual . . . and those arising from the interaction of man and environment."

2   BARRATT, DAVID. *C. S. Lewis and His World.* Grand Rapids, Mich.: Eerdmans, 46 pp. Reprint. London: Marshall Pickering.
    Barratt has written a glossy brief biography with many pictures of Lewis, his friends, and places important to him.

3   BILLINGSLEY, LLOYD. "Occasional Journalist." *Christianity Today* 31 (15 May):62.
    Reviewing *Present Concerns*, Billingsly says, "such pop anthologizing often falls flat with other authors, but it works with Lewis because of the breadth of his mind, the simplicity of his style, and the clarity of his faith."

4   CARNELL, CORBIN S[COTT]. "Large Aims and Modest Claims: The Inklings on Art." *CSL: The Bulletin of the New York C. S. Lewis Society* 18 (January):1–2.
    The Inklings agreed with Dorothy L. Sayers that humans create because they "have been made in the image of God who is a Maker." Lewis warned of the danger of loving art more than God. He felt Christian writers should have latent Christianity in their works to increase the reader's longing for spiritual truth.

5   CHRISTOPHER, JOE R. *C. S. Lewis.* Boston: Twayne, 150 pp.
    Two sides to Lewis's personality—the rationalistic and the romantic—flow through his work. He borrowed extensively from other writers, especially from his favorite poet, Dante. In this book Christopher surveys Lewis's autobiographical works, literary and lexical histories, generic criticism and literary theories, moral philosophies, apologetics, Christian essays, and fiction. Lewis's claim to greatness will be based on the Chronicles of Narnia,

Surprised by Joy, The Four Loves, The Screwtape Letters, and *Till We Have Faces*.

6   CHRISTOPHER, JOHN. "Notes on Joy." *Encounter* 68 (April):41–43.
     Christopher knew Joy Davidman Gresham quite well and heard her side of her relationship with Lewis. *Shadowlands* [1985.73] is in places misleading and inaccurate about their relationship. Joy was deeply in love with Lewis but felt there was no hope for anything other than friendship. When she was employed by Lewis as a housekeeper, "she engaged his interest as a woman." Lewis married Joy when she was dying to obtain guardianship of her sons; there was no "secret marriage preceding the marriage in the hospital." After the marriage Lewis's "fondness very quickly turned into a deep and rewarding love."

7   CLARK, JAMES ANDREW. "The Idea of the Good, Duality and Unity: A Study of C. S. Lewis, J. R. R. Tolkien, and Charles Williams." *Ashland Theological Journal* 19:1–33.
     Lewis, Tolkien, and Williams "held that the Good, or its representative, unites within itself the qualities of severity and largesses, great beauty and great dreadfulness." Lewis depicts Aslan in the Chronicles of Narnia and Cupid, the god of the mountain in *Till We Have Faces*, in terms of beauty and dreadfulness. In the Space Trilogy, the eldila are impressive and frightening creatures, and Ransom exhibits immortal beauty and wisdom. The three authors depict humans reacting to supernatural good with terror because it is an invasion of their self-made universes, is totally alien to them, means that they must choose between good and evil, and then must act on that choice. Humans also react to good with joy: Tolkien expresses this in the Consolation of the Happy Ending; for Williams "that Beatitude was one of communal and communicated glory . . . shared among individuals in some finely structured pattern of organization"; Lewis expresses it as Joy, a thirst made to be quenched.

8   CLASPER, PAUL. "C. S. Lewis and the Ministry of Spiritual Direction." *CSL: The Bulletin of the New York C. S. Lewis Society* 18 (October):1–7.
     The ministry of spiritual direction is an ongoing relationship between the directee, who desires being attentive to his or her spiritual life, and the director, whom the directee meets regularly for the purpose of being more attuned to God's presence. Lewis became a soul-friend to many people through his letter writing, and many people have found his writings to be helpful in personal matters. Spiritual direction has two primary concerns: discernment and encouragement of prayer. Discernment is a major theme of Lewis's writings; he is a helpful guide in discerning the mind of Christ from emotions. In his writings and in his vast correspondence Lewis explored the importance of prayer.

9 COBB, LAWRENCE W. "Courtly Love in *The Allegory*." *Mythlore* 14 (Autumn):43–45, 55.

In *The Allegory of Love* Lewis explains courtly love as being a pattern of adultery and seduction. Courtly love raised women to a place of ascendancy over men, a position that he did not believe was their natural or rightful place. Courtly love almost overthrew the institution of marriage, which was considered purely utilitarian. The essence of courtly love is that it is a "'reward freely given by the lady, and only our superiors can reward. But a wife is not a superior.'" Courtly love was also against the teachings of the Church; the authors of courtly love romances had to repent at the end of their works in order to remain in the good graces of the Church. Because of the tradition of courtly love, women will never again be considered a piece of property.

10 DAVEY, MARY ELLEN. "'My First School.'" *CSL: The Bulletin of the New York C. S. Lewis Society* 19 (December):1–3.

In the essay "My First School" in the collection *Present Concerns* Lewis shows two lessons learned: the difference between Joy and pleasure, and how to live for another world. His sermon "The Weight of Glory" contains two themes that directly parallel these two lessons: an intangible longing for something beyond ourselves and longing for another world.

11 DERRICK, CHRISTOPHER. "Some Personal Memories of C. S. Lewis, an Incarnational Man." *New Oxford Review* 54 (November):16–20.

Derrick knew Lewis for twenty-three years. He considered Lewis to be a superb lecturer; he "had an extraordinary talent for making his subject come alive and so for holding his audience enthralled." As a tutor he was dialectic, energetic, and combative. Lewis had some enemies among his colleagues who were envious of his great popularity. "He had a strong sense of hierarchy and the proper ordering of things," but did not stand on his dignity. He was an incarnational man, spiritual but earthy.

12 DUNLAP, BARBARA J. Review of *Present Concerns*. *Library Journal* 112 (1 March):77.

The work shows Lewis's ability to drive swiftly to the heart of the matter. While the articles add little to his canon, they are masterly examples of his "talent for establishing instant rapport with his readers and using it to lead them in directions they might otherwise have been reluctant to go."

13 EVANS, HILARY. *Gods, Spirits, Cosmic Guardians: A Comparative Study of the Encounter Experience*. Wellingborough, Northamptonshire: Aquarian Press, pp. 84–85.

There are several difficulties with Canon J. B. Phillips's seeing Lewis's ghost: the visits met a need of Phillips; "paranormally acquired knowledge seems to be involved"; Lewis's message, although helpful, is insubstantial; and Lewis's natural behavior suggests a planned illusion of reality. The case presents two choices: either Lewis did visit Phillips or Phillips imagined the incident.

14   FILMER, KATH. "From Belbury to Bernt-arse: The Rhetoric of the Wasteland in Lewis, Orwell and Hoban." *Mythlore* 14 (Winter):18–22.
  The rhetorical figure of "The Wasteland" is present in Lewis's *That Hideous Strength*, George Orwell's *Nineteen Eighty-Four,* and Russell Hoban's *Riddley Walker* (London: Cape, 1980). Lewis shows that the political system that permits jargon to distort meaning throws itself open to corruption, leaving a wasteland in its wake. Closely associated with jargon is "the psychological and biological manipulation of the human race." Lewis creates binary opposite images of the wasteland and the garden ideal. Orwell, like Lewis, argues against the tendency toward totalitarianism. However, unlike Lewis, Orwell sustains pessimism throughout his novel. Hoban's novel is centered on the fear of a nuclear holocaust. Like Lewis and Orwell, Hoban uses language to depict the wasteland. His emphasis is that "individuals have choices and true power is spiritual and psychological wholeness."

15   FISHER, MATT. "Maskull and Ransom: The Dark Night of the Soul." *Mythlore* 14 (Winter):30–31, 40.
  The Dark Night is a period of despair and doubt during a spiritual quest the hero must undergo in order to discover the truth. Maskull in David Lindsay's *A Voyage to Arcturus* (London: Methuen, 1920) undergoes the Dark Night in two stages and makes a transition from a feeling state to a state of relation. Ransom in *Out of the Silent Planet* and *Perelandra* undergoes the Dark Night, which is God's way of "breaking into the individual's life and inviting that person to participate in a unique relationship with the Holy."

16   FORD, PAUL FRANCIS. "C. S. Lewis, Ecumenical Spiritual Director: A Study of His Experience and Theology of Prayer and Discernment in the Process of Becoming a Self." Ph.D. dissertation, Fuller Theological Seminary, 197 pp.
  The most complete way of appreciating Lewis as a Christian writer is to understand him as a spiritual director who made rich use of his gifts of teaching, encouraging, discerning, and praying. George MacDonald, G. K. Chesterton, and Lewis had in common the idea that the spiritual world is home. Lewis was also attracted to Charles Williams's emphasis on self-sacrifice and self-forgetfulness. "Lewis's theology and experience of becoming a self is the key to understanding all of Lewis's work and life." He felt that self-absorption would lead to hell and only absorption in the Other, God, would lead us out of ourselves. In his theology of discernment, "what pleases God is a life of loving, peaceful, and joyful service." Examples of his discernment,

1987

one of his greatest gifts, are *The Screwtape Letters, The Great Divorce, That Hideous Strength*, his marriage to Helen Joy Davidman Gresham, and *The Four Loves*. Lewis's definition of prayer as "'*personal* contact between embryonic, incomplete *persons* (ourselves) and the utterly concrete *Person*'" shows the connection between his theology of self and of God. He felt that prayer is the process by which we become persons. He believed we need God; he felt that spiritual health means accepting the contingency of all created beings; he saw and answered communication, causality, and time problems with prayer. Lewis's major problem with prayer, why God grants some prayers and not others, was solved for him by MacDonald, who answered that God sometimes prepares us to receive and that He exercises a corrective granting of prayer.

17 FORTUNA, MARYANN. "A Descriptive Evaluative Study of Children's Modern Fantasy and Children's Science Fiction Using a Well-Known Example of Each." Ph.D. dissertation, Temple University, 102 pp.

   Lewis's *The Lion, the Witch and the Wardrobe* and Madeleine L'Engle's *A Wrinkle in Time* (New York: Farrar, Straus and Giroux, 1962) are outstanding examples of children's fantasy and children's science fiction, respectively. These novels are compared and contrasted using Charlotte Huck's "Guide for Evaluating Children's Literature" in *Children's Literature in the Elementary School* (3rd ed. New York: Holt, Rinehart and Winston, 1979). Although children's fantasy and children's science fiction have similarities in theme, style, and format, the differences between the two genres, where magic and the supernatural in fantasy and science in science fiction generate plot and influence setting, are significant enough that children's science fiction should not be categorized with children's fantasy.

18 GLOVER, J. DENIS. "A Young Reader's Letter Never Went Unanswered by C. S. Lewis." *The Christian Science Monitor* 27 July, p. 26.

   In this review of *C. S. Lewis Letters to Children*, Glover finds that the letters display childlike mirth as well as Christian faith and morality.

19 GOOCH, PAUL W. "'Conscience' in 1 Corinthians 8 and 10." *New Testament Studies: An International Journal* 33, no. 2:244–254.

   Lewis says the Greek word for conscience meant "internal consciring [*sic*] witness" before Paul used the term in Corinthians to mean moral conscience. However, translating the term as "bad feelings" resolves the moral perplexity about Paul's ethics evident in Corinthians.

20 GOSSEN, RUTH S. "C. S. Lewis's Humor: The Saving Grace." Ph.D. dissertation, 229 pp.

   Lewis's humor is an attitude of joy rather than a technique. Humor effectively bridges the moral discrepancy between sinners and God. In *The*

Pilgrim's Regress his satire is developed through conversations, exploiting the double meaning of allegory, and using logical fallacies. His targets in this work are the literary movements of the twenties, scientism, Freudianism, and current religious attitudes. In *The Screwtape Letters* "through Screwtape's humorous lack of proportion, lack of ability to see himself from the outside, Lewis points the way to the opposite, to God's saving grace." He uses four types of humor: Joy and Fun (which are divine), and the Joke Proper and Flippancy (which are human). In *The Great Divorce* Lewis depicts three kinds of wit: intelligence through the lack of reason in many of the characters; wit ingenium exemplified by the characters of George MacDonald and Sarah Smith; and dangerous wit portrayed by the bishop and the artist, who want to appear intelligent but are lacking in reason. In *That Hideous Strength* he uses irony, which "requires an intrinsic opposing relationship," in the parallel structure of the story, with parallel scenes, events, and characters; Lewis also uses the lives of Mark and Jane to illustrate a double irony with the theme of hierarchy and the rightness of roles.

21 GOUVEA, FERNANDO QUADROS. Review of *Boxen: The Imaginary World of the Young C. S. Lewis. Fantasy Review* 10 (January/February):45.

"Though fascinating to the Lewis scholar and to some Lewis fans, these stories do not really have enough substance to make for pleasant reading in themselves."

22 HALL, GRACE R. W. "Dynamic Life Choices in the Lewis Tapestries." In *Webs and Wardrobes: Humanist and Religious World Views in Children's Literature.* Edited by Joseph O'Beirne Milner and Lucy Floyd Morcock Milner. Lanham, Md.: University Press of America, pp. 47–55.

In the Chronicles of Narnia, "both Lewis' characters and his readers grow in awareness as they experience hardship, transformation, sacrifice, metamorphosis, and mission." He mixes fantasy with realistic descriptions and characters to create his world. "Lewis provides a purposeful view of mankind in which creation, invaded by evil, is aided by a god."

23 HARRIS, RICHARD. *C. S. Lewis: The Man and His God.* Wilton, Conn.: Morehouse-Barlow, 92 pp.

"There has been too much uncritical acceptance of Lewis's thought in Christian circles." He had an exacting sense of inner self-demand and this rubbed off on his image of God as demanding our prostration, an image that is inappropriate for the kind of deep personal relationship God desires with us. Lewis believed in devils but the existence of devils does not reconcile a belief in a God of love with the existence of evil; the idea of fallen angels seems fundamentally contradictory; and it seems morally repugnant to have devils leading us into sin. "The honest attempt to know ourselves, and the various forces at work within us, seems a more useful and healthy exercise than projecting the cunning of our unconscious onto devils." Lewis was a moralist, and while this is one of his strengths, it led him astray in understanding the role of suffering as coming directly from God to discipline us. When God chose to make a real creation he gave every atom a life of its own, therefore conflict and tragedy are inevitable outcomes and are not sent by God. Although Lewis did not undervalue the place of myth in religion, he did underestimate its attractive power in leading people to belief. In *Letters to Malcolm*, his best book of popular theology, "Lewis was able to turn his sensory experience into prayer." The strength of his approach in *The Four Loves* is the twin stress on love as being rooted in earthly instinct but needing to "be set under and ordered by the divine love." However, he does not have a full incarnational view of God, who puts Himself in the position of needing us. "It was in writing about glory that the passions of Lewis the Romantic and the Christian, the literary critic and the believer, fused together in a marvelous whole."

24   HYLES, VERNON. "On the Nature of Evil: The Cosmic Myths of Lewis, Tolkien and Williams." *Mythlore* 13 (Summer):9–13, 17.
      In the Space Trilogy the fundamental theme is the struggle between good and evil. Lewis depicts the nature of evil as sly and cunning, taking good and twisting it into something foul, replacing God with man. Lewis shows evil as existing on earth, shaping our life. Tolkien depicts evil as a perversion of God and His creation and declares that "hope is a viable alternative in the face of evil." For Williams, good and evil are two opposite poles struggling to "manipulate occult forces, to transcend the limitations of time and space, to control matter through mind, and to discover the secrets of life and death."

25   IVES, ROBERT B. "Some Notes on the Inklings." *CSL: The Bulletin of the New York C. S. Lewis Society* 18 (March):1–4.
      Three common threads define the Inklings: (1) they were an informal group but had structured meetings with people reading their manuscripts; (2) they primarily consisted of Lewis's friends; (3) they were drawn together by the shared interests of literature, religion, and culture. Ives provides a list of Inklings, divided into those involved from the beginning to the end, those who attended in the early period, those who attended during a transition period in the early 1940s, and those who attended from the mid-1940s (mostly sons and former pupils).

26   JONES, C[K]ARLA FAUST. "Paradox in Narnia: Unconscious But Inevitable." *CSL: The Bulletin of the New York C. S. Lewis Society* 18 (May):1–6.
      Lewis views life as a series of metaphysical paradoxes. There are three distinct paradoxes in the Chronicles of Narnia. *Sehnsucht* is experienced on earth but cannot be satisfied on earth. Another paradox is fatal beauty; the

association of beauty with evil is given a theological turn by Lewis. "The witches symbolize the objects of earthly beauty and desire which . . . divert potential Christians from the Kingdom of God and ultimately lead to their destruction." The third paradox is that of God at once terrible and good. Aslan's treatment of disobedient characters reveals the fearsome, harsh, and gentle aspects of God. Through paradox Lewis reveals theological truths about man's search for God, the attraction of evil, and the nature of God.

27 JONES, KARLA FAUST. "Girls in Narnia: Hindered or Human?" *Mythlore* 13 (Spring):15–19.
    Lucy Pevensie is the character closest to Aslan; she shows spiritual, physical, and emotional growth in the Chronicles. Susan Pevensie is a self-limited character who turns toward the world rather than toward Aslan. By depicting Aravis escaping the Calormen culture where women are forced to marry, Lewis supports a woman's right to develop her talents. Jill Pole is a leader, a soldier, and a guide. Polly Plummer is faithful, forgiving, and loyal. Although Lewis is occasionally guilty of sexist remarks, these are neutralized by the actions of his heroines, who are free to develop their talents without hindrance by social convention.

28 KAWANO, ROLAND M. "C. S. Lewis' *The Queen of Drum*." *Lamp-Post of the Southern California C. S. Lewis Society* 11, no. 3 (November):10–14.
    In Lewis's poem we see his concern with the pagan and Christian worlds as a struggle to choose sides without a reconciliation between the two. In the poem, "the Archbishop's interview with the Queen and his martyrdom diminish the strength of the major theme." Perhaps the alternatives the Queen is given between the faerie and the real world may be the same alternatives Lewis wrestled with before becoming a Christian. Perhaps he is describing a choice he made in his private life.

29 KING, DON. "The Wardrobe as Christian Metaphor." *Mythlore* 14 (Autumn): 25–27, 33.
    Lewis's use of the metaphor of the door in the Chronicles of Narnia has four characteristics: "1) Literal doors lead to the Door, Aslan; 2) Aslan is a two-way door," leading to Jesus Christ in the children's real world; "3) Passage through the different literal doors into Narnia is always unplanned; and 4) All who enter the doors are called into Narnia, but none are compelled to stay."

30 KNOWLES, SEBASTIAN DAVID GUY. "The Inklings in the War (2): C. S. Lewis and the Perversion of Purgatory." In "A Purgatorial Flame: British Literature of the Second World War." Ph.D. dissertation, Princeton University, pp. 233–247.
    In *The Great Divorce* Lewis depicts purgatory as "a vivid waiting, a

kinetic state. In this thoroughly original synthesis of Limbo and Purgatory, Lewis distills the essence of purgatorial waiting." As in Dante, each ghost represents a specific vice but the *Purgatorio* is turned upside down since all but one ghost fails the test and returns to hell. The novel is undoubtedly a product of the war; Lewis uses military metaphors to depict the diamantine hardness of the environment.

31 LINDBERG, LOTTIE. "Lewis's Images of the Plan of Creation, or C. S. Lewis: The Song and Dance Man." *CSL: The Bulletin of the New York C. S. Lewis Society* 19 (November):1–6.

Lewis shows "that the song is sung by the Creator, and that the dance is taken part in by the created." He also shows us we have the choice to hear the music and take part in the dance or not. Lindberg quotes passages dealing with music and dance from *The Magician's Nephew, The Lion, the Witch and the Wardrobe, Prince Caspian, Perelandra*, the essay "Equality" found in *Present Concerns, Reflections on the Psalms*, and *Mere Christianity*. "If music expresses the inexpressible, then perhaps dance helps us feel what we cannot understand."

32 LUSK, B. LYNN. "The Lion of Narnia." *Lamp-Post of the Southern California C. S. Lewis Society* 11, no. 1 (March):16–18.

In the Chronicles of Narnia Aslan reveals his deep love, is not meek or soft, is strong-minded, keeps his word, is joyful and loving, and is a true lion. "Through Lewis' portrayal of Aslan, I can see my Jesus; more of Him than I've seen before."

33 McMILLAN, LEX [O.]. "Grace Abounding to the Chief of Skeptics: C. S. Lewis as a Christian Prometheus." *CSL: The Bulletin of the New York C. S. Lewis Society* 18 (April):1–10.

Lewis's autobiography, *Surprised by Joy*, draws "the reader into the same process that led to his own conversion" through use of the strategy of "philosophic self-exploration." He develops the persona of Christian Prometheus, a heroic seeker of truth. *Spirits in Bondage* and *Dymer*, which have dominant themes of questing for truth, foreshadow the Christian Prometheus persona. In his autobiography, Lewis describes aspects of his character that are central to his persona of Christian Prometheus: "the English highbrow intellectual, the rugged individualist, and the son alienated from his father." Once establishing his credentials as a modern Promethean hero"—"skeptical, rational, fiercely individualistic—Lewis shows his conversion to Christianity as the result of these attributes and a consequence of his quest for truth. *Surprised by Joy* "is a masterful work of rhetoric and a great apologetic achievement because Lewis incarnates a figure of sacramental autobiography."

34 MANLOVE, C. N. *C. S. Lewis: His Literary Achievement.* New York: St. Martin's, 242 pp.

Lewis's fiction is more akin to his apologetics than to his criticism. Both take the reader through a learning process: the apologetics argue for a divine presence in the universe; the fiction shows characters finding it. They have similar qualities of diversity of impression and unity in complexity. *The Pilgrim's Regress* has a certain degree of patterning and organic imagination but ultimately fails because Lewis has not gotten inside the experience and uses allegory as an expression of his self-consciousness. *Out of the Silent Planet's* central theme is Ransom's acquisition of knowledge. *Perelandra* is "about the experience, growth, salvation and elevation to its rightful throne . . . of 'otherness.'" *That Hideous Strength's* central motif is concealment and penetration beneath deceptive surfaces. *The Great Divorce* portrays the differences between heaven and hell. The Chronicles of Narnia are successful because of Lewis's endless fertility of invention, his ability to create a consistent world, his beautiful handling of a transformation of reality, his depiction of joy and yearning, and "his power to capture great primal rhythms, Christian and pagan alike." Some weaknesses of the series are children characters behaving like adults, cloying animal characters, and oppressive moralizing. *Till We Have Faces* "has a far more complex and less judging awareness of the individual fallible personalities and of the moral uncertainties and ambiguities of existence than Lewis had admitted before." Lewis's works are Christian, involve a journey out of self toward "other," depict joy and the misinterpretations or refusals of it, and view evil as constriction and heaven as solidity, dance, and joy.

35 MORNEAU, ROBERT F. "Letters of Gratitude—III." *Review for Religious* 46 (May–June):429–440.

Lewis's gifted narration in *Surprised by Joy* holds our interest and helps us understand our own struggles. Courage is a virtue that consistently occurs in his literary works. His use of imagination unscrupulously draws many readers into the spiritual realm. Clarity and forceful use of analogy characterize his writing. Morneau includes quotations on various topics from *Surprised by Joy.*

36 MOYNIHAN, MARTIN. *The Latin Letters of C. S. Lewis to Don Giovanni Calabria of Verona and to Members of His Congregation, 1947 to 1961.* Longmont, Colo.: Bookmakers Guild, Inc., 64 pp.
Reprint of 1985.48.

37 MUSACCHIO, GEORGE. "Elwin Ransom: The Pilgrimage Begins." *Mythlore* 13 (Summer):15–17.

Out of the Silent Planet portrays Ransom's spiritual infancy. Four episodes transform Ransom. First is his journey to Malacandra, which changes

1987

his fear of outer space to an awareness of the living heavens and of Maledil as the source of all life. Second is his stay among the *hrossa* where he gains a new perspective on his fallen race and a new sense of his own manhood, and learns to obey the *eldila* rather than trusting his own judgment. Third is his learning about Maledil's system from the *sorns*. Fourth is his pilgrimage to speak with the chief *eldil* of the planet.

38 ———. "Fiction in *A Grief Observed.*" *Seven: An Anglo-American Literary Review* 8:73–83.
   This article is a slightly altered version of 1986.42.

39 MYERS, DORIS T. "What Lewis Really Did to *The Time Machine* and *The First Men in the Moon.*" *Mythlore* 13 (Spring):47–50, 63.
   In *The First Men in the Moon* (London: G. Newnes, 1901), H. G. Wells examines the effects of specialization and "how to balance the efficient [economic] functioning of a society with the happiness of individuals." In *Out of the Silent Planet* Lewis suggests that the "Old Western Man's emphasis on leisure pursuits would enable a society to have economic efficiency without destroying individualism." In *The Time Machine* (London: W. Heinemann, 1895), Wells sees evolution as the nature and destiny of mankind, shows the effects of class distinctions to indicate his preference for socialism, and depicts technology as a way man controls his environment. In *Perelandra* Lewis denies the ethical and moral conclusions drawn from evolution, shows the hierarchical authority structure is the natural state of man, and shows technology as augmenting the natural powers of man.

40 PROTHERO, JAMES. "A Portrait of Sudden Joy: A Comparison of James Joyce's *A Portrait of the Artist as a Young Man* and C. S. Lewis's *Surprised by Joy.*" *Lamp-Post of the Southern California C. S. Lewis Society* 11, no. 3 (November):3–9.
   Joyce's novel and Lewis's autobiography both portray what Lewis called transposition, experience funneled or transposed from a higher, spiritual plane, to a lower, physical one. Parallels between Joyce and Lewis's works include journeys of spiritual growth, similarities of tone, alienation of the protagonist from his father, settings of early twentieth-century Ireland and of public boarding school, and loss of faith with a fear of God and terror of going to hell. Joyce's protagonist undergoes the three traits Lewis specified in the essay "Transposition," the experience Lewis called Joy.

41 Review of *Present Concerns. Booklist* 83 (1 February):811.
   These brief meditations display Lewis's acute sense of how we live in God's world.

42   Review of *Present Concerns*. *Kirkus Reviews* 55 (15 January):112.
      "Impeccable, fanciful/polemical tidbits of Christian-oriented journalism.
      . . . What saves all this from deadly gravity is Lewis' quietly aristocratic dry
      humor . . . his astonishing command of the English language; and some star-
      tlingly unexpected views."

43   RIGA, FRANK P. "Self-Love in Augustine and C. S. Lewis." *Cithara: Essays
      in the Judaeo-Christian Tradition* 26, no. 2 (May):20–30.
      Lewis followed Augustine's concept of self-love, which has the love of
      God and the love of others as prerequisites. He is concerned with "the proper
      relationship of self-love to the love of God and neighbor" in *The Magician's
      Nephew* and *Till We Have Faces*.

44   ROOT, JERRY. Review of *C. S. Lewis Letters to Children*. *Seven: An Anglo-
      American Literary Review* 8:110.
      Lewis writes as a godfather, with warmth and insight. The letters are
      delightful, filled with good advice, and at times entertaining.

45   SAMMONS, MARTHA C. "Further in the Onion Skin: Lewis' Multi-leveled
      Models." *Lamp-Post of the Southern California C. S. Lewis Society* 11, no. 1
      (March):3–15.
      In *Perelandra* Weston argues that the universe has a thin rind of good
      things on the outside but nonentity on the inside, which we enter through
      death, and that God is outside this model. In *The Discarded Image* Lewis
      describes the medieval model of the universe with the earth as center sur-
      rounded by nine spheres, outside of which is the end of time and space. He
      believed this model should be turned inside out because the spatial order is
      opposite of the spiritual. In Lewis's inverted version of the medieval model,
      earth is not the center but outside everything, and space and the planets are the
      realm of myth and light. The result of the modern model, represented by
      Weston's view, is that God becomes an immaterial being who occupies no
      place and is unaffected by time. Lewis shows in the Chronicles of Narnia and
      the Space Trilogy that the center of the correct spiritual model is God, with the
      various worlds He has created radiating out from the center in concentric cir-
      cles and containing Him on varying levels. Lewis argues we must "choose
      whether God or self is to be at the center—whether our universe is to be
      anthropocentric like the ancient physical model, or theocentric, like the spiri-
      tual one."

46   SARROCCO, CLARA. "C. S. Lewis and the Latin Letters." *CSL: The Bulletin
      of the New York C. S. Lewis Society* 18 (February):1–6.
      Lewis wrote letters in Latin to Don Giovanni Calabria (Father John) of
      Verona, Italy. This article provides a brief biography of Calabria. The corre-

spondence began formally, with concerns for church unity, and evolved into a friendship, with exchanges about "their own personal struggles for salvation and joy in the Lord."

47   ———. "'Modern Man and His Categories of Thought.'" *CSL: The Bulletin of the New York C. S. Lewis Society* 19 (December):3–5.
   Lewis's main point in the essay, found in *Present Concerns*, is that there are six factors that have altered the modern mind and necessitate changes in the way Christianity is explained. These factors are a revolution in education that emphasizes the present, the emancipation of women, developmentalism or historicism leading to the idea that "the very standard of good is itself in a state of flux," proletarianism, practicality whereby it does not matter whether Christianity is true as long as it is socially useful, and skepticism about reason.

48   SAUDERS, PAULETTE G. "The Idea of Love in the Writings of C. S. Lewis." Ph.D. dissertation, Ball State University, 160 pp.
   Lewis's writings, especially his fiction, demonstrate a systematic doctrine of love. Most of his characters are personifications of the different kinds of loves and their perversions, which he discussed in *The Four Loves*. His purpose in his writings was to awaken a desire for love and goodness. In *Till We Have Faces* Orual personifies perverted affection and possessive Need-love in her relationships with Psyche, the Fox, and Bardia. The Fox is a model of affection, friendship, and Gift-love, while Psyche is an example of agape love, for which all humans should strive. In *The Great Divorce* most characters personify perversions of love; Sarah Smith, however, personifies Gift-love. In *The Screwtape Letters* the demons try to make the young man feel unselfish rather than loving toward others and try to turn his romantic love into the worship of being in love or into lust. In *Out of the Silent Planet* the harmony between the three species on Malacandra is due to their respect, or appreciative love, for each other. Friendship with affection, admiration, and Gift-love mixed in is evident in the relationship between Ransom and Hyoi. In *Perelandra* Gift-love, which Ransom personifies, is one of the major themes. *That Hideous Strength* deals with eros; at the beginning Mark and Jane personify what eros is not, each struggling alone with his or her problems, but at the end they personify true eros and true Gift-love. Lewis's didactic goal in his writings centered around love; every novel he wrote exemplifies love through its characters and is consistent with his portrayals of the right and wrong kinds of love.

49   SCHAKEL, PETER J. "That 'Hideous Strength' in Lewis and Orwell." *Mythlore* 13 (Summer):36–40.
   Both Lewis and Orwell deal with the dehumanization and despoliation of life under a proletarian regime. However, dehumanization is not Lewis's

main concern; his fundamental theme is the struggle between good and evil. While Orwell is concerned with the working classes, Lewis depicts no need for major social or political change. Lewis's interest is mainly in the moral-spiritual struggle of the upper-middle class. While *Animal Farm*, and to a lesser extent *Nineteen Eighty-Four*, are powerful twentieth-century myths, *That Hideous Strength* "lacks the simple, satisfying shape of myth."

50   SCHILDROTH, LISA. "An Annotated Bibliography of Criticism of C. S. Lewis's *Chronicles of Narnia* (Published since 1973)." *CSL: The Bulletin of the New York C. S. Lewis Society* 18 (July):1–6, 18; (August):1–5.

The two articles list in alphabetical order by author books, articles, theses, and essays containing criticism of the Chronicles of Narnia. Criticism of the Chronicles, compared to the period covered by the Christopher and Ostling bibliography [1974.9], has increased in quantity and quality. Post-1973 material deals with both the literary elements and religious meanings of the stories.

51   SCHOFIELD, STEPHEN. "'The Best Music in the World.'" *Canadian C. S. Lewis Journal*, no. 58 (Spring):16–17.

Schofield quotes Lewis's remarks about his favorite music as written to Arthur Greeves.

52   ———. "Girls, Music and Lewis." *Canadian C. S. Lewis Journal*, no. 58 (Spring):1–15.

For schools and universities Lewis's most valuable work is *A Preface to "Paradise Lost"*. His most striking qualities as a writer are absence of "malarkey" and gentleness. He avoided women because he had no sisters, his mother died when he was young, and he was placed in an all male environment as an adolescent. It is a "safe assumption that if English boarding schools had then included girls, which is surely conducive to easy and happy mixing of the sexes, he would have married in his twenties and not been forced into it as an act of charity [at] the age of fifty-eight."

53   SELLNER, EDWARD C. "Traditions of Spiritual Guidance: C. S. Lewis as Spiritual Mentor." *The Way* 27, no. 4:311–326.

Lewis is a model for the ministry of spiritual mentoring. He mentored others through teaching, letter-writing, and preaching. He was an effective spiritual mentor because of his warmth and hospitality, his sense of humor and magnanimity, and his willingness to share wisdom gained through personal experience. His greatest quality was his care, a deep and abiding concern. Friendship as a manifestation of his care was the foundation of his mentoring.

54   SMALLEY, WILLIAM E. "'Footprints of the Divine': A Study of Imaginative Literature as a Guide to the Spiritual Journey, with an Emphasis

1987

on *Prince Caspian* by C. S. Lewis." Ph.D. dissertation, Wesley Theological Seminary, 151 pp.

Imaginative literature can illuminate and guide the Christian's journey with God and allow him or her to recognize evidence of the Divine in daily life. The common narrative that defines and identifies people as a community is gone. Also lost is "THE STORY" of the redemptive work of God among His people. Story assists people in discovering who they are and is a means of becoming. In Narnia Lewis created a world that presents a metaphysical reality so that "readers may better know of their lives in relation to their Creator-Redeemer-God." The project reported is a weekend retreat exploring three major themes in *Prince Caspian*: loss and rediscovery of the story; longing, belief, and obedience; and joy and the great dance. Smalley provides the study guide for the project (including schedule outline, promotional materials, *Prince Caspian* reading guide, role-playing and game instructions, Narnian worship service, resource list) and evaluation reports.

55 SPIVAK, CHARLOTTE. "Images of Spirit in the Fiction of Clive Staples Lewis." *Mythlore* 14 (Winter):32–38.

The Spirit manifests itself through numinous figures in the Chronicles of Narnia, the Space Trilogy, *Till We Have Faces*, and *The Great Divorce*. The Spirit represents "'the relatively supernatural element which is given to every man at his creation—the rational element.'" Lewis's Spirit figures are variants of the traditional mythic wizard based on Merlin, the Jungian archetype of Wise Old Man, animal figures based on medieval iconography, and imagined species. The Spirit can also be perverted and irrational, such as Jadis, Weston, and the severed head of the criminal Alcasan.

56 TALBOTT, THOMAS. "C. S. Lewis and the Problem of Evil." *Christian Scholar's Review* 17 (September):36–51.

Beversluis's [1985.4] critique of *The Problem of Pain* misrepresents Lewis in inexcusable ways and ignores recent developments in philosophy that support Lewis. Since we cannot know what kinds of worlds are genuinely possible and were within God's power to create, Beversluis's pronouncement that an omnipotent God would have created things differently is presumptuous. The solution to the problem of evil lies in Lewis's assertion that God is wiser than we; He gives us what we need, not what we want. Suffering contributes to the perfection and reconciliation of the sufferer and those around him or her.

57 THORSON, STEPHEN, and DANIEL, JERRY [L.]. "Bibliographic Notes." *CSL: The Bulletin of the New York C. S. Lewis Society* 18 (March):6–7.

The notes provide a supplement to Hooper's bibliography [1979.48], listing books not included in, and additional data about books listed in, Hooper's bibliography. They include additional information on one short story listed in Hooper's bibliography. See the authors' earlier "Bibliographic Notes," 1983.76–77 and 1986.58–61.

58 WILLIS, JOHN RANDOLPH. "The Enduring Appeal of the Author C. S. Lewis." *Our Sunday Visitor* 75 (26 April):8.

Lewis appeals to Catholics primarily because of his writing style: his illustrations, creative approach to subjects, and ability to make dull subjects exciting. Heaven is one of his favorite themes. Lewis was known for his wit. He considered himself a Catholic but he stopped short of claiming to be a Roman Catholic.

1988

1 ADKISON, DANNY M. "C. S. Lewis and America's Inner Rings." *CSL: The Bulletin of the New York C. S. Lewis Society* 19 (September):1–5.

Lewis's essay "The Inner Ring" has political applications even though he was apolitical. He defined the inner ring as a clique and described the desire to be included in the local ring as being a dominant element in man's nature. Although the ring itself is neutral, the desire to be included in an inner ring is " 'the most skillful in making a man who is not yet a very bad man do very bad things.' " The desire to belong to the inner ring is the chief theme of *That Hideous Strength*. A theoretical application of Lewis's theory of inner rings can be found in the creation of America's Constitution. The Framers instituted checks and balances because they realized man acts out of self-interest. A specific application of the desire to belong to an inner ring is the Iran–Contra scandal; Oliver North sought not only the power and liberty to break rules but also "the delicious sense of secret intimacy."

2 ANDERSON, MARY JANELLE. "Toward a Christian Approach to Literature: The Critical Theories of C. S. Lewis as a Model for Christian Literary Criticism." Ph.D. dissertation, University of South Florida, 110 pp.

Lewis is the most significant critic for developing a Christian literary criticism because of his widespread acceptance of traditional Christian beliefs. He believed that art is form rather than content, that art should be objective, that moralistic literature without artistic value is worthless, and that the function of literary criticism is to encourage good reading. He had no respect for negative or evaluative criticism. He stressed the primacy of the literary text and the secondary position of the critic. He thought the author should be objective and free of emotion and should "mirror the wisdom and beauty already created in the universe by God." Lewis believed that the text should be meaningful rather than obscure or ambiguous, that it should not advance social or behavioral sciences, and that its literary value should be based on its artistry. He thought the reader should enjoy the author's perception, not his personality. He denounced psychoanalytical and anthropological criticism. Lewis emphasized reading and defined two kinds of readers: the literary, who receive the text, and the unliterary, who use it. He believed that literature was of secondary importance compared to the first priority of God, goodness, and moral behavior. Lewis's critical ideas are fully compatible with the teaching philosophies at even the most fundamental Christian academies.

3   BERRYHILL, DALE A. "Some Literary Sources of C. S. Lewis." *CSL: The Bulletin of the New York C. S. Lewis Society* 20 (November):6–7.
       Two minor sources for Lewis's lesson of the stalks in "Screwtape Proposes a Toast" are from Robert Browning's "Childe Roland to the Dark Tower Came" and Matthew Arnold's *Empedocles on Etna* [see 1986.23, 28 for the major source]. *Empedocles on Etna* is also the source for Lewis's essay "We Have No 'Right to Happiness,' " and for *The Problem of Pain*.

4   BIGGS, R. A. "The Lion, the Witch and Plato." *Times* 20 April, p. 10.
       The Chronicles of Narnia contain a profound Christian message. In the stories, Lewis communicates a glorious certainty. He also weaves "some key philosophical ideas from Plato's *Republic*" into the stories.

5   BLASDELL, HEATHER L. ". . . 'And There Shall the Lilith Repose.' " *Mythlore* 14 (Summer):4–6, 12.
       Lewis's characters of Jadis and the Emerald Witch in the Chronicles of Narnia and Williams's character of Lily Sammile in *Descent into Hell* (London: Faber & Faber, 1937) tempt males with promises of power and sexuality they have no intention of delivering. These characters abhor motherhood, are depicted as Queens of the Dead or Undead, and are associated with images of vampires. Although these Liliths are evil, both authors show good must always overcome evil.

6   BOENIG, ROBERT. "Critical and Fictional Pairing in C. S. Lewis." In *The Taste of the Pineapple: Essays on C. S. Lewis as Reader, Critic, and Imaginative Writer*. Edited by Bruce L. Edwards. Bowling Green, Ohio: Bowling Green State University Popular Press, pp. 138–148.
       Lewis transformed the critical method he used in his essay "What Chaucer Really Did to *Il Filostrato*" into a creative method in *Out of the Silent Planet*. In the essay he showed how Chaucer altered Boccaccio's story by developing the theme of courtly love in *Troilus and Criseyde*. In *Out of the Silent Planet* Lewis altered H. G. Wells's *The First Men in the Moon* (London: G. Newnes, 1901) "by adding a character who starts out believing in a Wellsian universe of blind violence and ends up believing in one of peace and order."

7   "Book Charges Fraud over C. S. Lewis." *Christianity Today* 32 (18 November):56.

In *The C. S. Lewis Hoax*, Kathryn Lindskoog accuses Walter Hooper of fraud in the publication of works after Lewis's death, especially *The Dark Tower*. [See 1988.40.] Paul Ford, founding director of the Southern California C. S. Lewis Society, is convinced Lewis wrote the work but calls for a forensic study of the original manuscript to clear up the controversy. Joe R. Christopher, a noted Lewis scholar, believes that many of the conjectures in Lindskoog's work are correct and that there will have to be major revisions in Lewis studies.

8   CARTER, MARGARET L. "Sub-Creation and Lewis's Theory of Literature." In *The Taste of the Pineapple: Essays on C. S. Lewis as Reader, Critic, and Imaginative Writer*. Edited by Bruce L. Edwards. Bowling Green, Ohio: Bowling Green State University Popular Press, pp. 129–137.

Lewis's early writings on Christianity and literature assign art a limited place in a Christian's life, while his later writings attach greater importance to art. His early writings defend the Christian's pursuit of art as a way of making a living, as a way to combat its misuse, for pleasure, and as a way for some to come to Christianity. In these writings Lewis sees art as a reflection of the one original good, a reflection of eternal beauty and wisdom. The rigor of his stand "is softened by a hint that mimesis may include an imaginative apprehension of some aspect of the Divine." In *An Experiment in Criticism* Lewis shows how literature is uniquely well suited as a path to the beatific vision, "since it enables us to share the Vision as experienced by minds other than our own." Fantasy, since it demands disinterested appreciation and as sub-creation "enables us to view the primary world with new eyes," plays a special role in the process.

9   CHERVIN, RONDA. "The Concept of Heroism in C. S. Lewis's Space Trilogy." *CSL: The Bulletin of the New York C. S. Lewis Society* 19 (February):1–7.

Lewis depicts heroism in the Space Trilogy by showing weak people, such as Ransom and Mark and Jane Studdock, becoming brave. Courage and heroism depend on trust in God. Fear results from the contingencies of living as a being with free choice. Fear is also due to introspective concern over self-image. Both Weston and Devine illustrate courage based on pride, and their desire for power leads to destruction of self and others. The actions of Ransom and the Studdocks show how God graces goodwill shown by weak heroes and heroines. Lewis demonstrates that performing heroic deeds makes "a person grow in strength of character to meet the next challenge with greater confidence."

1988

10 ———. "Paganism and Christianity: A Commentary on C. S. Lewis' Novel *Till We Have Faces.*" *Faith & Reason* 14 (Fall):243–253.

The novel sets up a dialectic "between primitive religion (the pagan 'thesis'), Greek philosophy (the pagan intellectual 'antithesis'), and Christianity (as the transformed 'synthesis')." Lewis depicts the divine in primitive religion as "personal, brutal, irrational, local, dark and supremely envious." In philosophical paganism the divine is impersonal, distant, and without jealousy, reality is dualistic, and a combination of skepticism and Stoicism is the correct response. It is Psyche who begins to understand that "the dark primitive rites of sacrifice might be combined with the philosophical idea of goodness."

11 CHRISTOPHER, JOE [R.] "J. R. R. Tolkien, Narnian Exile." *Mythlore* 15 (Autumn):37–45; (Winter):17–23.

Tolkien wrote that the Narnia Chronicles were outside the range of his sympathy. Humphrey Carpenter in *Tolkien: A Biography* (Boston: Houghton Mifflin, 1977) and in *The Inklings* [1978.4] says that Tolkien disliked them due to their failure of "sub-creation": they were hastily written, contained inconsistent details, and were not convincing in their depiction of a secondary world. However, since Carpenter does not give any sources, this explanation should be considered his interpretation rather than Tolkien's reason. Lewis was inconsistent in his development of Narnia because he did not plan a series when the first volume was written; he was more interested in the genre of fairy tale, which does not call for elaborations, than in creating a secondary world. Roger Lancelyn Green [1974.15] reports that Tolkien disliked Narnia because it distorted traditional mythology. While this is literally true, Lewis did create a symbolic pattern that fits his worldview. Nan C. L. Scott reports that Tolkien objected to the Narnia Chronicles because of their allegorical nature. Lewis denied they were "pre-planned allegories which set up Christian didacticism"; he is more interested in creating a thematic fiction. Tolkien's letter of "Sepuagesima 1948" is possibly about his jealous rejection of *The Lion, the Witch and the Wardrobe.*

12 ———. "Publishing Boxen." *Lamp-Post of the Southern California C. S. Lewis Society* 11, no. 4 (November):8–10.

The collection at the Wade Center contains photocopies of the Boxen materials. Three Boxen items remain to be published. Christopher believes Lewis used the spelling "Boscen" and "Bosconian." Hooper, in editing the Boxen material, supplemented the drawings from the Boxonian manuscripts with pictures from what the Lewis brothers called the "Leborough Studies" and shifted two pictures from one Boxonian work to another.

1988

13   COMO, JAMES [T.]. "The Centrality of Rhetoric to an Understanding of C. S. Lewis." *CSL: The Bulletin of the New York C. S. Lewis Society* 20 (December):1–2.

Lewis had "a 'rhetoric' characteristically his own: a set of tactics and strategies (analogy, disjunction, appeals to definition and experience, argument and appeal, beckoning and highly-imaged perorations) chosen from an inventory of devices and deployed as the 'situation' requires." He was also concerned with rhetoric as a scholar of literature. In addition, rhetoric was a cast of Lewis's mind; he used "himself to augment his *ethos*—his personal proof."

14   DALE, ALZINA STONE. "C. S. Lewis and G. K. Chesterton: Conservative Defendants as Critics." In *The Taste of the Pineapple: Essays on C. S. Lewis as Reader, Critic, and Imaginative Writer*. Edited by Bruce L. Edwards. Bowling Green, Ohio: Bowling Green State University Popular Press, pp. 206–218.

Lewis and Chesterton had similar lives, literary careers, and intellectual and imaginative outlooks. In their literary criticism both were "enthusiastic, not disparaging, critics who saw themselves as literature's 'defendants'" against literary amnesia. One philosophical difference between the two was Lewis's love of "Northerness" and Chesterton's dislike of its elitist orientation.

15   DANIEL, JERRY L. "C. S. Lewis as a Book Reviewer." *CSL: The Bulletin of the New York C. S. Lewis Society* 19 (April):1–7.

The major characteristics of Lewis's theory of criticism are illustrated in some of the forty-one book reviews he wrote, most of which are reviews of works of literary criticism. He deplored the search for sources and influences and the anthropological approach that looks for origins; while these may produce something of value, he did not believe that they are literary criticism. He vehemently rejected the modern emphasis on the author's personality. He condemned the modern tone of disillusionment in literature, although as a reviewer he avoided indulging his scorn of modern literature. He also attacked free verse and the obscurity of modern literature. As a reviewer Lewis tried "to be fair and to keep value judgement and analysis in rigidly separate categories."

16   ———. "The Taste of the Pineapple: A Basis for Literary Criticism." In *The Taste of the Pineapple: Essays on C. S. Lewis as Reader, Critic, and Imaginative Writer*. Edited by Bruce L. Edwards. Bowling Green, Ohio: Bowling Green State University Popular Press, pp. 9–27.

Lewis's "emphasis on the quiddity of things" provides an important insight into his approach as a reader, critic, and imaginative writer. When he read a work, the taste, feel, or atmosphere was of primary importance. His

1988

"criticism was based largely on his reading method." He saw modern critics "engaged in *avoiding* the essence of the works they criticized" through the anthropological approach, personal heresy, character criticism, source criticism, motif criticism, and authorship criticism. One type of commentary of which he did approve and that he furnished himself was a background to the culture and language of the period; this enabled the reader to prepare himself before reading an old work. In his imaginative writings Lewis wrote to communicate the vision filling his imagination and to elicit a stock response to that vision.

17 DONALDSON, MARA E[LIZABETH]. *Holy Places Are Dark Places: C. S. Lewis and Paul Ricoeur on Narrative Transformation.* Lanham, Md.: University Press of America, 146 pp.
    Revision of 1984.18.

18 DUNLAP, BARBARA J. Review of *The Essential C. S. Lewis. Library Journal* 113 (1 October):88.
    "Readers curious to judge the basis of Lewis's ever-increasing popularity can begin their explorations with this well-chosen reader."

19 EASTMAN, JACKIE F. "C. S. Lewis's Indebtedness to Edmund Spenser: The Labyrinth Episode as Threshold Symbol in *The Lion, the Witch and the Wardrobe.*" In *Proceedings of the Thirteenth Annual Conference of the Children's Literature Association, University of Missouri—Kansas City, May 16–18, 1986.* Edited by Susan R. Gannon and Ruth Anne Thompson. West Lafayette, Ind.: Education Department, Purdue University, pp. 140–143.
    In Spenser's *Faerie Queene* and in Lewis's novel, the labyrinth episodes serve as emblems of the change in consciousness needed to enter the "dream" world. Both have "clashing antitheses" in which the characters get their bearings by making mistakes. In both works the labyrinth at the threshold functions as a model of allegory. The labyrinths "prefigure the victory over death which is the essential narrative movement of both stories and source of their emotional impact."

20 EDWARDS, BRUCE L[EE, Jr.]. "Rehabilitating Reading: C. S. Lewis and Contemporary Critical Theory." In *The Taste of the Pineapple: Essays on C. S. Lewis as Reader, Critic, and Imaginative Writer.* Edited by Bruce L. Edwards. Bowling Green, Ohio: Bowling Green State University Popular Press, pp. 28–36.
    For the contemporary critical theory of deconstruction "the text and its author have no independent status or authority to demand that a reader 'understand' them in any particular manner." Lewis's stance is rehabilitative; he believed the author's text spoke out of its time, enabling readers to experience

the world evoked by the author. He made a distinction between enjoyment, the process of doing something, and contemplation, apprehending the object of the activity. Deconstructionists "confound the act of reading by trying to 'contemplate the enjoyed,' by merging criticism with reading." Lewis would say that by doing so, they lose the text.

21 FETHERSTON, PATIENCE. "C. S. Lewis on Rationalism: (Unpublished Notes)." *Seven: An Anglo-American Literary Review 9:87–89.*
    This article is a reprint of notes on rationalism Lewis sent to Fetherston in 1945.

22 FILMER, KATH. "The Masks of Lilith: A Comparison of C. S. Lewis's Reading of George MacDonald's *Lilith* and *Till We Have Faces*." *CSL: The Bulletin of the New York C. S. Lewis Society* 19 (January):1–5.
    Lewis saw the main lesson of *Lilith* (London: Chatto & Windus, 1895) as the need to die to self to be truly oneself and illustrated this in *Till We Have Faces*. The character of Ungit, like Lilith, is "the 'somehow spoiled' female image of Nature." Other instances of MacDonald's influence on Lewis's novel are less significant and include Orual and Mr. Van believing "they have been posed a riddle, when in fact they have been confronted by truth," the characters being led to the Deadlands by birds, and Psyche and Mr. Van being distracted by loved ones when they are performing their tasks. The influence of MacDonald on the theology of *Till We Have Faces* is profound and derives from his sermons, including the idea of shame leading to self-knowledge. The image of the Shadowbrute is related to MacDonald's image of God as a consuming fire.

23 ———. "*Out of the Silent Planet*: Reconstructing Wells with a Few Shots at Shaw." *Inklings: Jahrbuch für Literatur und Ästhetik* 6:43–54.
    Out of the Silent Planet parodies H. G. Wells's *The First Men in the Moon* (London: G. Newnes, 1901). Both novels have similar plot structure, but Lewis inverts or reconstructs Wells's ideas and attitudes. Wells's view of the cosmos is of endless silence and emptiness; Lewis shows the cosmos filled with life and supernatural energy. Lewis also reconstructs Wells's revolting, monstrous extraterrestrial beings (the possible end result of evolution as Wells saw it) with a redeemed, spiritually individuated human being. Lewis uses language as a powerful symbol to indicate the kind of person one is. He also "takes a few pot shots at the Bergson/Shaw philosophy of the Elan Vital (or 'Life Force')." Wells depicts a severely regulated extraterrestrial society in which "hatred of other castes is used to increase the productivity of any one group." Lewis depicts Malacandra as a world of agape love, where the three separate species each have a distinct role but are equal to and respected by the other species.

1988

24 ———. "The Polemic Image: The Role of Metaphor and Symbol in the Fiction of C. S. Lewis." In *The Taste of the Pineapple: Essays on C. S. Lewis as Reader, Critic, and Imaginative Writer*. Edited by Bruce L. Edwards. Bowling Green, Ohio: Bowling Green State University Popular Press, pp. 149–165.
    Reprint of 1986.15.

25 FRESHWATER, MARK EDWARDS. *C. S. Lewis and the Truth of Myth*. Lanham, Md.: University Press of America, 147 pp.
    Revision of 1985.26.

26 GRESHAM, DOUGLAS H. *Lenten Lands*. New York: Macmillan, 225 pp.
    Douglas is the second son of Helen Joy Davidman Gresham and William Lindsay Gresham. He first met Lewis in December 1953 after Joy divorced William and moved with her sons to England. He writes that Jack's [C. S. Lewis's] feelings for Joy rapidly developed into love, but a considerably longer time elapsed before Jack would admit it to himself. After their civil marriage, Jack and Joy made plans to move in together. Concerning his leaving Oxford, Jack told Doug that he took the position at Cambridge because he needed a higher salary to support a wife and family. "Mother and Jack, in the years between her initial recovery and the later reappearance of her sickness, found such beauty in their love for one another and their life together that outside intrusions were hard put to affect them within the sheltered, glowing care of their love." After Joy's death, Jack was never the same and concealed his grief from his friends. Lewis's housekeeper and her husband, the Millers, "began to worm their way into The Kilns' daily life." Doug, filled with self-pity after losing his mother, spent little time at the Kilns. In July 1963, Walter Hooper repeatedly visited Jack, and although Jack was ill and found Walter's enthusiasm somewhat irritating, Walter became popular with the household and helped Jack with his correspondence until he returned to America in August 1963. After Jack's death Douglas lived with a close friend of his mother and attended agricultural college. Warren, Lewis's brother, began to turn more frequently to drink, which the Millers encouraged so they could profit from him. Doug married and immigrated to Australia where he and his wife had four children. They farmed for a while, journeyed around Australia in a caravan while Doug did odd jobs, and then he worked for the Australian Broadcasting Commission. After Warren died in 1973, Doug found the Kilns thoroughly sacked, with everything taken, implicitly blaming the Millers.

27 GUTHRIE, BARBARA ANN BOWMAN. "The Spiritual Quest and Health and C. S. Lewis." Ph.D. dissertation, University of North Texas, 123 pp.
    The spiritual quest is the search for ultimate truth and the meaning of life. Health results from the interrelationship between body, mind, and spirit,

and involves four aspects—physical, psychological, social, and spiritual. Lewis defined health as the love of God, and felt that one's health was directly in proportion to one's love of God. His determination to know God can be found in his physical state, literary works, themes, friendships, ethics, marriage, and views on religion. Health for him is prayer, laughter, the sacraments, repentance, forgiveness, gratefulness, friendship, and loving others, all integrated into the behavior of the Tao. Lewis offers many gifts, including an explanation of how not to find God, his description of Joy as an invitation from God, the idea that feelings and sensations do not indicate God's presence or absence, and "the gift which Lewis offers anyone who opens many of his books; the experience of being *in* goodness and *with* God who is Good."

28   HANNAY, MARGARET P[ATTERSON]. "Provocative Generalizations: *The Allegory of Love* in Retrospect." In *The Taste of the Pineapple: Essays on C. S. Lewis as Reader, Critic, and Imaginative Writer*. Edited by Bruce L. Edwards. Bowling Green, Ohio: Bowling Green State University Popular Press, pp. 58–78.
        Reprint of 1986.21.

29   HERON, ALASDAIR I. C. "What Is Wrong with Biblical Exegesis? Reflection upon C. S. Lewis' Criticism." In *Different Gospels: Christian Orthodoxy and Modern Theologies*. Edited by Andrew Walker. London: Hodder & Stoughton, pp. 120–141.
        Rudolf Bultmann's attempt to demythologize the New Testament influenced academic theology in England after 1945, an effect that Lewis deplored. He believed it resulted in "a total evacuation of biblical meaning, a dissolution of theological substance, an abdication of evangelical conviction, and failure of Christian imagination." In his address "Fern-Seed and Elephants," Lewis states that New Testament critics lack literary judgment and are in error when they assume that only modern scholars understand the behavior and teachings of Christ. He says that these critics cannot speak with authority on the question of whether miracles or prophecies really occurred in the New Testament and that criticism that attempts to reconstruct the genesis of texts does not do so successfully. He fails to see that "it was critical literary and historical study of the Bible that delivered some of the main impulses to the critical study of other literature as well." The very character of the biblical documents makes it imperative to analyze how this complex literature came into being. Lewis was not a historian and "was therefore ill-equipped to appreciate the interest of historical-critical biblical study."

30   HODGENS, RICHARD M. "Lewis and Symonds on Boiardo, Ariosto and Tasso." *CSL: The Bulletin of the New York C. S. Lewis Society* 19 (March):1–5.
        Lewis's criticism of the three Italian Renaissance poets is found in *The*

1988

Allegory of Love and in *Studies in Medieval and Renaissance Literature*; John Addington Symonds's criticism is found in *Renaissance in Italy* (London: Smith, Elder, 1875–86). "On Boiardo they are in substantial agreement; [on] Ariosto they begin to diverge; the difference between their treatments of Tasso is an instructive gulf." Both critics admire Boiardo's novel use of ancient myth. Both consider Ariosto the greatest of the three, but Symonds finds no sublime motive in the *Orlando Furioso* while Lewis questions the English taste requiring high seriousness for a work of art to be considered great. Symonds commits the personal heresy with regard to Tasso and questions his sincerity while Lewis accepts Tasso's work for what it is, "not only a good story, but one with 'quite unforced nobility and piety.'"

31 HOLYER, ROBERT. "The Argument from Desire." *Faith and Philosophy* 5, no. 1 (January):61–71.

Lewis's argument from desire deserves more careful philosophical treatment than Beversluis gives it [1985.4]. Lewis claimed that "Joy is either a desire for a state of mind or for an external object." He failed to find fulfillment of his desire in the experience of Joy so he concluded that Joy must be a desire for an external object. He felt that the experience of Joy itself "will convince us that it is not simply a desire for a sum total satisfaction of our other desires," that it is a desire for God. Lewis argues that "for any type of natural desire there is a class of real objects that satisfy it. . . . Joy is a type of natural desire for an infinite object." The argument from desire survives "as an inductive argument of indeterminate force . . . Beversluis has not offered us good reason to impugn claims to know it."

32 ———. "C. S. Lewis—The Rationalist?" *Christian Scholar's Review* 18, no. 2:148–167.

The view of Lewis as a rationalist is a serious misrepresentation of him and his apologetic works. *Miracles* and *Case for Christianity* show that "not only was Lewis's claim for the rational credentials of Christianity rather more modest than we are often led to believe, but his own apologetic efforts cannot be rightly construed as an attempt to prove Christianity by the force of philosophical argument alone." His use of reason and argumentation was personally relative; he used argument because he possessed a logical mind. His "strategy was to convince the reader of the Christian vision as a whole," since not all Christian doctrines are individually provable. Because religious beliefs are produced not only by argument but also by emotions, Lewis tried to clarify and rekindle these emotions through the use of metaphor and analogy. He also attempted to remove imagination as an obstacle to faith by making Christianity more convincing to the imagination.

33 ———. "The Epistemology of C. S. Lewis's *Till We Have Faces.*" *Anglican Theological Review* 70 (July):233–255.

    The epistemology of the novel is embedded in the ways Orual, Psyche, and Fox "come to affirm, deny, and doubt the nature and reality of the Divine." The central question is how we know the existence and nature of God. The Fox conveys Lewis's criticism of the sort of rationalism that believes everything can be explained by natural causes. The central epistemological problem is "to read the signs of the Divine correctly and to find in them reasonable assurance sufficient to live faithfully with its irresolvable mystery and ambiguity." These signs are experiences of the holy, including fear and longing, the testimony of others, and religious experience. Since none of the evidence the characters have to consider proves decisive, they must affirm or deny the divine based on reason, by formulating beliefs about reality based on their experience of the world. The point of the novel is that "our grasp of ultimate truth must grow out of a grasp of the truth about ourselves."

34 HOOD, GWYNETH. "Husbands and Gods as Shadowbrutes: Beauty and the Beast from Apuleius to C. S. Lewis." *Mythlore* 15 (Winter):33–43, 60.

    The myth of Cupid and Psyche explores the relationship between husband and wife, and between human and divine. Apuleius was embarrased by the human-divine interpretation of the myth, and in his work chose instead to depict contemporary human society. Other similar tales from Eskimo, Zulu, Roman, French, Indian, and Norwegian cultures also work better when interpreted as stories "of adolescent struggles for independence with some class conflict thrown in," rather than as human-divine interaction since brutality is not part of the divine nature. In *Till We Have Faces* Lewis solved "the problem inherent in the myth by getting away from our modern conceptions of the divine and transporting us back to times when gods, like humans, were seen as bewildering blends of kindly and malignant traits." In the story he shows that Psyche, through a mystical union with the god of love, is given tasks that change her concept of the gods in her own mind and in the minds of Orual and the people of Glome.

35 HOUSTON, JAMES M. "The Prayer-Life of C. S. Lewis." *Crux* 24, no. 1 (March):2–10.

    Six traits characterize the personal prayer-life of Lewis: (1) his spirituality was earthy and full of realism, an expression of his no-nonsense kind of faith; (2) his prayer was practical and realistic; he was not concerned about being vocal or articulate in his prayers; (3) he had a natural, simple, and unstructured attitude to prayer; (4) he offered supplicatory prayers for others; (5) he saw prayer as friendship with God; (6) he saw that prayer matures through suffering. Two features of prayer he stressed most in his writings were the problem of causality and the nature of petitionary prayer. Prayer is an action in cooperation with God, not a direct action over nature. Lewis felt that one should concentrate on prayers that manifest the surrender of self.

36   HUTTAR, CHARLES A. "C. S. Lewis and the Demonic." *Perspectives* 3, no. 3 (March):6–10.
     Lewis replaced the modern caricature of the Devil "with a consistent and believable conception of the demonic" through his imaginative power in *The Screwtape Letters*, *Perelandra*, and *That Hideous Strength*. He characterizes demons as beings created by God whose existence is anguished because they have chosen evil over good, whose intelligence is impaired, and whose power is limited by God. In these works Lewis depicts demons interacting with humans through temptation, including supplying and preventing thoughts and blocking clear thinking; through illusory servitude, when they appear to be serving humans but instead the humans serve them; through demon possession; and through dominating society's structures and institutions, especially the educational system and the media.

37   KING, DON. "The Rhetorical Similarities of C. S. Lewis and Bertrand Russell." *Mythlore* 15 (Autumn):28–31.
     Both Lewis and Russell project winsome personas that "reflect intellectual honesty, openness, and curiosity." Both have developed an image of their audience as the "common person"—decently educated, pragmatic, sharp, able to "smell a rat," but not very patient. Both use argument by metaphor or analogy most effectively because it has the advantage of creating "an immediate mental image in the audience's mind that helps hold and focus the argument being considered." Although they use similar rhetorical devices, they hold opposite philosophical positions. Lewis "may have been using many of Russell's views as a springboard for his own counter arguments," fictionalizing Russell in his own popular works.

38   KRUEGER, JAMES. "'CSL and You'—The Society's Questionnaire." *CSL: The Bulletin of the New York C. S. Lewis Society* 19 (October):1–4.
     In this article Krueger reports his analysis of the questionnaire sent to all new members of the society. The first Lewis book most members read was *The Screwtape Letters*, followed by *Mere Christianity* and the Chronicles of Narnia. Most members are interested in Lewis's personal life and recommend him to others.

39   LEOPOLD, PAUL. "Fighting 'Verbicide' and Sounding Old-fashioned: Some Notes on Lewis's Use of Words." In *The Taste of the Pineapple: Essays on C. S. Lewis as Reader, Critic, and Imaginative Writer*. Edited by Bruce L. Edwards. Bowling Green, Ohio: Bowling Green State University Popular Press, pp. 110–127.

Two prominent features of Lewis's style are lucidity of argument and a defiant old-fashionedness, traits that are evident by his choice of vocabulary. His clarity owes much to the accuracy of his archaistic vocabulary, that is, his use of words and phrases no longer in current use; this practice gives "his style an extended range and a suggestion of timelessness (itself an old-fashioned ideal)." He also uses words and phrases that are becoming corrupt or extinct, and thus strikes a blow against verbicide. Lewis's use of "Edwardianisms," with their connotations of class, alienate the reader.

40 LINDSKOOG, KATHRYN [ANN]. *The C. S. Lewis Hoax*. Portland, Ore.: Multnomah, 175 pp.

The unfinished novel "The Dark Tower" "looks like a hoax because it is vastly inferior to all of Lewis's authentic fiction; it has not been demonstrated that anyone ever heard of it while Lewis was alive; it includes a suspicious echo of the 1962 children's classic *A Wrinkle in Time* [by Madeleine L'Engle (New York: Farrar, Straus and Giroux)]; and it is dissimilar to Lewis's other writing in style, content, and sexual orientation." The short story "The Man Born Blind," included in the collection *"The Dark Tower" and Other Stories*, contains writing "so flat, talky and amateurish that it seems impossible that Lewis could have written it." The film *Through Joy and Beyond*, produced by Hooper's friend Bob O'Donnell and co-written by Hooper and Anthony Marchington, contains a number of minor errors and some significant distortions. The 1976 edition of *The Screwtape Letters* published by Bob O'Donnell of Lord and King Associates and edited by Hooper has no warnings that Lewis's words and meanings have been changed. Hooper says he was Lewis's private secretary and lived with him and his brother during 1963. In reality he attended a summer course at Oxford from July 1 to August 9 that year and taught as a lecturer at the University of Kentucky during the spring and fall semesters of 1963. Hooper's handwriting can appear identical to that of Lewis. "For the literary executor of an important estate to own a private cache of papers from the great writer and also to be able to imitate that writer's penmanship is a potentially dangerous opportunity for fraud." Warren never met Hooper until Hooper returned to England after Lewis's death and was exasperated at Hooper's attempts to appear as one of Lewis's oldest and most intimate friends. Warren was opposed to Hooper's becoming an executor of Lewis's literary estate and was "upset about Hooper's 'quite astonishing talent for infiltration.'" Warren also objected to Hooper as the co-author of the official biography, which Hooper inexplicably delayed completing until after Warren's death. The biography gives the impression that Hooper was a central part of Lewis's life, which is a distortion of the truth: also distorted are Lewis's relationships with Mrs. Moore and Helen Joy Davidman. In 1979 Hooper published *They Stand Together: The Letters of C. S. Lewis to Arthur Greeves (1914–1963)*. Hooper's introduction culminates in an attack on Warren, emphasizing his alcoholism and quoting Lewis as saying Warren was unfit to look after his literary estate. *Boxen*, edited by Hooper, purports to contain all of Lewis's juvenilia. It contains an "Encyclopedia Boxoniana" that could not conceivably have been written by the adult Lewis as claimed, and that does not contain some materials for the book *C. S. Lewis: Images of His World* [1973.9] photographed while in Warren's possession.

41 LINDSKOOG, KATHRYN [ANN], and ELLWOOD, GRACIA FAY. "C. S. Lewis: Natural Law and the Law in Our Hearts." In *The Taste of the Pineapple: Essays on C. S. Lewis as Reader, Critic, and Imaginative Writer.* Edited by Bruce L. Edwards. Bowling Green, Ohio: Bowling Green State University Popular Press, pp. 195–205.
    Reprint of 1984.44.

42 LUSK, LINDA VANCE. "The Idea of Magnanimity in C. S. Lewis's Space Trilogy." *CSL: The Bulletin of the New York C. S. Lewis Society* 19 (July): 1–8.
    Ransom is a magnanimous hero in the tradition of Aristotle, Spenser, and Milton. "This magnanimity was once seen as a rightful pride which included courage, right acting, and a proper sense of one's relation to God and man." Aristotle's magnanimity is a public virtue, self-generated and self-sustained, the means by which humans may approach God, and has to do with action. Ransom in *Out of the Silent Planet* is like the Redcrosse Knight in Spenser's *The Faerie Queene*: the two activities in which Ransom most resembles Redcrosse are "overcoming fear by faith and making proper choices—after having made wrong ones." In *Perelandra* Ransom is like Christ in Milton's *Paradise Regained*: because the magnanimous man has "a proper sense of his identity in the likeness of God, he really does make choices based on a 'regard to [his] own dignity.'" Ransom in *That Hideous Strength* is like Spenser's, Milton's, and Williams's idea of Arthur.

43 McCLATCHEY, JOE. "The Affair of Jane's Dreams: Reading *That Hideous Strength* as Iconographic Art." In *The Taste of the Pineapple: Essays on C. S. Lewis as Reader, Critic, and Imaginative Writer*. Edited by Bruce L. Edwards. Bowling Green, Ohio: Bowling Green State University Popular Press, pp. 166–193.
    "Lewis sees iconographical art as a statement of life: 'an accompaniment, rather than a criticism' of it." His propensity for mingling Christian and pagan elements in *That Hideous Strength* enlivens its compelling iconographic imagery. The major categories of images in the novel are "(1) the False Cupid, (2) Antitypes to the False Cupid, (3) Forms of Human Adult Civilized Love, (4) Forms of Natural Appetite, (5) the Image of Evil, (6) the Image of Good, and (7) the Story of Arthur."

44   McLAUGHLIN, SARA PARK, and WEBB, MARK O. *A Word Index to the Poetry of C. S. Lewis*. West Cornwall, Conn.: Locust Hill Press, 232 pp.

The index covers poems published in *Spirits in Bondage*, *Poems*, and *Narrative Poems*. An abbreviation indicating the book and poem number, as well as the line number in which the word appears, follows each word indexed. A key to these abbreviations is given, indicating the book title and the poem title. There is also a list of words excluded, all foreign words, and insignificant English words.

45   MADDEN, LEO H. "Parallels Between C. S. Lewis's Surprised by Joy and Francis Thompson's 'The Hound of Heaven.'" *CSL: The Bulletin of the New York C. S. Lewis Society* 19 (June):1–5.

"Lewis's autobiography should be understood as a virtual re-telling of [Thompson's] epic poem in narrative form." The drama of both works is the soul's flight from the relentless approach of God. The soul retreats in philanthropy and kindness toward others, in the occult, "to seek comfort in the innocence and instinctive devotedness of children," and in nature. The surrender to God occurs when none of these contents the soul. The soul is passive in surrender, "made aware of the misery of human existence and of the Voice of God Himself who announces to the soul that He is the source of all human worth and merit." The overriding fear that caused the flight is the completeness of the terms of surrender, but the surrender to God becomes a victory, not a defeat. "One hands over to God one's liberty, memory, understanding . . . and one receives all back perfected and directed to their proper end."

46   MARTIN, JOHN. "C. S. Lewis: The Oracle of Elfland." *CSL: The Bulletin of the New York C. S. Lewis Society* 19 (August):1–7.

Lewis possessed "image magic, hard logic, and great knowledge"; in him the "Elf of imagination was always at work." *Till We Have Faces* is Lewis's great work, one only he could have written—"a work demanding deep thought, rich feeling, literary intuition, mythopoeic ingenuity, great classical knowledge, and supreme imagination." *The Pilgrim's Regress* has unforgettable moments and is a thinking man's surrealism. Lewis's ability to find the telling phrase, the illuminating image, makes him a useful guide to the existentially perplexed.

47   ———. "An Imaginary Interview." *CSL: The Bulletin of the New York C. S. Lewis Society* 20 (November):1–5.

Martin provides quotations from Lewis on religion, premarital sex, giving to the poor, life in outer space, reading of old books, and women as clergy.

48   ———. "Voices of Fire: Eliot, Lewis, Sayers and Chesterton." In *The Taste of the Pineapple: Essays on C. S. Lewis as Reader, Critic, and Imaginative*

1988

Writer. Edited by Bruce L. Edwards. Bowling Green, Ohio: Bowling Green State University Popular Press, pp. 219–239.
>   Reprint of 1982.35.

49   MARHESON, SUE. "C. S. Lewis and the Lion: Primitivism and Archetype in *The Chronicles of Narnia.*" *Mythlore* 15 (Autumn):13–18.
>   The Chronicles of Narnia are fantasy and should not be read as allegory but rather as symbolic narrative. Lewis participated in the imaginative response of primitivism, which "originates in a sense of cultural failure and takes the form of consequent attempts to restore vital symbols." The Lion is the archetype of the dying god, a primitivistic symbol based on "'the genesis of restoration from decay.'" Magic or enchantment alters the form of the subject, an alteration that is objective and real. The Lion is the enchanter; "he creates a world of which he is part, because that world is, in essence, himself." Dreams and enchantment, both experiences of self-transformation, are repeatedly connected in the Chronicles. Archetypal images "are designed to restore the psychic balance of the individual or epoch." The Lion heals characters in the stories both spiritually and physically, and reading the tales provides the reader a cleansing and healing experience.

50   MEYERS, ROBERT B. "'. . . the Abstractions Proper to Them': C. S. Lewis and Institutional Theory of Literature." In *The Taste of the Pineapple: Essays on C. S. Lewis as Reader, Critic, and Imaginative Writer*. Edited by Bruce L. Edwards. Bowling Green, Ohio: Bowling Green State University Popular Press, pp. 37–56.
>   *An Experiment in Criticism* makes the most sense when seen as institutional theory that considers what treatment readers give literary works as opposed to nonliterary works and who constitutes the literary audience. Lewis "adopts the ultimate institutional stance that literature is fundamentally a practice involving two primary elements: the work that has been offered as literature and the reader who reads it." He distinguishes between the unliterary reader, the high literary, and the middle literary; the last group has a high appreciation of literature but has a taste for realism that is "virtually the same as *having* a definition of literature in terms of preferred features, techniques, etc. Such a definition . . . excludes very much of what the literary of earlier periods once counted as literature," something Lewis was devoted to resisting. In *Experiment*, Lewis exposes the logical weaknesses of the critical theories of the middle literary, particularly the nature of tragedy. He also points out larger social factors contributing to leading the middle literary astray, and singles out the importance of English literature as an academic discipline in contributing enormously to the problem. Instead of an experiment, Lewis rediscovers "the basic relationship upon which the social practice of literature stands—the interaction [of] the received work with the literary reader."

51   MILWARD, PETER. "G. K. Chesterton and C. S. Lewis in Japan: A Personal Assessment." *Inklings: Jahrbuch für Literatur und Ästhetik* 6:165–175.

Milward recounts the history of the academic interest in Lewis and Chesterton in Japan, including what critical analyses were published, what conferences took place, and how Lewis and Chesterton societies were formed.

52   MITCHELL, KEITH. "Screwtape Revisited: Reflections on Re-Reading *The Screwtape Letters.*" *Priests & People* 2 (Fall):31–33.

The book's medium is brilliant and grippingly original. Some less attractive elements are traces of Puritan theology, the impression that God and the devil are equally powerful, and Lewis's personal quirks. Elements worthy of praise are the passages on virtues and humility, Lewis's insight, and his gift for aptly saying what needs to be said. *Screwtape* reminds us there is no substitute for personal sanctity and the temptation to make religion subordinate to worldly causes is deadly.

53   MORRISON, JOHN. "Oops." *CSL: The Bulletin of the New York C. S. Lewis Society* 19 (May):1–8.

Lewis, in his sermon "A Slip of the Tongue," considers the extent to which we long for temporal safety while pushing the eternal to the rear. We may protect ourselves against the temporal through common Christian usage—such as baptism, holy communion, and prayer—moral theology, rational thinking, the advice of good books, and a spiritual director.

54   MUSACCHIO, GEORGE. "Warfaring Christian." *Mythlore* 14 (Spring): 31–33.

Ransom undergoes momentous changes during his verbal and physical battles with the Un-man to prevent the fall of the Green Lady in *Perelandra*.

55   NELSON, MICHAEL. "C. S. Lewis and His Critics." *The Virginia Quarterly Review* 64, no. 1 (Winter):1–19.

Lewis's defense of his faith is logical and mythical. His boldness and outspokenness in his apologetics caused defects that are the excess of his virtues. He caricatured and bullied those with whom he disagreed, and his arguments were oversimplified. Most of his critics have been academic theologians who feel he is an intruder on their turf and who are jealous of his popularity and influence. Some of the broadsides aimed at Lewis by Beversluis hit home but ultimately his book [1985.4] founders. "He fundamentally misconstrues Lewis on the most important of issues, namely, whether Christianity is subject to rational proof." He slights Lewis's conviction that myth is vital to Christianity and misses the significance of faith qua faith to Lewis. Beversluis's treatment of *A Grief Observed* is unforgivable.

1988

56 O'HARE, JOAN, and WALLSGROVE, PAT. "Two Lewis Pupils." *Canadian C. S. Lewis Journal*, no. 64 (Autumn):1–4.

O'Hare found Lewis to be impeccably courteous, kind, and supportive. She found his greatest influence to have been *The Screwtape Letters*, which enabled her to be more tolerant of human frailties. Wallsgrove will always be grateful for knowing Lewis.

57 PACKER, J. I. "What Lewis Was and Wasn't." *Canadian C. S. Lewis Journal*, no. 64 (Autumn):7.

Reprint of 1988.58.

58 ———. "What Lewis Was and Wasn't." *Christianity Today* 32 (15 January):11.

Lewis's supreme achievement is the stark and stunning *The Pilgrim's Regress*. His fiction "lapses from the admirably adult to the archly adolescent, from the childlike to the childish." He was a Christian thinker without peer on three themes: "the reasonableness and humanity of Christian faith; the moral demands of discipleship; and heaven as home, the place of all value and all contentment." Reprinted: 1988.57.

59 PIEHLER, PAUL. "Visions and Revisions: C. S. Lewis's Contributions to the Theory of Allegory." In *The Taste of the Pineapple: Essays on C. S. Lewis as Reader, Critic, and Imaginative Writer*. Edited by Bruce L. Edwards. Bowling Green, Ohio: Bowling Green State University Popular Press, pp. 79–91.

In *The Allegory of Love* Lewis used an inconsistent definition of allegory; he considered allegory to be only a mode of expression and not a serious mode of thought. Piehler discusses a definition for allegory and traces the history of allegory. Lewis's interpretation of allegorical texts transcends his theoretical inconsistencies. "For, in spite of all his theoretical misgivings concerning the value of allegory, evidently he came to love and appreciate the form as no scholar had before him."

60 PIETRUSZ, JIM. "Rites of Passage: *The Chronicles of Narnia* and the Seven Sacraments." *Mythlore* 14 (Summer):61–63.

Lewis used the seven sacraments, "demarcation points in a person's spiritual growth," in the Chronicles. In *The Lion, the Witch and the Wardrobe* Edmund asks forgiveness from Aslan and his brother and sisters for his betrayal, depicting the sacrament of penance. *Prince Caspian* comes of age and accepts responsibility, depicting the sacrament of confirmation. In *The Voyage of the "Dawn Treader"* Eustace is baptized by Aslan. In *The Silver Chair* Prince Rilian undergoes extreme unction, the anointing of the critically ill. *The Horse and His Boy*, the most paradoxical story in the sacramental association, concerns the sacrament of marriage. In *The Magician's Nephew* Digory performs pastoral duties, depicting the sacrament of Holy Orders, and also the sacrament of Holy Eucharist by giving his mother the life-giving apple. *The Last Battle* does not depict a sacrament. "Seven sacraments in six books is not very symetrical," which illustrates the lack of organization in the series.

61 RATZINGER, CARDINAL JOSEPH. "Consumer Materialism and Christian Hope." *Canadian C. S. Lewis Journal*, no. 63 (Summer):4–5.

Lewis predicted the dangers of the collapse of the foundations of morality. He emphatically stated that "the moral character of being itself and the necessity for harmony between human existence and the message of nature is common to all the great civilisations."

62 Review of *The Essential C. S. Lewis*. *Booklist* 85 (15 September):113.

"A satisfactory overview of a prolific genius."

63 SADLER, GLENN EDWARD. "C. S. Lewis." In *Writers for Children: Critical Studies of Major Authors Since the Seventeenth Century*. Edited by Jane M. Bingham. New York: Scribner, pp. 357–364.

In the Chronicles of Narnia Lewis explores extensively the traditional good/evil dualism of the fairy tale. On repeated readings his ransacking of traditional myths for content is annoying and distracts the reader from the plot. *The Lion, the Witch and the Wardrobe*, *The Magician's Nephew*, and *Prince Caspian* smoothly integrate myth and fairy tale and are the most convincing of the stories. *The Last Battle* is more a futuristic myth; the plot is overloaded with too much religious and philosophical symbolism. The underlying theme in the Chronicles is that myth and fact are uniquely related. "For the child reader it is the recurring conflict between truth and falsity, real and make-believe, reality and appearances, that makes the *Narnia* stories so continually appealing." Lewis's creation of Aslan "is one of his most moving fictional achievements." The Chronicles have not been fully appreciated for their insights on parent-child psychology. Limitations include the interruption of action for dialogue and the lack of purpose in the way the myth of Narnia flows. Lewis's treatment of death and immortality is his most notable theme. "The *Chronicles of Narnia* continue to be Lewis' great literary tribute to the enduring power of a child's mind."

64 SAMMONS, MARTHA C. *"A Better Country": The Worlds of Religious Fantasy and Science Fiction*. Contributions to the Study of Science Fiction and Fantasy, no. 32. New York: Greenwood Press, 168 pp.

The theories and techniques used by Lewis, Tolkien, and MacDonald, who founded the genre of religious fantasy and science fiction, can also be illustrated in the works of contemporary writers. An important element of religious fantasy is the invention of a secondary world that shows the reality of the supernatural, spiritual world. The central theme of the genre is the war between good and evil. "The basic plot is that of an ordinary hero who undergoes adventures in a strange landscape, has a goal or quest . . . undergoes a series of tests or obstacles, and eventually restores order." One main purpose of religious fantasy is to put the reader "'on the road to God,'" a direction achieved by having the main character become converted. For the story to be effective the theology "must be presented through narrative action and embodied in situations so the work has a dramatic quality." One common technique of religious fantasy is to present Christian cosmology and biblical truths in a different way by creating a new mythology. Important influences on the genre are fairy tales, the Bible, medieval morality plays, the Arthurian legend, the dream voyage, the beast fable, and historical fantasy. Science fiction, because it uses rational rather than supernatural explanation, is rarely used by contemporary authors to discuss theological themes. However, it is ideally suited to religious themes because it is more interested in ideas and is "a natural type of literature to speculate about religions on other planets or in the future." Lewis felt the ideal form of fantasy was myth because it must be experienced, not read for abstract meaning. The effects of fantasy are recovery by allowing the reader to see the world in a new way, restoration of value by giving meaning to human existence, satisfaction of desires for the spiritual and supernatural, and consolation in "'a sudden glimpse of the underlying reality or truth,'" which pierces the reader with joy.

65 SAYER, GEORGE. "C. S. Lewis and George MacDonald." *Inklings: Jahrbuch für Literatur und Ästhetik* 6:65–77.

MacDonald's *Phantastes: A Faerie Romance for Men and Women* (London: Smith, Elder, 1858) influenced *Dymer*'s quest for the feminine. "Probably Lewis learnt more about the sort of death that leads to birth into new life from MacDonald than from any other writer." Lewis was interested in the devotional aspects of *The Diary of an Old Soul* (1880) and *Unspoken Sermons* (London: Straham, 1867). *The Great Divorce* is Lewis's most important literary tribute to MacDonald; "its very structure is designed to accommodate, even show off, some of MacDonald's ideas."

66 ———. *Jack: C. S. Lewis and His Times*. San Francisco: Harper & Row, 278 pp.

This detailed biography provides new perspective on Lewis's relationships with his father, his brother, Mrs. Moore, and Joy Davidman. It contributes interesting insights into Lewis's motivation and character, incorporates political and social history of the times, and discusses Lewis's works. Sayer, a pupil and longtime friend of Lewis, makes extensive use of "The Lewis Papers," a collection of family papers assembled by Albert Lewis and edited and typed by Warren. The book includes bibliographies of Lewis's works and books and periodicals about him. Reprinted in part: 1988.67.

67   ———. "Preface: Our First Meeting." *Canadian C. S. Lewis Journal*, no. 62 (Spring):4–5.
      Reprinted from 1988.66.

68   SCHAKEL, PETER J. Review of *Boxen: The Imaginary World of the Young C. S. Lewis. Seven: An Anglo-American Literary Review* 9:137–138.
      "The pieces do highlight, by their absence, the qualities that make Lewis's mature work successful."

69   SCHOFIELD, STEPHEN. "Breaking Bachelors' Barriers." *Canadian C. S. Lewis Journal*, no. 63 (Summer):9–10.
      "America is a land of informal candor and camaraderie, a natural trait of two women [the Duchess of Windsor and Joy Lewis] who thus, it seems, at least in part, broke through and induced into matrimony two gentlemen of the Old World, Edward VIII and C. S. Lewis."

70   ———. "Milton, Lewis & the Press." *Canadian C. S. Lewis Journal*, no. 61 (Winter):4–7.
      Lewis inadvertently reached the English masses when the *Daily Mirror* printed, without permission, his essay on sex and Christianity. He advises reading the original literature rather than criticism about it, but his *A Preface to "Paradise Lost"* is easier and more delightful than Milton. He "is more illuminating and readable than Milton himself."

71   ———. "'Pride Forbids Using a Stick'." *Canadian C. S. Lewis Journal*, no. 62 (Spring):8–9.
      Lewis walked about twenty miles a day while on holiday. He was quite lyrical about his walks. This article quotes from Lewis's letters to Arthur Greeves about his walks.

72   STEWART, DAVID H. "Style and Substance in the Prose of C. S. Lewis." In *The Taste of the Pineapple: Essays on C. S. Lewis as Reader, Critic, and Imaginative Writer*. Edited by Bruce L. Edwards. Bowling Green, Ohio: Bowling Green State University Popular Press, pp. 92–109.
      The secret of Lewis's effectiveness lies in his revisions, his images, and the oral quality of his work. His revisions follow "a logical-lexical-aural process, with each element clarifying meaning and enhancing the poem." His use of homely images for analogues of grand objects creates a delightful, surprising, and illuminating congruity. The oral quality of his writing approximates a dialogue with the reader. Instead of "blocking the view with his own ego, he tried to remove himself, to become a 'clean' lens or mirror."

73   "Take That Look Off Your Face: A Note on Lewis and Joyce." *CSL: The Bulletin of the New York C. S. Lewis Society* 20 (December):4–5.
      Lewis patterned *Surprised by Joy* after James Joyce's *Portrait of the*

1988

Artist as a Young Man to emphasize the different outcomes the authors reached: Lewis underwent a conversion to Christianity and Joyce was unable to embrace religion.

74 TALIAFERRO, CHARLES. "A Narnian Theory of the Atonement." *Scottish Journal of Theology* 41:75–92.

Aslan's ransom of Edmund in *The Lion, the Witch and the Wardrobe* fits the classic ransom theory of atonement. "The ransom theory conceives of Christ's redemption of us as a dramatic deliverance from the power of the evil one, Satan." The Narnian version of the ransom theory is that evildoers become hostage to Satan, who demands Jesus in exchange for them. Jesus gives himself to Satan, and through this self-donation overthrows Satan. Aslan's death and resurrection is not identical to the Christian's understanding of Christ's. The ransom theory has advantages over two competing theories of atonement: the Abelardian and the Anselmian. The Narnian ransom theory maintains that Satan is not equal to God and that by doing evil, creatures place themselves in discord with God and harmony with Satan; Satan acts in ignorance by demanding Christ's sacrifice, the very thing that destroys him; creatures do not lose their free will; and God's choosing to save us in this costly manner shows His love. Ransom theory enshrines a pre-eminently Christian act, provides a coherent understanding of the atonement, and highlights a realistic view of freedom and evil.

75 THORSON, STEPHEN. " 'Knowledge' in C. S. Lewis's Post-Conversion Thought: This Epistemological Method." *Seven: An Anglo-American Literary Review* 9:91–116.

Lewis's post–conversion epistemology is based on reason, experience, and authority, and he never changed his views. In *Miracles* he argued that reason is objective and "gives us genuine insight into reality." He also believed that moral values are objective, "are independent of the causal connections of a deterministic Nature," and are therefore part of a supernature. Lewis's basic point in *The Abolition of Man* is that "one cannot judge Moral Reason from outside it." He was not arguing that if one accepts one part of the Tao one must accept it all as Nuttall [1984.50] claims. Lewis did not believe all knowledge comes from reason but "that knowledge depends on the *validity* of reasoning." He believed we receive facts to reason about from our own physical, psychological, or spiritual experiences or from an authority. Schakel [1984.59] is wrong about Lewis coming to accept a subjective path toward knowledge.

76 TRUPIA, ROBERT C. "Learning Christian Behavior: The Way of Virtue in The Chronicles of Narnia." *Lamp-Post of the Southern California C. S. Lewis Society* 11, no. 4 (November):3–8.

The first three novels of the Chronicles present the "theological" virtues and the last four the "cardinal" virtues. *The Lion, the Witch and the Wardrobe* is concerned with charity, *Prince Caspian* focuses on faith, *Voyage of the "Dawn Treader"* presents hope, *The Silver Chair* covers prudence, *The Horse and His Boy* depicts justice, *The Magician's Nephew* highlights temperance, and *The Last Battle* explores fortitude.

77 TYNAN, KENNETH. "Exhilaration." *Canadian C. S. Lewis Journal*, no. 61 (Winter):10–14.
    Reprint of 1979.112–113; 1983.79.

78 VELDMAN, MEREDITH. "C. S. Lewis and J. R. R. Tolkien: Fantasy as Protest Literature." In "Romantic and Religious Protest in a Secular Society: Fantasy Literature, the Campaign for Nuclear Disarmament, and Eco-Activism in Britain, 1945–1980." Ph.D. dissertation, Northwestern University, pp. 7–82.
    Fantasy provides insight into ultimate reality and criticizes the existing social system. In his Space Trilogy and in the Chronicles of Narnia, Lewis builds his myth from the medieval model, warns of the consequences of severing the connection between humanity and the natural world, affirms the sanctity of the natural world, and depicts the importance of each individual. In these works he argues that the modern Western world has "lost touch with mythical reality, and so with the spiritual and natural realms." Lewis and Tolkien's fantasies were moral protests against collectivism, the cult of progress, and the cult of science and technology. Readers recognize this moral protest and respond to Lewis and Tolkien's works based on their own appraisal of contemporary society.

79 YANCY, PHILIP. "Hearing the World in a Higher Key." *Christianity Today* 32 (21 October):24–28.
    There seems to be no difference between the natural and supernatural worlds so why believe in an unseen world? The theme of two worlds runs throughout Lewis's works but is found particularly in "Transposition." He defines the problem as the continuity between natural and spiritual things and claims that spiritual events manifest themselves in natural phenomena. Modern science reduces both natural and supernatural phenomena to their component parts. To avoid this reduction we must acknowledge the power of reductionism, realize that the natural world is not superior to the higher world, and be aware that the reality of the spiritual world is carried by the faculties of the natural world.

Index

1981.65, 75; 1982.5, 66; 1983.82;
1984.46; 1985.4, 55, 68–69;
1987.23–34, 56; 1988.5, 74
Evolution, 1975.2, 5, 8, 53; 1984.42;
1985.40; 1987.39
Experiment in Criticism, An
Criticism of, 1977.8; 1988.50
Summaries of, 1979.111; 1986.20

Fairy tales, 1972.9; 1974.50; 1977.9;
1981.3, 25, 36; 1983.44;
1984.19; 1985.36, 75; 1988.11,
63–64
Faith, 1974.27; 1975.3, 37; 1976.20, 32,
37; 1977.12, 14; 1978.27; 1979.2,
23, 42, 77, 93, 107; 1981.52–53,
68, 75; 1982.27, 64; 1983.81;
1984.26, 31, 47, 68; 1985.4, 26, 58,
74–75, 80; 1986.38, 42; 1988.33,
35, 55, 58, 76
Fantasy, 1972.23; 1973.46; 1974.5, 41;
1975.2, 17, 23, 31, 36, 52, 55;
1976.11, 16; 1977.15, 32, 40, 45;
1979.107; 1980.10; 1981.8, 70;
1982.1, 52; 1983.18, 60;
1984.55–56, 58, 66–67; 1985.21,
36, 83; 1986.8, 41, 49–50; 1987.1,
17, 22; 1988.8, 49, 64, 78
Farrell, Eleanor M., 1986.14
Farrer, Austin, 1979.37
Fernandez, Irene, 1982.18
Fetherston, Patience, 1988.21
Fichte, Joerg O., 1975.15
Fiction
Characterization, 1972.22; 1976.15;
1979.82; 1981.2; 1984.37; 1985.32;
1987.55
Criticism of, 1973.32; 1974.41; 1975.17,
23, 31, 55; 1976.43; 1978.45;
1979.107; 1980.10; 1981.22, 25;
1982.11; 1983.43, 80; 1984.30, 58,
66; 1985.11, 21; 1986.15, 17;
1987.34; 1988.46, 78
Genre of, 1975.52; 1977.57; 1978.40;
1981.18; 1984.55; 1988.64
Images and symbols, 1980.40
Inspiration, 1982.21
Political aspect of, 1972.23; 1984.58
Sources of, 1972.22; 1983.51; 1984.17
Summaries of, 1972.22; 1973.46;
1978.20, 45; 1980.22; 1981.49;
1983.44, 49
Themes of, 1974.41; 1980.28; 1984.54
Celtic myth, 1983.51
Christopoesis, 1975.54

Christian Platonism, 1981.58
Dance, 1976.22; 1986.56; 1987.31
Dionysus and Christ, 1985.74
Discernment, 1986.5
Evil, 1974.37; 1978.5; 1981.75;
1988.36
Free will, 1977.46
Glory, 1981.31
Good, 1987.7
Humor, 1987.20
Love, 1987.43, 48
Masculine and feminine, 1973.25;
1977.13, 18; 1978.16; 1982.45
Model of the universe, 1987.45
Moral order, 1978.18
Mother, 1984.34
Music, 1987.31
Mythopoesis, 1975.55
Salvation, 1981.75
Shadow myth, 1975.13
Substitution, 1983.30
Tao, 1980.63; 1983.43
Violence, 1974.33
Filmer, Kath, 1984.19; 1985.24–25;
1986.15; 1987.14; 1988.22–23
Fischer, Philip C., 1980.15
Fish, Stanley, 1986.16
Fisher, Judith L., 1983.19
Fisher, Matt, 1987.15
Fisher, Robert, 1984.20
Fitton, Toby, 1979.38
Fitzgerald, Dorothy Hobson, 1980.16;
1981.20; 1983.20; 1984.21
Fitzpatrick, John, 1973.6; 1981.21; 1983.21
Flieger, Verlyn, 1986.17
Forbes, Cheryl, 1976.11
Ford, Paul Francis, 1980.17; 1983.22;
1984.25; 1987.16
Ford, Peter, 1974.12–13
Foreman, Frank, 1984.22–23
Foreman, Lelia, 1984.24
Forgiveness, 1977.14; 1981.78; 1982.37;
1983.72; 1988.27, 60
"Form of Things Unknown, The"
Criticism of, 1983.21; 1984.24
Fortuna, Maryann, 1987.17
Four Loves, The
Summaries of, 1978.14; 1981.67
Fowler, Alastair, 1977.22
Franceschelli, Amos, 1973.7; 1978.12
Free will, 1973.5; 1974.19; 1977.25, 28,
46; 1983.49; 1985.68; 1986.64;
1988.74
Freshwater, Mark Edwards, 1985.26
Freud, Jill, 1980.18

Freud, Sigmund
  About, 1972.16; 1973.18–19, 33
Friendship, 1972.22; 1973.2, 11; 1974.15;
    1978.4, 14; 1979.17; 1981.54, 77;
    1985.1, 6, 50–51; 1987.48, 53;
    1988.27
Friesen, Garry L., 1983.24
Frost, Naomi, 1975.16; 1977.23
Fryer, W. R., 1980.19; 1982.19; 1984.26
Fuller, Edmund, 1974.14; 1983.26
Fuller, Edmund, and Jones, Alan, 1981.32
Futch, Ken, 1977.24; 1978.13; 1980.20

Gardiner, Katherine, 1985.28
Garner, Ross, 1972.9
Gebbert, Vera M., 1979.39
Geiger, William A., Jr., 1980.21
Geisler, Norman L., 1983.27
Gestalt psychology, 1985.80
Gibran, Jean, 1985.29
Gibson, Evan K., 1980.22
Gilbert, Douglas, and Kilby, Clyde S.,
    1973.9
Gilmore, Charles, 1979.40
Glover, Donald E., 1981.22
Glover, J. Denis, 1987.18
Glusman, John A., 1983.28
God, 1972.8, 21; 1973.3–5, 8, 16, 23, 25,
    35, 39; 1974.4, 29, 41, 44–45;
    1975.8, 17, 28, 39–40, 44, 51, 54;
    1976.32; 1977.18, 28, 36, 46, 56,
    62–63; 1978.9, 16, 22, 49; 1979.2,
    36, 42, 71; 1980.8, 22, 24–25, 29,
    54, 60; 1981.19, 28, 31, 52–53, 65,
    78; 1982.1, 37, 41, 63, 65; 1983.24,
    43, 47, 49, 81–82; 1984.26, 28, 42,
    44, 68; 1985.3–4, 7, 46, 70, 80;
    1986.11, 32, 56; 1987.16, 23, 26,
    45, 54, 56; 1988.27, 33, 45
  Doctrine of prevenient grace, 1976.9
  Doctrine of reciprocity, 1975.44
  Relationship with man, 1979.83;
    1980.52; 1981.39; 1983.37, 83;
    1984.75; 1988.34, 42
God in the Dock
  Reviews of, 1984.51; 1986.43
Gooch, Paul W., 1987.19
Good, 1974.33, 37, 41; 1975.12, 28;
    1976.13, 16; 1977.20; 1978.5;
    1979.52, 83, 107; 1980.61;
    1981.29, 47, 58; 1982.1, 5, 66;
    1983.1, 3, 14, 37, 60; 1984.19, 37,
    67; 1985.4, 13, 24, 46, 68, 75, 77,
    82; 1987.7, 24, 26, 48–49; 1988.5,
    8, 10, 27, 43, 63–64

Goodknight, Glen H., 1984.27
Goodknight, Glen H., and Brenion,
    Frederick, 1973.10
Gossen, Ruth S., 1987.20
Gough, John, 1977.25
Gouvea, Fernando Quadros, 1987.21
Graham, W. Fred, 1975.17
Great Divorce, The
  Characterization of, 1972.8
  Criticism of, 1976.1
  Literary parallels, 1975.7; 1983.4
  Sources of, 1974.28
  Summaries of, 1972.25; 1981.8
  Symbolism of, 1974.47
  Themes of, 1977.69; 1979.116; 1983.14;
    1986.64; 1987.30
Green, Carole, 1972.10
Green, Roger Lancelyn, 1975.18;
    1979.41
Green, Roger Lancelyn, and Hopper,
    Walter, 1974.15
Greenfield, Robert, 1976.12
Greeves, Arthur
  Biography, 1985.27
Gresham, Douglas H., 1988.26
Grief Observed, A
  Criticism of, 1975.37; 1983.81; 1984.68;
    1986.42
Griffin, Brian, 1975.19
Griffin, Emilie, 1978.14; 1980.23–24
Griffin, Henry William, 1986.18–19
Griffin, William, 1977.27
Griffiths, Alan Bebe, 1979.42; 1984.28
Gruber, Loren C., 1975.20
Gruenler, Royce Gordon, 1974.16
Gurney, Stephen, 1983.29
Gussman, Neil, 1986.20
Guthrie, Barbara Ann Bowman,
    1988.27

Hajjar, Jacqueline Accad, 1982.20
Haldane, J. B. S.
  Criticism of, 1972.12
Hales, E[dward] E[lton] Y[oung]
  Chariot of Fire, 1979.19
Hall, Grace R.W., 1987.22
Hall, Susan, 1976.13
Hall, Thomas G., 1975.21
Hallan, Leila, 1980.25
"Hamlet: The Prince or the Poem,"
    1975.10
Hanger, Nancy C., 1983.30
Hannay, Margaret Patterson, 1973.11;
    1976.14–15; 1977.28; 1981.23;
    1986.21

Hardie, Colin, 1985.30
Harms, Paul W. F., 1973.12
Harris, Mason, 1976.16
Harris, Richard, 1987.23
Hart, Dabney A., 1984.29–30; 1985.31
Hartt, Walter F., 1981.24
Harwood, A. C., 1974.17; 1975.22
Havard, Robert E., 1979.45
Hawkins, Peter, 1984.31
Haynes, Jack, 1974.18
Heaven, 1972.21; 1973.5, 16, 23;
    1974.12; 1975.7; 1976.3–4, 19;
    1977.56, 58; 1979.56, 84; 1981.1,
    8, 29, 53; 1982.27, 54, 59, 69;
    1983.14, 82; 1984.17, 65, 72;
    1987.34, 58; 1988.58
Heidelberger, Patricia, 1979.46
Helfrich, John W., 1980.26; 1984.32
Hell, 1972.25; 1973.5, 23; 1974.47;
    1975.7; 1976.4, 19, 30; 1977.6;
    1979.84, 116; 1982.27, 59;
    1983.14, 82; 1984.9, 17; 1985.55;
    1986.11, 64; 1987.16, 34, 40
Helms, Randel, 1981.25
Hendrickson, David, 1973.13; 1976.18
Henthorne, Susan Cassandra, 1985.32
Heron, Alasdair I. C., 1988.29
Hierarchy, 1973.24; 1974.17; 1975.26, 49;
    1976.30; 1978.51; 1982.20;
    1983.24, 45; 1984.45; 1985.32;
    1987.11, 20
Hilderbrand, Gary, 1974.19
Hilderbrand, Gerald, 1972.11
Hinman, Myra, 1985.33
Hipolito, Jane, 1974.20
History, 1974.13; 1975.5, 53; 1977.71;
    1982.36; 1984.42, 45; 1985.40, 54
  Philosophy of, 1975.5; 1984.42; 1985.40
Hodgens, Richard M., 1972.12–13;
    1976.19; 1978.15; 1979.47;
    1982.21; 1985.34; 1986.22;
    1988.30
Hoffecker, W. Andrew, and Timmerman,
    John H., 1978.16
Hogan, Patrick G., Jr., 1977.29
Holbrook, David, 1973.14; 1978.17
Holiness, 1973.2; 1977.63; 1981.76
Hollwitz, John Charles, 1980.27; 1985.35
Holmer, Paul L., 1976.20
Holyer, Robert, 1988.31–33
Homosexuality, 1973.11, 45
Hood, Gwyneth, 1988.34
Hooper, Walter, 1974.21–22; 1976.21;
    1977.30; 1979.48–51; 1981.26;
    1982.22

As trustee of Lewis's literary estate,
    1981.26
  Bibliography, 1973.10
  Questions about, 1978.23; 1979.5, 28;
    1979.67, 98–100; 1980.56, 58–59;
    1988.7, 40
Hooper, Walter, and Green, Roger
    Lancelyn, 1974.15
Horse and His Boy, The
  Summaries of, 1973.39; 1982.63
  See also Chronicles of Narnia
Horsman, Gail, 1981.27
Houston, James M., 1983.32; 1988.35
Houtman, Marcia K., 1981.28–29;
    1982.23
Houtman, Marcia K., and Johnson,
    William G., 1986.24
Howard, Andrews, 1977.32
Howard, Thomas, 1978.18; 1980.28;
    1981.30
Hughes, Larry Raymond, 1980.29
Humanism, 1972.4; 1973.1; 1978.29;
    1982.31, 36, 61; 1983.27
"Humanitarian Theory of Punishment,
    The"
  Criticism of, 1973.43; 1979.56; 1985.67;
    1986.7
  Summaries of, 1972.1; 1974.26, 49;
    1984.8
Hume, Kathryn, 1974.23
Humility, 1975.42; 1977.47; 1981.76;
    1982.26; 1983.3, 81; 1984.41, 64;
    1985.51; 1988.52
Humor, 1973.2, 12, 39; 1974.29, 42, 44;
    1975.39; 1976.40; 1979.13;
    1980.32; 1983.73; 1984.31, 67;
    1985.62, 82; 1986.46; 1987.20, 42,
    53
Hunt, David, 1983.33
Huttar, Charles A., 1977.33; 1980.30;
    1986.23; 1988.36
Hutton, Muriel, 1972.14
Hyles, Vernon, 1987.24
Hyms, 1974.25
Hynes, Samuel, 1979.52

Imagination, 1973.12, 21, 46; 1974.4, 24,
    41; 1975.1, 11–12, 21, 24, 29, 54;
    1976.11, 38; 1977.22, 35, 43, 61,
    68, 72; 1978.1, 46; 1979.20, 23, 55,
    61, 93, 107; 1980.32; 1981.42, 65;
    1982.26, 33; 1983.56, 66, 75;
    1984.30, 58–59, 66; 1985.37;
    1986.15, 36, 62; 1988.32
Imbelli, Robert, 1984.33

Lang, Andrew
History of English Literature from "Beowulf" to Swinburne, 1975.18
Language, 1972.3; 1973.12, 20, 41; 1974.41; 1977.43; 1978.21–22, 32; 1979.13, 20; 1980.29, 32, 43, 52; 1981.40, 59, 61; 1982.41; 1983.56, 73; 1984.30; 1985.24–25, 70, 82; 1988.23
Last Battle, The
Sources of, 1980.41
Summaries of, 1977.58; 1985.23
Themes of, 1976.24; 1984.65
See also Chronicles of Narnia
LeGuin, Ursula K., 1977.37
Earthsea Trilogy, 1979.10; 1986.14; 1987.1
"Learning in War-time," 1983.22
Lecturer, Lewis as, 1979.75
Leinster, Murry
"Sidewise in Time," 1978.7
Leitenberg, Barbara, 1975.28
Leopold, Paul, 1983.39; 1988.39
Letters, 1979.36; 1980.9; 1984.31; 1985.19, 48; 1987.46
Letters to an American Lady
Summaries of, 1977.14; 1981.76; 1986.37
Letters to Malcolm: Chiefly on Prayer
Summaries of, 1984.32
Lewis collections, 1974.40; 1979.96, 121; 1981.4. *See also* Marion E. Wade Center
Lewis scholarship, 1981.11
Lewis, Albert
Biography, 1985.27
Lewis, Florence Hamilton
Biography, 1985.27
Lewis, Naomi, 1979.62
Lewis, Warren Hamilton, 1982.28
Bibliography, 1972.18
Biography, 1974.22; 1982.12; 1985.27
Criticism of his works, 1972.18
Diaries, 1982.28
Leyerle, John, 1979.63
Leyland, Margaret M., 1977.38
Lieb, Laurie, 1974.30
Life after death, 1974.12; 1975.16; 1976.3; 1978.11, 36; 1982.59; 1984.65; 1986.11
Light, 1974.47; 1975.13, 29; 1977.56
Lindberg, Lottie, 1986.29; 1987.31
Linden, William, 1974.31
Lindsay, David A.
About, 1975.52

Voyage to Arcturus, A, 1974.31; 1978.7; 1982.51; 1987.15
Lindskoog, Kathryn Ann, 1973.23; 1975.29; 1976.27; 1978.23; 1979.64–65, 67, 69; 1981.37; 1983.40; 1985.42; 1986.30–31; 1988.40
Lindskoog, Kathryn [Ann], and Ellwood, Gracia Fay, 1984.44
Lindvall, Terrence Roy, 1980.32
Linton, Calvin D., 1973.24
Lion, the Witch and the Wardrobe, The
Criticism of, 1972.10; 1982.47; 1984.19
Literary parallels, 1983.11, 60; 1987.17; 1988.19
Summaries of, 1986.31
Themes of, 1983.63; 1985.78; 1988.74
See also Chronicles of Narnia
Literary criticism
Criticism of, 1984.7, 30
Reception in Germany, 1975.15
Summaries of, 1977.5, 43; 1978.34; 1980.12; 1981.3; 1982.17, 62; 1983.18; 1984.70; 1985.31; 1988.14–15, 20
Literary parallels
Lewis Carroll and Lewis, 1981.35
G[ilbert] K[eith] Chesterton and Lewis, 1981.14, 68; 1988.14
Johannes Eckhart and Lewis, 1984.14
T[homas] S[tearns] Eliot and Lewis, 1982.14
Gerard Manley Hopkins and Lewis, 1981.68
George MacDonald and Lewis, 1981.36
Flannery O'Connor and Lewis, 1981.47
Bertrand Russell and Lewis, 1988.37
J[ohn] R[onald] R[euel] Tolkien and Lewis, 1981.35
Literary theory
Summaries of, 1974.50; 1976.20; 1977.24; 1979.55; 1981.17, 22, 24-25, 43; 1982.71; 1988.2, 8, 16
Lloyd, Charles E., 1981.38
Lloyd, Joan, 1973.25
Lobdell, Jared C., 1973.26
Logan, Darlene, 1982.29
Loganbill, Dean, 1975.30
Logres, 1973.28; 1977.47, 62; 1983.57
Logsdon, Mike J., 1986.32
Loney, John Douglas, 1983.43
Love, 1973.23; 1974.28; 1975.35; 1976.10, 15, 30; 1977.31, 36, 44, 47, 65; 1978.14, 51; 1979.19, 107;

Missionary theology, 1981.10
Mitchell, Keith, 1988.52
Mitchell, L. J., 1983.47
Mobley, Jonnie Patricia, 1973.28
Moen, Peggy, 1985.47
"Modern Man and His Categories of
   Thought," 1987.47
Monick, Stanley, 1978.29
Montgomery, John Warwick, 1974.36
Moore, Jane King, 1976.27; 1977.1, 38;
   1979.46, 59, 72; 1980.18; 1986.46;
   1988.40, 66
More–Tyndale Controversy, 1980.35
Morgan, Gerald, 1976.33
Morneau, Robert F., 1987.35
Morris, Clifford, 1973.29
Morris, Daniel L., 1986.39
Morris, Francis J., 1977.43
Morris, William
  Criticism of, 1974.1; 1983.18
Morrison, John, 1976.34; 1979.77;
   1982.37; 1984.48; 1988.53
Moynihan, Martin, 1984.49; 1985.48
Muggeridge, Malcolm, 1981.46
Murdoch, Brian, 1986.40
Murphy, Brian, 1976.35; 1983.49
Murphy, Patrick D., 1986.41
Murrin, Michael, 1982.38
Musacchio, George, 1977.44; 1978.30;
   1980.36; 1983.50; 1986.42;
   1987.37; 1988.54
Music, 1974.25; 1975.32; 1979.22;
   1981.59; 1983.10; 1987.31, 51
"My First School," 1987.10
Myers, Doris T., 1985.49; 1987.39
Myers, W. A., 1975.34
Mysticism, 1975.25; 1978.6; 1979.42;
   1981.19; 1982.27
Myth, 1972.7; 1973.6; 1974.24; 1975.13,
   30; 1976.6, 14, 41, 43; 1977.15, 17,
   29, 34, 43; 1978.4, 18, 29, 39;
   1980.27, 30, 40, 55; 1981.18,
   41–42; 1982.33, 65; 1983.7, 10, 80;
   1984.5, 30, 54; 1985.21, 26;
   1986.36; 1987.23; 1988.34, 55,
   63–64

Nair, Devan, 1985.50
Nakao, Setsuko, 1977.45; 1978.31;
   1979.78; 1985.51
"Nameless Isle, The" 1984.36
Nardo, A. K., 1979.79
"Nativity," 1983.40
Nature, 1973.4, 23; 1974.19; 1975.7;
   1976.5, 8, 31; 1977.62, 68; 1978.9;

   1980.29; 1981.59; 1982.42;
   1983.47, 58, 62; 1985.41, 75;
   1986.36, 41
Nelson, Marie, 1978.32
Nelson, Michael, 1988.55
Neuleib, Janice Witherspoon, 1974.37;
   1975.35–36; 1977.46; 1978.33;
   1980.37; 1981.47
Noel, Henry, 1972.19; 1973.30–31;
   1974.38; 1981.48
Nolan, Charles J., Jr., 1974.39; 1977.47;
   1979.80; 1980.38
Northernness, 1973.1; 1976.36
Numinous, 1972.7; 1973.4; 1975.23;
   1976.5, 37; 1977.15; 1979.50;
   1981.2; 1984.7; 1985.24, 75, 80
Nuttall, A. D., 1984.50

Objectivity, 1973.27, 35; 1974.29, 34;
   1975.34; 1976.20, 29, 38; 1977.49,
   56, 68; 1978.1; 1979.23, 51, 80, 83,
   107, 114; 1980.29, 63; 1981.65;
   1982.26, 42; 1983.1, 43, 66;
   1984.50; 1985.54; 1986.36; 1988.2,
   20, 75
Occult, 1974.7; 1988.45
Of This and Other Worlds
  Reviews of, 1982.55, 64, 67; 1983.78
O'Hare, Colman, 1973.32; 1979.81
O'Hare, Joan, and Wallsgrove, Pat,
   1988.56
Olsen, Dorothy Anne, 1978.34
"On Science Fiction," 1978.33
"On Stories"
  Summaries of, 1974.50
*On Stories: And Other Essays on
  Literature*
  Reviews of, 1982.43–44, 46, 57;
   1983.28, 59
  Summaries of, 1982.32
"On the Reading of Old Books," 1979.108
O'Reilly, James D., 1977.48
Ormrod, Richard, 1985.52
Ostling, Joan K., and Christopher, Joe R.,
   1974.8–9
Otto, Rudolf
  The Idea of the Holy, 1981.11
Oury, Scott, 1977.49
Out of the Silent Planet
  Characterization, 1987.37
  Criticism of, 1975.49; 1985.24, 35;
   1986.33; 1988.6
  Images, 1979.118
  Literary parallels, 1975.36, 49; 1980.4;
   1986.50; 1987.39; 1988.6, 33

Out of the Silent Planet (*continued*)
Summaries of, 1977.70
Themes of, 1975.38; 1983.19; 1984.46
See also Ransom Trilogy
Overby, Charles, 1984.51
Oxbury, Harold, 1985.53
Oxford University, 1980.19; 1981.62;
 1982.19, 49; 1983.32

Packer, J. I., 1988.58
Paganism, 1973.13; 1974.4, 24; 1977.36;
 1981.15; 1982.4, 33; 1983.63;
 1984.20; 1987.28; 1988.10, 43
Patrick, James, 1985.54
Patterson, Nancy-Lou, 1976.36; 1979.82;
 1980.39–40; 1981.50; 1983.51;
 1984.52–53; 1985.55–57;
 1986.43–45
Pauline, Sister, 1981.49
Paxford, F. W., 1986.46
Payne, Leanne, 1979.83
Pedagogy, 1982.65
 Characterization, 1981.6, 45; 1985.33;
 1988.54
 Criticism of, 1972.7; 1975.31; 1977.28;
 1979.47; 1984.11; 1985.14, 34
 Genre of, 1983.37
 Literary parallels, 1977.28; 1982.29–30;
 1987.39
 Sources of, 1975.48
 Summaries of, 1977.44
 Themes of, 1976.26; 1978.46; 1981.52;
 1982.1; 1983.19; 1984.57; 1985.9,
 68–69
See also Ransom Trilogy
Personal Heresy, The
 Summaries of, 1976.25; 1978.21
Personality, 1976.2; 1978.6; 1979.7;
 1985.51; 1987.16
Peters, John, 1985.58
Petersen, William J., 1985.59
Peterson, Jan, and White, William Luther,
 1973.44
Phelps, Russ A., 1980.41
Philip, Neil, 1985.60; 1986.47
Philip, Peter, 1980.42
Phillips, J. B.
 Seeing Lewis's ghost, 1987.13
Philosophy, 1985.54
Piehler, Paul, 1988.59
Pieper, Josef, 1980.43
Pietrusz, Jim, 1988.60
Pile, Joan B., 1980.44
Pilgrim's Regress, The
 Criticism of, 1986.22

Summaries of, 1986.36
Themes of, 1976.41; 1985.54
Pippert, Wesley G., 1974.40
Pittenger, Norman, 1981.51
Pitter, Ruth, 1980.45
Pitts, Mary Ellen, 1982.39
Plank, Robert, 1973.33
Poetry
 Criticism of, 1972.20; 1980.45; 1982.25;
 1986.35
 Summaries of, 1976.19; 1979.57
 Word index, 1988.44
"Poison of Subjectivism," 1976.29
Politics, 1981.66; 1983.2; 1984.22, 77
Prayer, 1973.23; 1974.6; 1975.40;
 1976.32; 1977.14; 1978.11; 1979.2;
 1981.10, 53, 76; 1983.82; 1985.7;
 1987.8, 16; 1988.27, 35
Preface to "Paradise Lost," A
 Criticism of, 1972.6, 21; 1988.70
 Summaries of, 1972.17; 1973.34;
 1976.14; 1986.16
Present Concerns
 Reviews of, 1987.3, 12, 41–42
Presley, Horton, 1984.54
Price, Geoffrey, 1986.48
Price, Meredith, 1982.40
Price, Steven, 1981.52
Prince Caspian
 Summaries of, 1974.44
 Themes of, 1987.54
See also Chronicles of Narnia
Problem of Pain, The
 Criticism of, 1983.81; 1987.56
 Language, 1980.43
 Sources of, 1988.3
 Summaries of, 1973.4; 1980.25; 1986.32
Process theology, 1978.49
Prothero, James, 1987.40
Psalms, 1974.35; 1978.3; 1979.15;
 1980.46; 1983.62
Psychoanalysis, 1972.16; 1973.18–19, 33
Punishment, 1972.1; 1973.43; 1974.26,
 49; 1979.56; 1984.8; 1985.67;
 1986.7
Purcell, James Mark, 1972.20; 1973.34
Purgatory, 1973.16; 1978.11; 1979.56, 84;
 1980.60; 1982.27; 1984.73;
 1987.30
Purtill, Richard L., 1974.41; 1977.50;
 1981.53; 1984.55
Pyles, Franklin Arthur, 1978.35; 1983.56
"Queen of Drum, The"
 Criticism of, 1976.19; 1982.6; 1987.28
 Summaries of, 1976.4

Taylor, A. J. P., 1979.110
Taylor, Maurice, 1985.76
Technology, 1973.5, 42; 1974.46; 1976.5;
    1977.58; 1980.52; 1982.41–42;
    1983.13, 19; 1984.42; 1987.39;
    1988.78
Teichert, Marilyn Chandler, 1984.68
Temperance, 1981.64
Tennyson, G. B., 1974.46
Tetreault, James, 1976.42; 1986.57
That Hideous Strength
  Characterization, 1979.82; 1981.47;
      1986.44
  Criticism of, 1973.42; 1977.50;
      1981.50
  Literary parallels, 1981.50; 1985.25;
      1986.38; 1987.49
  Structure of, 1980.62
  Themes of, 1977.47
    Arthurian legends, 1973.28; 1977.62;
        1983.57; 1985.77
    Beauty, 1979.80
    Child motif, 1974.39
    Freedom, 1982.20
    Iconographic art, 1988.43
    Love, 1974.18
    Marriage, 1980.38
    Masculine and feminine, 1982.45;
        1986.45
    Mind and body, 1974.30
    Scientism, 1982.53; 1986.10
    Self, 1980.37
    Wasteland, 1987.14
  See also Ransom Trilogy
"The Great War" with Owen Barfield,
    1975.1; 1978.1; 1983.75; 1984.1,
    69. *See also* Anthroposophy
Theology, 1973.5; 1974.16, 33; 1977.40,
    72; 1979.107; 1981.10, 24, 29,
    42–43, 65; 1983.47, 82; 1984.48,
    72; 1985.54, 70, 80; 1987.16;
    1988.29, 64
Thesing, William B., and Brown,
    Christopher C., 1983.8
*They Stand Together: The Letters of C. S.
    Lewis to Arthur Greeves
    (1914–1963)*
  Editing, 1979.51
  Reviews of, 1979.4, 8, 17–18, 31, 38,
      62, 120; 1980.15, 20, 48–49;
      1981.38, 1982.3
  Summaries of, 1979.72
Thienes, John, 1982.59
Thompson, Raymond H., 1985.77
Thomson, Patricia, 1980.64

Thorson, Stephen, 1981.70; 1983.75;
    1984.69; 1988.75
Thorson, Stephen, and Daniel, Jerry L.,
    1983.76–77; 1986.58–61;
    1987.57
Till We Have Faces
  Archetypes, 1977.16
  Characterization, 1981.19; 1983.72
  Criticism of, 1975.11; 1976.37; 1977.36;
      1980.47, 55; 1982.4, 54; 1984.18,
      59; 1985.21; 1986.34
  Literary parallels, 1982.60
  Sources of, 1977.32, 65; 1988.22, 34
  Structure of, 1975.6
  Study guide, 1976.6
  Summaries of, 1984.40; 1986.36
  Themes of, 1975.41
    Biblical doctrines, 1980.51
    Epistemology, 1977.61; 1983.66;
        1988.33
    Evil, 1975.35
    God, 1979.71; 1988.10
    Love, 1984.5
    Mystic experience, 1975.25
    Myth, 1975.30; 1976.41, 43; 1978.6;
        1981.19
    Substitution, 1981.20
    Truth, 1982.20
Tillyard, E[ustace] M[andeville] W[eten-
    hall]
  Personal Heresy, 1976.25; 1978.21
Timmerman, John H., 1975.44;
    1977.61–62
Timmerman, John H., and Hoffecker, W.
    Andrew, 1978.16
Tixier, Eliane, 1977.63
Tolkien, J[ohn] R[onald] R[euel]
  Biography, 1981.35, 54; 1985.27
  Dislike of Chronicles of Narnia, 1988.11
  Fellowship of the Ring, 1982.40
  Fiction, 1973.32; 1974.41; 1975.13, 55;
      1981.24–25, 49, 58; 1983.10, 51;
      1984.66; 1986.56; 1988.78
  Themes of, 1978.32; 1984.6; 1987.7, 24
Tollefsen, Olaf, 1979.111
Totton, Nick, 1977.64
Translations of Lewis's works, 1973.44
"Transposition," 1974.16; 1988.79
Travis, Byron M., 1982.60
Trease, Geoffrey, 1983.78
Trickett, Rachel, 1984.70
Tripp, Raymond P., Jr., 1975.45–46
Trupia, Robert C., 1988.76
Turney, Austin, and Turney, Ruth,
    1982.61

Turney, Ruth, and Turney, Austin, 1982.61
Tutor, Lewis as, 1974.42; 1977.21; 1979.11, 13, 26, 88, 112; 1980.42, 64; 1981.16; 1983.5; 1984.9–10, 28; 1985.5; 1987.11; 1988.56
Tynan, Kenneth, 1979.112

Ulreich, John C., 1983.80
Unrue, John C., 1975.47
Utopia, 1975.28; 1983.19; 1986.2, 50

Van Der Weele, Steve J., 1977.65
Van Waasdijk, E. J., 1972.24
Vanauken, Sheldon, 1977.66; 1981.71
Vanauken, Sheldon and Jean
  About, 1977.12, 66
Veldman, Meredith, 1988.78
Vidal, Jaime, 1975.48
Visionary Christian: 131 Readings from C. S. Lewis, The
  Reviews of, 1981.55–57; 1982.72
Viswanatham, K., 1982.62
Vogelpohl, Jan, 1982.63
Voyage of the "Dawn Treader," The
  Literary parallels, 1978.9
  Summaries of, 1975.39
  Themes of, 1986.14, 49
  See also Chronicles of Narnia

Wade Center. *See* Marion E. Wade Center
Waggoner, Diana, 1978.45
Wain, John, 1980.65
Walker, Jeanne Murray, 1978.46; 1985.78
Walking, 1988.71
Wall, Robert Walter, 1983.81
Wallsgrove, Pat, and O'Hare, Joan, 1988.56
Walsh, Chad, 1977.67; 1978.47; 1979.114–115; 1981.74
War, 1979.97; 1981.5, 63; 1983.22, 84; 1984.23
Ward, Patricia A., 1978.48
Ward, Samuel Keith, 1977.68
Warnock, Mary, 1986.62
Warren, Eugene, 1977.69
Watkins, Duff, 1978.49
Watson, George, 1982.64
Watson, James D., 1981.75
Watt, Donald, 1975.49
"We Have No 'Right to Happiness'"
  Sources of, 1988.3
Weaver, Mary Jo, 1979.116
Webb, Mark O., and McLaughlin, Sara Park, 1988.44

Webber, Robert E., 1985.79
"Weight of Glory, The," 1987.10
Well, Calvin Richard, 1985.80
Wells, H[erbert] G[eorge]
  First Men on the Moon, The, 1975.36, 49; 1980.4; 1987.39; 1988.6, 23
  Time Machine, The, 1980.4, 1987.39
Wennberg, Robert, 1973.43
Wertz, Sharon, 1980.66
Westerlund, Lois, 1974.47; 1977.70
"What Chaucer Really Did to *Il Filostrato*," 1988.6
"What Christmas Means to Me," 1983.40
White, John
  Iron Sceptre, The, 1985.71
  Tower of Geburah: A Children's Fantasy, 1985.71
White, T[erence] H[anburg]
  Fiction, 1977.15
White, William Luther, and Peterson, Jan, 1973.44
Widmer, Cynthia, 1985.82
Wilcox, Steven Michael, 1982.65
Wilkinson, Robin, 1982.66
Williams, Charles
  Biography, 1980.16; 1981.54; 1985.27
  Descent into Hell, 1981.20; 1982.40; 1986.64; 1988.5
  Fiction, 1973.32; 1975.13, 55; 1981.58; 1983.51; 1984.66; 1986.56
  Figure of Arthur, The, 1984.21
  Themes of, 1975.16; 1981.31; 1983.30; 1987.7, 24
Williams, Donald T., 1979.117
Williams, Jan, 1974.48; 1981.76
Williams, Terri, 1972.25; 1974.49–50; 1975.50; 1977.71; 1978.50–51; 1981.77
Willis, John Randolph, 1980.67; 1983.82; 1987.58
Wilson, A. N., 1982.67
Wirt, Sherwood, 1975.51
Wissler, Steven Paul, 1980.68; 1981.78
Witcher, Geraldine, 1985.82
Wolfe, Gary K., 1975.52; 1979.118
Wolfe, Gregory, 1983.83; 1984.71; 1986.63
Women
  Attitude toward, 1976.15–16, 27; 1977.39; 1980.54; 1981.46; 1986.3; 1987.52
  Characterization of, 1979.82; 1981.45, 71; 1984.37; 1985.32; 1987.27
Wong, Fran, 1972.26